To Learn More Abou

If you would like more information on other EBRI publications, or information on becoming a member of EBRI, please fill out this form and fax it to EBRI

Fax to (202) 775-6312

Name _____

Title _____

Company _____

Type of Organization _____

Address _____

City/State/ZIP _____

Phone _____

Fax _____

Specific Areas of Interest _____

_____

_____

**Look for information about EBRI on our web site at
www.ebri.org**

Fundamentals, Sixth Edition

So that we can let you know when updates for
Fundamentals of Employee Benefit Programs will be
available, please fill out this card and fax it to EBRI.

Fax to (202) 775-6312

Name _____

Title _____

Company _____

Type of Organization _____

Address _____

City/State/ZIP _____

Phone _____

Comments about this publication _____

_____

_____

What would you like to see included in the next edition? _____

_____

_____

**EBRI members have access to EBRI publications on
our web site at www.ebri.org**

EBRI
EMPLOYEE
BENEFIT
RESEARCH
INSTITUTE

An EBRI-ERF Publication

Fifth Edition

Fundamentals of Employee Benefit Programs

© 1997 Employee Benefit Research Institute
Education and Research Fund
2121 K Street, NW, Suite 600
Washington, DC 20037-1896
(202) 659-0670
web site www.ebri.org

Library of Congress Cataloging-in-Publication Data

Fundamentals of Employee Benefit Programs. — 5th ed.
    p.   cm.
Includes bibliographical references and index.
ISBN 0-86643-085-7 (pbk. : alk. paper)
1. Employee fringe benefits—United States. I. Employee Benefit Research Institute
(Washington, D.C.)
HD4928.N6F86   1997   96-32342
331.25'5'0973—dc20   CIP

Table of Contents

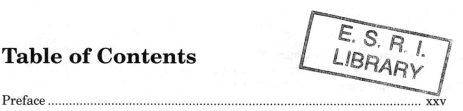

PART ONE
OVERVIEW

PART TWO
RETIREMENT BENEFITS

Chapter 4
Pension Plans

Chapter 5
Defined Benefit and Defined Contribution Plans: Understanding the Differences

Chapter 6
Profit-Sharing Plans

Chapter 7
Thrift Plans

Chapter 8
401(k) Cash or Deferred Arrangements

Chapter 9
Employee Stock Ownership Plans

Chapter 10
Cash Balance Pension Plans and Other Hybrid Retirement Plans

Chapter 11
Simplified Employee Pensions

Chapter 12
Nondiscrimination, Minimum Coverage, and Participation Requirements for Pension Plans

Chapter 17
Retirement Plans for the Self-Employed

Chapter 18
Planning for Retirement

PART THREE
HEALTH BENEFITS

Chapter 19
Health Insurance

Chapter 20
Dental Care Plans

Chapter 21
Prescription Drug Plans

Chapter 22
Vision Care Plans

Chapter 23
Health Maintenance Organizations

Chapter 24
Preferred Provider Organizations

Chapter 25
Managing Health Care Costs

Chapter 26
Mental Health and Substance Abuse Benefits

Chapter 27
Retiree Health Insurance

Chapter 28
Health Promotion Programs

PART FOUR
OTHER BENEFITS

Chapter 29
Employee Assistance Programs

Chapter 30
Disability Income Plans

Chapter 31
Long-Term Care Insurance

Chapter 32
Group Life Insurance Plans

Chapter 33
Survivor Benefits

PART FIVE
PUBLIC-SECTOR BENEFITS

Chapter 40
Defined Benefit Pension Plans in the Public Sector

Chapter 41
Supplemental Savings Plans in the Public Sector

Chapter 42
Health Insurance in the Public Sector

Chapter 43
Life Insurance and Related Protection in the Public Sector

Chapter 44
Leave Programs in the Public Sector

PART SIX
PUBLIC POLICY ISSUES

Chapter 45
Pension Tax Expenditures

Chapter 46
Health Insurance Portability and COBRA Expansion

Chapter 47
Medical Savings Accounts: Issues to Consider

Preface

New relationships among employers, employees, and the government are emerging rapidly as the economic landscape responds to organizational restructuring, global competition, and the introduction of new technology that is transforming the nature of work. In this evolving environment, changes in employee benefit programs often tend to be driven less by legislation than they were in the past: many employers are moving forward and designing and implementing benefit programs that work for their organizations rather than waiting for government permission or approval.

A number of companies have adopted an organizational philosophy that emphasizes a movement away from paternalism and toward individual responsibility, creating a new "social contract" between employers and employees.

Yet amid these abundant signs of change there is considerable continuity in the basic employment system. Employee benefit programs continue to be an important component of total compensation, addressing workers' economic security needs in a number of ways. They provide protection against loss of family income because of illness, disability, unemployment, and premature death. They also offer health insurance plans for workers and their families and provide the opportunity for workers to accrue sufficient funds to ensure a comfortable life in retirement. Other benefits assist employees in such areas as education and dependent care.

Pension, health care, and other reform measures currently being debated will undoubtedly alter the form of many benefits, but they will do so without changing their basic purpose of fostering workers' economic security.

I am proud to introduce the fifth edition of the Employee Benefit Research Institute's (EBRI) *Fundamentals of Employee Benefit Programs,* which is designed, as were the earlier editions, to educate readers about the extent and importance of employee benefits and the many changes being made by employers and by lawmakers.

This edition offers a detailed description of private- and public-sector employee benefit programs as they exist today, providing the reader a perspective from which to view whatever alterations the future brings. The book discusses and interprets the legislative, regulatory, and tax policy changes that these programs have undergone since the publication of the fourth edition in 1990. It also includes descriptions of emerging new directions such as the growing popularity of hybrid retirement plans that accommodate the needs of a diverse work force while meeting employers' requirements for flexibility, equity, and cost control. In addition, the book's scope has been expanded to include a section on public policy issues, discussing the reform measures that are currently under debate or the subject of legislative initiatives. The consequences of comprehensive tax reform and various health care reform proposals for employee benefits and income security could be vast, and they need to be examined as the deliberation process continues.

In keeping with its goal to educate readers on the whole range of employee benefits and related public policy issues in the most accessible manner possible, *Fundamentals* is divided into six sections: Overview, Retirement Benefits, Health Benefits, Other Benefits, Public-Sector Benefits, and Public Policy Issues. Chapters within the sections are designed to be read separately, with each including definitions of key terms used within it. Every chapter includes bibliographical references and suggested sources for additional information. A comprehensive index makes this book a thorough and practical reference, particularly when used in conjunction with the *EBRI Databook on Employee Benefits*.

Fundamentals is, however, a primer. It does not provide legal, investment, or employee benefit plan design advice or advice concerning compliance with federal regulations, and it should not be used for such purposes. Due to constant economic, legal, and regulatory changes, individuals should always seek specific legal, financial planning, and employee benefit information from legal counsel, financial institutions, and employee benefit professionals. The applicability of the information in this book to a specific plan, plan sponsor, or plan participant must be determined by legal counsel.

We wish to thank EBRI members, who generously made their benefit experts available to oversee the technical information in this project. We are particularly grateful to the following individuals, who served as reviewers and technical advisors: Bill Bolger, Harry Conaway, Susan DiLiddo, Cynthia Drinkwater, Barbara Wright Duggan, Jim Durfey, Cathy Eitelberg, Mary Feldman, Neil Grossman, Camille Haltim, Jennifer Harris, Diana Jost, J. Michael Keeling, Adrienne LaBombarde, Bill Link, Marie Lipari, Linda Lund, Frank McArdle, John McCormack, Diane Oakley, Melvyn Rodrigues, Bob Seraphin, Larry Sher, Peter Schmidt, Jerry Uslander, Dave Veeneman, Kurt Walton, Sue Velleman, John Woyke, John Vlajkovic, and Clark Yaggy.

We also wish to express appreciation to the EBRI staff, who contributed to the book's publication: Sharyn Campbell, Paul Fronstin, Deborah Holmes,

Ken McDonnell, Cheri Meyer, Cindy O'Connor, Carolyn Pemberton, Edina Rheem, EBRI Fellow Jack VanDerhei, and Paul Yakoboski.

The views expressed in this book should not be attributed to those whose assistance is acknowledged or to the officers, trustees, members, or other sponsors of EBRI, its Education and Research Fund, or their staffs.

Dallas L. Salisbury
President
January 1997

PART ONE
OVERVIEW

1. Employee Benefits in the United States: An Introduction

Employee benefits are intended to promote economic security by insuring against uncertain events and to raise living standards by providing targeted services. Employee benefit programs also add to economic stability by helping to secure the income and welfare of American families, which helps the economy as a whole.

The U.S. employee benefit system is a partnership among businesses, individuals, and the government. Most employment-based benefits, such as pensions and health insurance, are provided voluntarily by businesses. The government supports these voluntary employment-based benefits by granting them favorable tax treatment. Other benefits, including Social Security, unemployment insurance, workers' compensation, and family and medical leave, are mandatory. The government also supports individual financial security programs through individual retirement accounts, favorable taxation of life insurance contracts, and tax-free death benefits.

A Brief History

Employee benefit programs have existed in the United States since colonial times. Early programs include the Plymouth Colony settlers' military retirement program in 1636; Gallatin Glassworks' profit-sharing plan in 1797; American Express Company's private employer pension plan in 1875; Montgomery Ward's group health, life, and accident insurance program in 1910; and Baylor University Hospital's formalized prepaid group hospitalization plan in 1929. The federal government's involvement in the provision of such benefits further expanded coverage. In 1935, Congress mandated basic retirement income protection under the Social Security program; In 1956, it added income protection for disabled workers and their dependents; in 1965, it added health insurance for the elderly and disabled under the Medicare program. Moreover, voluntary employment-based benefit programs became more prevalent as federal tax preferences for employee benefits coincided with rising tax rates, strengthening incentives to provide private benefits.

The Role of Employee Benefits

Today's employment-based benefit programs represent a national commitment to provide some measure of income security and access to certain services (especially medical care) to active workers, displaced and disabled workers, retirees, and their families.

Income Security—A family's income security can be threatened if a wage earner dies or becomes disabled. Group life insurance and long-term disability insurance, often provided voluntarily by employers, can help to alleviate such unexpected financial losses. Employment-based pension and savings plans can also help to provide economic security for workers who look forward to a period of voluntary retirement in old age. Mandatory government programs also address the need for income security. The Social Security Old-Age, Survivors, and Disability Insurance (OASDI) program provides an income base, in the form of a lifetime annuity, to nearly all retired and disabled workers and their surviving spouses. Workers who become unemployed or disabled may qualify for temporary unemployment insurance or workers' compensation payments, respectively.

Nearly all Americans will benefit from one or more private and public income security programs during their lifetimes. In 1993, 67 million workers (57 percent of all workers) worked for an employer that sponsored a retirement plan. Of these 67 million workers, 76 percent participated in an employment-based retirement plan (Yakoboski et al., 1994b). In 1994, 53.8 percent of all elderly (aged 65 and over) married couples and 35.1 percent of all unmarried elderly individuals had income from employment-based pensions.

Mandatory government programs provide nearly universal coverage. In 1994, the Social Security system covered 139.0 million employees and self-employed persons, and 42.9 million persons, including the elderly, disabled, and their dependents and survivors, were receiving benefits. An estimated 93 percent of elderly married couples and elderly unmarried individuals received income from Social Security in 1994.

Access to Important Services—The U.S. employee benefit system also seeks to provide American workers and their families with lifelong access to certain vital services, especially medical care. Many American workers participate in group health insurance programs sponsored voluntarily by their employers. Coverage may be limited to acute hospital care or may include such routine services as dental exams and physician visits. Often, an employee's dependents are covered. Sixty-four percent of the civilian population under age 65, or 145.9 million persons, were covered by employment-based health insurance in 1994 (Fronstin and Rheem, 1996). Among full-time, full-year workers, 80.1 percent had employment-based coverage.

Some employers sponsor health insurance benefits to retired employees. In 1993, among workers aged 45 and over whose employer sponsored a health insurance plan, 41.4 percent had health insurance available at group rates on retirement throughout their retirement years (Yakoboski et al., 1994a). For some workers, the employer provides health insurance in retirement only until the retiree reaches age 65, the age at which an individual becomes eligible for Medicare, the federally sponsored medical insurance program for the elderly and disabled. In 1993, 17.3 percent of workers aged 45 and over whose employer sponsored health insurance in retirement had the health insurance available on retirement until age 65. In 1994, 95.5 percent of the elderly population received health insurance coverage through the Medicare program. However, Medicare does not cover all medical services, e.g., it does not cover maintenance prescription drugs. Therefore, some employers provide health insurance coverage to their retirees who are aged 65 and over, providing them with coverage for services not covered by Medicare.

Employee benefit programs are not limited to income security and health insurance. Specialized benefit programs help provide access to a wide range of important services, including ongoing education and training, child care, long-term care, and legal assistance. Other employee benefits, such as subsidized parking, product discounts, and relocation expense reimbursement, can provide convenience and cost savings for employees. Employee benefits also include paid sick leave, holidays, vacations, and maternity or paternity leave.

A list of employment-based benefits is presented in chart 1.1. Although not exhaustive, the list shows the variety and range of the U.S. employee benefit system. Chart 1.1 also distinguishes between voluntary and mandated employee benefit programs and shows the wide variety of tax treatments that apply to these benefits.

Tax Treatment

Federal tax provisions for employee benefit programs are relatively new. The tax code has provided tax incentives since 1921 for employment-based pension plans, since 1939 for compensation received for injuries or sickness, and since 1942 for health plans. The Social Security program, as initially

Chart 1.1
Selected Benefits

Types of Benefits by Tax Treatment	Types of Benefits by Function

Types of Benefits by Tax Treatment

Mandatory
- Social Security retirement (OASI)
- Social Security disability (DI)
- Medicare Part A (Social Security HI)
- Workers' compensation
- Unemployment insurance
- Medicaid[a]
- Supplemental Security Income (SSI)[a]
- Public assistance[a]

Voluntary
  Fully Taxable
- Vacations
- Paid lunch
- Rest periods
- Severance pay
- Cash bonuses and awards

  Tax Exempt[b]
- Employee and dependent health insurance
- Retiree health insurance
- Dental insurance
- Vision insurance
- Medicare Part B (Social Security SMI)
- Educational assistance[c]
- Legal assistance
- Child care
- Discounts
- Flexible spending accounts
- Parking
- Cafeteria facility
- Meals

  Tax Deferred[b]
- Keogh plans
- Defined benefit pension plans
- Defined contribution pension plans
    money purchase pension plans
    deferred profit-sharing plans
    savings and thrift plans
    employee stock ownership plans
    stock bonus plans
    simplified employee pension plans
    individual retirement account plans
    cash or deferred arrangements
        401(k)
        403 (b)

  Other Tax Preferred[b,d]
- Life insurance
- Long-term disability insurance
- Sick leave or sickness and accident insurance
- Other leave (maternity, funeral, jury, etc.)

Types of Benefits by Function

Retirement Income Benefits
- Social Security retirement (OASI)
- Supplemental Security Income (SSI)[a]
- Keogh plans
- Defined benefit pension plans
- Defined contribution pension plans
    money purchase pension plans
    deferred profit-sharing plans
    savings and thrift plans
    employee stock ownership plans
    stock bonus plans
    simplified employee pension plans
    individual retirement account plans
    cash or deferred arrangements
        401(k)
        403 (b)

Health Care
- Employee and dependent health insurance
- Retiree health insurance
- Dental insurance
- Vision insurance
- Medicare (Social Security HI, SMI)
- Medicaid[a]

Other Benefits
- Social Security disability (DI)
- Long-term disability insurance
- Life insurance
- Workers' compensation
- Unemployment insurance
- Public assistance[a]
- Severance pay
- Child care
- Vacations
- Sick leave or sickness and accident insurance
- Other leave (maternity, funeral, jury, etc.)
- Paid lunch
- Rest periods
- Legal assistance
- Education
- Flexible spending accounts
- Bonuses and awards
- Parking
- Cafeteria facility
- Meals
- Discounts

(continued)

enacted in 1935, provided retirement income to workers and their spouses; in 1956, the program was extended to provide income to disabled workers (their dependents were included in the program in 1958); and in 1965, the program was extended again to provide health insurance coverage to the elderly, disabled, and low-income individuals.

The general tax treatment of employee benefit programs has remained relatively consistent over the years. Employer contributions to health insurance remain tax exempt to employees and tax deductible to employers; in addition, the benefits received under employment-based health plans are tax free. Taxes on most retirement programs are deferred until benefit receipt. Other benefits, such as life insurance, dependent care, and educational assistance, are tax exempt up to specified dollar limits. Vacations and other time-off benefits, bonuses and awards, and severance pay are fully taxable (chart 1.1).

Meeting Changing Needs

Given such a wide range of options, compensation packages can be tailored to achieve employer and employee goals and can change in response to workers' needs and preferences. Demographic changes in the American work force and general population have influenced and are likely to continue influencing the provision and design of employee benefit programs.

An Aging Population—One change in progress is the shift in the U.S. population's age distribution. Members of the large baby boom cohort (individuals born between 1946 and 1964) currently compose a disproportionately large part of the overall work force, especially in new and fast-growing industries. As this cohort ages, and the smaller baby bust cohort (individuals born between 1964 and 1975) enters the labor force, the age distribution of the work force will shift toward older workers, whose needs and preferences may differ from those of younger workers. As the baby boom cohort begins to retire, an increasing proportion of Americans will be elderly and living longer and will depend on sources other than employment for income and vital services. These forces will affect both income security and health care insurance programs.

Developments in the retirement plan market may in part represent a response to work force changes. It has been well documented that, in the private sector, participation in defined contribution plans (which promise a specified contribution to an employee's account) is growing faster than participation in traditional defined benefit pension plans (which promise a specified benefit at retirement). The number of active participants in a defined benefit plan where the defined benefit plan was the primary plan declined slightly between 1975 and 1992 (from 27 million to 25 million), while the number of active participants in a defined contribution plan where the defined contribution plan was the primary plan grew during those years (from 4 million to 19 million) (U.S. Department of Labor, 1996).

Defined contribution plans historically have offered faster vesting than defined benefit plans, and defined contribution lump-sum benefits are more portable than defined benefit plan deferred annuities. Thus, younger workers may anticipate future job changes and therefore place a higher value on faster vesting and benefit portability common to defined contribution plans. In addition, young families may be attracted to defined contribution plan provisions that allow access to money in the account prior to retirement in cases of financial hardship and on termination of employment (although preretirement and hardship withdrawals are generally subject to a 10 percent excise tax and regular income tax). However, as the baby boom cohort ages and the work force becomes weighted more toward older workers, preferences may shift again toward defined benefit plans, which are generally characterized as providing more secure retirement protection than defined contribution plans for long-tenure employees working at the same company until retirement. Also, it is possible to save more money in the last several years before retirement in a defined benefit plan than it is in a defined contribution plan.

The effects of the aging population on retirement programs can already be seen in the Social Security Old-Age and Survivors Insurance (OASI) program. Partly as a result of increased life expectancies, past population shifts are reflected in a decrease in the ratio of OASDI-covered workers to OASDI beneficiaries from 16.5 in 1950 to 3.7 in 1970 to 3.3 in 1995. Under intermediate assumptions, the ratio of OASDI workers to beneficiaries is expected to decrease to 2.4 in 2020 and to 1.8 in 2070 (U.S. Department of Social Security, 1996). In response, taxes imposed on employers and employees to finance the pay-as-you-go OASI system were raised from 1.5 percent in 1950 to roughly 4.8 percent in 1983. The rates were revised again under the Social Security Amendments of 1983 and increased incrementally to 5.6 percent in 1993. Moreover, in anticipation of the baby boom's retirement, the retirement age will rise incrementally to age 67 by 2022 for people reaching age 62 in 2000 or later. (For more detail on Social Security retirement age, see chapter 2 on Social Security and Medicare.)

Health care benefit programs are also affected by the aging of the population. The elderly generally require more health care than the working age population. The effects of this trend on medical expenditures are exacerbated by the rapid pace of health care price inflation. Between 1982 and 1995, the price level of medical services and commodities rose 130 percent, compared with a 55 percent increase in consumer prices overall. Propelled by these factors, national health expenditures reached 13.7 percent of the U.S. Gross Domestic Product in 1994, up from 7.4 percent in 1970. Between 1960 and 1994, employer spending for health insurance (excluding Medicare) increased an average of 13.6 percent per year, to $263.6 billion (Employee Benefit Research Institute, 1995). In response to these developments, employers are taking steps to slow the growth of their health care costs. Increasingly, employers are requiring employees to share the cost of health insurance premiums and/or pay a larger portion of health costs out of pocket. It is hoped that cost sharing and other cost management measures will discourage unnecessary utilization of health care services.

The Medicare program, like OASI, has already been affected by demographic shifts and rapid health care inflation. The employer/employee tax rate for Medicare Hospital Insurance (HI) increased from 0.6 percent in 1970 on a maximum taxable amount of $7,800 of annual earnings to 1.45 percent in 1996, with no cap on the maximum amount of annual earnings subject to the tax. In anticipation of further cost increases, Congress changed Medicare's reimbursement system in 1983 to the prospective payment system (PPS) for inpatient hospital care and in 1989 to the resource based relative value system (RBRVS) for outpatient physician services. Nonetheless, according to the 1995 Social Security board of trustees' report, the HI trust fund is projected to be depleted by 2001, given intermediate economic and demographic assumptions.

As the population ages, the proportion requiring nursing home care or other long-term care will increase. Currently, private insurance for such health care needs is not widely available, and federal financing for nursing home care is generally available only under the Medicaid program, with eligibility subject to stringent means tests. Many find this situation unacceptable, and pressure is building to make other provisions for financing long-term care, either through expanded provision of voluntary private insurance (perhaps through employers), through a mandatory government program, or both.

Balancing Work and Family—Family structure has changed radically from the days when it typically consisted of a father who was the sole wage earner, a mother who stayed at home, and two children. Today, both husband and wife often work, children are in day care, and there are many single-parent families. The increase in labor force participation by women, especially those with young children, has implications for employee benefits that cannot be overlooked. In 1950, 12 percent of women with children under age 6 were in the labor force, compared with 62 percent in 1994 (U.S. Department of Commerce, 1995). In 1994, out of a total of 66.7 million children, 27.3 million (40.9 percent) lived in a two-parent family in which both parents worked; 13.5 million (20.3 percent) lived in a two-parent family where one parent worked; 10.3 million (15.5 percent) lived in a one-parent family in which the parent worked; and 3.8 million (5.6 percent) lived in a one- or two-parent family in which the parent or parents were unemployed.

These trends have led to public and private responses that attempt to help workers better balance work and family needs. Legislation has been enacted at the federal and state levels that requires employers to provide a minimum period of parental leave and to promote federal and more state involvement in child care access, affordability, and quality.

Flexibility—Another response to a changing work force is the growing use of flexible benefit plans. Within such arrangements, employees are permitted choices among benefits and/or benefit levels. Employees thus may exchange benefits that they consider less valuable for others better suited to their needs. Employee benefit programs, whether public or private, that address these and other needs can enhance the economic security of individual workers and their families. The provision of benefits such as child care and parental leave can help smooth career progress, to the overall advantage of labor markets. Thus, these and other benefits can help families and employers reconcile the personal needs of the home with the economic needs of the work place.

Benefits and the Federal Budget

The expansion of federal tax incentives for employee benefits that occurred in the 1970s has dramatically slowed and is unlikely to be repeated during this decade unless the current federal budget situation eases. Faced with billions of dollars in federal budget deficits, legislators are concerned with tax losses attributable to tax-favored employee benefit programs. Because some benefits are tax exempt (health) and others are not subject to taxes until some future time (pensions), the current tax revenue loss to the U.S. Treasury can be substantial. Thus, employee benefits are often targets in legislative revenue-raising efforts. Employee benefit programs will remain an important piece of total compensation, but changes in employee benefit and tax policy appear to be continuing. Keeping up with and understanding the changes and their effects will be important not only for sponsors of benefit programs but for employees as well.

Bibliography

Employee Benefit Research Institute. *EBRI Databook on Employee Benefits.* Third edition. Washington, DC: Employee Benefit Research Institute, 1995.

_____. *Retirement in the 21st Century... Ready or Not... .* Washington, DC: Employee Benefit Research Institute, 1994.

Fronstin, Paul, and Edina Rheem. "Sources of Health Insurance and Characteristics of the Uninsured: Analysis of the March 1995 Current Population Survey." *EBRI Issue Brief* no. 170 (Employee Benefit Research Institute, February 1996).

Levit, Katharine, et al. "National Health Expenditures, 1994." *Health Care Financing Review* (Spring 1996): 205–242.

Mamorsky, Jeffrey D. *Employee Benefits Handbook.* Third edition. Boston, MA: Warren, Gorham & Lamont, 1992.

Rosenbloom, Jerry S., ed. *The Handbook of Employee Benefits: Design, Funding, and Administration.* Third edition. Homewood, IL: Dow Jones-Irwin, 1992.

U.S. Department of Commerce. Bureau of the Census. *Statistical Abstract of the United States, 1995.* Washington, DC: U.S. Government Printing Office, 1995.

U.S. Department of Labor. Bureau of Labor Statistics. *Employee Benefits in Medium and Large Private Establishments, 1993.* Washington, DC: U.S. Government Printing Office, 1994a.

_____. *Employee Benefits in Small Private Establishments, 1992.* Washington, DC: U.S. Government Printing Office, 1994b.

_____. *Employee Benefits in State and Local Governments, 1992.* Washington, DC: U.S. Government Printing Office, 1994c.

U.S. Department of Labor. Pension and Welfare Benefits Administration. *Private Pension Plan Bulletin. Abstract of 1992 Form 5500 Annual Reports.* Washington, DC: U.S. Government Printing Office, 1996.

U.S. Department of Social Security. *1996 Annual Report of the Board of Trustees of the Federal Old-Age and Survivors Insurance and Disability Insurance Trust Funds.* Washington, DC: U.S. Government Printing Office, 1996.

Yakoboski, Paul, and Celia Silverman. "Baby Boomers in Retirement: What Are Their Prospects?" *EBRI Special Report SR-23 / Issue Brief* no. 151 (Employee Benefit Research Institute, July 1994).

Yakoboski, Paul, et al. "Employment-Based Health Benefits: Analysis of the April 1993 Current Population Survey." *EBRI Special Report SR-24 / Issue Brief* no. 152 (Employee Benefit Research Institute, August 1994a).

_____. "Employment-Based Retirement Benefits: Analysis of the April 1993 Current Population Survey." *EBRI Special Report SR-25 / Issue Brief* no. 153 (Employee Benefit Research Institute, September 1994b).

Additional Information

American Federation of Labor and Congress of Industrial Organizations
815 16th Street, NW
Washington, DC 20036
(202) 637-5000

Association of Private Pension and Welfare Plans
1212 New York Avenue, NW, Suite 1250
Washington, DC 20005
(202) 289-6700

The Business Roundtable
1615 L Street, NW, Suite 1100
Washington, DC 20036
(202) 872-1260

Conference Board
845 Third Avenue
New York, NY 10022
(212) 759-0900

ERISA Industry Committee
1400 L Street, NW, Suite 350
Washington, DC 20005
(202) 789-1400

International Foundation of Employee Benefit Plans
P.O. Box 69
18700 West Bluemound Road
Brookfield, WI 53008-0069
(414) 786-6700

National Association of Manufacturers
1331 Pennsylvania Avenue, NW, Suite 1500
Washington, DC 20004
(202) 637-3000

Society for Human Resource Management
606 North Washington Street
Alexandria, VA 22314
(703) 548-3440

Society for Professional Benefit Administrators
2 Wisconsin Circle, Suite 670
Chevy Chase, MD 20815
(301) 718-7722

U.S. Chamber of Commerce
1615 H Street, NW
Washington, DC 20062
(202) 463-5620 (economics)
(202) 659-6000 (policy)

2. Social Security and Medicare

Introduction

The Social Security Act was signed by President Franklin Delano Roosevelt on August 14, 1935; it became effective on January 1, 1937, and benefits were first payable in 1940. The national social insurance system was significantly broadened with the addition of the Disability Insurance program in 1956. The system was further expanded when Medicare was established by the Social Security Amendments of 1965, with benefits first available in July 1966. The original pieces of legislation have been amended many times and have become a complex set of laws and regulations that affect the lives of almost all Americans. This chapter briefly discusses the current Social Security and Medicare systems, their benefits, and their costs.

What Are Social Security and Medicare?

The *Social Security Handbook*, published by the Social Security Administration (SSA), provides a detailed explanation of the Social Security Act and its operation. In describing Social Security, the *Handbook* states:

The Social Security Act and related laws establish a number of programs which have the basic objectives of providing for the material needs of individuals and families, protecting aged and disabled persons against the expenses of illnesses that could otherwise exhaust their savings, keeping families together, and giving children the opportunity to grow up in health and security. These programs include:

Retirement insurance

Survivors insurance

Disability insurance

Hospital and medical insurance for the aged, the disabled, and those with end-stage renal disease

Black lung benefits

Supplemental Security Income

Unemployment insurance

Public assistance and welfare services

—Aid to needy families with children

—Medical assistance

—Maternal and child health services

—Child support enforcement

—Family and child welfare services

—Food stamps

—Energy assistance

The federal government operates the Old-Age, Survivors, and Disability Insurance (OASDI) programs (administered by SSA); Medicare, which consists of the Hospital Insurance (HI) and Supplementary Medical Insurance (SMI) programs (administered by the U.S. Health Care Financing Administration); the black lung benefit program (administered by SSA and the U.S. Department of Labor); and the Supplemental Security Income (SSI) program (administered by SSA). The remaining programs are operated by the states, with the federal government cooperating and contributing funds. Medicaid, for example, is a federal-state matching entitlement program that provides medical assistance for certain individuals and families with low incomes and resources.

This chapter focuses on OASDI and Medicare. These programs are financed primarily by the Social Security and Medicare payroll taxes paid by employees, employers, and self-employed persons. An exception to this financing method is Medicare SMI, also known as Part B, which is financed by premiums paid by those electing to be covered by SMI and by general revenues.

Participation

Who is covered by Social Security and thereby eligible for OASDI and Medicare benefits? When Social Security became effective in 1937, it applied only to workers in nonagricultural industry and commerce—about 60 percent of all working persons. Since then, there has been a steady movement toward covering all workers. Currently, about 95 percent of all jobs in the United States are covered. In 1994, about 139 million persons worked in employment or self-employment covered under the OASDI program (U.S. Social Security Administration, 1995b).

The Social Security Act originally excluded all state and local government employees from coverage because of uncertainty concerning whether the federal government could legally tax state employers. Workers for certain nonprofit organizations that are traditionally exempt from income and other taxes were also excluded. Federal government employees were excluded because they were covered by the Civil Service Retirement System, which was established in 1920.

In the 1950s, coverage was extended to most self-employed persons, farm and household workers, and members of the armed forces. Legislation enacted in 1950 (and thereafter) provided that employees of state and local governments and nonprofit organizations could be covered by Social Security on a voluntary basis under certain conditions. The Social Security Amendments of 1983 changed the law to *require* coverage of employees of all nonprofit organizations. This legislation also mandated that, once state and local governments elected to become covered by Social Security, they could not later withdraw from the program. Additionally, beginning in 1984, new federal government employees became covered by Social Security.

The majority of workers currently excluded from coverage fall into five major categories: (1) federal civilian employees hired before January 1, 1984,[1] (2) railroad workers, (3) certain employees of state and local governments who are covered under a retirement system, (4) household workers and farm workers whose earnings do not meet certain minimum requirements, and (5) persons with very low net earnings from self-employment.

Benefits

Because of the complexity of the Social Security and Medicare programs, this section gives a necessarily brief overview of their benefits. (Consult the bibliography at the end of this chapter for more detailed information.)

Social Security replaces a portion of covered earnings (discussed in the section on How Social Security and Medicare Are Funded) that may be lost as a result of a person's old age, disability, or death. Medicare pays a portion of the medical expenses of aged and disabled persons. Social Security and Medicare provide a much wider variety of benefits than is generally recognized. In fact, 59 percent of the OASDI benefits awarded in 1994 were awarded to persons other than retired workers (U.S. Social Security Administration, 1995b).

Old-Age, Survivors, and Disability Insurance—The following benefits are provided under OASDI programs:

---

[1] Notable exceptions include employees who returned to service after 1983 after a break in service of at least a year and employees who elected to transfer to the Federal Employees Retirement System (established for employees hired after 1983).

- monthly benefits to insured workers[2] aged 62 or over and to their eligible spouses and dependents,
- monthly benefits to disabled insured workers and to their eligible spouses and dependents, and
- monthly benefits to the eligible survivors of a deceased insured worker.

(For more information on disability income and Social Security survivor benefits, see chapters 30 and 33.)

A worker must be fully insured to receive most types of benefits. In general, a fully insured person is one who has at least as many credits[3] (acquired at any time after 1936) as the number of full calendar years elapsing between age 21 and age 62, disability, or death, whichever occurs first. For those who attained age 21 before 1951, the requirement is one credit for each year after 1950 and before the year of attainment of age 62, disability, or death. In general, today's workers will become fully insured (i.e., eligible to receive full retirement benefits) after acquiring 40 credits (about 10 years of work). In 1996, one credit will be acquired for each $640 in covered earnings. The earnings figure is updated annually, based on increases in average wages. A worker can acquire up to four credits per year.

Benefits are based on the primary insurance amount (PIA). The PIA is the monthly benefit amount payable to the worker on retirement at age 65 or on entitlement to disability benefits. The PIA is also the base figure from which monthly benefit amounts payable to the worker's family members or survivors are determined. The PIA is derived from the worker's annual taxable earnings, averaged over a time period that encompasses most of the worker's adult years.

A person aged 62 or over who has not acquired sufficient earnings to receive benefits on his or her own record can nevertheless collect a benefit based on a spouse's earnings record, provided the spouse has applied for benefits. This benefit is equal to an extra 50 percent of the primary retiree's PIA if the recipient is aged 65 or over. If the recipient is aged 62, he or she can receive permanently reduced benefits, currently 37.5 percent of the primary retiree's PIA. An individual who is entitled to a benefit on the basis

---

[2] An individual is not required to be retired in order to receive benefits at age 62, but benefits may be reduced due to the earnings limitation, which applies until age 70. For more information on the earnings limitation, see the discussion later in this section.

[3] Social Security credits were previously called quarters of coverage.

of his or her own earnings and also to a spousal benefit is entitled to receive whichever amount is greater.

A provision for divorced spouses became effective in 1985. In the past, a divorced woman, for example, could receive a spouse's benefit if she had been married at least 10 years to her former husband, but only if he had retired and started receiving his benefits. This created severe problems in cases where the former husband did not retire; the ex-spouse was thus ineligible for benefits. Currently, if the husband is not retired, the ex-spouse can receive the benefit if they both are at least age 62, were married 10 years, were divorced at least two years, and the former husband worked under Social Security long enough to qualify for benefits.

Receipt of a spouse's benefits by a former spouse does not reduce the amount available to a current spouse. Each can receive a spouse's benefit, although, as noted earlier, the current spouse must wait until the benefit earner retires.

The 1983 Social Security Amendments made significant changes in benefit eligibility. While reduced benefits will continue to be paid at age 62, the age for receiving full benefits—now age 65—will be increased in the future. The following table illustrates the increase in the full benefit age:

Year in Which Worker Attains Age 62	Age at Which 100 Percent of PIA is Payable
2000	65 and 2 months
2001	65 and 4 months
2002	65 and 6 months
2003	65 and 8 months
2004	65 and 10 months
2005–2016	66
2017	66 and 2 months
2018	66 and 4 months
2019	66 and 6 months
2020	66 and 8 months
2021	66 and 10 months
2022 and later	67

Source: U.S. Social Security Administration, 1995b.

The early retirement benefit amount, which is payable at age 62, will be reduced over this period. The maximum reduction for early retirement benefits will increase from its present 20 percent to 30 percent for those who reach age 62 in the year 2022 or later.

Monthly benefit amounts are related to the average earnings on which a worker pays Social Security taxes throughout his or her career years. When computing benefits, a worker's average earnings are indexed to changes that have taken place in national average earnings over the worker's career years. To assist in achieving *social adequacy,* benefits replace a larger percentage of indexed preretirement earnings for persons with low average indexed earnings than for persons with high average indexed earnings.

Social Security benefits are reduced or eliminated altogether if a participant under age 70 works after retiring and earnings from such work exceed specified amounts (called the earnings limitations) in any given year. In 1996, retirees aged 65 to 69 could earn up to $12,500[4] annually without a reduction in Social Security benefits. Benefits were reduced by $1 for each $3 earned in excess of this amount. For those under age 65, the earnings limitation for 1996 was $8,280. Benefits were reduced by $1 for every $2 earned in excess of this amount. In the first year that an individual is entitled to benefits, an alternative monthly test based on monthly earnings will apply, if more favorable. During that year, beginning with the month of entitlement, individuals can receive the benefit for any month that they do not earn over one-twelfth of the earnings limitation. In 1996, the alternative monthly test was based on $1,042 for those aged 65 to 69 and on $690 for those under age 65. If an individual earns more than one-twelfth of the annual limit, benefits are not payable for that month unless they are payable under the regular annual test. There is no limit on the amount an individual aged 70 or over may earn and still receive Social Security benefits.

Once monthly benefits begin, they generally are adjusted automatically each December to reflect changes in the cost of living. Cost-of-living adjustments are normally payable beginning in January. Prior to 1986, these adjustments generally occurred only if the consumer price index (CPI) increased by 3 percent or more since the last automatic adjustment. In 1986, Congress passed legislation eliminating the requirement that the CPI had to rise at least 3 percent before a cost-of-living benefit increase would take effect. Under the 1986 law, any rise in the CPI in the preceding 12-month measurement period calls for an equivalent percentage increase in benefits, applicable to persons eligible for benefits.

---

[4]Increases in the earnings limit for retirees aged 65 through 69 will be phased in gradually until the limit reaches $30,000 in 2002. After 2002, increases in the earnings limitation will be based on the growth of average wages.

Social Security benefits were not subject to federal, state, or local income taxes (or to Social Security tax) prior to the 1983 amendments. As a result of the 1983 amendments and the Omnibus Budget Reconciliation Act of 1993 (OBRA '93), taxpayers are subject to income taxes on their Social Security benefits based on how their provisional income compares with certain base amounts. Provisional income is equal to adjusted gross income (before Social Security and Railroad Retirement Tier 1 benefits are considered) plus certain nontaxable income (such as tax-exempt interest income) plus one-half of Social Security and Railroad Retirement Tier 1 benefits. For single taxpayers, up to 50 percent of benefits are subject to federal income taxes if their provisional income is over $25,000 but not more than $34,000. If their provisional income is over $34,000, up to 85 percent of benefits are subject to taxation. For married persons filing jointly, the base amounts are $32,000 and $44,000. Married taxpayers filing separately who live with their spouses any time during the tax year have base amounts of $0.

Social Security was not designed to meet all financial needs that arise from a person's old age, disability, or death. It is intended to serve as a supplement to private savings and employer-sponsored retirement plans. This applies particularly to persons who earn higher-than-average incomes during their working years because of the limit on covered earnings and the benefit formula tilt, which favors lower-paid workers. The following table illustrates the monthly benefits payable to individuals who retired at ages 62 and 65 in 1996 with various final annual earnings. The figures in the example assume that the individuals worked steadily and received pay raises at a rate equal to the U.S. average throughout their working careers.

1996 Final Annual Earnings	1996 Annual Benefit at Age 62		1996 Annual Benefit at Age 65	
	Dollar amount	As a percentage of final annual earnings	Dollar amount	As a percentage of final annual earnings
$15,000	$6,010	40%	$7,464	50%
36,000	10,666	30	13,200	37
62,700	12,355	20	14,976	24

Source: Dale R. Detlefs, Robert J. Myers, and J. Robert Treanor, *1996 Mercer Guide to Social Security and Medicare* (Louisville, KY: William M. Mercer, Inc., 1996).

During calendar year 1994, $316.8 billion in OASDI benefits were paid to 42.9 million persons, including retired and disabled workers and their families and survivors of deceased workers (U.S. Social Security Administration, 1995a).

Hospital Insurance and Supplementary Medical Insurance—The Medicare program has two parts: Part A, the mandatory program of Hospital Insurance (HI), and Part B, the voluntary program of Supplementary Medical Insurance (SMI). Part A benefits are provided automatically on the basis of past work. Part B benefits are available only if individuals choose to pay a monthly premium. These are two separate but coordinated health insurance plans for individuals aged 65 or over. Medicare coverage was extended to certain severely disabled persons under age 65 and to certain persons suffering from kidney disease by the 1972 Social Security Amendments.

In July 1994, 36.5 million persons were enrolled for Medicare Part A and 35.2 million under Medicare Part B. For both programs, approximately 90 percent of the enrollees are aged and the rest are disabled. Medicare benefit payments for 1994 totaled $161.9 billion, of which HI accounted for 64 percent.

The HI program pays part of the costs of inpatient hospital care, certain post-hospital care, home health care, and hospice care. Those eligible for HI benefits at age 65 include: individuals eligible for Social Security or Railroad Retirement benefits as well as workers and their spouses in federal, state, or local government employment with a sufficient period of Medicare-only coverage;[5] disabled beneficiaries (but not their dependents) who have been entitled to Social Security or Railroad Retirement disability benefits for at least 24 months; government employees with Medicare-only coverage who have been disabled for more than 29 months; and insured workers (and their spouses and children) with end-stage renal disease requiring dialysis or a kidney transplant.

Individuals who did not work long enough to qualify for HI coverage can purchase HI coverage if they are aged 65 or over, are U.S. residents, are either citizens or have lawfully lived in the U.S. for five consecutive years, and if they also enroll in Part B coverage, described in the following paragraph. The monthly premium for those who purchase HI coverage is $289 in

---

[5] These individuals are covered, regardless of Social Security coverage, if they have sufficient earnings credits.

1996. This is reduced to $188 a month for uninsured persons who have at least 30 quarters of coverage.

Medicare Part B, SMI, primarily covers physicians' fees, most outpatient hospital services, and certain related services. All persons (except aliens who have not lawfully resided in the United States for five consecutive years) aged 65 or over and all disabled persons entitled to coverage under HI are eligible to enroll in the SMI program on a voluntary basis by paying a monthly premium.

Additionally, beginning in 1983, all federal civilian employees became covered under HI, and state and local government employees hired after March 31, 1986, and whose jobs were not already covered under Social Security were covered by HI beginning April 1, 1986.

For additional information on Medicare plan design, see chapter 27 on retiree health benefits.

How Social Security and Medicare Are Funded

Social Security and Medicare are financed primarily by payroll taxes paid by employees, employers, and the self-employed. These taxes are held by special trust funds established exclusively to pay Social Security and Medicare program benefits and administrative expenses. Any trust fund assets not needed to meet current costs are invested in special issue U.S. government securities.

In 1994, the OASDI program received income from the following sources: payroll taxes, 90.4 percent; interest earnings, 8.2 percent; taxation of OASDI benefits, 1.4 percent (as a result of the 1983 amendments, in 1984 the OASDI trust fund began receiving income from the taxation of up to 50 percent of some recipients' OASDI benefits); and payments from the general fund of the Treasury, less than 1 percent.

Similarly, the HI program received income from payroll taxes, 87.0 percent; interest earnings, 9.8 percent; taxation of OASDI benefits, 1.5 percent (as a result of OBRA '93, additional revenue resulting from taxing 50 percent to 85 percent of some recipients' OASDI benefits is credited to the HI trust fund); railroad retirement account transfers, less than 1 percent; payments from the general fund of the Treasury, less than 1 percent; and premiums from voluntary enrollees, less than 1 percent.

Unlike the other Social Security programs, SMI is not financed by payroll taxes. Approximately 65.1 percent of all SMI income comes from general revenue contributions, 31.3 percent from the premiums paid by the enrollees, and 3.6 percent from interest earnings of the SMI trust funds.

General revenue contributions increased as a result of the 1983 Social Security amendments, which included a provision for shifting amounts equal to federal income tax liabilities on Social Security benefits from the general fund to the Social Security trust funds. Also, general revenues contribute amounts equal to the employer share of the Social Security tax with respect to coverage of federal employment.

The 1983 Social Security amendments also increased payroll tax rates for employers, employees, and the self-employed. To lessen the burden of the tax increases, tax credits (against Social Security tax liability) were provided to employees (in 1984 only) and to self-employed persons from 1984 through 1989 (2.7 percent in 1984, 2.3 percent in 1985, and 2.0 percent in 1986–1989).

In 1996, participating (non-self-employed) workers paid Federal Insurance Contributions Act (FICA) taxes of 7.65 percent (6.2 percent is for OASDI and 1.45 percent is for HI) on the first $62,700 of earnings. The employer paid an equal amount. No OASDI taxes are withheld on earnings over $62,700 (adjusted annually). This limit is called the maximum taxable earnings base, or covered earnings. This base rises in future years at the same rate as national average earnings. As a result of OBRA '93, there is no maximum taxable earnings base for the HI tax rate; i.e., the HI tax rate of 1.45 percent is paid on all earnings, including those above $62,700.

Self-employed persons have the same maximum taxable earnings base as other workers but pay higher tax rates since they pay both as an employer and an employee. The Self-Employed Contributions Act (SECA) tax rate for 1996 was 15.30 percent. The income tax credit for the self-employed was terminated beginning in 1990 but is replaced with an income tax deduction for one-half the SECA contribution. In addition, the self-employed may deduct 50 percent of their Social Security and Medicare self-employment tax as a business expense on their income tax return.

In 1996, the SMI premium was $42.50 per month. For those individuals receiving Social Security benefits, the SMI premium is ordinarily deducted from the Social Security benefits. Otherwise, an individual is billed by the government quarterly in advance.

Recovering the Value of Social Security and Medicare Taxes

More and more public attention is being focused on what kind of value

Social Security and Medicare provide each generation of workers in relation to the Social Security and Medicare taxes they pay. A variety of illustrations of the amount of time it takes to recover the value of taxes paid are possible, depending on the variation of several factors, including: what parts of the Social Security and Medicare taxes are counted (i.e., OASI, OASDI, OASDHI); whether Social Security and Medicare taxes include the employer's share; whether the taxes are adjusted for forgone interest; whether the benefits are adjusted to reflect cost-of-living adjustments; and whether the effect of the taxation of benefits is included. The range of possibilities covered by such illustrations implies that the illustrations should be interpreted with caution.

A 1995 memorandum from the Social Security Press Office provides information on the number of months it took or will take workers retiring at normal retirement age in 1975, 1995, and 2015 to recover the accumulated value of OASDHI employee and employee-employer taxes.[6] A hypothetical worker with average earnings who retired in January 1975[7] at age 65 with an eligible spouse[8] recovered the value of employee OASDHI taxes after 1.4 years. It took the same hypothetical worker 2.8 years to recover the value of employee-employer OASDHI taxes. For a hypothetical worker with average earnings who retired in January 1995[9] at age 65 with an eligible spouse, the corresponding time frames were 6.7 years and 15.3 years. For a

---

[6] The worker's total taxes (or combined employer-employee taxes) are accumulated with interest from the time they were paid up to the date of retirement. After retirement, the accumulated value of the taxes, less any benefits received, continues to earn interest. Benefit payments receive an annual increase equal to the increase in the Consumer Price Index. Interest rates equivalent to the average effective yield on investments in the OASDI Trust Funds in each year are used in the calculation. Projected effective interest rates, average wages, and benefit increases are based on the alternative II set of assumptions from the 1995 Social Security Trustees Report.

[7] Worker is assumed to have had earnings from 1937 through the year before retirement. Average earnings in each year are defined to equal the average wage used for Social Security indexing purposes.

[8] Spouse is assumed to be the same age as the worker and not to have worked outside the home.

[9] Worker is assumed to have had earnings from age 22 through the year before retirement. Average earnings in each year are defined to equal the average wage used for Social Security indexing purposes.

hypothetical worker with average earnings who will retire in January 2015[10] at age 65 with an eligible spouse, the corresponding time frames are projected to be 11.2 years and 26.1 years.

These figures illustrate the relative relationship of payback times of past, current, and future beneficiaries. It is fairly clear that it will take significantly longer for future retirees to recover the value of taxes paid, however they are measured. This is ameliorated somewhat by the projection that future retirees are expected to live longer and thus collect benefits longer. Social Security and Medicare supporters defend the phenomenon of lengthening payback times by arguing that the programs should not be viewed as annuities but as "social insurance" that provides fundamental financial protection to the nation's workers and their families. They point out that the social benefits of giving a measure of economic independence to the elderly, orphaned children, surviving spouses, and the disabled should not be disregarded. Some feel that it is incorrect to evaluate the Social Security program's worth simply by measuring the speed or rate of return of the "typical" worker's contributions, because such computations do not adequately reflect the program's social features, such as its antipoverty value. Critics of Social Security and Medicare view these social welfare features as basic flaws in the programs and argue that by combining the goals of social adequacy (which is welfare-related) with individual equity (which loosely ties benefits to taxes paid), the program is unable to accomplish either goal well. Inequities cited include the claim that future beneficiaries will on the whole receive retirement benefits inferior to those that the equivalence of their taxes could purchase in the private sector and the claim that when interest is included, some categories of workers will not recoup what they and their employer paid in taxes on their behalf.

Social Security Benefit Estimates

Since September 30, 1995, SSA has been required by law to automatically send personal earnings and benefit estimate statements (PEBES) to individuals aged 60 and over who do not already receive Social Security benefits. Additional mailings will be sent each year to individuals reaching age 60 until 1999, when PEBES will thereafter be sent annually to all individuals aged 25 and over. The SSA statement will contain the following information:

---

[10] Ibid

- the amount of wages paid to, or self-employment earnings reported by, the individual;
- an estimate of the aggregate FICA contributions made by or on behalf of the individual;
- a separate estimate of the aggregate contributions for Medicare coverage; and
- an estimate of the individual's potential monthly Social Security old-age benefit, disability, and survivors' benefits, plus a description of Medicare Part A coverage.

Workers who are younger than age 60 may continue to request such earnings and benefit information by filing Form SSA–7004–SM (Request for Earnings and Benefit Estimate Statement) that can be obtained by calling 1-800-772-1213, toll free. The Social Security Administration recommends that individuals request this information every three years to verify the accuracy of their records.

Social Security benefit estimates can also be obtained by using a personal computer program developed by the SSA's Office of the Actuary. The program, called ANYPIA, works on IBM and compatible PCs to produce the Social Security PIA for an old-age, survivor, or disability insurance benefit.

Outlook

The development of Social Security and Medicare is a continuing process. The programs are products of the decisions made by policymakers living in an ever-changing social and economic environment.

When the men and women on the leading edge of the postwar baby boom begin to reach retirement age in approximately 2011, social and economic conditions are likely to be quite different than they are today or have been in the past. Accordingly, it is reasonable to expect society to begin now to make the changes necessary to assure that the Social Security and Medicare programs will be appropriate for the future social and economic environment.

We may, for example, anticipate that as we move into the next century there will be increased public debate regarding the appropriate normal retirement age. Some observers will criticize the higher normal retirement age of 67 as being unreasonably punitive to certain individuals, particularly those working in arduous occupations. Others will be in favor of raising the normal retirement age even further (e.g., to age 70), arguing that there are more jobs today in the service sector and that manufacturing and agricultural jobs have benefited from new technology and are therefore less strenuous than in the past. There may also be discussion regarding raising the early retirement age, currently age 62, to perhaps age 65.

It is argued that alleged inequities of the Social Security system could be improved significantly by reforming the rules applying to spouses, working couples, divorced persons, and retirees who work. One suggested change favored by individuals of younger generations is the option to divert some of their Social Security and Medicare contributions into private retirement accounts, e.g., an individual retirement account (IRA). Those who oppose such a change argue that Social Security is designed to be the guaranteed floor of retirement income, and exposing Americans to investment risk would jeopardize that guarantee.

Other groups have suggested that Social Security should be means tested (i.e., that it should be phased out for retirees whose income exceeds some threshold level). Opponents point out that Social Security is financed, at least in part, by the employee's own contributions and therefore should be considered as something earned by the employee.

The 1994–1995 Advisory Council on Social Security[11] devised three reform recommendations, including a plan that would increase benefit taxes in conjunction with direct investment of Social Security funds in equities; a proposal (known as the individual accounts plan) that would layer small-scale mandatory individual accounts on top of the present system; and a plan that would gradually replace the present defined benefit system with large-scale defined contributions held outside the Old-Age, Survivors, and Disability Trust Funds that could be invested in equities. Although the council recommendations are not binding, lawmakers often use them as a guide to forming legislation.

There will also be increased attention given to certain aspects of the Disability Insurance program, due to its rapid growth, delays in processing

---

[11] Sec. 706 of the Social Security Act requires the Secretary of Health and Human Services to appoint an advisory council every four years to examine issues affecting the Social Security and Medicare programs. Under the provisions of the Social Security Independence and Program Improvements Act of 1994 (P.L. 103-296), which separated SSA from the Department of Health and Human Services and established SSA as an independent agency, this is the last advisory council to be appointed. P.L. 103-296 also established a seven-member bipartisan Social Security Advisory Board to review policies related to the OASDI and SSI programs and make recommendations to the Commissioner of Social Security.

claims, court decisions that have altered agency policies, and concern that payments to alcoholics and drug addicts are being used to perpetuate their habits.

Regarding the Medicare program, potential cost-saving changes include increasing the premiums and other payments by retirees, cutting payments to doctors and hospitals, or raising the eligibility age. Other proposed changes could include managed care and HMOs, medical savings accounts, or insurance vouchers.

In order to increase trust fund revenues, some argue for expanding the Social Security and Medicare tax base to include employee benefits (health insurance premiums and other forms of nonwage compensation). Others favor raising the limit on maximum earnings subject to the OASDI tax (there is no limit on earnings subject to the HI tax), although such an option involves only modest revenue gains and discriminates against the self-employed. Still others suggest allowing part of the trust fund assets to be invested in private capital market investments instead of in the special Treasury bonds in which the assets are now invested. These and other issues, reflecting changing social and economic patterns, will influence the inevitable modifications to the Social Security program.

Public understanding or misunderstanding will play a more important role in determining the future shape of the programs than it did in the past, when Social Security and Medicare taxes were relatively low and the average worker was less questioning. For many American workers, the payroll tax burden for Social Security and Medicare exceeds their federal income tax liability (when both employer and employee rates are combined).

One problem confronting Social Security and Medicare is a lack of public understanding about the programs—their basic rationale, the type and level of benefits they provide, the tenuous relationship between individual taxes paid and individual benefits received, the method of financing, and the significance of projected high future costs. The better individuals understand Social Security and Medicare, the greater their chances that the programs will be modified to coincide with their needs. Public acceptance will be necessary for programs that are scheduled to pay benefits and to require tax collections amounting to trillions of dollars during the next several years.

The Social Security Administration has expanded its efforts to educate the public. In addition, a number of advisory groups and commissions regularly study the various aspects of Social Security and Medicare. This attention and scrutiny may result in a certain amount of turmoil; however, in the long run it should improve the Social Security and Medicare programs.

Conclusion

The changes in Social Security legislated in the 1983 Social Security amendments helped solve the financial crisis that plagued the OASDI program at that time. This legislation also strengthened the financing of the HI program. Unfortunately, both the OASDI and the HI programs are projected to experience financial difficulties in the not-too-distant future. Under intermediate assumptions,[12] the actuarial estimates made by the Social Security Board of Trustees in 1995 projected that OASDI benefit payments will exceed income from payroll taxes and taxation of benefits beginning in 2013. This date is important for budget policy because it marks the year in which government would have to provide cash to the program rather than receive surplus cash from it. Congress will have to raise taxes or borrow from the public in order to pay promised benefits. According to the 1995 OASDI Trustees Report, the OASDI trust fund is expected to be completely exhausted by 2030. The funding of Social Security will continue to be a matter of controversy and hence be subject to change well before that date of 2013 is reached, since the buildup of Social Security's reserves, resulting from the 1983 and previous amendments, has in itself set off a public debate.

As part of the Social Security amendments of 1983, operations of the OASDI and HI trust funds were removed from the Unified Budget after fiscal year 1992. Subsequent legislation removed OASDI effective fiscal year 1986. As noted earlier, annual excesses of income over outgo in the Social Security and Medicare trust funds are invested in special issue U.S. Government securities. Hence, although the Social Security and Medicare trust funds are off-budget, investment of the trust fund excesses in federal government securities means that Social Security and Medicare financing is intricately related to the federal government's budgetary and fiscal policies. In an effort to separate Social Security policymaking from economic and budgeting decisions affecting the rest of the federal government, the Social Security Independence and Program Improvements Act of 1994 was signed into law by President Bill Clinton on August 15, 1994. The Social Security

---

[12] The intermediate assumptions represent the Social Security Board of Trustees' "best estimates" of likely future economic and demographic conditions.

Agency became an independent federal agency effective March 31, 1995.

The Medicare program could be a much greater problem. According to the 1995 Trustees' Report, the HI program moved into negative cash flow in 1992 as benefit costs began exceeding payroll tax revenue. The HI trust fund is projected to be exhausted by the year 2002 (under intermediate assumptions). Although the SMI trust fund is adequately funded on a limited year-to-year basis, it is experiencing a growth rate that is unsustainable.

Social Security and Medicare are large, well established, and recognized as an integral part of the national socioeconomic structure. Nevertheless, important questions remain. Will the Social Security and Medicare programs grow in a way that best reconciles beneficiaries' economic needs with taxpayers' financial abilities—or will they be curtailed because of heavy financial burdens? Will there be a more concerted effort in the future to formulate a more comprehensive national retirement policy that takes into account projected Social Security benefits as well as the retirement benefits that employees expect to receive from employment-based plans and their individual savings initiatives (IRAs, thrift plans, etc.)? Will health care and Medicare be comprehensively reformed on a national basis? The answers depends largely on the dialogue and decisions of an informed citizenry.

Bibliography

Detlefs, Dale R., Robert J. Myers, and J. Robert Treanor. *1996 Mercer Guide to Social Security and Medicare.* Louisville, KY: William M. Mercer, Inc., 1996.

Employee Benefit Research Institute. *Databook on Employee Benefits.* Third edition. Washington, DC: Employee Benefit Research Institute, 1995.

_____. *Retirement in the 21st Century ... Ready or Not ... .* Washington, DC: Employee Benefit Research Institute, 1994.

_____. "Are Workers Kidding Themselves? Results of the 1995 Retirement Confidence Survey." *EBRI Issue Brief* no. 168 (Employee Benefit Research Institute, December 1995).

Employee Benefit Research Institute/The Gallup Organization, Inc. "Public Attitudes on Social Security, 1995." *EBRI/Gallup Survey* G-62 (Washington, DC: Employee Benefit Research Institute, March 1995).

_____. "Public Attitudes on Social Security, Part I, 1994." *EBRI/Gallup Survey* G-56 (Washington, DC: Employee Benefit Research Institute, April 1994).

_____. "Public Attitudes on Social Security, Part II, 1994." *EBRI/Gallup Survey* G-57 (Washington, DC: Employee Benefit Research Institute, May 1994).

Hay/Huggins Company. *1995 Social Security Summary.* Philadelphia, PA: Hay/Huggins Company, 1995.

Kingson, Eric R., and Edward D. Berkowitz. *Social Security and Medicare: A Policy Primer.* Westport, CT: Auburn House, 1993.

Kollmann, Geoffrey. *How Long Does It Take New Retirees to Recover the Value of Their Social Security Taxes?* CRS Report for Congress. Washington, DC: Congressional Research Service, January 3, 1995.

_____. *Social Security: The Relationship of Taxes and Benefits for Past, Present, and Future Retirees.* CRS Report for Congress. Washington, DC: Congressional Research Service, January 9, 1995.

Myers, Robert J. *Summary of the Provisions of the Old-Age, Survivors, and Disability Insurance System, the Hospital Insurance System, and the Supplementary Medical Insurance System.* Louisville, KY: William M. Mercer, Inc., 1994.

Social Security and Medicare Boards of Trustees. *Status of the Social Security and Medicare Programs: A Summary of the 1995 Annual Reports.* Washington, DC: U.S. Government Printing Office, 1995.

Steuerle, C. Eugene, and Jon M. Bakija. *Retooling Social Security for the 21st Century: Right & Wrong Approaches to Reform.* Washington, DC: The Urban Institute Press, 1994.

U.S. Department of Health and Human Services. Health Care Financing Administration. *1995 Annual Report of the Board of Trustees of the Federal Hospital Insurance Trust Fund.* Washington, DC: U.S. Government Printing Office, 1995.

_____. *1995 Annual Report of the Board of Trustees of the Federal Supplementary Medical Insurance Trust Fund.* Washington, DC: U.S. Government Printing Office, 1995.

U.S. Department of Health and Human Services. Social Security Administration. *Social Security Bulletin* (Winter 1993). Washington, DC: U.S. Government Printing Office, 1993.

U.S. Social Security Administration. *1995 Annual Report of the Board of Trustees of the Federal Old-Age and Survivors Insurance and Disability Insurance Trust Funds.* Washington, DC: U.S. Government Printing Office, 1995a.

_____. *Social Security Bulletin Annual Statistical Supplement, 1995.* Washington, DC: U.S. Government Printing Office, 1995b.

_____. *Social Security Courier* (November 1995). Washington, DC: U.S. Government Printing Office, 1995c.

_____. *Social Security Handbook, 1995.* Twelfth edition. Washington, DC: U.S. Government Printing Office, 1995d.

Zayatz, Tim. "Illustrative Social Security Retirement Benefit Amounts, and Number of Months to Recover the Value of Past Social Security Taxes, for Beneficiaries Retiring in 1975, 1985, 1995, 2015, and 2035." *Memorandum.* Baltimore, MD: Social Security Administration Press Office, April 12, 1995.

Additional Information

American Association of Retired Persons
601 E Street, NW
Washington, DC 20049
(202) 434-2277

National Academy of Social Insurance
1776 Massachusetts Avenue, NW, Suite 615
Washington, DC 20036
(202) 452-8097

U.S. Department of Health and Human Services
Health Care Financing Administration
200 Independence Avenue, SW
Washington, DC 20201
Public Affairs: (202) 690-6113
Publications: (410) 966-7843
Medicare Hotline: (800) 638-6833

U.S. Social Security Administration
6401 Security Boulevard
Baltimore, MD 21235
(800) 772-1213

3. Employee Retirement Income Security Act

Introduction and Overview

President Gerald Ford signed the Employee Retirement Income Security Act (ERISA) into law on Labor Day, September 2, 1974. It remains the most comprehensive employee benefits legislation enacted in the United States, affecting the millions of Americans who are covered by employee benefit programs.

ERISA has a long history. President John F. Kennedy appointed a cabinet-level committee in 1962 to study private pension plans. In releasing the report, the committee concluded "that private pension plans should continue as a major element in the nation's total retirement security program. Their strength rests on the supplementation they can provide to the basic public system." But the committee also noted that the pension system was inadequate in certain areas, such as participant rights, funding, benefit protection, and oversight. The report led to investigations by various congressional committees that spanned nearly 10 years.

During its investigations, Congress found that there were a substantial number of benefit plans that were important to the well-being and security of millions of American workers and their dependents. Most plans were operated for the benefit of participants and beneficiaries, Congress found, but a small number were not. Congress determined that participants generally received insufficient information about their benefit plans and that there was inadequate protection of their rights.

In designing ERISA, Congress wanted to address these problems but at the same time promote "a renewed expansion of private retirement plans" and increase the number of participants receiving benefits. ERISA established standards that employee benefit plans must follow to obtain and maintain their tax-favored status. ERISA created standards for reporting and disclosure, funding, fiscal responsibility, and employee eligibility and vesting. ERISA set up a new government agency to insure most vested benefits against plan termination and established contribution and benefit limits for retirement plans.

ERISA primarily applies to private retirement plans, but almost all employee benefit plans are subject to some provisions of the act. The legislation affects welfare plans, such as health insurance, group life insurance, sick pay, and long-term disability income, and retirement plans, such as pension and profit-sharing plans, thrift plans, stock bonus plans, and employee stock ownership plans.

ERISA supersedes all state law otherwise applicable to pension (and welfare) plans covered by the reporting, disclosure, fiduciary responsibility, eligibility, vesting, funding, and termination insurance provisions of ERISA. This is what is commonly called "ERISA preemption." It does not apply to state law regulating insurance, banking, or securities. ERISA does not apply to state and local government plans, church plans, or those covering only self-employed persons (except for certain rules dealing with qualified plans).

The U.S. Departments of Labor and the Treasury have primary responsibility for administering ERISA. The Department of Labor (DoL) has primary jurisdiction over reporting, disclosure, and fiduciary matters, while the Treasury Department has primary jurisdiction over eligibility, vesting, and funding. The Pension Benefit Guaranty Corporation (PBGC), an agency of the federal government, administers the plan termination insurance program.

ERISA standards are set out in four titles to the act: Title I—Reporting, Disclosure, and Minimum Standards Administered by the Labor Department; Title II—Minimum Standards Administered by the Treasury Department (Internal Revenue Code provisions); Title III—Jurisdiction and Administration; and Title IV—Plan Termination Insurance.

This discussion is not intended to provide legal guidance or a guide to compliance. It provides a basic overview of the areas governed by ERISA. Further discussion of many areas is found in other chapters. The Additional Information list at the end of this chapter lists futher sources to consult.

ERISA and Health and Welfare Plans

A first important step to understanding ERISA and how it relates to employee health plans is to understand the terms used in ERISA that relate to employee health plans. The term *employee benefit plan* applies to employee pension plans and employee welfare plans. Both terms are given very broad meanings. The term *employee welfare plan* applies to any kind of nonpension employee benefit plan, including health plans (both insured and not insured), life insurance, disability plans, etc. Under the terms of ERISA, all employment-based health plans, insured or not insured, are ERISA plans except for health plans maintained by government entities for the employees of federal, state, and local governments and church plans maintained for the employees of the church.

The key provisions of ERISA that relate to employment-based health plans are found in sec. 514. Sec. 514(a) of ERISA, known as the "preemption" clause, states that, "the provisions of this title and Title 4, shall supersede any and all state laws insofar as they may now or thereafter relate to any employee benefit plan." The preemption by ERISA of state regulations is very broad. Under current law, there is only one way for a state to get around ERISA's preemption and that is by an act of Congress with the president's signature. To date, only Hawaii's Prepaid Health Plan has an exemption from ERISA preemption. Sec. 514(b), known as the "savings" clause, exempts state regulation of insurance from ERISA preemption. Sec. 514(c), known as the "deemer" clause, states that a state cannot deem an employee health plan as insurance to avoid ERISA preemption.

The results of these term definitions and sec. 514 are that all private-sector nonchurch employment-based health plans are ERISA plans and therefore exempt from state regulation. However, given that ERISA does not preempt state regulation of insurance, states indirectly regulate ERISA health plans that purchase an insurance contract (the state regulates the insurance contract not the employment-based health plan).

An employer can avoid any state regulation of its health plan by self-funding, or self-insuring, the health plan. Under this funding arrangement, the employer assumes the financial risk for the health plan. Under a fully insured arrangement, the employer shifts the financial risk of the health plan to another party, usually an insurance company. The term *self-funding*, although commonly used, can be misleading. The term *self-fund* leaves one to believe that the employer sets up a separate fund from which the employer pays health benefit claims. However, most employers that self-fund their health benefit plans pay health benefit claims on a pay-as-you-go basis out of general funds. Also, not all employers that choose to self-fund their health plan are fully self-funded. Some employers find that it is more cost effective to carve out certain segments of their health plan, e.g., mental health benefits or prescription drugs, and purchase an insurance contract to cover the funding of these benefits. By doing this, the carved-out segment of the employer's plan is now indirectly regulated by the state in which the benefit is available.

Another way self-funded plans may be partially insured is through the purchase of stop-loss coverage. To cover against catastrophic losses, some companies that self-fund their health plans purchase stop-loss coverage.

There are two types of stop-loss coverage: specific stop-loss coverage, which insures against the risk that any one claim will exceed a certain amount, and aggregate stop-loss, which insures against the entire plan's losses exceeding a certain amount. Most plans purchase both types of stop-loss coverage.

When an employer self-funds its employee health plan, the health plan is exempt from taxes and other assessments that states levy on insurers. Nearly all states (except Michigan and Utah) assess a premium tax on commercial insurers that operate in that state. These taxes range from 1 percent to 4 percent of premiums collected. All states operate a guaranty fund that pays outstanding claims when an insurer fails. Depending on their competitiveness and market strategy, many insurers are able to pass this cost on to their customers. These funds get their moneys from assessments on insurers in the state. By self-funding, an employer can avoid these costs.

Self-funded employers are also exempt from state regulations. The most widely known state regulations are the state mandated benefits. State mandated benefits are legal requirements that insurers operating in that state must offer specific health services or the services provided by specified providers. The mandates are generally narrowly defined and apply to all commercial insurers, Blue Cross and Blue Shield Plans, and health maintenance organizations (HMOs). As of 1995, there were over 1,000 state mandated benefits. Research shows that state mandated benefits increase claims costs, yet their impact on premium costs is unclear.

A further complication of the issue arises when a self-funded health plan contracts with an HMO. State regulation of HMOs varies greatly from state to state. Some states regulate HMOs as they would insurance companies, while other states do not consider HMOs to be insurance. The issue of whether self-funded health plans that contract with HMOs are regulated by the states is still unclear.

Two commonly asked questions regarding self-funded health plans are: how many employers self-fund their health plan and how many individuals are covered by a self-funded health plan? Data on the number of employers that self-fund their health plan are not available. Among the reasons are: current federal reporting requirements focus on pension plans and not health plans, health plans with fewer than 100 participants are generally exempt from reporting, and inconsistencies exist among the data reported for health plans (U.S. General Accounting Office, 1995).

As to the number of individuals covered by a self-funded health plan, the Bureau of Labor Statistics (BLS) employee benefits surveys indicate that, in survey years 1992 and 1993, 21,983,900 full-time employees, or 29.1 percent of all full-time employees in private industry and state and local governments, participated in a self-funded health benefit plan (U.S. Department of Labor, 1994a and 1994b). However, these data represent only full-time employees and do not give information on their dependents or part-time employees covered by a self-funded health plans. The U.S. General Accounting Office (GAO) estimated that 44 million individuals (workers and their dependents) were covered by a self-funded health plan in 1993.[1]

ERISA and Pension Plans

Reporting and Disclosure—ERISA's extensive reporting and disclosure requirements are rooted in a belief that availability of information serves two important needs. First, adequate communication about the plan to participants can lead to employees having more realistic expectations of their benefits. Second, periodic reporting to government helps officials monitor legal compliance.

Employee benefit plan sponsors subject to ERISA are required to provide summary plan descriptions (SPDs) to plan participants and beneficiaries. The summary must be written so that the average participant can understand it, and must be accurate and detailed enough to reasonably inform participants and beneficiaries of their rights and obligations.

The law does not dictate the exact form the SPD should take. However, it does require inclusion of specific information. For example, among other things, an SPD must include:
- the name and address of the employer or employee organization maintaining the plan;
- the name and/or title and business address of each trustee;
- plan requirements for participation and benefit accrual eligibility;
- a description of provisions for nonforfeitable pension benefits;
- information regarding credited service and breaks in service (defined

---

[1] The General Accounting Office (GAO) number comes from a model the GAO developed using data from the Bureau of Labor Statistics employee benefit surveys, the March supplement to the 1994 Current Population Survey, data from the Form 5500 filings, a 1994 Rand, Inc. survey of 10 states done for the Robert Wood Johnson Foundation, and various consulting firm data (Foster Higgins and KPMG Peat Marwick). See U.S. General Accounting Office, *Employer-based Health Plans: Issues, Trends, and Challenges Posed by ERISA* (Washington, DC: U.S. General Accounting Office, 1995).

later); and

- a description of situations that may result in disqualification, denial, loss, or forfeiture of benefits.

In addition to the SPD, each participant and beneficiary must have access to financial information about the plan. This information is provided in summary form (summary annual report), drawn from a more extensive annual report (Form 5500 series) filed with the Internal Revenue Service (IRS), a division of the U.S. Department of the Treasury. Such information is intended to give participants and beneficiaries an awareness of the plan's financial status. (The full annual report, which IRS sends to DoL, includes detailed information on the number of plan participants; plan benefit obligations; distributions made to participants and beneficiaries; financial, actuarial, and insurance data; and the amount and nature of the plan's assets. Participants may obtain the full report from DoL.)

Participants are also entitled to see other documents relating to the plan (e.g., insurance contracts, trustee reports, etc.). Once a year, participants and beneficiaries may request a written statement of accrued and vested benefits. A plan participant who terminates service with vested benefits that are not paid at that time must be given a statement showing the amount of accrued and vested benefits. A participant who requests such material and does not receive it within 30 days may file suit in a federal court. The court may require the plan administrator to furnish the materials, and it may impose a penalty of up to $100 a day until the materials are received.

Other reports must be filed when certain events occur. DoL, for example, must be notified when a new plan is established (through the SPD) or when an existing plan is revised (through the Summary of Material Modifications). PBGC must be notified when private defined benefit plans are terminated.

Fiduciary Requirements—Employers who sponsored retirement plans before ERISA were subject to one general fiduciary standard: plans had to be operated for the exclusive benefit of participants and beneficiaries. ERISA expanded this principle and applied it to almost all employee benefit plans. Fiduciaries are broadly defined as those who exercise control or discretion in managing plan assets; those who render investment advice to the plan for direct or indirect compensation or have authority to do so; and those who have discretionary authority in administering the plan. They may include individual employers and officers and will include trustees and plan administrators. Attorneys, actuaries, accountants, and consultants would generally not be considered fiduciaries when performing their normal professional services.

In fulfilling their responsibilities, fiduciaries must act in the exclusive interest of plan participants and plan beneficiaries, diversify the plan's assets to minimize risk of large losses, and act in accordance with documents that govern the plan.

Fiduciaries must act with the care, skill, prudence and diligence under the circumstances then prevailing that a "prudent man" acting in a like capacity and familiar with such matters would use in the conduct of an enterprise of a like character and with like aims. This standard is frequently referred to as ERISA's prudent man rule. Because the performance standard is so high, the prudent man rule is often referred to as the prudent expert rule.

Fiduciaries must meet this test in performing any aspects of plan operation for which they are responsible—from selecting the individual or institution that will handle plan asset investment to setting investment objectives. A fiduciary who violates ERISA's standards may be personally liable to cover any losses resulting from failure to meet responsibilities and may be required to return any personal profits realized from his or her actions. Additionally, fiduciaries may be liable for the misconduct in some circumstances, e.g., if they know about such misconduct and fail to take appropriate remedial action.

DoL is responsible for enforcing these standards. In certain situations, DoL may bring suit on behalf of participants in plans that do not satisfy ERISA's fiduciary standards. DoL may also assess a monetary penalty for any breach of fiduciary responsibility even with respect to a person other than a fiduciary who knowingly participates in the wrongdoing.

Certain transactions between a pension plan and parties in interest are prohibited. Parties in interest include, but are not limited to, a fiduciary, a person providing services to the plan, an employer whose employees are covered in the plan, an owner of 50 percent or more of the business, a relative of any of the above parties, or a company at least 50 percent owned by any individual noted above. Prohibited transactions include: the sale, exchange, or leasing of property; lending money or extending credit; furnishing goods, services, or facilities; use of plan assets; and acquisition of qualifying employer securities and real property in excess of allowable limits.

ERISA provides specific exemptions for certain circumstances as well as a process for applying to the DoL for an administrative exemption. ERISA prohibits anyone, including the employer, from discriminating against a participant to prevent the participant from obtaining benefit rights or for the exercise of his or her benefit rights. If a participant is fired or otherwise discriminated against in violation of this provision, he or she may seek assistance from DoL or may file suit in federal court.

Assignment of Benefits—The assignment of benefits to another person (also called alienation) under a pension plan is prohibited, with certain exceptions, including: the assignment of up to 10 percent of a benefit that is in pay status; the use of an employee's vested benefit as collateral for a plan loan (if not a prohibited transaction); and payment pursuant to a qualified domestic relations order (QDRO). A QDRO assigns to an alternate payee (spouse, former spouse, or dependent) the right to receive all or a portion of the benefits payable to a participant (even where the participant is still employed).

Minimum Standards and Other Qualified Plan Rules—ERISA also sets specific standards for eligibility, coverage participation, vesting, benefit accrual, and funding of retirement plans. Most of these represent minimum requirements (thus the term *minimum standards*); employers may adopt plans with more liberal standards.

General Eligibility—A pension plan may require that an employee meet an age and service requirement before becoming eligible for participation. However, the employer cannot require the employee to be over age 21 or to have completed more than one year of service with the employer, typically defined as at least 1,000 hours of work in a 12-month period. An exception applies to plans with immediate vesting; such plans may require completion of up to two years of service.

Coverage and Participation—An employer has some flexibility in determining who will be covered under the pension plan(s). For example, employee groups may be defined on the basis of pay (hourly vs. salaried), job location, or unionization. An employer may have one plan covering all these types of groups (and others) or separate plans. However, tax-qualified plan(s) must generally satisfy a set of nondiscrimination rules (under IRC sec. 401(a)(4), 410(b), and, in some cases, 401(a)(26)) designed to ensure that the plan arrangement does not discriminate in favor of highly compensated employees in coverage, participation, and benefits provided. (For more information on coverage and participation requirements, see chapter 12.)

Vesting—Participants generally attain nonforfeitable and nonrevocable—vested—rights to pension benefits after satisfying specific service (or years of participation) or age and service requirements. Once vested, an employee's rights generally cannot be revoked. ERISA requires a plan to adopt vesting standards for the employee's benefit (the account balance under a defined contribution plan or the accrued benefit under a defined benefit plan) at least as liberal as one of the following two schedules: full vesting (100 percent) after five years of participation in the plan (with no vesting prior to that time, known as cliff vesting) or graded (gradual) vesting of 20 percent after three years of service and an additional 20 percent after each subsequent year of service until 100 percent vesting is reached at the end of seven years of service. These rules apply to benefits attributable to employer contributions to a single-employer pension plan. Benefits attributable to employee contributions to either defined contribution or defined benefit plans and investment income earned on employee contributions to defined contribution plans are immediately vested.

Multiemployer plans, which cover the workers of two or more unrelated companies under a collective bargaining agreement, currently may use a 10-year cliff vesting schedule. This schedule means that employees do not attain vested rights to benefits attributable to employer contributions until they have completed 10 years of service but become 100 percent vested at that time. However, effective for plan years beginning on or after the earlier of (1) January 1, 1997, or expiration of the collective bargaining agreement under which the plan is maintained, whichever is later or (2) January 1, 1999, multiemployer plans will be subject to these same vesting rules as other qualified plans. Multiemployer plans may provide for cancellation of part of a vested benefit when the participant's employer withdraws (see section on plan termination insurance).

Full vesting must also occur when a participant reaches the plan's normal retirement age (commonly age 65, but sometimes earlier) or (to the extent the benefit is then funded) if the plan is terminated; some plans provide for it on early retirement, death, or disability. Loss or suspension of benefits can occur in some situations, however. If a participant and spouse have both waived the preretirement survivor option (discussed later in this chapter), the spouse will not be entitled to any benefit based on employer promises or contributions in a qualified retirement plan should the participant die before retirement. Additionally, benefits paid to retired participants may be suspended during reemployment with the same employer. Participants who take their own contributions out of the plan may—if they are not sufficiently vested—lose their rights to employer plan contributions but must be permitted to buy back the forfeited benefits on repayment of contributions and interest.

In many cases, an employee who is not vested can have a break in service (temporary cessation of covered employment) without losing credit for previous years of service.[2] Revised break-in-service rules were legislated under the Retirement Equity Act of 1984 and require prior service to be reinstated unless the number of consecutive one-year breaks in service is equal to, or exceeds, the greater of five years or the number of prebreak years of service. Benefit credit is further protected while an employee is on parental leave.

Form of Benefit Payment—ERISA requires retirement plans that offer an annuity as a payment option to provide a qualified joint and survivor (J&S) annuity for married participants as the normal method of benefit payment. This provides the surviving spouse with a lifetime monthly income equal to at least one-half the amount of the employee's benefit. To pay for this protection, the employee's benefit usually is reduced. In order to select a pension paid over the duration of the participant's life only (or any other payment form), both the participant and the spouse must refuse the J&S option in writing. (The spouses' signatures must be notarized or made before a plan administrator.) The J&S need not be provided unless the participant has been married at least one year.

Plans may make additional death benefits available to vested participants in the form of a life insurance contract or a cash distribution as long as these benefits are incidental to the pension plan, which is defined explicitly by IRS.

Most plans must also provide preretirement survivor benefits to the spouse of a vested participant who dies before retirement. The benefit is payable in the form of an annuity for the life of the surviving spouse beginning at what would have been the employee's normal retirement date or, at the election of the surviving spouse, as early as the employee's earliest retirement date or death, whichever is later.[3] Unless both spouses waive this benefit option in writing, these benefits will be provided to the surviving spouse even if the participant had named someone else as his or her

---

[2] If an employee completes fewer than 1,000 hours of service within a computation period, credit need not be given for a year of service, and the employee need not be given any benefit accrual for the period in question. However, if the employee has completed at least 501 hours of service in the computation period, this will prevent the employee from incurring a "break in service." Whether the employee has incurred a break in service is significant in terms of eligibility and vesting of benefits.

[3] Profit-sharing plans generally do not have to comply with spousal provisions, if the surviving spouse is the beneficiary.

heir. The annuity must be equal to at least one-half of the participant's accrued benefit at the time of his or her death. To reflect the cost of providing survivor protection, employers are allowed to provide a lower benefit to the participant. Preretirement survivor benefits need not be provided unless the participant has been married at least one year.

Benefit Accrual—ERISA requires that plans use one of three alternative formulas to determine the minimum speed at which defined benefit pension benefits accrue to participants. In general, benefit amounts in a defined benefit plan accrue over the period of an employee's plan participation, but they do not have to accrue evenly over that time. The law focuses only on the rate of benefit accrual, generally forbidding benefits to accrue disproportionately at the end of an employee's career; it does not mandate any specific benefit levels. However, benefit accruals may not be reduced or discontinued because of age. Thus employees who work beyond normal retirement age will continue to receive credit for time worked and contributions made to their plan, but the employer is allowed to restrict the number of years of benefit accrual.

Funding—Assets in qualified pension plans must be kept separate from the employer's general assets.[4] A plan may be maintained through one of a number of vehicles. One method is to establish a trust agreement with a bank or similar institution. In this case, the trust holds the plan's money and invests it, and the employer does not have access to the funds. A plan may also be maintained with an insurance company through allocated or unallocated accounts. If the allocated arrangement is used, separate accounts are established for each plan participant prior to retirement, and total contributions are divided among participants. Under an unallocated arrangement, a pool of funds is established and benefits are paid from it. Pension plans may also be maintained through individual policies issued on each participant's life. Sometimes both arrangements are used.

To ensure that pension plans have sufficient assets to pay benefits when participants retire, ERISA established minimum funding standards for defined benefit and some defined contribution plans. Money purchase and target benefit plans are covered under these requirements but not profit-

---

[4]The Small Business Job Protection Act of 1996 requires the Department of Labor to promulgate regulations clarifying which assets of an insurance company become subject to ERISA if that insurance company provides policies to an ERISA-covered employee benefit plan. New policies issued after 1998 will be subject to the fiduciary obligations under ERISA.

sharing, stock bonus, or most employee stock ownership plans.[5] For money purchase and target benefit plans, the minimum contribution is the amount set out in the plan formula. Single-employer defined benefit plans must make at least a minimum contribution equal to the normal cost of the plan plus amounts necessary to amortize in equal installments any unfunded past service liabilities, any experience gains or losses, any waived funding deficiencies, any changes in actuarial assumptions, and other items.[6] The amortization period for past service liabilities is generally 30 years and for experience gains or losses and funding deficiencies 5 years. For changes in actuarial assumptions, the amortization period is 10 years. The contribution must be made through quarterly payments.[7] Employers and their corporate affiliates that do not make the necessary contribution are subject to an excise tax on the unpaid amount. The IRS can grant waivers of the minimum funding contribution in limited circumstances of employer business hardship. A company cannot obtain more than three waivers in any 15 consecutive years.

Accelerated contributions are required for certain underfunded plans (other than those with fewer than 100 participants). Although originally modified as part of the Omnibus Budget Reconciliation Act of 1987, several flaws in the methodology required additional modification. The Retirement Protection Act of 1994 (RPA) imposed more stringent minimum funding requirements for these plans and reduced their flexibility in choosing interest rate and mortality assumptions. For a more detailed discussion of

---

[5] In a money purchase plan, employer contributions are mandatory and are usually based on each participant's compensation. A stock bonus plan is similar to a profit-sharing plan but usually makes benefit payments in the form of company stock. A target benefit plan is a cross between a defined benefit plan and a money purchase plan, with an initial defined retirement benefit target as in a defined benefit plan but with contributions allocated similarly to a money purchase plan. An employee stock ownership plan must be invested primarily in employer stock.

[6] The normal cost equals the cost of pension benefits earned that year and administrative costs. Past service liabilities occur when credit for an employee's past service prior to the inception of the plan is granted. Experience gains or losses result from changes in actuarial assumptions or methods.

[7] Technically, only underfunded plans incur a financial penalty for missing a quarterly contribution. Moreover, the RPA of 1994 introduced a new liquidity requirement that must be recalculated each quarter. For more details on this topic, see William M. Mercer (1994). Subsequent to the passage of the RPA, the Treasury Secretary was given the flexibility to waive the liquidity shortfall excise tax upon a showing of reasonable cause for failure to meet the liquidity requirement.

these calculations, see William M. Mercer (1994).

The funding rules for multiemployer plans are somewhat different from those for single-employer plans. For example, multiemployer plans may amortize experience gains and losses over 15 years rather than 5 years, and contributions to cover their required minimum funding do not have to be made in quarterly installments. Multiemployer plans are not subject to the special accelerated contribution rules noted above. (For further discussion of these rules, see chapter 14 on multiemployer plans.)

There are also maximum funding limits on tax-deductible contributions. For defined contribution plans other than profit-sharing plans, the amount deductible may not exceed the limit on annual additions to the plan. (For further explanation of funding limits, see chapter 4 on pension plans.) For profit-sharing plans, the maximum annual limit for deduction purposes is 15 percent of compensation.

For defined benefit plans, the maximum is normal cost plus 10-year amortization of unfunded past service liabilities, up to the the full-funding limit. The full-funding limit is essentially the lesser of roughly 100 percent of projected benefits (100 percent of benefits based on projected salary increases) or 150 percent of the plan's current liability, which essentially is all existing liabilities to employees and beneficiaries, except for benefits contingent on certain unpredictable events. Furthermore, in the case of a plan (other than a multiemployer plan) that has more than 100 partici-pants, the maximum deductible contribution will never be less than the plan's unfunded current liability.

There is a 10 percent excise tax on nondeductible employer contribu-tions. In practice, employers generally contribute no more than they can currently deduct. If both a defined benefit pension plan and a defined contribution plan exist, with overlapping payrolls, the total amount deduct-ible in any taxable year under both plans cannot exceed 25 percent of the compensation paid or accrued to covered employees for that year. However, the Retirement Protection Act of 1994 waives the excise tax if the nonde-ductible contribution to the defined contribution plan is no more than 6 percent of compensation. If the contribution is larger, the excise tax would apply to any amount over 6 percent.

Contributions and Benefits—ERISA also set maximum limits on annual contributions and benefits that qualified retirement plans may provide for each participant. The limits are known as sec. 415 limits, referring to the IRC section that defines them. There are separate limits for defined benefit and defined contribution plans. (For a description of these limits, see chapter 4 on pension plans.)

Plan Termination Insurance—Title IV of ERISA established the PBGC to insure payment of certain pension plan benefits in the event a covered (i.e., private-sector defined benefit) plan terminates with insufficient funds to pay the benefits. Covered plans or their sponsors must pay annual premiums to PBGC to provide funds from which guaranteed benefits can be paid. Both single-employer and multiemployer plans are covered under Title IV, but under separate insurance programs. Coverage is mandatory if the employer is in interstate commerce or the plan has been determined to be qualified for tax-favored status. Certain plans are exempt, including defined contribution plans, government and church plans, plans established by fraternal societies to which no employer contributions are made, and plans established and maintained by a professional service employer with 25 or fewer participants in the plan. The contributing sponsor or plan administrator must pay the premiums imposed by the PBGC. If the contributing sponsor of any plan is a member of a controlled group, each member is jointly and severally liable for any premiums.

ERISA set the premium for single-employer plans at $1 per plan participant per year. The rate, which must be legislated by Congress, has subsequently been increased a number of times. The Omnibus Budget Reconciliation Act of 1987 (OBRA '87) not only increased the premium but significantly changed the premium structure for single-employer pension plans. Certain provisions of OBRA '87, also known as the Pension Protection Act, raised the base premium to $16 per participant. In addition, for plans with more than 100 participants, a variable-rate premium of $6 was imposed for each $1,000 of unfunded vested benefits, rising to a maximum total premium of $50 per participant per year.

The Omnibus Budget Reconciliation Act of 1989 (OBRA '89) made further modifications. For plan years beginning after 1990, the single-employer flat-rate per-participant premium was increased to $19. The additional premium required of underfunded plans was increased to $9 per $1,000 of unfunded vested benefits, rising to a maximum additional premium of $53 per participant per year. However, the Retirement Protection Act of 1994 will gradually eliminate this cap. Technically, for plan years beginning on or after July 1, 1994, 20 percent of the variable rate premium over $53 must be paid. The rate increases to 60 percent in the following year, and for plan years beginning on or after July 1, 1996, the cap is eliminated.

The Retirement Protection Act of 1994 also required changes in several of the assumptions and methods for purposes of determining the value of vested benefits. Prior to 1995, the sponsor was allowed to use the mortality table used for funding in determining its unfunded vested benefits. For plan years beginning on or after January 1, 1995, plans must adopt a specified mortality table, and they eventually will need to adopt a new mortality table that will be issued by the Treasury Department. Prior to 1995, the plan was required to use an interest rate between 90 percent and 110 percent of the weighted average of 30-year Treasury securities during the four-year period prior to the beginning of the plan year. The Retirement Protection Act of 1994 lowers the maximum interest rate that can be used for this purpose for plan years beginning on or after January 1, 1999, to 105 percent of the weighted average described above. For the 1995, 1996, 1997, and 1998 plan years, this percentage is 109 percent, 108 percent, 107 percent, and 106 percent, respectively, of the weighted average.

Multiemployer premium rates, originally set at $.50 per plan participant per year, were raised by the 1980 Multiemployer Pension Plan Amendments Act (MPPAA) to $1.40, with scheduled increases reaching $2.60 in 1989. PBGC could have accelerated the move to $2.60 to protect the multiemployer program's financial soundness but found that was not needed and thus to date has not asked Congress for an increase beyond the $2.60 rate.

Termination Policy—Voluntary terminations of single-employer plans are restricted to two cases: a standard termination and a distress termination. (PBGC may, at its discretion, force a termination in certain situations. This is known as an involuntary termination.) A standard termination is permitted only if the plan has sufficient assets to pay all of the plan's benefit liabilities. These include all accrued basic benefits, including those that were not vested at the time of termination, and could include other benefits as well. The term *benefit liabilities* is to be defined by IRS, although it is a key element in PBGC's program.

Underfunded plans may only terminate in a distress situation, which is allowed only if the entire corporate (controlled) group would not be able to pay its debts pursuant to a plan of reorganization without the termination or would be unable to continue business outside the Chapter 11 reorganization process. A distress termination is only possible with the approval of the bankruptcy court or PBGC.

For multiemployer plans, PBGC provided insurance coverage on a discretionary, plan-by-plan basis to participants of terminating plans until 1980, when MPPAA established an automatic benefit guarantee for all terminating covered multiemployer plans.[8]

Covered Plans and Benefits—PBGC guarantees certain nonforfeitable retirement benefits, and any death, survivor, or disability benefit either owed or in payment status at plan termination, under defined benefit plans covered by Title IV should such a plan terminate. Benefit guarantees are expressed in terms of life annuities, which are regular payments beginning at age 65 and made over the life of the beneficiary.

There are certain restrictions on the monthly benefit amount PBGC will pay. In general, payment of guaranteed benefits is limited to a maximum dollar amount that is adjusted annually to reflect increases in workers' wages. The maximum monthly benefit in 1995 is $2,573.86. The limit applies to a participant's total guaranteed benefit under all plans in which he or she is covered; it is not possible to receive separate insurance protection under several plans and, thus, to increase the total guaranteed benefit.

Insurance on new benefit provisions (i.e., benefits resulting from newly established plans or recent plan amendments) is phased in at 20 percent per year (or $20 per month if higher). Therefore, full insurance coverage may not apply to some benefits until they have been in effect for five years prior to plan termination. The guarantee pertains exclusively to benefits earned while the plan is qualified for favorable tax treatment. Additionally, benefits are guaranteed up to the stipulated maximum.

For multiemployer plans, MPPAA established a level of guaranteed benefits that is much lower than single-employer plan benefit guarantees. No portion of a multiemployer plan benefit is guaranteed until it has been in effect for five years; the maximum amount guaranteed per year of service is 100 percent of the first $5 in monthly benefit rate plus 75 percent of the lesser of the next $15 of the accrual rate in excess of $5 (i.e., a maximum of $20 per month for each year of service, or $600 per month for a 30-year employee). For a multiemployer plan, the guarantee only applies at the point of plan insolvency.

Employer Liability to PBGC—If a plan terminates in a distress situation with insufficient assets to meet all benefit liabilities, the contributing plan sponsor and each member of the controlled group is jointly and severally liable to PBGC for the total amount of unfunded liabilities plus interest

---

[8] Under the Employee Retirement Income Security Act's 1974 provisions, certain plans that were maintained by more than one employer were treated as single-employer plans. The Multiemployer Pension Plan Amendments Act allowed these plans to irrevocably elect—within one year of the act's enactment—to remain classified as single-employer plans.

on such liabilities from the termination date.

Different rules apply for multiemployer plans. MPPAA imposes liability, payable to the plan, on an employer for withdrawal from a multiemployer plan that is less than fully funded for vested benefits. Withdrawal liability is a legal obligation requiring an employer that discontinues or sharply reduces its contributions to a multiemployer plan to pay for its share of the plan's unfunded vested benefits. The employer must continue to make annual payments for 20 years or until the liability is satisfied, whichever occurs first.

Under MPPAA, full withdrawal occurs when an employer's contribution obligation to a plan permanently ceases, or if all of an employer's covered operations under a plan permanently cease. Partial withdrawal occurs when there is a defined reduction in an employer's contribution base (i.e., if there is a 70 percent decline in the number of contribution units—e.g., hours worked) continuing for three years. Partial withdrawal also results when an employer is no longer obligated to contribute under one of two or more collective bargaining agreements even though work continues that previously required contributions under the expired agreement, or because one or more (but not all) of an employer's facilities withdraws from a plan even though work continues at the withdrawing facility. PBGC assumes liability only when the entire plan is in financial difficulty. Thus, for multiemployer plans, plan insolvency, rather than plan termination, is the insured event. Plan trustees are responsible for identifying withdrawing employers, calculating the amount of the withdrawal liability, and collecting this liability.

Multiemployer plan trustees can adopt one of four methods set forth by PBGC for computing the employer's share of the unfunded vested benefits or develop their own computation method subject to PBGC approval. If plans do not choose a method, MPPAA requires that they use a presumptive rule.

Some limited exemptions from withdrawal liability apply to the building, construction, entertainment, trucking, moving, and warehousing industries. A de minimis rule also applies. Under this rule, withdrawal liability is waived for an employer whose share is less than $50,000 or 0.75 percent of the plan's total unfunded liability, whichever is smaller, and reduced if the allocated liability is larger (up to $150,000).

Conclusion

ERISA is the most comprehensive employee benefits law ever implemented. Since it became law, thousands of plans have been amended to comply with its requirements. As areas that were initially overlooked or treated inadequately have been identified, the law has been amended. More changes can be anticipated.

Bibliography

Allen, Everett T., Joseph J. Melone, Jerry S. Rosenbloom, and Jack L. VanDerhei. *Pension Planning: Pensions, Profit-Sharing, and Other Deferred Compensation Plans.* Seventh edition. Homewood, IL: Richard D. Irwin, Inc., 1992.

Pension Benefit Guaranty Corporation. *Employer's Pension Guide.* Washington, DC: Pension Benefit Guaranty Corporation, n.d.

_____. *A Legislative History of Public Law 45-214, 95th Congress.* Washington, DC: Pension Benefit Guaranty Corporation, 1978.

_____. *Your Guaranteed Pension.* Washington, DC: Pension Benefit Guaranty Corporation, 1994.

William M. Mercer. *New Rules for Underfunded Pension Plans: The Retirement Protection Act of 1994.* William M. Mercer, 1994.

U.S. Department of Labor. Bureau of Labor Statistics. *Employee Benefits in Medium and Large Private Establishments, 1993.* Washington, DC: U.S. Government Printing Office, 1994a.

_____. *Employee Benefits in State and Local Governments, 1992.* Washington, DC: U.S. Government Printing Office, 1994b.

U.S. General Accounting Office. *Employer-based Health Plans: Issues, Trends and Challenges Posed by ERISA.* Washington, DC: U.S. General Accounting Office, 1995.

Additional Information

ERISA Industry Committee
1400 L Street, NW, Suite 350
Washington, DC 20005
(202) 789-1400

Self-Insurance Institute of America
17,300 Redhill Avenue, Suite 100
Irvine, CA 92714
(714) 261-2553

U.S. Department of Labor
Pension and Welfare Benefits
Administration
200 Constitution Avenue, NW
Washington, DC 20210
(202) 219-8776

PART 2
RETIREMENT BENEFITS

4. Pension Plans

Introduction

The first pension plan in the United States was established in 1759 to benefit widows and children of Presbyterian ministers. But it was more than a century later, in 1875, before the American Express Company established a formal corporate plan (Allen, et al., 1992). During the next century, some 400 plans were established, primarily in the railroad, banking, and public utility industries. The most significant growth has occurred since the mid 1940s. In 1992, private pension plans numbered more than 708,000 and covered more than 45 million active participants (Employee Benefit Research Institute, 1995).

The statutory tax treatment of pensions was formally legislated through the Revenue Act of 1921, which exempted interest income of stock bonus and profit-sharing plans from current taxation and deferred tax to employees until distribution. Statutes enacted since 1921 have permitted employers to deduct a reasonable amount in excess of the amount necessary to fund current pension liabilities (1928); made pension trusts irrevocable (1938); and established nondiscriminatory eligibility rules for pension coverage, contributions, and benefits (1942). These provisions were incorporated into the Internal Revenue Code (IRC) of 1954 and, along with major modifications made by the Tax Reform Act of 1986 (TRA '86), constitute the basic rules governing the tax qualification of pension plans.[1]

The tax treatment accorded qualified plans provides incentives both for employers to establish such plans and for employees to participate in them. In general, a contribution to a qualified plan is immediately deductible in computing the employer's taxes but only becomes taxable to the employee on subsequent distribution from the plan. In the interim, investment earnings on the contributions are not subject to tax. This preferential tax treatment is contingent on the employer's compliance with rules set out in the Employee Retirement Income Security Act of 1974 (ERISA) and administered by the U.S. Department of the Treasury (under the IRC) and the U.S. Department of Labor (under ERISA). Plans not meeting ERISA qualification requirements may also be used to provide retirement income.

---

[1] For a list and description of laws governing the tax treatment of pensions, see Employee Benefit Research Institute (1995).

Nonqualified plans are generally governed by trust law rather than the tax code.[2]

Types of Plans

Defined Benefit Plans—In a defined benefit plan, the employer agrees to provide the employee a nominal benefit amount at retirement based on a specified formula. The formula is usually one of three general types: a flat-benefit formula, a career-average formula, or a final-pay formula.

- *Flat-Benefit Formulas*—These formulas pay a flat dollar amount for each year of service recognized under the plan.
- *Career-Average Formulas*—There are two types of career-average formulas. Under the first type, participants earn a percentage of the pay recognized for plan purposes in each year they are plan participants. The second type of career-average formula averages the participant's yearly earnings over the period of plan participation. At retirement, the benefit equals a percentage of the career-average pay, multiplied by the participant's number of years of service.
- *Final-Pay Formulas*—These plans base benefits on average earnings during a specified number of years at the end of a participant's career; this is presumably the time when earnings are highest. The benefit equals a percentage of the participant's final average earnings, multiplied by the number of years of service. This formula provides preretirement inflation protection to the participant but can represent a higher cost to the employer.[3]

Flat-benefit formulas are common in collectively bargained plans or plans covering hourly paid employees. Career-average and final-pay formulas are most common in plans covering nonunion employees. Under pay-related formulas, an employer has some discretion in defining pay for plan purposes provided the definition does not discriminate in favor of highly compensated employees, subject to the statutory and regulatory definition of compensation used in testing for nondiscrimination. Under ERISA's minimum standards, there is also some leeway in determining what employment

---

[2] The discussion in this chapter focuses on qualified plan rules. For a review of nonqualified plans, see Rosenbloom (1996).

[3] Very few private-sector defined benefit plans provide postretirement indexed benefits, compared with public-sector plans. (For more information on public-sector defined benefit pension plans, see chapter 40).

period will be recognized in the benefit formula. The benefit may reflect only the plan participation period or may be based on the entire employment period.

Defined Contribution Plans—In a defined contribution plan, the employer makes provision for contributions to an account established for each participating employee. The final retirement benefit reflects the total of employer contributions, any employee contributions, and investment gains or losses. Sometimes the accumulated amount includes forfeitures resulting from employer contributions forfeited by employees who leave before becoming vested. (For a definition of this term, see chapter 3 on ERISA). As a result, the level of future retirement benefits cannot be calculated exactly in advance. Employer contributions to defined contribution plans are often based on a specific formula such as a percentage of participant salary or of company profits. The plans may be designed to include pretax or after-tax employee contributions, which may be voluntary or mandatory. There are several types of defined contribution plans. In a money purchase plan, employer contributions are mandatory and are usually stated as a percentage of employee salary. In a profit-sharing plan, total contributions to be distributed are often derived from a portion of company profits. Stock bonus plans are similar to profit-sharing plans but usually make contributions and benefit payments in the form of company stock. A target benefit plan is a cross between a defined benefit plan and a money purchase plan—with a targeted benefit used to determine the level of contributions but with contributions allocated to accounts as in a money purchase plan. A thrift, or savings, plan is essentially an employee savings account, often with employer matching contributions. In a 401(k) arrangement, an employee can elect to contribute, on a pretax basis, a portion of current compensation to an individual account, thus deferring current income tax on the contribution and the investment income earned. In an employee stock ownership plan (ESOP), employer contributions to employee accounts must be primarily in company stock.

Contributions and Benefits

Individual Participant Limits—ERISA originally set limits on the contribution and/or benefit amounts that retirement plans could provide to individual participants on a tax-deductible basis under IRC sec. 415. Under defined benefit plans, the original maximum annual benefit at age 65 was set at the lesser of $75,000 per year or 100 percent of the participant's average compensation over the three consecutive highest earning years. Under defined contribution plans, the maximum annual contribution (including a portion of employee contributions) was originally limited to the lesser of $25,000 or 25 percent of compensation. Before 1983, the maximum limits were adjusted annually to reflect increases in the cost of living. The Tax Equity and Fiscal Responsibility Act of 1982 (TEFRA) imposed new benefit and contribution limits beginning in 1983 and froze them at these levels until 1985. The Deficit Reduction Act of 1984 extended the freeze on cost-of-living adjustments until 1988. TRA '86 made further changes, setting the dollar annual benefit limit under a defined benefit plan to $90,000, adjusted for changes in the consumer price index (CPI). (The 1996 limit is $120,000.) The annual dollar contribution limit for defined contribution plans is $30,000 and will also increase in the future as the CPI increases. A special limit applies to participants covered by a defined benefit and a defined contribution plan maintained by the same employer; however, this limit is generally repealed for "limitation" years beginning after December 31, 1999.[4]

Employee Contributions—Both pretax and after-tax employee contributions are included in computing the above limits. Furthermore, each of these has its own separate limits. Employee pretax contributions are limited to $9,500 in 1996 (adjusted for inflation) for 401(k) arrangements and 403(b) tax-deferred annuities. After-tax contributions in practice may be limited by nondiscrimination rules under IRC sec. 401(k) and 401(m). (For further discusiion of employee contributions, see chapter 8 on 401(k) arrangements.) There is an overall limit of $150,000 on annual compensation that can be considered for calculating benefit and contribution limits. This, too, is adjusted for changes in the cost of living.

Top-Heavy Plans—TEFRA established a new category of plans known as top-heavy plans. A plan is top heavy if more than 60 percent of the accounts or accrued benefits under the plan are attributable to key employees.[5] A key employee is defined as: an officer with annual compensation in excess of 50 percent of the annual defined benefit annual limit; 1 of the 10 employees owning the largest number of shares of the employer and having compensation in excess of the annual defined contribution limit; a

---

[4] See Allen, et al. (1992) for an explanation of the formula.

[5] Top-heavy rules do not apply to savings incentive match plan for employees (SIMPLE plans). (See chapter 8 on 401(k) cash or deferred arrangements for details.)

5 percent owner of the employer; or a 1 percent owner of the employer whose compensation exceeds $150,000.

A top-heavy plan must satisfy special requirements for vesting and for contributions and benefits. The required vesting schedules for a top-heavy plan are accelerated to three-year cliff and six-year graded (compared with five-year cliff and seven-year graded for non top-heavy plans. (For a description of these terms, see chapter 3 on ERISA).

Top-heavy plans must also provide a minimum benefit (for defined benefit plans) or a minimum contribution (for defined contribution plans) to nonkey employees. Under a top-heavy defined benefit plan, the annual retirement benefit of a nonkey employee must not be less than his or her average compensation[6] multiplied by the lesser of 2 percent times the number of years of service[7] or 20 percent. Under a top-heavy defined contribution plan, the employer's contribution for each nonkey employee must not be less than 3 percent of compensation. However, if the highest contribution percentage rate for a key employee is less than 3 percent of compensation, the 3 percent minimum contribution rate is reduced to the rate that applies to the key employee.

Plan Qualification Rules

Pension plans must satisfy a variety of rules to qualify for tax-favored treatment. These rules, created under ERISA and discussed in chapter 3, are designed to protect employee rights and to guarantee that pension benefits will be available for employees at retirement. The rules govern requirements for reporting and disclosure of plan information, fiduciary responsibilities, employee eligibility for plan participation, vesting of benefits, form of benefit payment, and funding. In addition, qualified plans must satisfy a set of nondiscrimination rules (under IRC sec. 401(a)(4), sec. 410(b), and in some cases sec. 401(a)(26)) designed to insure that a plan does not discriminate in favor of highly compensated employees. The nondiscrimination rules are satisfied through a series of complex rules that

---

[6] A participant's average compensation means the participant's average compensation averaged over a period of no more than five consecutive years during which the participant had the greatest aggregate compensation from the employer.

[7] However, the following years of service are not taken into account for determining the minimum annual retirement benefits: a year of service within which ends a plan year for which the defined benefit plan is not top heavy; and a year of service completed in a plan year beginning before 1984.

must be tested annually to ensure that the classification of employees who are eligible for participation (i.e., covered) is nondiscriminatory, and the proportion of eligible employees who actually participate in a plan is nondiscriminatory. In addition, the level of contributions and benefits under the plan(s) tested to ensure that they do not disproportionately accrue to the highly compensated. A highly compensated employee for a particular year is an employee who is a 5 percent owner (or who was a 5 percent owner in the preceding year), or any employee who in the prior year had compensation in excess of $80,000 (indexed) and who, if the employer elects to apply the top 20 percent rule, was in the top 20 percent of employees on the basis of compensation for the prior year.

The top 20 percent group is calculated by eliminating certain employees, such as seasonal or part-time employees, from the count.

Types of Distributions and Tax Treatment

Pension plans generally offer retiring participants a choice between two payment options: an annuity, in which the benefit is paid out in a stream of regular payments, usually monthly and usually over the life of the participant (or lives of the participant and spouse) but sometimes over some other specified period; or in a lump sum. The type of distribution and when it is taken determines the tax treatment.

Distributions in the Form of an Annuity—Benefits from a qualified plan payable in the form of an annuity are only included in the employee's income as payments are received. A portion of any after-tax employee contribution to the plan is considered a return of the contribution and therefore is not taxable.[8] An individual computes the tax-free portion of each year's distribution by dividing the individual's contributions and other amounts previously taxed by a specified factor. This factor is generally tied to the age of the participant when the payments begin.

The rules apply to distributions from pension or 401(k) plans, as well as

---

[8] Technically, there are two other components that may be received tax free: loans from the qualified retirement plan to the participant that were treated as taxable distributions and PS-58 costs (the amount of a participant's current taxable income as a result of receiving life insurance protection under a company's qualified retirement plan).

[9] In general, when the annuity starting date was prior to 1997, the tax free portion is derived using a formula that relates the amount of the participant's after-tax contribution (known as the investment in the contract, or basis) to the expected

distributions from sec. 403(b) arrangements. These rules do not apply to distributions from IRAs.[9]

Lump-Sum Distributions—A lump sum is commonly offered in defined contribution plans for distribution at retirement, death, or disability. Some defined contribution plans also provide an annuity option for their participants. However, if such an alternative exists and the benefit amount exceeds $3,500, the employer may not cash out the benefit unilaterally.

For tax years beginning prior to January 1, 2000, a lump-sum distribution may be entitled to special tax treatment if it is a distribution of an employee's total accrued benefit from all plans that is paid within a single tax year and made on the occasion of the employee's death, attainment of age $59^{1}/_{2}$, or separation from the employer's service (separate treatment applies to money purchase plans). Self-employed individuals may receive lump-sum distribution treatment only in the case of death, disability, or the attainment of age $59^{1}/_{2}$. A distribution of an annuity contract from a trust or an annuity plan may be treated as a lump-sum distribution. The distribution must occur within one year of the qualified event.

TRA '86 substantially changed the tax treatment of lump-sum distributions. Under prior law, which is still applicable to certain individuals covered by a transition rule, favorable capital gains treatment and 10-year forward income averaging applied. Amounts distributed as lump sums from qualified plans were separated into pre-1974 amounts and post-1973 amounts. This computation was made by multiplying the amount distributed by a fraction: the numerator was the number of months of active participation in the plan before January 1, 1974, and the denominator was the total number of months of active participation. The resulting sum was deemed the pre-1974 portion and, in the absence of the election described later, was taxed as a long-term capital gain. Such treatment may have been favorable to the taxpayer because only 40 percent of such capital gain was subject to tax. The balance of the lump-sum distribution was deemed the

return to the participant (which is based on life expectancy tables). The ratio of the basis to the expected return is multiplied by the annual annuity payment provided under the plan to derive the nontaxable portion of the annuity. An employee may not exclude from taxation amounts exceeding his or her total contribution to the plan. Thus, once the total amounts excluded from taxation equal the employee's basis, any remaining payments are taxable. There are also special provisions for a one-time deduction if the participant dies before the entire basis is collected (viz., the participant dies prior to his or her life expectancy). See Allen, et al. (1992) for details.

post-1973 portion and was treated as ordinary income.

An employee participating in the plan for 5 or more years prior to distribution could elect to use a special 10-year forward income averaging method to compute the amount of tax on the post-1973 amount. Under this special income averaging rule, a separate tax was computed at ordinary income rates assuming single status on one-tenth of the post-1973 amount (less a minimum distribution allowance[10]), and the resulting figure was multiplied by 10. Because of the progressive income tax rates and the fact that this tax was computed separately from the taxpayer's other income, the 10-year forward income averaging rule could result in substantial tax savings.

A separate election could be made to treat all pre-1974 amounts as ordinary income eligible for 10-year forward income averaging. Such an election could be advantageous since, depending on the amount of the distribution, 10-year forward income averaging might have produced a lower tax on the pre-1974 amount than would capital gains treatment. The election was irrevocable and applied to all subsequent lump-sum distributions received by the taxpayer.

TRA '86 phased out capital gains treatment for lump-sum distributions over 6 years beginning January 1, 1987, and eliminated 10-year forward averaging for taxable years beginning after December 31, 1986. Instead, it permits a one-time election of five-year forward averaging for a lump-sum distribution received after age 59½. Under a transition rule, a participant who attained age 50 by January 1, 1986, is permitted to make one election of 5-year forward averaging or 10-year forward averaging (at 1986 tax rates) with respect to a single lump-sum distribution without regard to attainment of age 59½ and to retain the capital gains character of the pre-1974 portion of such a distribution. Under the transition rule, the pre-1974 capital gains portion would be taxed at a rate of 20 percent.

Distributions from some tax-favored retirement plans are not currently eligible for lump-sum treatment and five-year averaging for qualified lump-sum distributions will be repealed for all plans effective for tax years beginning after December 31, 1999.[11] (Consult the chapters on other types of pension plans for more information on this issue.)

---

[10] See Allen, et al. (1992) for details.

[11] Grandfathered 10-year averaging and existing capital gains provisions for those who attained age 50 by January 1, 1986 will be retained.

Distributions for Special Events—Most pension plans pay benefits when events other than normal retirement or separation from service occur. Most of the benefit distributions are not mandatory. The amount of such benefits is usually based on the participant's accrued benefit at the time of the event.

- *Early Retirement*—Early retirement benefits are generally payable when a participant satisfies certain age and/or age and service requirements. The early retirement benefit is usually the accrued benefit reduced to reflect a participant's increased duration of benefit receipt. Sometimes, to encourage early retirement, subsidized early retirement benefits are paid until the participant is eligible for Social Security retirement benefits. This type of benefit may be limited to participants with long service or to those who are retiring because of a plant shutdown or staff reduction. The maximum benefit payable from a defined benefit plan under IRC sec. 415 must be actuarially reduced for retirees who claim benefits before the Social Security normal retirement age, which is currently 65 but scheduled to rise gradually to age 67 beginning in the year 2000.

- *Disability Benefits*—Plans generally pay full benefits on disability. Disability benefits may be tied to age and/or age and service requirements and are usually contingent on satisfying the plan's definition of disability. The definition of disability for plan purposes may be linked to the definition of disability under Social Security. (For further discussion of disability benefits, see chapter 2 on Social Security and Medicare.) The benefit may be a flat-dollar amount that continues until the participant's normal retirement date (assuming he or she remains disabled); then, at the normal retirement date, the normal retirement benefit would become payable. Or, the plan may pay the participant the unreduced, accrued benefit during the period before he or she reaches normal retirement age. Under yet a different method, the plan may reduce the participant's accrued benefit to reflect that benefits are paid before normal retirement. In some plans, disabled participants continue to accrue benefits from the time they become disabled through their normal retirement age. Where an employer also provides a long-term disability (LTD) plan, the pension plan benefit is usually postponed until the LTD benefit stops to avoid duplicate payments. (For further discussion of LTD plans, see chapter 30 on disability income.)

- *Late Retirement Benefits*—Most pension plans specify age 65 as the normal retirement age for plan participants, but employers may not force employees to retire because of age. These plans must reflect how benefits will be calculated for participants who remain employed beyond age 65. A plan must now recognize earnings and/or service after age 65 for pension contribution and benefit purposes.

- *Death Benefits before Retirement*—Some plans must provide a preretirement survivor benefit to the spouse of a vested participant who dies before retirement. The benefit is payable in the form of an annuity for the life of the surviving spouse, beginning at what would have been the employee's earliest retirement date, or death, whichever is later. The annuity must be equal to at least one-half of the participant's accrued benefit at the time of his or her death. To reflect the cost of providing survivor protection, the law permits employers to provide a lower benefit to the participant. Written spousal consent is needed to elect out of the coverage. A preretirement survivor annuity need not be provided unless the participant has been married at least one year and is at least 35 years old.
- *Death Benefits after Retirement*—Retirement benefits must be paid to married persons as a joint and survivor (J&S) annuity (if an annuity is a payment option). This provides the surviving spouse with monthly income equal to at least one-half the amount of the participant's benefit. To reflect the cost of the survivor protection, the participant's benefit is usually reduced. Both the participant and the spouse must give written consent to waive the J&S annuity, either to select a pension paid over the duration of the participant's life only or to elect that pension payments be paid to a nonspouse or be paid over a specified period. The J&S need not be provided unless the participant has been married at least one year and is at least 35 years old. Typically, any participant contributions (exceeding employer contributions) are refunded to a beneficiary if a participant dies before receiving his or her benefits.
- *Estate Benefits*—At one time, all except the portion of pension benefit attributable to employer money was free of estate tax, subject to certain limits on contributions and other rules. However, under current law, pension plan payments are included in a decedent's gross estate and taxed accordingly, subject to regular estate tax deductions (including one for the spouse).
- *Premature (Early) Distributions*—A 10 percent penalty tax is imposed on most pension plan distributions paid to individuals prior to age

$59^{1}/_{2}$. The penalty is designed to discourage the use of these funds prior to retirement. Distributions under certain conditions are exempt from the tax, including amounts rolled over to an individual retirement account (IRA) or other qualified plan, as are most distributions in the form of an annuity. Also exempt from penalty tax are payments made on the participant's death or disability; made after the participant has separated from service on or after age 55; used for medical expenses to the extent deductible for federal income tax purposes (IRC sec. 213); made in the form of distributions in substantially equal amounts over the life of the individual or the joint lives of the individual and the spouse, without regard to the age of the individual at the time of the distribution; or made to or on behalf of an alternate payee pursuant to a qualified domestic relations order.

The Unemployment Compensation Amendments Act of 1992 (UCAA) affects qualified pension plan distributions in four ways. Effective January 1, 1993, UCAA: liberalizes rollover rules; establishes a method of transferring eligible rollover distribution amounts between plans and IRAs in what will be referred to as directed rollovers; modifies the timing and content of the rollover notice required under IRC sec. 402(f); and imposes mandatory 20 percent income tax withholding on eligible rollover distributions that are not transferred as directed rollovers. The act also requires plans to be amended to allow participants the option of electing directed rollovers. However, qualified plans are not required to accept directed rollovers.[12] Final regulations have recently been issued for these tax law changes.[13]

- *Loans*—The availability of loans to participants is an exception to ERISA's general principle that transactions between a plan and parties in interest—such as participants—are prohibited because of potential abuse of funds earmarked for retirement. Plan loans are generally not treated as taxable distributions and are restricted to limited circumstances defined under IRC sec. 72 and ERISA sec. 408(b)(1).

  A plan loan must be described in writing. The amount of a new loan

---

[12] See David G. Shipp, "Easier Rollover Rules Also Bring New Mandatory Withholding Requirements," *Benefits Quarterly* (First Quarter 1993): 71–76.

[13] See "Final Regs. Explain Latest Rollover Requirements," *Taxation for Accountants* (November 1995): 306–307.

plus the outstanding balance of any other plan loans cannot exceed the lesser of $50,000 or the greater of one-half of the present value of the employee's nonforfeitable accrued benefit under the plan or $10,000. The $50,000 limit is reduced by the excess of the highest outstanding loan balance during the one-year period ending on the day before the new loan is made, over the outstanding balance on the date of the loan. A plan is permitted to impose a minimum loan amount as high as $1,000.

Loans must be repaid within five years. A longer term is available only for loans used to acquire the participant's principal residence. The loan must require substantially level amortization payments, payable at least quarterly. The interest rate must reasonably reflect rates charged on comparable loans made on a commercial basis. Interest paid to the plan also does not increase the individual's basis in the plan or tax-deferred annuity. Loans to owner-employees from Keogh plans continue to be prohibited transactions. The loan must be adequately secured so that, in the event of a default, the participant's retirement income is preserved and loss to the plan is prevented. Up to 50 percent of a participant's vested accrued benefit may be loaned without additional security being required.

- *Rollovers*—In general, lump-sum distributions from a qualified pension plan may be rolled over tax free into an IRA or another retirement plan. The transfer must be made within 60 days of the participant's receipt of the distribution from the first plan.

Timing of Distributions—Distributions of qualified plan balances must generally begin by April 1 of the year following the later of (1) the year in which the individual attains age $70^1/2$ or (2) the year the employee retires.[14] A minimum distribution is required to be paid out each year, loosely equal to the value of the individual's account divided by the individual's life expectancy, if the form of benefit payment is a lump sum. If the form of benefit is an annuity, the required distribution is the amount of annual annuity payment. A 50 percent nondeductible excise tax is imposed on the individual in any taxable year on the difference between the amount required to be distributed and the amount actually distributed. There is also

---

[14]Five percent owners and individual retirement account holders will be required to receive distribution by April 1 of the year following the year they attain age $70^1/2$, even if they are not yet retired.

a limit on the total annual amount that an individual may receive in retirement plan distributions. If total withdrawals in one year from all retirement plans (including IRAs) are over $155,000 (indexed), a 15 percent excise tax is imposed on the excess. The excess distributions tax is suspended for distributions received during 1997, 1998, and 1999.

A separate limit is used for any distribution that includes a lump-sum distribution in which forward averaging or capital gains treatment is elected. In this case, the lump-sum distribution is treated separately from the other distributions and is subject to a limit that is five times greater than the applicable limit for the year. A special rule allows a portion of an individual's benefit accrued before August 1, 1986, to be grandfathered, i.e., exempt from the tax.

Integration

Social Security benefits replace a greater proportion of preretirement earnings for lower paid employees than for higher paid employees. This is caused by two factors. Social Security taxes and benefits are based on earnings up to the taxable wage base rather than on all earnings. In addition, the Social Security benefit formula produces higher benefits—relative to earnings—for lower paid employees. Thus, to help compensate for greater Social Security benefits for lower paid employees, employers are permitted to provide proportionately higher pension benefits to higher paid employees. This benefit coordination is known as integration. (For further discussion of pension plan integration with Social Security, see chapter 13.)

Plan Termination

Although pension plans must be established with the intent that they will be permanent, employers are permitted to terminate their plans. If a defined benefit plan terminates with assets greater than the amount necessary to pay required benefits, the employer may recover the excess assets and use them for business or other purposes. A 50 percent excise tax is imposed on the amount recovered.[15] ERISA established plan termination

---

[15] This penalty is reduced to 20 percent if: 25 percent of the otherwise recoverable reversion is transferred to another qualified retirement plan that covers at least 95 percent of the active participants of the terminated plan; 20 percent of the otherwise recoverable reversion is used to provide pro rata increases in the benefits accrued by participants under the terminated plan; or (3) the employer is in Chapter 7 bankruptcy liquidation.

insurance to protect participants' benefits in the event a plan terminates with insufficient assets to pay benefits. (For a detailed discussion of termination insurance, see chapter 3 on ERISA.)

Bibliography

Allen, Everett T., Joseph J. Melone, Jerry S. Rosenbloom, and Jack L. VanDerhei. *Pension Planning: Pensions, Profit-Sharing, and Other Deferred Compensation Plans.* Seventh edition. Homewood, IL: Richard D. Irwin, Inc., 1992.

Employee Benefit Research Institute. *EBRI Databook on Employee Benefits.* Third edition. Washington, DC: Employee Benefit Research Institute, 1995.

Rosenbloom, Jerry S. *The Handbook of Employee Benefits: Design, Funding and Administration.* Homewood, IL: Dow Jones-Irwin, 1996.

Additional Information

Association of Private Pension and Welfare Plans
1212 New York Avenue, NW, Suite 1250
Washington, DC 20005
(202) 289-6700

Pension Benefit Guaranty Corporation
1200 K Street, NW
Washington, DC 20005
(202) 326-4000

U.S. Department of Labor
Pension and Welfare Benefits Administration
200 Constitution Avenue, NW
Washington, DC 20210
(202) 219-8776

U.S. Department of the Treasury
1500 Pennsylvania Avenue, NW
Washington, DC 20220
(202) 622-2000

5. Defined Benefit and Defined Contribution Plans: Understanding the Differences

Introduction

Both defined benefit and defined contribution pension plans offer various advantages to employers and employees. The features of each are generally distinct and quite different. This chapter describes the basics of each plan type, then looks at the specific factors that make each approach different.

Defined Benefit Plans

In a defined benefit plan, each employee's future benefit is determined by a specific formula, and the plan provides a nominal level of benefits on retirement. Usually, the promised benefit is tied to the employee's earnings, length of service, or both. For example, an employer may promise to pay each participant a benefit equal to a percentage of the employee's final five-year average salary times number of years of service at retirement, or the employer may pay a flat dollar amount per year of service. A defined benefit plan is typically not contributory—i.e., there are usually no employee contributions. And there are usually no individual accounts maintained for each employee. The employer makes regular contributions to the plan to fund the participants' future benefits. The employer bears the risk of providing the guaranteed level of retirement benefits. In 1993, 56 percent of full-time employees of medium and large private establishments were covered by defined benefit plans (U.S. Department of Labor, 1994).

Defined benefit plan sponsors may choose from several formulas for determining final retirement benefits. These include:
- *Flat-Benefit Formulas*—These formulas pay a flat-dollar amount for every year of service recognized under the plan.
- *Career-Average Formulas*—There are two types of career-average formulas. Under the first type, participants earn a percentage of the pay recognized for plan purposes in each year they are plan participants. The second type of career-average formula averages the participant's yearly earnings over the period of plan participation. At retirement, the benefit equals a percentage of the career-average pay,

multiplied by the participant's number of years of service.

- *Final-Pay Formulas*—These plans base benefits on average earnings during a specified number of years at the end of a participant's career (usually five years); this is presumably the time when earnings are highest. The benefit equals a percentage of the participant's final average earnings, multiplied by the number of years of service. This formula provides the greatest inflation protection to the participant but can represent a higher cost to the employer.

Defined Contribution Plans

In a defined contribution plan, employers generally promise to make annual or periodic contributions to accounts set up for each employee. (Sometimes defined contribution plans are referred to as individual account plans.) The current contribution is guaranteed but not a level of benefits at retirement, as in a defined benefit plan. In 1993, 49 percent of full-time employees in medium and large private establishments participated in one or more defined contribution plans, up from 45 percent in 1988 (U.S. Department of Labor, 1994).

The contribution to a defined contribution plan may be stated as a percentage of the employee's salary and/or may be related to years of service. Sometimes there are only employer contributions, sometimes only employee contributions, and sometimes both. The benefit payable at retirement is based on money accumulated in each employee's account. The accumulated money will reflect employer contributions, employee contributions (if any), and investment gains or losses. The accumulated amount may also include employer contributions forfeited by employees who leave before they become fully vested, to the extent such contributions are reallocated to the accounts of employees who remain. These are called forfeitures.

There are several types of defined contribution plans, including money purchase plans, profit-sharing plans, 401(k) arrangements, savings plans, and employee stock ownership plans (ESOPs). These are described briefly below. (For more detail, consult individual chapters on these plans.)

Savings, or Thrift, Plan—A savings, or thrift, plan is essentially an employee-funded savings plan. An employee generally makes contributions on an after-tax basis to an account set up in his or her name. The contributions are often stated as a percentage of pay. The contributions may be matched (in full or in part) by the employer, but there is no statutory obligation for employer contributions.

Profit-Sharing Plan—A profit-sharing plan provides for contributions to the plan sometimes based on annual profits for the previous year. However, profits are not required for contributions, and a company is under no obligation to make contributions on a regular basis. Contributions are typically divided among participants in proportion to their respective earnings.

Money Purchase Pension Plan—Employer contributions are mandatory in a money purchase plan. They are usually stated as a percentage of employee salary. Retirement benefits are equal to the amount in the individual account at retirement.

Employee Stock Ownership Plan—An ESOP is a tax-qualified employee benefit plan that provides shares of stock in the sponsoring company to participating employees. An ESOP is required to invest primarily in employer stock and is permitted to borrow money on a tax-deductible basis to purchase this stock.

401(k) Arrangement—A qualified cash or deferred arrangement, under sec. 401(k) of the Internal Revenue Code (IRC), allows an employee to elect to have a portion of his or her compensation (otherwise payable in cash) contributed to a qualified profit-sharing, stock bonus, or pre Employee Retirement Income Security Act of 1974 (ERISA) money purchase pension plan. The employee contribution is most commonly treated as a pretax reduction in salary.

An employer may adopt a defined contribution plan:
- as a step toward achieving employees' retirement income security;
- to supplement an existing defined benefit plan;
- to avoid the long-term funding and liability commitments, as well as the more burdensome regulations, of a defined benefit plan; and
- to create a program that provides benefits for short-term workers.

To illustrate the basic differences between the two approaches, the discussion in this chapter will focus on the major considerations involved in an employer's selection of a plan and the differences for employees. These include achievement of objectives, plan cost, ownership of assets and investment risk, ancillary benefit provisions, postretirement benefit increases, employee acceptance, employee benefits and length of service, plan administration, taxes, and regulations.

Achievement of Objectives

A foremost objective for many employers in adopting a retirement plan is to provide future retirement income to employees. Another is to help to maintain organizational efficiency and vitality. Sometimes a goal is to help reward long-term employees. Such goals usually require plans to be available for long periods of benefit accumulation.

A defined benefit plan can provide a meaningful retirement benefit for employees who remain with one employer throughout their career. An employee's earnings generally grow over the years, and if years of service are calculated, the longer the employee works for one employer, the greater the benefit. In addition, employees who begin employment with a new employer later in life can benefit from a defined benefit plan that is based on final average pay or career earnings. However, for employees who change jobs frequently, especially at younger ages, a defined contribution plan offers more portability. A defined contribution plan often has a shorter vesting period—i.e., the period of service required before the employee becomes entitled to the benefit.

Plan Cost

In adopting a defined benefit plan, an employer accepts an unknown cost commitment. Numerous factors determine the cost of promised benefits, including the rates of return on investment, the number of employees working until they become vested in a benefit, the nature of future government regulatory changes, and future employee pay levels. The unknown cost aspect of defined benefit plans is sometimes considered a deterrent. Employers estimate the unknown cost by projecting future interest earnings, mortality rates, personnel turnover, and salary increases; thus, they attempt to establish a reasonably level funding pattern. Moreover, the plan's assets and liabilities are evaluated periodically (usually annually), and contribution adjustments can be made on a regular basis. Within legal limits, the employer is permitted to vary contributions from year to year. Therefore, defined benefit plan sponsors are permitted a certain amount of contribution flexibility.

Defined contribution plan sponsors generally know the plan's cost on a yearly basis. The employer pays a set amount—usually on a regular basis. This cost control feature appeals to many employers, particularly newer and smaller companies. Some funding flexibility is possible under some types of defined contribution plans by basing employer contributions on profits, thus allowing the employer to temporarily forgo contributions during economic hardship.

Ownership of Assets and Investment Risk

The ownership of plan assets differs between defined benefit and defined contribution plans. In a defined contribution plan, contributions can be viewed as a deferred wage once an employee has become vested. The full vested value of each participant's account can be considered owned by the employee. Vested benefits are often distributable to employees on employment termination. Under defined contribution plans it is the employee who bears the investment risk. Favorable investment results will increase benefits, while unfavorable results will decrease benefits.

In a defined benefit plan, vested benefits can again be viewed as a deferred wage. It is here, however, that the difference in investment risk becomes important. Defined benefit plan sponsors assume an obligation for paying a stipulated future benefit. Consequently, the employer accepts the investment risk involved in meeting this obligation. If the pension fund earns a lower-than-expected yield, the employer will have to make additional contributions in order to provide the promised benefits. If the pension fund investment results are better than expected, the employer can reduce annual contributions or increase the level of benefits, perhaps on an ad-hoc basis. (See the following section on postretirement benefit increases.)

Ancillary Benefit Provisions

Although retirement plans are intended first and foremost to provide retirement income, they must, under some circumstances, make some provision for paying benefits in the event of a participant's death. (For further discussion of death benefits, see chapter 4 on pension plans.) Most plans provide early retirement benefits as well.[1] To receive ancillary benefits, employees may be required to satisfy certain eligibility requirements, although the law places limits on such requirements.

Defined contribution thrift and profit-sharing plans usually pay a vested employee's individual account balance in full on death, employment termination, retirement, or disability. Defined benefit plans frequently distribute the vested benefit as a stream of level monthly payments for life or for some stated period beginning at the time the employee retires early, at the normal age, or later. This is called an annuity.

---

[1] Disability benefits may also be provided.

Postretirement Benefit Increases

During periods of inflation, the pensioner's financial position is brought into sharp focus. In such periods, retired employees living on fixed pensions, or on incomes derived from investing lump-sum retirement distributions, have been affected by the dollar's declining value. Automatic Social Security benefit increases have helped, but they frequently have not provided total retirement income increases comparable with inflationary increases for above-average earners.

Most employers are concerned about their retired workers' financial problems. However, few sponsors of defined benefit plans can afford the uncertainty of providing automatic cost-of-living adjustments under their plans. If resources are available, many employers are willing to voluntarily grant ad hoc benefit increases after retirement to help offset inflation. Defined contribution thrift and profit-sharing plan sponsors usually provide the option of lump-sum distributions at retirement. Money purchase pension plans may require that pension benefits be taken in the form of an annuity.

Employee Acceptance

By nature, defined benefit plans are complex. The formulas are often complicated. The legal documents explaining the plan and employee rights under the plan can be difficult to understand. Numerous government regulations have added more and more complexity to the operation of defined benefit plans, making them more difficult to understand. Sometimes, promised future benefits may seem remote to the employee, and the current dollar value of benefits is not clear.

Defined contribution plans can also be complex, but their complexity is less apparent to employees. Defined contribution plan participants have individual accounts; their accounts usually have known values expressed in dollars rather than benefit formulas. And the ability of employees to take accumulations in a lump sum at employment termination is often appealing.

Pension Benefits and Length of Service

Defined contribution plans offer distinct advantages to employees who change jobs frequently. Vesting provisions in these plans are generally more liberal than those for defined benefit plans. Many defined contribution plans provide at least partial vesting of employer contributions after two or three years of service. Employee contributions are always immediately and fully vested—as they are in defined benefit plans. Additionally, vested benefits under thrift and profit-sharing plans are normally paid in a lump sum at employment termination, but under defined benefit plans they are usually paid as an annuity.

Alternatively, defined benefit plans often have cliff vesting, with no vesting of benefits promised by the employer until employees work a certain number of years (capped by law). And defined benefit plans do not usually provide payment of vested benefits at employment termination; participants receive deferred monthly income when they become eligible to retire from employment. However, the benefit amount is usually frozen at termination, and the employee is exposed to future inflation unless the benefit is indexed to reflect cost-of-living adjustments.

Defined benefit plan benefit formulas may anticipate late-age hirings; they may be designed to provide adequate retirement benefits for employees with fewer years of service. This offers an advantage for the employee making a permanent job commitment relatively late in his or her career. Under defined contribution plans, employees hired later in life are less likely to accrue meaningful retirement benefits.

Plan Administration

Both defined benefit and defined contribution plans can be complex to administer; they usually require trained internal staffs and/or outside advisors. Defined contribution plans offer some administrative advantages over defined benefit plans. First, defined benefit plans require the use of actuarial projections that take into account the future number of employees, ages, life span, earnings, and other demographic characteristics. Defined contribution plans do not. Second, provisions of the tax code and ERISA tend to have less impact on defined contribution plans than on defined benefit plans. For example:

- Defined benefit plans must satisfy both minimum and maximum funding standards. (For more information on funding standards, see chapter 3 on ERISA.) Generally, defined contribution plans do not have to satisfy these standards.
- Most defined benefit plans must calculate and pay insurance premiums to the Pension Benefit Guaranty Corporation (PBGC) to protect pension benefits in the event of plan termination. Defined contribution

plans are by nature fully funded; therefore, they do not present the risks of defined benefit plans and are not subject to the pension insurance program. This also makes it administratively easier to terminate a defined contribution plan because approval by PBGC is not necessary. (For further information on PBGC premiums, see chapter 3 on ERISA.)

- ERISA originally set limits on the maximum benefits that could be paid from defined benefit plans and on maximum contributions to defined contribution plans. Several laws since ERISA have made changes to those benefit limits but with generally fewer and less restrictive limits on defined contribution plans. The calculation of these limits can be quite complicated.

- Defined benefit plans usually must provide more detailed and complicated actuarial disclosure reports than defined contribution plans. But, for defined contribution plans, recordkeeping can also pose complications, especially when employees are allowed different investment options or when loan and/or withdrawal provisions are provided.

Taxes

For employers, the tax impact under defined benefit and defined contribution plans is quite different. Under a defined contribution plan, employer contributions are a deductible business expense in the year they are paid to participants' accounts, subject to certain statutory limits. In a defined benefit plan, an employer must contribute a minimum amount to fund the future benefit, for which a tax deduction is also allowed. But the employer may not overfund the plan and has a maximum limit that cannot be exceeded without tax penalty.

For employees, the tax considerations associated with each plan are essentially the same. Employees do not pay taxes on employer contributions, investment income, or capital gains of retirement plan assets until they receive benefits. However, employees in defined benefit plans have traditionally paid taxes on their own plan contributions in the year such income was earned. Most private defined benefit plans do not require employee contributions, but public-sector defined benefit plans commonly do.

Under defined benefit and defined contribution plans, benefits are subject to income taxation when received by the employee. The tax consequences depend on the form of benefit payment, not on the type of plan. Lump-sum distributions are treated the same, for example, whether paid from a defined benefit or a defined contribution plan. If the benefit is in the form of an annuity, which is typical under defined benefit plans, ordinary income tax rates apply. (A portion of any employee contribution to the plan is considered a return of the contribution and therefore is not taxable.) The advantage here is that traditionally the employee has been in a lower income tax bracket when retired than during his or her working years, although this has become less likely under current tax laws. A distribution in the form of a lump sum may qualify for special tax treatment. Lump-sum distributions are common in defined contribution plans, especially for smaller amounts. (For further discussion of the taxation of lump sums and annuities, see chapter 4 on pension plans.)

Legislation and Regulations—Since the passage of ERISA, Congress has enacted many laws that have increased the complexity and administrative burden of pension plans, especially defined benefit plans. Such laws include the Economic Recovery Tax Act of 1981; the Tax Equity and Fiscal Responsibility Act of 1982; the Deficit Reduction Act of 1984; the Retirement Equity Act of 1984; the Consolidated Omnibus Budget Reconciliation Act of 1985; the Tax Reform Act of 1986; the Omnibus Budget Reconciliation acts of 1986, 1987, and 1989; and the Retirement Protection Act of 1994. Many observers agree that continuing legislative and regulatory change has added unnecessary complexity and uncertainty to plan sponsorship. The Small Business Job Protection Act of 1996 represents a significant change in direction toward simplification.

Conclusion

In the past, defined benefit plans were generally adopted as the primary vehicle for meeting employees' retirement income needs. More recently, due to changes in legislation, employee attitudes, and the mobility of the work force, there is more interest in defined contribution plans. Over the last 10 years, the number of defined contribution plans has grown at a much faster rate than that of defined benefit plans (Employee Benefit Research Institute, 1995). Some employers believe that the most effective retirement program combines the two types of plans, making maximum use of the particular cost and benefit advantages of each.

An employer could, for example, adopt a defined benefit plan that provides a modest level of benefits and supplement these benefits with a defined contribution thrift, profit-sharing, or 401(k) plan. The employer's cost risk under the defined benefit plan is decreased, while the two plans combine benefits to satisfy income adequacy standards.

Employers might also adopt a single plan that incorporates characteristics of both defined benefit and defined contribution plans. One type is a cash balance pension plan. (For a discussion of cash balance and other hybrid plans, see chapter 10.) Relatively new to the field, it is a defined benefit plan with features common to defined contribution plans. Another type is a target benefit plan, which is a defined contribution plan that has defined benefit plan features.

Defined benefit and defined contribution plans have distinctly different features that offer various advantages and disadvantages for both employers and employees. A close examination of all these features is important for employers in deciding whether to adopt a plan and for employees in understanding the plan in which they participate.

Bibliography

Allen, Everett T., Joseph J. Melone, Jerry S. Rosenbloom, and Jack L. VanDerhei. *Pension Planning: Pensions, Profit Sharing and Other Deferred Compensation Plans.* Seventh edition. Homewood, IL: Richard D. Irwin, Inc., 1992.

Burkhauser, Richard V., and Dallas L. Salisbury, eds. *Pensions in a Changing Economy.* Washington, DC: Employee Benefit Research Institute, 1993.

Employee Benefit Research Institute. *EBRI Databook on Employee Benefits.* Third edition. Washington, DC: Employee Benefit Research Institute, 1995.

Milne, Deborah, Jack VanDerhei, and Paul Yakoboski. "Can We Save Enough to Retire? Participant Education in Defined Contribution Plans." *EBRI Issue Brief* no. 160 (Employee Benefit Research Institute, April 1995).

Salisbury, Dallas L., and Nora Super Jones, eds. *Retirement in the 21st Century...Ready or Not....* Washington, DC: Employee Benefit Research Institute, 1994.

Silverman, Celia. "Pension Evolution in a Changing Economy." *EBRI Special Report* SR-17/*Issue Brief* no. 141 (Employee Benefit Research Institute, September 1993).

U.S. Department of Labor. Bureau of Labor Statistics. *Employee Benefits in Medium and Large Private Establishments, 1993.* Washington, DC: U.S. Government Printing Office, 1994.

Yakoboski, Paul. "Retirement Program Lump-Sum Distributions: Hundreds of Billions in Hidden Pension Income." *EBRI Issue Brief* no. 146 (Employee Benefit Research Institute, February 1994).

Yakoboski, Paul, et al. "Employment-Based Retirement Income Benefits: Analysis of the April 1993 Current Population Survey." *EBRI Special Report* SR-25/*Issue Brief* no. 153 (Employee Benefit Research Institute, September 1994).

Yakoboski, Paul, and Annmarie Reilly. "Salary Reduction Plans and Individual Saving for Retirement." *EBRI Issue Brief* no. 155 (Employee Benefit Research Institute, November 1994).

Yakoboski, Paul, and Sarah Boyce. "Pension Coverage and Participation Growth: A New Look at Primary and Supplemental Plans." *EBRI Issue Brief* no. 144 (Employee Benefit Research Institute, December 1993).

Additional Information

Association of Private Pension and Welfare Plans
1212 New York Avenue, NW, Suite 1250
Washington, DC 20005
(202) 289-6700

The Conference Board
845 Third Avenue
New York, NY 10022
(212) 872-1260

International Foundation of Employee Benefit Plans
P.O. Box 69, 18700 West Bluemound Road
Brookfield, WI 53008-0069
(414) 786-6700

Profit Sharing Council of America
10 S. Riverside Plaza, Suite 1460
Chicago, IL 60606
(312) 441-8550

6. Profit-Sharing Plans

Introduction

A profit-sharing plan is a type of defined contribution plan that is sometimes used as a supplement to a primary defined benefit plan. Sometimes these plans are structured in such a way that employees share in their companies' profits and potentially gain a greater interest in their firms' success.

About 100 years ago, Pillsbury Mills and Procter & Gamble each established a cash (defined below) profit-sharing plan. In 1916, Harris Trust & Savings Bank in Chicago established the first deferred (defined below) profit-sharing plan. In 1939, legislation clarified the tax status of deferred plans. This legislation and the World War II wage freeze resulted in rapid growth of profit-sharing plans in the 1940s. The Employee Retirement Income Security Act of 1974 (ERISA) furthered the growth by imposing less burdensome regulations on profit-sharing plans than on defined benefit pension plans, thus increasing their attractiveness.

Types of Plans

There are three basic types of profit-sharing plans.

Cash Plan—At the time profits are determined, contributions are paid directly to employees in the form of cash, checks, or stock. The amount is taxed as ordinary income when distributed.

Deferred Plan—Profit-sharing contributions are not paid out currently but rather are deferred to individual accounts set up for each employee. Benefits—and any investment earnings accrued—are distributed at retirement, death, disability, and sometimes at separation from service and other events.

Combination Plan—In this type of plan the participant has the option of deferring all or part of the profit-sharing allocation. That portion taken as a deferral is placed into the participant's account, where it and investment earnings accrue tax free until withdrawal. Any amount taken in cash is taxed currently. For tax purposes, Internal Revenue Service (IRS) qualification of profit-sharing plans is restricted to deferred or combination plans. Therefore, the remainder of this chapter will focus primarily on these two types of profit-sharing arrangements.

Plan Qualification Rules

Profit-sharing plans, as other retirement plans, must meet a variety of requirements to qualify for preferential tax treatment. These rules, created under ERISA and discussed in chapter 3, are designed to protect employee rights and to guarantee that pension benefits will be available for employees at retirement. The rules govern requirements for reporting and disclosure of plan information, fiduciary responsibilities, employee eligibility for plan participation, vesting of benefits, form of benefit payment, and funding. In addition, qualified plans must satisfy a set of IRS nondiscrimination rules (under Internal Revenue Code (IRC) secs. 401(a)(4), 410(b), and, in some cases, 401(a)(26)) designed to insure that a plan does not discriminate in favor of highly compensated employees.[1]

Contributions

Employer Contributions—Plans must define how employer contributions will be allocated to employee accounts. The allocation formula is generally based on compensation. Sometimes the allocation is a flat percentage of pay, or it may be determined by calculating the proportion of each employee's compensation relative to the total compensation of all plan participants. For example, if the employee earns $15,000 annually and total annual compensation for all participants is $300,000, he or she would receive 5 percent of the employer's annual contribution.

Some plans base their allocations on compensation and service credits. These plans must be careful to assure that the wage/service formula meets the regulatory scheme for demonstrating that the formula does not discriminate in favor of highly compensated employees. Whether a plan uses compensation or both compensation and service in determining allocations depends on an employer's objectives. If employee retention is a primary goal, this can be reflected in a pay-and-service allocation formula. Allocation formulas may be integrated with Social Security within prescribed limits. (For more information about integration with Social Security, see chapter 13.)

Maximum annual contributions (employer and employee, if any) on behalf of each plan participant are limited by the defined contribution limits under IRC sec. 415—the lesser of 25 percent of compensation or $30,000.

---

[1] A highly compensated employee is defined in chapter 4.

(For further details on contribution limits, including future increases in the dollar amount, see chapter 4 on pension plans.) But the total amount of contributions for all employees that an employer may deduct for federal tax purposes is limited to 15 percent of all covered employees' compensation.

Until recently, an employer's contribution to a profit-sharing plan was limited to the extent of an employer's current or accumulated profits. Currently, an employer does not have to have profits to establish a profit-sharing plan, and total contributions are not restricted to total profits. However, plan documents must specify that the plan is a profit-sharing plan.

If an employer's contribution for a particular year is less than the maximum amount for which a deduction is allowed, the unused limit may not be carried forward to subsequent years unless the carryforward existed as of December 31, 1986. These limit carryforwards may be used to increase the general deduction limit to 25 percent until the carryforwards are exhausted.

A deduction carryforward of contributions in excess of the deduction limit for a particular year may be deductible in succeeding taxable years to the extent allowed. However, such contributions may be subject to a 10 percent nondeductible excise tax. Excess contributions are defined as the sum of total amounts contributed for the taxable year over the amount allowable as a deduction for that year plus the amount of excess contributions for the preceding year, reduced by amounts returned to the employer during the year, if any, and the portion of the prior excess contribution that is deductible in the current year. In other words, if an excess contribution is made during a taxable year, the excise tax would apply for that year and for each succeeding year to the extent that the excess is not eliminated. Excess contributions for a year are determined at the close of the employer's taxable year, and the tax is imposed on the employer.

Employee Contributions—Pure profit-sharing plans do not require employee contributions, but some may permit voluntary employee contributions up to certain limits. The plan then generally looks more like a thrift plan. (See chapter 7 for a discussion of thrift plans.) Employee contributions in the form of a salary reduction are becoming increasingly popular. When pretax salary reduction is allowed, the plan must follow rules for 401(k) arrangements (see chapter 8 for a discussion of 401(k) plans).

Taxation—Employer contributions to a profit-sharing plan are deductible by the company as a business expense (up to the limits noted previously). Employees are not taxed on the deferred contributions—and any interest accrued—until distribution. Any allocation (all or part) taken in cash is taxed on a current basis.

Investments

Profit-sharing funds may be invested in a wide variety of vehicles including corporate stocks, bonds, real estate, insurance products, and mutual funds. In general, retirement plans may not hold more than 10 percent of their assets in employer securities. However, an exception exists for profit-sharing plans, stock bonus plans, thrift plans, and employee stock ownership plans, as well as money purchase plans that were in existence before ERISA's enactment and invested primarily in employer securities at that time. Therefore, contributions are frequently invested in employer securities. This practice may give participants an increased interest in the firm's success.

Individual account assets can be held in one fund or in several funds. The plan sponsor usually has responsibility for developing broad investment policies. The trustee (e.g., a bank) is usually responsible for the actual investment of plan assets. Some employers permit participants to select among several investment options. In addition, participants may be given individual direction within certain limits set forth in Department of Labor regulations.

Distributions

Retirement, Disability, and Death Benefits—The law requires that participants' account balances fully vest at retirement. In addition, plans generally provide for benefits on death and disability. The plan's vesting provisions determine whether an employee will receive full or partial benefits on other types of employment termination. However, if the plan is contributory (i.e., employees make contributions), the employee will always receive the benefits that are attributable to his or her own contributions. Profit-sharing plans typically give retiring participants and beneficiaries of deceased participants a choice between a lump-sum payment and installments. Usually, those who terminate employment for reasons other than retirement, death, or disability receive lump-sum distributions, although if the benefit exceeds $3,500, the participant cannot be forced to take an immediate benefit. Distributions from profit-sharing accounts must follow the distribution rules for all qualified retirement plans. Distributions must generally begin by the year following the attainment of age $70^{1/2}$, unless the individual has not retired. There are minimum and maximum limits on the amount of annual distribution, both subject to penalty taxes if not followed. (See chapter 4 for a complete description of pension plan distributions.)

In-Service Withdrawals—Some profit-sharing plans provide for partial account withdrawals during active employment. Plans allowing participants to elect account withdrawals impose certain conditions, which vary widely. But generally the funds must be held in the plan for two years before a withdrawal is allowed.

A 10 percent additional income tax applies to most early distributions made before age $59^1/_2$. The 10 percent additional tax does not apply to distributions that are: (1) due to the participant's death or disability; (2) in the form of an annuity or installments payable over the life or life expectancy of the participant (or joint lives or life expectancies of the participant and the participant's beneficiary); (3) made after the participant has separated from service on or after age 55; (4) used for payment of medical expenses deductible under federal income tax rules; (5) made to or on behalf of an alternate payee pursuant to a qualified domestic relations order; or (6) rolled over to an individual retirement account or another qualified plan within 60 days.

Loans—Some plans permit employees to borrow a portion of their vested benefits. In general, the employee must repay the loan according to a level amortization schedule, with payments made at least quarterly. If loans are permitted, they must be available to all participants on a comparable basis and must bear a reasonable interest rate. (For a detailed explanation of loan requirements, see chapter 4 on pension plans.)

Conclusion

Profit sharing offers employees a chance to share in their company's success. The level of company success is directly related to profits, which often define the amount of profit-sharing allocation. So the greater the profits of the company, the larger the potential allocation. However, profit-sharing plans can serve several goals. If the plan is cash only, it is generally viewed as a form of bonus. If profits are good, benefits are paid. However, these can become viewed as certain, and employees may spend anticipated benefits before they materialize. Deferred plans are generally intended to supplement other pension plans and thus are generally more appropriate for retirement purposes.

Because of their advantages to both employees and employers, profit-sharing plans will probably continue to play an important role in employee benefits planning.

Bibliography

Allen Everett T., Joseph J. Melone, Jerry S. Rosenbloom, and Jack L. VanDerhei. *Pension Planning: Pensions, Profit-Sharing, and Other Deferred Compensation Plans.* Seventh edition. Homewood, IL: Richard D. Irwin, Inc., 1992.

Bureau of National Affairs. *Non-Traditional Incentive Pay Programs.* Washington, DC: Bureau of National Affairs, 1991.

Employee Benefit Research Institute. *Databook on Employee Benefits.* Third edition. Washington, DC: Employee Benefit Research Institute, 1995.

Kruse, Douglas L. *Does Profit Sharing Affect Productivity?* Cambridge, MA: Bureau of Economic Research, 1993.

U.S. Department of Labor. Bureau of Labor Statistics. *Employee Benefits in Medium and Large Private Establishments, 1993.* Washington, DC: U.S. Government Printing Office, 1994.

_____. *Employee Benefits in Small Private Establishments, 1992.* Washington, DC: U.S. Government Printing Office, 1994.

Watson Wyatt. *Top 50: A Survey of Retirement, Thrift and Profit Sharing Plans Covering Salaried Employees at 50 Large U.S. Industrial Companies as of January 1, 1995.* Washington, DC: The Wyatt Company, 1996.

Additional Information

Profit Sharing Council of America
10 S. Riverside Plaza, Suite 1460
Chicago, IL 60606
(312) 441-8550

Pension Research Council
307 Colonial Penn Center
University of Pennsylvania
Philadelphia, PA 19104-6218
(215) 898-7620

7. Thrift Plans

Introduction

A thrift, or savings, plan is a type of defined contribution plan. The Internal Revenue Code (IRC) qualifies thrift plans as a type of profit-sharing plan, and they are similar in many ways. The chief differences from an employer's perspective are that thrift plans generally require participants to make contributions, while profit-sharing plans do not. Employees generally make periodic contributions to thrift plans. Employee contributions are sometimes matched (completely or in part) by employer contributions. These contributions are placed in a trust fund and invested. For recordkeeping purposes, each participant's savings and earnings are assigned to an individual account. The tax-favored treatment of employer contributions and employer and employee investment gains make these plans attractive and effective vehicles for retirement savings.

Plan Qualification Rules

Thrift plans, like other retirement plans, must satisfy a set of rules to qualify for tax-favored treatment. These rules, created under the Employee Retirement Income Security Act of 1974 (ERISA), are designed to protect employees' rights and to guarantee that pension benefits will be available for employees at retirement. (For further discussion of these rules, see chapter 3 on ERISA.) The rules govern requirements for reporting and disclosure of plan information, fiduciary responsibilities, employee eligibility for plan participation, vesting of benefits, form of benefit payment, and funding. In addition, qualified plans must satisfy a set of Internal Revenue Service (IRS) nondiscrimination rules (under IRC secs. 401(a)(4), 410(b), and, in some cases, 401(a)(26)) designed to insure that a plan does not discriminate in favor of highly compensated employees. (For a discussion of nondiscrimination requirements, see chapter 12.)

Contributions

Employee Contributions—Most thrift plans are contributory; i.e., to participate, eligible employees agree to make voluntary contributions. Employee contributions to thrift plans are of two types: basic contributions, which are sometimes matched by employer contributions; and supplemental contributions, which are not matched by employer contributions. Depending on the plan's structure, the employee's contributions can be made from after-tax income or through pretax income in the form of salary reduction. Employee contributions are generally made through payroll deductions. If the thrift plan utilizes this salary reduction feature, the plan must follow special rules for 401(k) arrangements. (For further discussion of 401(k) arrangements, see chapter 8.) Sometimes the employer requires participants to contribute a specified percentage of pay. Alternately, the employer may be able to choose a contribution level between certain limits, e.g., between 1 percent and 10 percent of pay. Employees are usually permitted to change or suspend contributions at some time during the plan year.

Employer Contributions—Employers can make contributions to a thrift plan through a number of arrangements. Employer contributions usually are defined as a fixed percentage of each dollar of basic employee contributions, although they can be defined as a flat dollar amount. The matching percentage may be the same for all employees, or it may increase with years of service or participation. Employer matching contributions, together with employee contributions, are subject to a special nondiscrimination rule under IRC sec. 401(m). Under a different approach, employers may provide a contribution matched (partially or fully) to an employee's contribution and a supplemental contribution based on profits. Under a relatively uncommon approach, employer contributions are based entirely on profits. Many surveys suggest that the level of the employer's matching contribution is an important factor in determining employees' participation and their level of contributions.

Limits—As with other defined contribution plans, annual employer and employee contributions to thrift plans are limited under IRC sec. 415. Annual contributions per participant cannot exceed 25 percent of compensation, or $30,000, whichever is less. Compensation up to $150,000 (indexed) is used in computing the limit. The $30,000 will also be indexed. (For further discussion of contribution limits, see chapter 4 on pension plans.) A further limit applies if an employee participates in both a defined benefit and a defined contribution plan. Employee contributions are limited separately. In practice, any employee contributions—and matching employer contributions—are limited by nondiscrimination rules under IRC sec. 401(m) unless a safe harbor test is satisfied (see chapter 8 on 401(k) cash or deferred arrangements for details).[1] These rules limit the employee

---

[1] The safe harbor is available for years beginning after December 31, 1998.

after-tax contributions of highly compensated employees and the employer contributions for highly compensated employees to a proportion of the amount nonhighly compensated employees contribute. The rules are very similar to those for 401(k) cash or deferred arrangements and include a prescribed method for distributing to highly compensated participants amounts exceeding the permitted limits. (For further discussion of 401(k) cash or deferred arrangements, see chapter 8.) An employer is also limited in the amount of contributions that are eligible for a tax deduction. Each year total employer contributions are deductible as a business expense up to 15 percent of total employee compensation (IRC sec. 404).

Taxation—Employer contributions to a thrift plan are deductible by the company as a business expense up to the limits noted above. Employees generally make contributions with after-tax money; therefore, federal income, Social Security, and other payroll taxes apply. However, any employer contributions and investment earnings on all contributions accrue tax free until distribution.

Investments—Most thrift plans offer the participant several investment options. In some cases, employer contributions must be placed in a designated investment vehicle, and flexibility is permitted only with regard to employee contributions. Common investment vehicles include guaranteed investment contracts through insurance companies; company stock; balanced funds, which invest in a mix of stocks and bonds; equity funds; and bond funds. Many plans permit employees to change their investment vehicles. Where permitted, such changes may be limited to investment of future contributions or may apply to both past and future contributions. Often there is a restriction on the frequency of change.

Distributions

Retirement, Disability, and Death Benefits—The law requires that participants' account balances fully vest at retirement. In addition, plans generally provide for benefits on death and disability. The plan's vesting provisions determine whether an employee will receive full or partial benefits on other types of employment termination. However, if the plan is contributory (i.e., employees make contributions), the employee will always receive the benefits that are attributable to his or her own contributions. Usually, those who terminate employment for reasons other than retirement, death, or disability receive lump-sum distributions. Distributions from profit-sharing accounts must follow the general distribution rules for all qualified retirement plans. Distributions generally must begin by the April 15 following the attainment of age 70½ unless the individual has not retired. There are minimum limits on the amount of annual distribution, subject to penalty taxes if not followed. (For a complete description of distribution rules, see chapter 4 on pension plans.)

In-Service Withdrawals—Some profit-sharing plans provide for partial account withdrawals during active employment. Plans allowing participants to elect account withdrawals impose certain conditions, which vary widely. But generally the funds must be held in the plan for two years before a withdrawal is allowed. A 10 percent additional income tax applies to most early distributions made before age 59 1/2. The 10 percent additional tax does not apply to distributions that are: (1) due to the participant's death or disability, (2) in the form of an annuity or installments payable over the life or life expectancy of the participant (or joint lives or life expectancies of the participant and the participant's beneficiary); (3) made after the participant has separated from service on or after age 55; (4) used for payment of medical expenses deductible under federal income tax rules; (5) made to or on behalf of an alternate payee pursuant to a qualified domestic relations order; or (6) rolled over to an individual retirement account or another qualified plan within 60 days.

Loans—Some plans permit employees to borrow a portion of their vested benefits. In general, the employee must repay the loan according to a level amortization schedule with payments made at least quarterly. If loans are permitted, they must be available to all participants on a comparable basis, and must bear a reasonable interest rate. (For a detailed explanation of loan requirements, see chapter 4 on pension plans.)

Plan Administration

The administrative complexity of a thrift plan depends on its design. Individual participant account records must be maintained, and annual account statements must be provided to employees. Administrative complexity varies with the number of options (e.g., contribution rates, investment vehicles, and the frequency of permitted changes). Administrative responsibilities are often divided between the employer and an outside organization. As a plan matures and its trust fund grows, it is frequently necessary to hire an investment manager and an internal liaison.

Conclusion

Thrift plans can play an important role in a firm's total benefit program. They may function as the principal retirement income vehicle, or they may provide supplemental retirement income. While employer contributions are not required, they provide an incentive for employee participation and add to the employees' retirement savings potential. Nevertheless, even without employer contributions, thrift plans are a tax-effective way for employees to save and are less costly for employers in such cases.

Bibliography

Allen, Everett T., Joseph J. Melone, Jerry S. Rosenbloom, and Jack L. VanDerhei. *Pension Planning: Pensions, Profit Sharing, and Other Deferred Compensation Plans*. Seventh editon. Homewood, IL: Richard D. Irwin, Inc., 1992.

Burkhauser, Richard V., and Dallas L. Salisbury, eds. *Pensions in a Changing Economy*. Washington, DC: Employee Benefit Research Institute/ National Academy on Aging, 1993.

Employee Benefit Research Institute. *EBRI Databook on Employee Benefits*. Third edition. Washington, DC: Employee Benefit Research Institute, 1995.

U.S. Department of Labor. Bureau of Labor Statistics. *Employee Benefits in Medium and Large Private Establishments, 1993*. Washington, DC: U.S. Government Printing Office, 1994.

_____. *Employee Benefits in Small Private Establishments, 1992*. Washington, DC: U.S. Government Printing Office, 1994.

Additional Information

Association of Private Pension and Welfare Plans
1212 New York Avenue, NW, Suite 1250
Washington, DC 20005
(202) 289-6700

International Foundation of Employee Benefit Plans
P.O. Box 69
18700 West Bluemound Road
Brookfield, WI 53008-0069
(414) 786-6700

8. 401(k) Cash or Deferred Arrangements

Introduction

A qualified cash or deferred arrangement under sec. 401(k) of the Internal Revenue Code (IRC) allows an employee to elect to have a portion of his or her compensation (otherwise payable in cash) contributed to a qualified retirement plan. The employee contribution is treated not as current income but most commonly as a pretax reduction in salary, which is then paid into the plan by the employer on behalf of the employee. In some cases, an employer allows employees to elect to have profit-sharing allocations contributed to the plan. In both instances, the employee defers income tax on the 401(k) plan contribution until the time of withdrawal. Whatever portion is not contributed to the 401(k) arrangement may be taken in cash, which is considered current income and taxed accordingly.

Various forms of deferred compensation have existed for many years. As early as the mid-1950s, cash or deferred profit-sharing plans using pretax employee contributions were permitted by the Internal Revenue Service (IRS) as long as at least one-half of the participants electing to defer were in the lowest paid two-thirds of all plan participants. It was not until the late 1970s that the U.S. Congress acted to sanction cash or deferred arrangements, formalize their design, and provide for regular guidance. The Revenue Act of 1978 added sec. 401(k) to the IRC—hence the commonly used reference to this type of arrangement as a 401(k) plan. These arrangements are a popular vehicle for retirement savings. They provide employees the ability to save on a tax-effective basis by deferring current taxes until a future time when taxes might be lower and permit employers some flexibility in pension plan design and contribution levels.

More than 38.9 million workers were covered by 401(k) or 401(k)-type arrangements in 1993, up from 7.1 million in 1983.[1] Growth in 401(k)s has

---

[1] These numbers are derived from the employee benefit supplements to the Census Bureau's May 1983 and April 1993 Current Population Surveys, cosponsored by the Employee Benefit Research Institute and various federal agencies. Further references to 1988 data are from the latter survey. 401(k)-type arrangements include salary deferral plans of state and local governments (sec. 457 plans) and tax-exempt organizations (403(b) plans). For further information on the surveys and participation in 401(k) arrangements, see Salisbury (1989).

been broad based, occurring across industries, earnings groups, and firm sizes. Nevertheless, 401(k) arrangements are most popular in larger firms. In smaller firms, where there is less likely to be a pension of any kind, 401(k) arrangements are less prevalent. In 1993, 12.1 percent of workers in firms with between 10 and 24 employees were covered by 401(k)s, while among workers in firms with more than 1,000 employees, 54.3 percent were covered (Yakoboski, et al., 1994).

Eligibility

Most private firms may establish 401(k) arrangements. State and local governments may not maintain 401(k) arrangements unless they were adopted before May 6, 1986, but can set up somewhat similar plans under IRC sec. 457. Employees become eligible to participate in 401(k) arrangements usually after meeting a service requirement. For a 401(k) arrangement, the maximum service period is one year. Vesting—the employee's attainment of nonforfeitable rights to benefits—of employee contributions and some employer contributions must be immediate. Other types of contributions are subject to minimum vesting standards under the Employee Retirement Income Security Act of 1974 (ERISA). (For more information on eligibility and vesting rules, see chapter 3 on ERISA.)

Types of 401(k) Arrangements

There are essentially two ways a 401(k) arrangement can be designed: through an actual salary reduction or through a profit-sharing distribution. In a salary reduction arrangement, the employee may elect to have a percentage of salary contributed to the plan (otherwise payable in cash), thereby reducing current salary and reducing the base on which federal income and some state taxes are calculated. These arrangements must be included in an employer's profit-sharing, stock bonus, pre-ERISA money-purchase, or rural electric cooperative plan. They can be designed to include employee contributions only, employer contributions only, or both employee and employer contributions. In a cash or deferred profit-sharing arrangement, the employee is offered the option of deferring a profit-sharing distribution (or some portion of it) to a trust account or taking the distribution in cash. In both arrangements, the deferral and any income thereon accrue tax free until distribution. Any distribution taken in cash from the profit-sharing arrangement is currently taxed.

Contributions

Four types of contributions are normally paid to 401(k) plans.

- *Elective*—tax-deferred employee contributions (made by the employer on behalf of the employee) in the form of a salary reduction.
- *Matching*—employer contributions that match employee contributions, although the employer does not always provide a full dollar-for-dollar match.
- *Nonelective*—contributions other than matching made by the employer from employer funds. Sometimes these are made to help satisfy nondiscrimination tests (see following discussion).
- *Voluntary*—after-tax employee contributions not made through salary reduction.

Plan participants may be allowed to direct the investment of 401(k) contributions (sometimes just their own contributions; sometimes the employer contributions as well). Investment options commonly include: a fixed (or guaranteed investment contract (GIC)) fund, which invests in a guaranteed interest contract with an insurance company; a balanced fund, which is designed to provide stability as well as growth through an investment mix of stocks and bonds; and an equity fund, which historically has demonstrated the most potential for growth but also the most risk. Investments in this fund are made in common stocks. The different funds allow the participant the option to direct investments toward his or her individual retirement planning goal. Other options sometimes available include bond funds, money market funds, fixed income securities, and company stock.

Employee elective contributions to a 401(k) arrangement are limited (to $9,500 in 1996) and are coordinated with elective contributions to simplified employee pensions, sec. 457 state and local government plans, tax-deferred 403(b) annuities, and sec. 501(c)(18) trusts. The limit is adjusted for inflation to reflect changes in the consumer price index. Employee after-tax contributions and employer matching contributions are limited under IRC sec. 401(m).

The limit on total employer and employee contributions to a qualified 401(k) plan is governed by the same rules as other defined contribution plans under IRC sec. 415. In general, the sum of the employer's contribution (including the amount the employee elected to contribute through salary reduction plus any employer matching contributions), any after-tax employee contributions, and any additions from former employee's forfeitures may not exceed the lesser of 25 percent of an employee's compensation or

$30,000 (indexed).[2] Only compensation up to $150,000 (in 1996, indexed) is used in determining the limit.

Nondiscrimination Requirements

Like other qualified retirement plans, 401(k) arrangements must be designed to insure that a plan does not discriminate in favor of highly compensated employees in terms of coverage and participation in the plan and contributions provided. The rules for coverage and participation are the same as those for other qualified retirement plans (under secs. 410(b) and 401(a)(26)). However, a special test for 401(k)s that limits elective contributions of highly compensated employees replaces the general plan rules prohibiting discrimination in contributions and benefits (under sec. 401(a)(4)). The test, known as the ADP (or actual deferral percentage) test, must be run annually. The Small Business Job Protection Act of 1996 will eventually provide two alternatives to the ADP test. Effective for taxable years beginning after 1996, 401(k) nondiscrimination requirements may be satisfied by adopting a savings incentive match plan for employees (SIMPLE) plan (see Appendix A for details). Effective for years beginning after December 31, 1998, two *alternative* safe-harbor methods of meeting the ADP tests will be available. (See Appendix B for details.) Certain of the other rules under the sec. 401(a)(4) regulatory scheme may be applicable to 401(k) arrangements.

The ADP test works this way: The eligible group of employees (defined as those employees who are eligible for employer contributions under the plan for that year) is divided into the highly compensated and the nonhighly compensated. Then, within each group, the percentage of compensation that is contributed on behalf of each employee is determined.[3] The percentages for the employees are totaled and averaged to get an ADP for the group. The ADP for the highly compensated group is then compared with the ADP for the nonhighly compensated group. The ADP test may be satisfied in one of two ways.

---

[2] If a plan participant terminates, the nonvested benefits are forfeited and become available for other plan uses. They may be reallocated among employees or used to reduce employer contributions. (For further discussion of sec. 415 limits, see chapter 4 on pension plans.)

[3] The permitted deferrals for highly compensated employees may be based on the preceding year's deferrals of the nonhighly compensated employees, rather than the current year's deferrals.

Test 1: The ADP for the eligible highly compensated may not be more than the ADP of the other eligible employees multiplied by 1.25 (the basic test).

Test 2: The excess of the ADP for the highly compensated over the nonhighly compensated may not be more than 2 percentage points, and the ADP for the highly compensated may not be more than the ADP of the nonhighly compensated multiplied by 2 (the alternative test).

For example, if the ADP for the nonhighly compensated group is 4 percent, and the ADP for the highly compensated group is 6 percent, are the nondiscrimination rules satisfied?

Test 1: Because 6 percent (the ADP of the highly compensated) is greater than 5 percent (4 percent x 1.25), test 1 is not satisfied.

Test 2: Because 6 percent (the ADP of the highly compensated) is not more than 2 percentage points more than 4 percent (the ADP of the nonhighly compensated) and 6 percent is not more than 8 percent (the ADP of the nonhighly compensated multiplied by 2), test 2 is satisfied.

Because one of the tests has been satisfied, the nondiscrimination rules are, therefore, satisfied. As mentioned earlier, these rules apply to employee elective deferrals. Employee after-tax and employer matching contributions in 401(k) arrangements and any other qualified retirement plan are subject to a parallel rule called the actual contribution percentage (ACP) test under IRC sec. 401(m). The test is essentially the same as the ADP test applied to elective contributions. If the 401(k) arrangement consists of both elective and nonelective contributions, there are further tests that must be satisfied.[4]

Table 8.1 illustrates the maximum ADPs allowed for the highly compensated employees, assuming various ADPs for the nonhighly compensated.

Distributions

The ability to withdraw funds is more restricted in a 401(k) arrange-

---

[4] If a plan must meet both the actual deferral percentage and actual contribution percentage tests, there is a restriction on the multiple use of the alternative limitation. For more details, see VanDerhei (1996).

Table 8.1
Maximum Actual Deferral Percentages (ADPs) for Top Paid Employees

If the Average ADP and Any Employer Contribution for the Lower Paid Is:	The Maximum Average ADP (Including Any Employer Contribution) for the Top Paid Will Be:	
	Test 1	Test 2
$1/2$%	$5/8$%	1%
1	$1^1/4$	2
2	$2^1/2$	4
3	$3^3/4$	5
4	5	6
5	$6^1/4$	7
6	$7^1/2$	8
7	$8^3/4$	9
8	10	10
9	$11^1/4$	11
10	$12^1/2$	12

ment than in other types of pension plans. In general, distributions of employee elective contributions (and any nonelective or matching contributions used to satisfy the ADP test) may be made before age $59^1/2$ only in the case of death, disability, separation from service, plan termination if there is no establishment or maintenance of another defined contribution plan (other than an employee stock ownership plan), sale of a subsidiary or substantially all the business' assets (as long as the employee remains in employment with the corporation acquiring the assets), or financial hardship. Voluntary employee after-tax contributions, matching employer contributions, and applicable earnings are not subject to these rules.

Hardship Defined—When the term *financial hardship* was originally defined in 1981 by the IRS in proposed regulations, a two-part definition was set out that said that the participant must (1) have an "immediate and heavy" financial need and (2) have no other resources "reasonably" available. These rules required the employer to investigate the individual circumstances of the hardship applicant. Until 1988, the only other regulatory guidance came from individual plan IRS revenue rulings. In August 1988, IRS issued final regulations in which it retained the two-part definition of hardship but clarified the conditions under which each of these would be met. Each part may be satisfied through either a "facts and circumstances" test or safe harbor rules. The safe harbors provide a set of events that may be deemed automatically to cause an "immediate and heavy financial need" and that would satisfy the "other resources" provision.

Immediate and Heavy Need—Under the facts and circumstances rule, a need is defined as immediate and heavy if the need can be determined by the facts and circumstances surrounding the hardship request. Under the safe harbor test, a distribution will be deemed to be immediate and heavy if it is for medical expenses; purchase of a principal residence for the employee; tuition for post-secondary education, but only for the next quarter or semester; and prevention of eviction or mortgage foreclosure.

Determining Financial Need from Reasonably Available Resources—To determine that a financial need cannot be met by other reasonably available resources under the facts and circumstances test, the employee must show that (1) the distribution does not exceed the amount required to meet the need and (2) the need cannot be met from other reasonably available resources (including assets of the employee's spouse and minor children). An employer may demonstrate that these provisions are met without an independent investigation of the applicant's financial affairs if the employer reasonably relies on the participant's representation that the need cannot be relieved by insurance, reasonable liquidation of other assets, the cessation of employee contributions under the plans, and other plan distributions or loans from either the plan or commercial sources.

The safe harbor rules for establishing financial need are satisfied if:
- the hardship withdrawal does not exceed the amount needed;
- the employee has obtained all distributions (other than for hardship) and all nontaxable loans available from all of the employer's plans;
- the employee's contributions under all other employer plans are suspended for 12 months after the hardship withdrawal; and
- the dollar limit on pretax contributions for the year after the hardship withdrawal is reduced by the amount of pretax contributions made during the year in which the hardship occurred.

Furthermore, the amount available for a hardship distribution consists only of employee elective contributions and investment earnings that have accrued through December 31, 1988. Most hardship withdrawals are subject to the early distribution penalty tax, discussed later in this chapter.

Loans—An employee may be able to borrow funds from the plan if the plan permits. The rules governing loans from a 401(k) are essentially the same as those for other qualified plans. However, certain of the restrictive distribution rules with respect to 401(k) accounts may come into play.

Taxation

Contributions—Elective, nonelective, and matching contributions to a qualified sec. 401(k) arrangement are excludable from the employee's gross income until distribution. The employee thus defers federal income tax until the time the benefit is distributed. The deferral of taxation applies also to some states and municipality tax provisions but not to Social Security and unemployment taxes. Voluntary employee after-tax contributions are taxable on a current basis. Earnings generated by any of these contributions are not taxed until withdrawal.

An employer may claim a business deduction for contributions to a 401(k) plan up to statutory limits defined under IRC sec. 404(a). If the 401(k) is part of a profit-sharing plan, the maximum annual deduction is generally limited to 15 percent of the total compensation of participating employees. (For a complete discussion of deduction limits, see chapter 6 on profit-sharing plans.)

Distributions—Distributions of 401(k) funds prior to age 59^1/2 are subject to a 10 percent penalty tax (in addition to regular income tax) unless the distribution is (1) on the participant's death or disability, (2) in the form of an annuity payable over the life or life expectancy of the participant (or the joint lives or life expectancies of the participant and the participant's beneficiary), (3) made after the participant has separated from service after attainment of age 55, (4) made to or on behalf of an alternate payee pursuant to a qualified domestic relations order, (5) for payment of a medical expense to the extent deductible for income tax purposes under IRC sec. 213 (expenses that exceed 7^1/2 percent of adjusted gross income), or rolled over to an individual retirement account (IRA) or another qualified plan within 60 days. Hardship distributions are subject to the 10 percent penalty tax unless for medical expenses to the extent deductible for federal income tax purposes. Distributions of 401(k) accumulations received after the attainment of age 59^1/2 are taxed just as other qualified plan distributions. (For a detailed discussion of these rules, see chapter 4 on pension plans.)

Plan Administration

The installation and operation of a qualified 401(k) plan can require detailed recordkeeping and account maintenance procedures. Proposed regulations set forth specific requirements for the administration of each plan participant's 401(k) account. Under the regulations, a 401(k) plan must maintain separate accounting between the portion of the employee's accrued benefit that is subject to the special vesting and withdrawal rules and any other (after-tax) benefits.

In each participant's account, depending on the structure of the plan, there may need to be a separate record for deductible employer contributions (elective and nonelective), nondeductible voluntary employee contributions, and vested and nonvested company contributions. Special rules exist for contributions made before 1980.

Conclusion

In today's mobile society, 401(k) arrangements can be particularly effective in meeting retirement income needs among workers who change jobs frequently and workers with intermittent labor force participation. Employee elective contributions to the plans are fully and immediately vested. When employees terminate employment or change jobs, they can roll over the accumulated contributions and earnings of the plan to an IRA or another qualified plan. As a result, 401(k) arrangements may particularly benefit young workers with high labor force mobility and women who leave the labor force for a protracted time. Sec. 401(k) arrangements are also used by employers as a way to provide supplemental retirement security for their employees without increasing overall pension costs. This may be accomplished by supplementing the employer's primary pension (often a defined benefit) plan with a 401(k) arrangement that has little or no employer contribution.

Bibliography

Allen, Everett T., Jr., Joseph J. Melone, Jerry S. Rosenbloom, and Jack L. VanDerhei. *Pension Planning: Pensions, Profit-Sharing, and Other Deferred Compensation Plans.* Seventh edition. Homewood, IL: Richard D. Irwin, Inc., 1992

Salisbury, Dallas L. "Individual Saving for Retirement: The 401(k) and IRA Experiences." *EBRI Issue Brief* no. 95 (Employee Benefit Research Institute, October 1989).

VanDerhei, Jack L. "Cash or Deferred Plans." In Jerry S. Rosenbloom, ed., *Handbook of Employee Benefits.* Third edition. Homewood, IL: Dow Jones-Irwin, 1996.

Yakoboski, Paul J., et al. "Employment-Based Retirement Income Benefits:

Analysis of the April 1993 Current Population Survey." *EBRI Special Report* SR-25/*Issue Brief* no. 153 (Employee Benefit Research Institute, September 1994).

Additional Information

The 401(k) Association
1 Summit Square
Doublewoods Road and Rt. 413
Langhorne, PA 19047
(215) 579-8830

Association of Private Pension and Welfare Plans
1212 New York Avenue, NW, Suite 1250
Washington, DC 20005
(202) 289-6700

International Foundation of Employee Benefit Plans
P.O. Box 69
18700 West Bluemound Road
Brookfield, WI 53008-0069
(414) 786-6700

Pension Research Council
307 Colonial Penn Center
University of Pennsylvania
Philadelphia, PA 19104-6218
(215) 898-7620

9. Employee Stock Ownership Plans

Introduction

An employee stock ownership plan (ESOP) allows companies to share ownership with employees without requiring the employees to invest their own money. With an ESOP, shares of company stock are contributed to the ESOP on behalf of the employees. Although other employment-based plans, such as stock bonus and profit-sharing plans (covered in chapter 6), may contain company stock, an ESOP is required to invest primarily in company stock.

ESOPs are unique among employee benefit plans in another way: they may borrow money. This feature can be beneficial as a corporate finance tool. Because of special tax benefits accorded ESOPs, they can also lower the cost of financing corporate transactions.

Louis O. Kelso is generally credited with creating the ESOP concept. Kelso believed that by providing employees with access to capital credit, ESOPs would broaden the distribution of wealth through free enterprise mechanisms. Employees who were made owners of the productive assets of the business where they work, Kelso reasoned, would benefit from the wealth produced by those assets and would thus acquire both a capital income and an incentive for being more productive.

Kelso attracted a powerful ally in Sen. Russell Long (D-LA), who used his influence to spearhead legislative efforts to promote ESOPs. Political support for the ESOP concept has grown steadily, and through the end of the 1980s Congress encouraged ESOPs through a number of favorable laws, including the Employee Retirement Income Security Act of 1974 (ERISA), the Tax Reduction Act of 1975, the Tax Reform Act of 1976, the Revenue Act of 1978, the Economic Recovery Tax Act of 1981, the Deficit Reduction Act of 1984, and the Technical and Miscellaneous Revenue Act of 1988. However, in 1989, ESOPs came under congressional scrutiny when the large amount of debt incurred by some ESOPs was connected with heavy corporate takeover activity. Congress considered major ESOP changes that would have dramatically reduced their attractiveness to corporations but ultimately passed relatively minor tax changes in the Omnibus Budget Reconciliation Act of 1989 (OBRA '89). These changes are discussed later in this chapter.

Types of ESOPs

Leveraged ESOPs—An ESOP that borrows funds to acquire stock is called a leveraged ESOP and usually works in the following way.

Funds are borrowed to acquire employer securities. This can be accomplished in one of two ways (chart 9.1). An employer may arrange to sell the ESOP a specified amount of qualified employer securities at fair market value. The ESOP then borrows the funds needed to purchase the stock. The lender may be a bank or regulated investment company or the employer or shareholders in the employing company. The loan may be guaranteed by the employer, or the stock may be pledged as collateral; it is common for both to occur. The loan is typically repaid with the employer's tax-deductible contributions to the ESOP. Non tax-deductible funds may be used to repay the loan, although it is not a very common practice. As the ESOP loan is repaid, shares of stock are allocated to participants' accounts. Unallocated

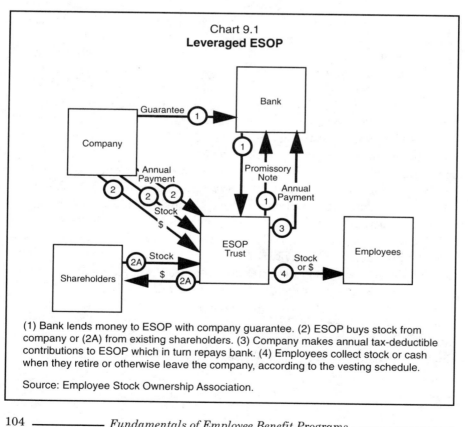

Chart 9.1
Leveraged ESOP

(1) Bank lends money to ESOP with company guarantee. (2) ESOP buys stock from company or (2A) from existing shareholders. (3) Company makes annual tax-deductible contributions to ESOP which in turn repays bank. (4) Employees collect stock or cash when they retire or otherwise leave the company, according to the vesting schedule.

Source: Employee Stock Ownership Association.

shares remain in the ESOP trust and can continue to serve as collateral for the remaining loan balance.

Alternatively, the employer may borrow the money and transfer stock to the ESOP in exchange for the promissory note. The employer makes deductible contributions to the ESOP, which uses these contributions to pay off the note. These repayments to the employer, in turn, are used to pay off the employer's loan.

In contrast to a nonleveraged ESOP, where stock is acquired slowly through employer contributions, a leveraged ESOP generally acquires a large block of stock purchased with the borrowed funds; the shares are held in trust and allocated to participants as the loan is repaid. A leveraged ESOP can acquire a large share of ownership in a company much faster than a nonleveraged ESOP. Furthermore, if the loan is used to buy stock from the employer (rather than from outside existing stockholders), the ESOP transaction provides a cash infusion for the employer.

Leveraged ESOPs have been responsible for much of the overall growth of ESOPs over the past several years. The National Center for Employee Ownership attributes this growth to several factors.

- There was a general increase at the end of the 1980s in merger and acquisition activity, of which leveraged ESOPs are sometimes a part.
- Tax incentives passed in 1984 and 1986 have made leveraged ESOPs a more attractive means of borrowing money and nonleveraged ESOPs less attractive in general.
- For a minority of the companies (probably under 1 percent of all ESOPs and 15 percent of public company ESOPs), ESOPs are part of a defense against hostile takeovers.
- Many employers have come to believe that sharing ownership with employees helps to create a more productive work environment.

Other ESOPs—Some companies establish ESOPs that are not leveraged. A company sets up a trust, to which it periodically contributes. The company may contribute stock directly or cash, which the fund uses to purchase the stock. The stock is allocated to individual accounts for employees. ESOPs that are not leveraged but can be are sometimes called leverageable ESOPs.

The Tax Reduction Act of 1975 allowed an extended investment tax credit equal to qualified contributions to a special nonleveraged ESOP called a TRASOP (Tax Reduction Act stock ownership plan); the allowed credit was increased in the Tax Reform Act of 1976. Under the Economic Recovery Tax Act of 1981, beginning in 1983 the basis for the allowed tax credit was shifted from investment to payroll, replacing the TRASOP with the PAYSOP (payroll-based employee stock ownership plan). However, the Tax Reform Act of 1986 repealed the PAYSOP tax credit for compensation paid or accrued after December 31, 1986.

Plan Qualification Rules

ESOPs are a type of defined contribution plan and qualify with the Internal Revenue Service as either a stock bonus plan or a stock bonus/money purchase pension plan combination. As with all tax-qualified plans, ESOPs must establish a trust to receive the employer's contributions to the plan, and the plan must be created exclusively for the benefit of employees.

ESOPs are subject to the general ERISA rules governing eligibility, vesting, participation and coverage, and reporting. (See chapter 3 on ERISA and chapter 12 on pension plan nondiscrimination and particpation requirements.) But ESOPs also must comply with additional requirements aimed at the plans' specific characteristics.

Investment of Assets—As mentioned earlier, ESOPs must invest primarily in qualified securities of the employer. In practical terms, this means that at least 51 percent of a plan's assets must be so invested. Qualified employer securities may include readily tradeable common stock, stock with voting power and dividend rights, preferred stock that is convertible into qualified common stock, and stock of affiliated corporations if certain requirements are met. Debt instruments are not included.

Diversification—For stock acquired after 1986, ESOPs must provide means for qualified participants nearing retirement to diversify part of their ESOP account balance. In general, beginning with the plan year following the participant's attainment of both age 55 and 10 years of participation, the participant must be provided the opportunity to diversify at least 25 percent of the total account. Five years later, the participant must be allowed to diversify at least 50 percent. Alternatively, the ESOP may distribute the amount that could be diversified.

Voting Rights—ESOP participants must be allowed certain voting rights. For stock that is readily tradeable (stock of a public company), full voting rights for all allocated shares must be passed through to participants. For stock of closely held companies (those whose voting stock is held by a few shareholders), voting rights must be passed through on all major corporate issues, specifically those that must be decided by more than a majority vote. Shares not voted by participants may be voted by the

ESOP trustee.

Distributions—ESOPs are permitted to make distributions in either stock or cash. Unless the sponsoring company's charter or bylaws require that substantially all of the company's stock be owned by employees, participants must be allowed to take their distributions in stock.[1] Generally, the full amount must be paid out over no more than five years, although the participant can elect to extend this period. Also, the period can be extended up to an additional five years for account balances in excess of $500,000, as indexed.

A participant receiving nonpublicly traded stock must be given an option to sell the stock to the employer at an independently appraised fair market value (a put option). For stock acquired after 1986, the employer can pay for the stock in annual installments, over a period of up to five years (beginning no later than 30 days after the sale), and pay interest at a reasonable rate. The employer must provide security for the unpaid balance of deferred payments. The employer and the ESOP may exercise a right of first refusal to repurchase nonpublicly traded stock distributed by the ESOP.

Special Tax Advantages

ESOPs enjoy a variety of tax advantages over other defined contribution plans.

Deductions for Contributions—ESOP contributions that are used to repay an ESOP loan are not subject to the usual 15 percent of covered compensation deduction limit. (For further discussion of deduction limits, see chapter 4 on pension plans). Instead, employers can deduct contributions used to pay the loan principal, up to 25 percent of compensation. Unlimited deductions are permitted for contributions used to pay loan interest.

Dividend Deduction—Employers generally may also deduct dividends paid on ESOP stock to the extent that the dividends are distributed in cash to participants or used to repay the principal on the ESOP loan. However, to be deductible, the dividends must be on employer securities acquired with

---

[1] Unless the separating participant elects otherwise, distributions attributable to stock acquired after December 31, 1986, must begin within one year following the plan year in which the participant retires, dies, or becomes disabled or within five years after the participant separates from service for any other reason (if not reemployed with the same company).

the ESOP loan (generally effective for securities acquired after August 4, 1989). These liberal deduction limits are designed to help accelerate the rate at which ESOPs can repay loans, thereby allowing more rapid allocation of ESOP stock to participants' accounts.

Lender Incentive—Under prior law, qualified lenders—banks and regulated investment companies—could exclude from gross income 50 percent of the interest earned on ESOP loans. Some of this advantage was passed on to the ESOP through lower interest rates. However, OBRA '89 permits this interest exclusion only if three conditions are satisfied: (1) the ESOP owns more than 50 percent of each class of outstanding stock of the corporation issuing the securities or more than 50 percent of the total value of all outstanding stock of the corporation immediately after the acquisition of employer securities with the proceeds of such loans; (2) the term of the loan is not more than 15 years; and (3) voting rights on allocated shares are passed through to participants. The provision is generally effective for loans made after July 10, 1989. Certain exceptions apply for loans pursuant to certain written binding commitments in effect on that date (or on June 6, 1989) and for loans after which the ESOP owns at least 30 percent of the company and the loan was made by November 17, 1989.

The Small Business Job Protection Act of 1996 repealled the exclusion for new loans. Any loans in effect before June 10, 1996 were grandfathered under the previous law. Certain refinancing of ESPO loans will be exempt from the changes.

A number of other tax incentives are provided to encourage the use of ESOPs to broaden corporate ownership, as follows.

Incentives for Sale of Stock to an ESOP—Shareholders of corporate stock can defer taxes on the gain from the sale of stock to an ESOP if, on the completion of the sale, the ESOP owns at least 30 percent of the company and the seller reinvests the proceeds from the sale in qualified domestic securities within one year after (or three months before) the sale. In addition, the seller must have held the securities for at least three years before the sale of the stock (effective for sales after July 10, 1989). This provision allows owners of closely held businesses who are approaching retirement age to, in essence, create a market for their stock and to diversify their investments, on a tax-deferred basis, while providing their employees with a significant benefit and assuring the continued independence of the business.

Until 1989, estates that sold employer stock to an ESOP could exclude from taxes 50 percent of the proceeds received on the sale, up to $750,000. This was repealed in OBRA '89, effective for estates of decedents dying after December 19, 1989.

Early Distribution Tax—Lump-sum distributions paid to ESOP participants prior to January 1, 1990, are exempt from the 10 percent penalty tax imposed on employees for early withdrawal (prior to age $59^{1}/_{2}$).

Conclusion

ESOPs can provide employees with substantial financial benefits through stock ownership while providing companies with attractive tax advantages and a powerful corporate finance tool. By making employees partial owners of the business, a company also may realize productivity improvements, since workers benefit directly from corporate profitability and are thus working in their own interest.

Although the advantages of ESOPs are attracting growing numbers of companies, there is also some risk to consider. Because the ESOP is invested primarily in employer securities, its success depends on the long-term performance of the company and its stock. There is, therefore, a greater degree of risk involved because of the concentration of employee capital.

An ESOP is not appropriate in every circumstance, but the many benefits of employee ownership and ESOP financing merit close consideration of this concept.

Bibliography

Blasi, Joseph R. *Employee Ownership: Revolution or Ripoff?* Cambridge, MA: Ballinger, 1988.

Employee Benefit Research Institute. *Databook on Employee Benefits.* Third edition. Washington, DC: Employee Benefit Research Institute, 1995.

Council of Institutional Investors. *Does Ownership Add Value? 100 Empirical Studies.* Washington, DC: Council of Institutional Investors, 1994.

Kelso, Louis O., and Patricia Hetter Kelso. *Democracy and Economic Power: Extending the ESOP Revolution Through Binary Economics.* Lanham, MD: University Press of America, 1991.

Piacentini, Joseph S. "Employee Stock Ownership Plans: Impact on Retirement Income and Corporate Performance." *EBRI Issue Brief* no. 74 (Employee Benefit Research Institute, January 1988).

Quarrey, Michael. *Employee Ownership and Corporate Performance.* Oakland, CA: National Center for Employee Ownership, 1991.

Rosen, Corey, and Karen M. Young, eds. *Understanding Employee Owner-ship*. Ithaca, NY: ILP Press, 1991.

Young, Karen, ed. *The Expanding Role of ESOPs in Public Companies*. New York, NY: Quorum Books, 1990.

Additional Information

Employee Stock Ownership Association
1726 M Street, NW
Washington, DC 20036
(202) 293-2971

National Center for Employee Ownership
1201 Martin Luther King, Jr. Way
Oakland, CA 94612
(510) 272-9461

10. Cash Balance Pension Plans and Other Hybrid Retirement Plans

Introduction

An increasing number of employers have been offering retirement plans that combine features of both defined benefit and defined contribution plans. There are a variety of these plans, called hybrid plans, the most well-known of which is the cash balance plan. Other hybrid plans (including pension equity, life cycle, floor-offset, age-weighted profit-sharing, new comparability profit sharing, and target benefit) are discussed briefly at the end of this chapter.

Cash balance and pension equity plans are classified as defined benefit plans but have many defined contribution plan characteristics, whereas age-weighted profit-sharing, new comparability profit-sharing, and target benefit plans are classified as defined contribution plans but have some defined benefit plan characteristics. Floor-offset plans consist of two separate but associated plans rather than a single plan design with both defined benefit and defined contribution plan characteristics.

Cash Balance Pension Plans

The concept of a cash balance pension plan first became widely known when Bank of America adopted a cash balance plan in the mid-1980s as an alternative to the more traditional retirement vehicles. The bank believed that the best vehicle to satisfy its needs would be a less traditional plan that combined the best features of both a defined benefit plan and a defined contribution plan. Data from the Bureau of Labor Statistics indicate that 3 percent of full-time defined benefit plan participants in medium and large private establishments had the cash account method of determining retirement payments in 1993 (U.S. Department of Labor, 1994).

A cash balance plan is a defined benefit plan that bears a close resemblance to a defined contribution plan. (For more information on pension plans, see chapter 4.) Each participant has an account that is credited with a dollar amount that resembles an employer contribution and is generally determined as a percentage of pay. Each participant's account is also credited with interest. The plan usually provides benefits in the form of a lump-sum distribution or annuity.

Despite the similarities to a defined contribution plan, a cash balance plan is actually quite different because it defines future pension benefits, not employer contributions. Each account expresses the current lump-sum value of the participant's accrued benefit; in so doing, the account is merely a bookkeeping device and does not relate directly to plan assets. Similarly, employer contributions are based on actuarial valuations, so they may be less than the sum of the additions to participants' accounts. Finally, interest is credited at a rate specified in the plan and is unrelated to the investment earnings of the employer's pension trust.

Benefits—

- *Credits to Accounts*—The annual benefit accrual in a cash balance plan is expressed as a lump-sum amount and is added to each participant's account balance. This cash balance credit is usually a percentage of the participant's pay but may also be a flat dollar amount. The cash balance credits are often age or service related and may be integrated with Social Security.[1] Some organizations credit different amounts for various components of pay or base the credits on company performance.

  The second type of credit, the interest credit, is specified by the plan. The interest rate is either a specified rate or a rate related to some index, such as the consumer price index (CPI) or the rate on U.S. Treasury bills. The interest credit may vary from year to year, recognizing current economic conditions, and may be communicated to participants before the start of the year.

- *Transitional Benefits*— Generally, cash balance plans that are converted from traditional final pay defined benefit plans provide special transitional benefits for employees nearing retirement. These grandfather provisions are necessary, since the accrual pattern under a cash balance plan (a career average defined benefit plan) is such that benefits accrue at a faster rate early in the career and at a lower rate later in the career, when compared with a final average defined benefit plan.[2] Without the grandfather provision, older and/or longer service

---

[1] Integration is a feature of some qualified retirement plans that coordinates plan benefits or contributions with Social Security. (For more information on pension plan integration, see chapter 13.)

[2] For a discussion of career-average and final-average defined benefit plan formulas, see chapter 5 on defined benefit and defined contribution plans.

employees could lose benefits due to the conversion. In addition, most cash balance plans do not have subsidized early retirement benefits, whereas defined benefit plans often have this feature, so grandfathering employees who are nearing retirement may be necessary or these benefits would be lost.

- *Investment of Assets*—The sponsor determines how the plan assets will be invested and bears all of the risk and reward. Investment gains and losses will eventually affect the amount the sponsor contributes. If the rate of return on plan assets is higher than expected, the employer may be able to cut back on future contributions or increase benefits in the cash balance plan. If the cash balance plan suffers an investment loss, or returns are less than expected, a sponsor will amortize the loss over a period of years. The sponsor promises to credit each participant's account with the interest rate specified in the plan and then hopes to achieve a rate of return higher than or equal to that credited to the accounts. Although the sponsor may not achieve the set interest rate in any one year, the goal over time is to get a return on investment that is greater than or equal to the set rate. As with other defined benefit plans, the sponsor seeks the highest long-term return consistent with appropriate levels of risk.
- *Sec. 415 Limits*—Cash balance plan benefits are limited by Internal Revenue Code (IRC) sec. 415 in the same manner as any other defined benefit plan (see chapter 4 on pension plans). These limits are applied to the annuity equivalent of the cash balance account, not—as in a defined contribution plan—to the annual addition to the account.

Minimum Standards— Cash balance plans are subject to the same Employee Retirement Income Security Act of 1974 (ERISA) requirements as other defined benefit plans, including minimum standards for eligibility, vesting, and funding. (These standards are described in detail in chapter 3 on ERISA.) The following discussion addresses areas specific to cash balance plans.

- *Vesting*—Like other qualified retirement plans, a cash balance plan is required to meet ERISA's minimum vesting requirements of full vesting after five years (cliff) or graded vesting over years three through seven. Many cash balance plans provide earlier vesting than other defined benefit plans, which often only provide the minimum required vesting schedule. Usually cash balance plans provide cliff vesting rather than graded vesting.

- *Funding*—Minimum funding requirements apply to cash balance plans in the same manner as for other defined benefit plans (i.e., the normal cost plus amounts required to amortize any unfunded accrued liability over a period of years, subject to the full-funding limit). (See chapter 4 for a detailed discussion of pension funding.)

Distributions—Cash balance plans generally provide participants the option of receiving their vested account balances in the form of a lump-sum distribution or as an annuity at the time of retirement or employment termination.[3] If the distribution is lump sum, it is usually equal to the participant's vested account balance. If the distribution is in the form of an annuity, the amount of the annuity is actuarially equivalent to the account balance. The lump-sum option is another characteristic of cash balance plans that is different from traditional defined benefit plans and similar to defined contribution plans. Lump-sum distributions are popular with participants (especially in the case of employment termination), since they can be rolled over into an individual retirement account (IRA) or into a new employer's retirement plan, enabling the benefit to continue to grow with investment earnings. Since lump-sum distributions do not guarantee that retirees will have continuing retirement benefits, some sponsors encourage the selection of an annuity by specifying a favorable actuarial basis to convert accounts into annuities. Terminating employees may also elect to leave their balances in the plan, accruing interest credits, until retirement.

The usual joint and survivor and preretirement survivor requirements apply to cash balance plans. (For further discussion of these requirements, see chapter 4 on pension plans.) Thus, in general, benefits for a participant with an eligible spouse must be paid in the form of a qualified joint and survivor annuity unless the participant and spouse elect otherwise. The preretirement survivor annuity requirements apply to cash balance plans in the same manner as to other defined benefit plans. However, almost all cash balance plans go beyond the minimum requirements and pay the full account balance in the event of the employee's death.

Loans—Loans to participants are permitted under cash balance plans, but as a practical matter may be complicated to administer—just as with other defined benefit plans. Under a defined contribution plan, when a distribution is made, the loan can be automatically paid off, but under a

---

[3] By law, cash balance plans must provide an annuity option, although the lump-sum option is provided at the employer's discretion.

defined benefit plan, if the participant elects a monthly annuity, there is no way to assure repayment of the loan.

Plan Termination Insurance—Like any defined benefit plan, a cash balance plan is subject to plan termination insurance and must pay annual premiums to the Pension Benefit Guaranty Corporation (PBGC). Also, as with other defined benefit plans, a cash balance plan may be terminated only if plan assets are sufficient to cover all benefit liabilities (i.e., all accrued benefits), unless the employer is in distress.

On standard termination of a cash balance plan, all participant accounts vest to the extent funded, and plan assets are allocated among plan participants. If the plan has residual assets, these may be used to provide additional benefits or may revert to the employer, whichever the plan provides.

If plan assets are less than the sum of account balances (either because plan assets declined in value or because the employer contributed less than the sum of the additions to individual accounts), the plan can terminate only in a distress situation. Several areas remain unclear, including how, under a distress termination, the PBGC would determine guaranteed benefits, allocate plan assets, and value benefit liabilities. (See chapter 3 on ERISA for more information about plan termination insurance.)

Comparison with Defined Contribution Plans—A cash balance plan is similar in many ways to a defined contribution plan, particularly a money purchase plan or a profit-sharing plan, under which the employer contributes at a fixed rate. An employer's cost under a cash balance plan is typically lower than the cost under a defined contribution money purchase plan with the same level of additions to participant accounts, because the actuary may anticipate both forfeitures and investment earnings in excess of the rates to be credited to account balances. To the extent experience differs from the actuarial assumptions, future contributions to a cash balance plan will be adjusted, which may lead to more cost volatility. The employer's pension expense must be determined in accordance with the Financial Accounting Standards Board's accounting rules for all defined benefit plans. (See Allen et al., 1992, for a detailed explanation of these rules.) If a defined contribution plan is qualified as a profit-sharing plan, elective salary deferrals are permissible under IRC sec. 401(k), but this is not permitted under a cash balance plan.

A defined contribution plan is not subject to PBGC premiums and plan termination insurance provisions. Because all benefits are always fully funded under a defined contribution plan, plan termination insurance is not needed. Under a cash balance plan, as in a defined benefit plan, it is possible for participants to lose part of their accrued benefits on plan termination in spite of the plan termination insurance.

A cash balance plan will generally be less difficult and expensive to administer than a defined contribution plan. Account recordkeeping is much simpler under a cash balance plan because there is no need to reconcile account balances with trust assets, and there are typically no employee contributions, loans, withdrawals, or fund transfers. However, an actuarial valuation is required. Defined contribution plans and cash balance plans are attractive to younger, shorter service employees, who generally find the accounts concept attractive and who may have little interest in retirement or in a traditional defined benefit plan.

Annuities can be paid directly from the trust of a cash balance plan and are generally larger than the policies employees could obtain from an insurance company themselves using their account balances. Under a defined contribution plan, an employee wishing an annuity must have his or her balance transferred to an insurance company.

Comparison with Defined Benefit Plans—Under a typical defined benefit plan, two employees with equal pay but differing ages will earn the same amount of retirement income for each year of service. Because the money invested for a younger employee can grow with interest for many more years than that invested for an employee close to retirement, the cost of funding the pension earned for a younger employee is less than that for an older employee. For employees who terminate employment at younger ages, both the accrued benefits and the costs are low. The lower benefits are likely one of the reasons younger employees place low value on traditional defined benefit plans.

Traditional pension plan benefit formulas are oriented to the total retirement benefit, taking retirement age and length of service into account. In contrast, cash balance plans emphasize annual accumulations and may therefore not be as flexible as traditional plans in providing specified levels of retirement income.

A cash balance plan may be more difficult and costly to administer than a traditional defined benefit plan. Records of plan accounts must be kept. In practice, the cost may be more or less than a traditional defined benefit plan, depending on the number of employees, plan design, and data processing facilities.

Pension Equity Plans

Pension equity plans[4] first became widely known when RJR Nabisco implemented one in 1993. Both cash balance and pension equity plans define benefits in terms of a current lump-sum value rather than a deferred annuity, but a pension equity plan is a final-average lump-sum plan, whereas a cash balance plan is a career-average lump-sum plan. Furthermore, a pension equity plan does not have the individual accounts and interest credits associated with cash balance plans. For each year worked under a pension equity plan, employees are credited with a percentage that will be applied to their final average earnings. As an employee ages or as an employee's years of service increase, the percentage earned increases. Organizations may also choose to apply additional percentages to earnings above a threshold amount to provide an additional benefit for the portion of pay not eligible for Social Security benefits. On termination of employment or retirement, most employers allow employees to receive a lump-sum benefit that is equal to final average earnings multiplied by the sum of the percentages earned during a career (since lump-sum distributions do not guarantee that retirees will have continuing retirement benefits, some employers offer only annuities[5]). Employees can take the lump sum as cash, convert it to an annuity under the plan, or roll it over into either an IRA or another employer's retirement plan.

Life Cycle Pension Plans and Retirement Bonus Plans[6]

The concept of a life cycle or retirement bonus plan is very similar to that of a pension equity plan. A life cycle/retirement bonus plan is a final average salary pension plan in which benefits are determined according to salary near retirement and years of service. A participant earns credits for each year of service. The total of the credits is considered a percentage, which is multiplied by the participant's final average salary to determine what lump sum will be paid at retirement or termination. These plans can be changed to meet the needs of a specific employer by reducing benefits on payment before retirement eligibility, providing higher credits for older

---

[4] According to Geisel (1995), about 15 employers have set up pension equity plans.

[5] By law, pension equity plans must provide an annuity option, although the lump-sum option is provided at the employer's discretion.

[6] Also known as mobility bonus pension plans.

employees, integrating with Social Security covered compensation, or coordinating with other retirement benefits. Any accrued benefit earned under a defined benefit plan prior to the effective date of the life cycle/ retirement bonus plan can be preserved as transition credits that may be added to the regular credits in calculating the lump-sum benefit. Like a pension equity plan, the benefit under a life cycle/retirement bonus plan is based on final average pay (rather than career average pay), enabling it to provide protection against inflation and to recognize the accelerated earnings of fast-track employees. The necessity of recordkeeping to account for individual account balances is eliminated.

Floor-Offset Pension Plans

A floor-offset plan (also known as a feeder plan) differs from most other hybrid arrangements in that it actually consists of two *separate* (but associated) plans—a defined benefit "floor" plan and a defined contribution "base" plan—rather than a *single* plan design with both defined benefit and defined contribution plan characteristics. The defined benefit plan uses a standard formula (which may take into account age, service, and/or compensation) to establish a minimum benefit level that is dependent on the employer's objectives and constraints. If the defined contribution plan provides a benefit that equals or exceeds the minimum established by the defined benefit floor plan, the participant receives the balance in the defined contribution account and no benefit is payable from the floor plan. However, if the defined contribution plan provides less than the minimum benefit (perhaps as a result of investment performance or inflation), the floor plan makes up the difference between what the defined contribution plan *is* able to provide and the minimum benefit.[7] In other words, the benefit provided by the defined benefit plan is reduced by the value of the participant's account in the defined contribution plan. Just about any defined contribution plan can function as the base plan,[8] although the defined contribution

---

[7] The defined benefit formula is usually offset by 100 percent of the defined contribution plan benefits, although it may be offset by only a portion of the defined contribution plan benefits.

[8] A notable exception is the TRA '86 restriction that IRC sec. 401(k) cash or deferred arrangements cannot be included in a floor-offset arrangement, although TRA '86 also included a special rule for "qualified offset arrangements" consisting of a cash or deferred arrangement and a defined benefit plan that were in existence on April 16, 1986.

portion of a floor-offset plan is often a standard profit-sharing plan. The defined benefit formula is unrestricted. The investment risk in a floor-offset plan is usually borne by the employer; i.e., the employer is typically responsible for the investment of assets in both the defined benefit and defined contribution plans. According to Robinson and Small (1993), the majority of firms with floor plans in 1993 had between 5,000 and 20,000 employees. Such plans typically provided a floor benefit for a career employee of between 40 percent and 60 percent of preretirement compensation.

Age-Weighted Profit-Sharing Plans

This hybrid combines the flexibility of a profit-sharing plan with the ability of a defined benefit pension plan to skew benefits in favor of older employees. While cash balance and pension equity plans are generally attractive to large employers, age-weighted profit-sharing plans are primarily small employer plans. Unlike a typical profit-sharing plan in which each participant receives a contribution based on compensation, employees in *age-weighted* profit-sharing plans have an age factor applied to the profit-sharing plan allocation formula in order to compensate older employees who have fewer years to accumulate sufficient funds for retirement. At first glance, this type of formula might appear to violate nondiscrimination regulations, since it permits larger contributions for older employees, who tend to receive higher compensation. However, under the regulations, these contributions can be converted to "equivalent benefits" and can pass the general nondiscrimination test. Since annual allocations are projected to retirement age with interest, they will vary according to the plan participants' ages. All of the basic requirements that apply to regular profit-sharing plans also apply to age-weighted profit-sharing plans.

New Comparability Profit-Sharing Plans

The new comparability plan divides employees into separate and distinct allocation groups in order to provide larger percentage contributions for certain select employees than for other employees. (In some cases, as much as 80 percent or 90 percent of the employer's contribution can be allocated to the select group.) Unlike an age-weighted profit-sharing plan, a new comparability plan does not necessarily relate the amount of the contribution to the employee's age. However, age spreads among the allocation groups can have an impact. By using the allocation group technique, a plan can be designed to provide one contribution rate to a select allocation group of employees, with a different and much lower rate for employees who are not in the select group. The allocation groups may be based on any reasonable criteria, including percentage of ownership, status as key or highly compensated employee, job description, length of service, age, etc. The allocation groups can be tailored to satisfy specific objectives since they can be set up for owners, officers, supervisors, managers, long-service employees, or salaried employees. The structure of the allocation groups must be defined in the plan document and may be changed periodically by plan amendment. Each allocation group has its own allocation method. Within each allocation group, the contribution is allocated uniformly (either as a flat dollar amount or as a percentage of pay). The annual allocation method must also be defined in the plan document and may be changed by plan amendment, provided no individual's accrued benefit is reduced. Nondiscrimination testing is satisfied by dividing employees into "rate groups"[9] (not to be confused with allocation groups). If each rate group satisfies the IRC sec. 410(b) minimum coverage test,[10] the allocation as a whole passes the IRC sec. 401(a)(4) general test. New comparability plans usually require annual testing and are very sensitive to employee demographics.

Target Benefit Plans

Target benefit plans, also known as target plans, are technically defined contribution plans (specifically money purchase pension plans[11]) but operate as hybrids of defined benefit and defined contribution plans. A target benefit plan sets a "target" benefit (e.g., 1.5 percent of final average salary times years of service) for each participant at normal retirement age (usually age 65) using a defined benefit plan formula, and employer contri-

---

[9] For more information on adjusted equivalent accrual rates, see Grubbs (1994).

[10] The plan must pass either the ratio percentage test or the facts and circumstances test to meet the 410(b) regulations. For more information on these two tests, see Grubbs (1994), and Londergan et al. (1994).

[11] A money purchase pension plan is a type of defined contribution plan under which employer contributions are usually determined as a fixed percentage of pay. The benefits for each employee are the amounts that can be provided by the sums contributed to his or her account plus income from investment gains. Forfeitures for separation of service prior to full vesting can be used to reduce the employer's contributions or be reallocated among remaining employees.

butions are determined actuarially—just like a defined benefit plan—so that they become a fixed obligation of the employer. An acceptable actuarial cost method (along with acceptable assumptions stated in the plan) is used to determine a contribution rate for each employee assumed to be sufficient to provide the targeted benefit. Contribution rates may differ considerably among the individual plan participants. Up to this point, the target plan is essentially defined benefit in nature. However, the target benefit for each participant is not guaranteed as it would be in a defined benefit plan—it is merely a goal to be achieved, not a promise to the participant of a fixed benefit. As in a defined contribution plan, individual accounts are established for employees, and investment gains and losses are credited to their accounts. Most target benefit plans leave investment decisions in the hands of the participants. Ultimate retirement benefits are determined by actual account balances, which may be higher or lower than the targeted benefit. Employers only have an obligation to make the contribution required by the plan formula; if the rate of return on plan assets is less than what was assumed, the employer is *not* obligated to provide funding that will restore the balance to the targeted level. The accounts may provide for several investment options and for both fixed and variable annuities, and benefits may vary substantially among similar participants. There is considerable flexibility in target plan design. Target formulas may be based on years of service and/or compensation (final year's salary, final average salary, or career average salary). Plan designs may also include provisions for past-service benefits and integration with Social Security under the rules that apply to defined benefit plans. In most respects, a target plan is treated as a money purchase plan and is subject to the rules pertaining to such plans. U.S. Department of Labor data indicate that in 1992, there were 219,000 participants (202,000 active) in 10,137 target benefit plans (U.S. Department of Labor, 1996).

Conclusion

Hybrid plans offer a compromise between conventional defined benefit plans and defined contribution plans and can be designed to fit almost any organization's needs. The emergence of hybrid retirement vehicles such as cash balance plans and pension equity plans signifies how dramatically the pension marketplace is changing. The lack of appreciation by young workers for traditional pension plans, the desire for pension portability, and the complexities associated with conventional defined benefit plans, among other factors, have combined to make hybrid plans more attractive to both employers and employees. As employee demographics, legal requirements, and benefit costs continue to change, hybrid plans have the potential to become more popular as an alternative to traditional pension plans.

Bibliography

Allen, Everett T., Jr., Joseph J. Melone, Jerry S. Rosenbloom, and Jack L. VanDerhei. *Pension Planning: Pensions, Profit-Sharing, and Other Deferred Compensation Plans.* Seventh edition. Burr Ridge, IL: Richard D. Irwin, Inc., 1992.

Buck Consultants, Inc. "Hybrid Pension Plans—A Solution for Some Employers." *For Your Benefit...* no. 124 (May 1995): 1–8.

Campbell, Sharyn. "Hybrid Retirement Plans: The Retirement Income System Continues to Evolve." *EBRI Special Report* SR-32/*Issue Brief* no. 171 (Employee Benefit Research Institute, March 1996).

Charles D. Spencer & Associates, Inc. "Floor-Offset Arrangements Combine Profit-Sharing Plan, Defined Benefit 'Floor' Plan to Guarantee Minimum Benefit." *Spencer's Research Reports on Employee Benefits* (February 11, 1994): 217.2.-1–217.2.-4.

Geisel, Jerry. "Pension Equity Plans Another Option When Traditional Pension Doesn't Fit." *Business Insurance* (August 14, 1995): 11.

Grubbs, Donald S., Jr. "Age-Weighted Plans and New Comparability Plans." *Journal of Pension Planning & Compliance* (Summer 1994): 1–28.

Karlin, Michael. "The Life Cycle Pension Plan: A Step Ahead." *Pension World* (May 1992): 24–26.

King, Francis P., and Michael Heller. "Target Benefit Plans." *Benefits Quarterly* (Fourth Quarter 1989): 9–15.

Lloyd, Michael E., and Mark K. Dunbar. "Benefits Testing: The Dawn of a New Day for Defined Contribution Planning." *Journal of Pension Planning & Compliance* (Fall 1993): 42–47.

Londergan, Edward F., and Paul Vickers. " 'New Comparability': Increased Flexibility for Profit Sharing Plans?" *Journal of the American Society of CLU & ChFC* (March 1994): 44–49.

Mamorsky, Jeffrey D., ed. *Employee Benefits Handbook.* Third edition. Boston, MA: Warren, Gorham & Lamont, 1992.

O'Donnell, George F., and Thomas W. Meagher. "Cash Balance Plans: A New Solution for the 1990s." *Journal of Compensation and Benefits* (November–December 1994): 11–20.

Robinson, Pati, and William S. Small. "The Floor Offset Retirement Plan: Versatile and Tested, It Merits More Attention." *Compensation and Benefits Review* (May/June 1993): 28–33.

Rosenbloom, Jerry S., ed. *The Handbook of Employee Benefits: Design, Funding, and Administration.* Fourth edition. Vol. 1 and 2. Homewood, IL: Business One Irwin, 1996.

U.S. Department of Labor. Bureau of Labor Statistics. *Employee Benefits in Medium and Large Firms,* 1988 and 1989. Washington, DC: U.S. Government Printing Office, 1989 and 1990.

_____. *Employee Benefits in Medium and Large Private Establishments,* 1991 and 1993. Washington, DC: U.S. Government Printing Office, 1993 and 1994.

U.S. Department of Labor. Pension and Welfare Benefits Administration. *Private Pension Plan Bulletin* (Winter 1993, Summer 1993, Winter 1995, and Winter 1996).

The Wyatt Company. "Pension Equity Plan Meets Needs of Changing Workforce." *Wyatt Insider* (November 1992): 8–9.

Additional Information

American Society of Pension Actuaries
4350 North Fairfax Drive, Suite 820
Arlington, VA 22203
(703) 516-9300

Association of Private Pension and Welfare Plans
1212 New York Avenue, NW, Suite 1250
Washington, DC 20005
(202) 289-6700

International Foundation of Employee Benefit Plans
P.O. Box 69
18700 West Bluemound Road
Brookfield, WI 53008-0069
(414) 786-6700

11. Simplified Employee Pensions

Introduction

Many small businesses have been reluctant to establish a qualified retirement plan for their employees. Some fear the potential burdens associated with administering a plan and complying with complex federal regulations. The U.S. Congress sought to remove some of these obstacles for small businesses in the Revenue Act of 1978, which established a new tax-favored retirement plan aimed primarily at small employers—the simplified employee pension (SEP).

SEPs are arrangements under which an individual retirement account (IRA) is established for each eligible employee. The employee is immediately vested in employer contributions and generally directs the investment of the money. These arrangements are sometimes called SEP-IRAs.

A principal difference for individuals between a SEP and an employer-sponsored IRA is the larger annual contribution available for a SEP (discussed below). SEPs must also meet some qualified retirement plan rules for eligibility, coverage, vesting, and contributions that do not exist for employment-based IRAs. (For further discussion of IRAs, see chapter 16).

SEPs offer employers an alternative to more complex and costly qualified pension plans. Paperwork, recordkeeping, and reporting requirements are kept to a minimum.

SEPs may be set up by corporations, unincorporated businesses and partnerships, and self-employed persons. Although companies of any size may create SEPs, the simplicity of the arrangement is designed to interest small businesses.

Eligibility

Employer contributions must be made for each employee who has reached age 21, has worked for the employer during at least three of the preceding five years, and has received at least $300 in compensation from the employer during the year. The $300 figure is indexed to increases in the cost of living (the figure for 1996 is $400). Any period of service during a year, even if only one day, qualifies as work for the year. The employer must contribute for employees who worked some period during the year even if they have left the company by the time the employer makes the contribution. Employees covered by collective bargaining agreements and nonresident aliens may be excluded from eligibility. All eligible employees must participate in the SEP, including eligible part-time employees. If at least one eligible employee elects not to participate, the employer is not permitted to contribute to accounts for the other employees.

Contributions

Employers—Under the Revenue Act of 1978, the maximum an employer could contribute for each employee was the lesser of $7,500 or 15 percent of compensation. The limit on compensation that could be considered for calculating the annual contribution was $100,000.

The dollar limit on contributions to SEPs was raised to $15,000 and the compensation limit to $200,000 by the Economic Recovery Tax Act of 1981. The Tax Equity and Fiscal Responsibility Act of 1982 raised the dollar limit on contributions to $30,000. The limit includes the amount an employee elects to contribute through salary reduction. The Omnibus Budget Reconciliation Act of 1993 decreased the compensation limit to $150,000 (which is still the limit for 1996), but this limit will be indexed to the cost of living in the future.

Employer contributions are considered discriminatory unless the same percentage of compensation is allocated to all eligible employees. In plans integrated with Social Security, a limited disparity is permitted (see section on plan design). An employer may contribute to a SEP in addition to contributing to other qualified pension plans. However, SEP contributions are included in the total contribution and deduction limits on all qualified plans, under Internal Revenue Code secs. 415 and 404. One of the most flexible features of a SEP from an employer's standpoint is that there is no required annual contribution. For example, if a company has a poor year and profits are low, the employer can decrease the contribution or simply not make one. Employees are fully and immediately vested in the employer's contributions and investment earnings on the contributions. Therefore, the employee has nonforfeitable rights to the funds and will not lose any on separation from service.

Employees—When SEPs were first created, if the employer contribution was less than the maximum contribution permitted for IRAs that year, the employee was permitted to make up the difference with a tax-deductible contribution to the SEP. In addition, an employee could also contribute up to the maximum tax-deductible level to his or her own IRA. Under rules established by TRA '86, an employee covered under a SEP may not be able to make the full $2,000 deductible contribution to his or her own IRA if his or her adjusted gross income exceeds $25,000 (single) or $40,000 (married filing jointly). (For further discussion of IRAs, see chapter 16.)

TRA '86 considerably broadened the incentives for employee participation in a SEP by providing a salary reduction option. The provision authorizing salary reduction for SEPs was repealed by the Small Business Job Protection Act of 1996.

Distributions

From their inception, SEPs have been subject to the same penalties on early withdrawals (those made prior to age 59½) that have applied to IRAs. In 1986, this tax was expanded to apply not only to SEPs and IRAs but to all qualified employment-based retirement plans. A 10 percent excise tax is imposed on amounts withdrawn before age 59½, unless in the form of an annuity, or on the death or disability of the covered worker. To avoid penalties, SEP distributions must generally begin by April 1 of the calendar year following the calendar year in which an individual attains age 70½ unless the individual has not retired. Loans cannot be made from SEPs.

Taxation

Until the end of 1986, employees had to include as gross income on their tax returns the amounts contributed by their employers to a SEP account and claim an offsetting deduction for the amount; employers included the contributions on employees' W-2 forms. Effective in 1987, employer contributions and employees' elective deferrals to SEPs are excluded from employees' taxable income. Contributions and earnings accumulate tax free until withdrawn. Employer contributions to a SEP are not subject to Social Security (FICA) taxes or to unemployment (FUTA) taxes, but employee elective deferrals are included as wages for FICA and FUTA purposes. An employer may elect to operate a SEP on the basis of a calendar year or the employer's taxable year. Contributions for a taxable year may be made no later than the due date (including extensions) for filing the return for that taxable year.

Integration

Until 1989, employers were permitted to take a portion of the Social Security taxes paid by the employer for each employee into account in calculating the SEP contribution for the employee. That is, the employer could subtract a portion of the Social Security tax paid in a given year from the SEP contribution. This enabled employers to make SEP contributions that were a higher percentage of compensation for higher paid employees (assuming that their compensation exceeded the maximum taxable wage base) because the Social Security tax is a smaller percentage of their total compensation than it is for lower paid workers. Effective in 1989, TRA '86 prescribed new integration rules for defined contribution plans that also apply to the nonelective portion of SEP contributions. These rules permit a limited disparity between the percentage contribution above and below the Social Security wage base. (For a discussion of integration requirements, see chapter 13 on integrating pension plans with Social Security.)

Conclusion

Pension coverage is less common among small businesses than among medium-sized and large businesses. In 1993, only 19 percent of workers in firms with fewer than 25 employees were covered by an employer pension plan, compared with 46 percent among firms with 25–99 employees and 83 percent among firms with 100 or more employees (Employee Benefit Research Institute, 1995). Despite attempts by Congress since 1978 to stimulate interest in SEPs by increasing contribution limits, many of the very firms to which SEPs are targeted know little about them. Among employers that have heard of SEPs, interest in flexibility of contributions and simplicity of administration may be tempered by concern about the nondiscrimination requirements. The employer must make contributions on behalf of employees who may not remain long with the employer, thus diverting funds the employer might wish to use to reward longer service employees. Because employees vest immediately in employer contributions, employers may feel that such a retirement arrangement does little to encourage employees to remain with the employer. Employees have the advantage of immediate vesting, but, as with other retirement arrangements, they face penalties and taxation if they withdraw the contributions and earnings before age $59^{1}/2$.

Bibliography

Allen, Everett T., Jr., Joseph J. Melone, Jerry S. Rosenbloom, and Jack L. VanDerhei. *Pension Planning: Pensions, Profit-Sharing, and Other Deferred Compensation Plans.* Seventh edition. Homewood, IL: Richard D. Irwin, Inc., 1992.

Andrews, Emily. *Pension Policy and Small Employers: At What Price Coverage?* Washington, DC: Employee Benefit Research Institute, 1989.

Employee Benefit Research Institute. *EBRI Databook on Employee Benefits.* Third edition. Washington, DC: Employee Benefit Research Institute, 1995.

Krass, Stephen J. *The Pension Answer Book.* Seventh edition. New York, NY: Panel Publishers, Inc., 1992.

Littell, David A., Donald C. Cardamone, and Wilhelm L. Gruszecki. *Retirement Savings Plans: Design, Regulation and Admininstration of Cash or Deferred Arrangements.* New York, NY: John Wiley & Sons, 1993.

U.S. General Accounting Office. *Private Pensions: Changes Can Produce a Modest Increase in Use of Simplified Employee Pensions.* Washington, DC: U.S. General Accounting Office, 1992.

Additional Information

Association of Private Pension and Welfare Plans
1212 New York Avenue, NW
Suite 1250
Washington, DC 20005
(202) 289-6700

U.S. Department of Labor
Pension and Welfare Benefits Administration
200 Constitution Avenue, NW
Washington, DC 20210
(202) 219-8776

12. Nondiscrimination, Minimum Coverage, and Participation Requirements for Pension Plans

Introduction

Qualified pension plans have long been subject to statutory and regulatory requirements designed to ensure that the tax advantages would result in broad-based coverage of employees—as opposed to plans set up to benefit only the highly paid employees and/or managers of a firm. Although these requirements have met with various degrees of success, legislators sought to accelerate this progress and further broaden employee access to employment-based pension plans through various provisions of the Tax Reform Act of 1986 (TRA '86). This chapter deals with three specific criteria that must be simultaneously satisfied for a plan to have tax-qualified status: nondiscrimination, minimum coverage, and minimum participation requirements. The regulations on the nondiscrimination rules, which provide a three-part test to ensure that contributions or benefits provided under the plan do not discriminate in favor of highly compensated employees are discussed first. This is followed by an examination of the regulations on the minimum participation requirements and a discussion of the minimum coverage requirements that consider overall employee participation in pension plans.

Nondiscrimination Rules

Overview—Sec. 401(a)(4) of the Internal Revenue Code (IRC) provides that a plan is qualified only if the contributions or benefits provided under the plan do not discriminate in favor of highly compensated employees. The regulations for sec. 401(a)(4) set forth three requirements a plan must meet to satisfy this condition:

- either the contributions or the benefits provided under the plan must be nondiscriminatory in terms of their amount;
- the benefits, rights, and features provided under the plan must be available to employees in the plan in a nondiscriminatory manner; and
- the effect of the plan in certain special circumstances (e.g., plan amendments, grants of past service credit, and plan terminations) must be nondiscriminatory.

Each of these requirements is explored in more detail in the following paragraphs.

Nondiscrimination in Amount of Contributions or Benefits— Although separate rules are provided for determining whether contributions and benefits are nondiscriminatory, it is generally permissible for a pension plan to satisfy this requirement by showing that either the contributions or the benefits are nondiscriminatory. An exception to this general rule applies to plans subject to sec. 401(k) or 401(m) and employee stock ownership plans (ESOPs). (For further discussion of 401(k) arrangements and ESOPs, see chapters 8 and 9, respectively.) In these cases, the plan must prove that contributions are nondiscriminatory.

Nondiscrimination in Amount of Contributions—The regulations for sec. 401(a)(4) provide two safe harbor tests for defined contribution plans. The first applies to a defined contribution plan with a uniform allocation formula that provides employees with uniform allocation rates. Permitted disparity that is explicitly taken into account under the allocation formula may be taken into account in applying this test. The second regulation permits a defined contribution plan with a uniform allocation formula weighted for age or service to satisfy the requirement if the average rate of allocation for highly compensated employees under the plan does not exceed the average rate of allocation for nonhighly compensated employees under the plan.

If a plan does not satisfy one of these safe harbor tests, the requirement will be met if no highly compensated employee under the plan has an allocation rate exceeding that of any nonhighly compensated employee under the plan. For the purpose of this calculation, permitted disparity under sec. 401(l)—i.e., differences in rates that occur due to integration with Social Security—may generally be taken into account by imputation. (For further discussion of integrating pension plans with Social Security, see chapter 13.) Also, considerable flexibility is provided to employers in applying this general test under the grouping and restructuring tests. However, plans subject to sec. 401(k) or sec. 401(m) must satisfy the special rules provided for them.

Nondiscrimination in Amount of Benefits—The regulations contain four safe harbors under which a plan is considered nondiscriminatory with respect to the amount of benefits. All require that the plan have a uniform benefit formula, that any subsidized early retirement or joint and survivor benefit be provided on similar terms to substantially all covered employees, that the formula base benefits on a nondiscriminatory definition of compensation, and that the plan have a uniform retirement age for all employees.

Two safe harbors apply to unit credit plans that provide a benefit for each year of service based on a fixed percentage of pay or a fixed dollar amount. The first is for plans that provide for the accrual of these benefits on a unit credit basis, and the second is for plans using the fractional accrual rule. The other two apply to flat benefit plans that satisfy the fractional accrual rule. An example of such a plan is one that provides a benefit of 50 percent of compensation accrued evenly over all years of service or participation. Such a plan satisfies the safe harbor only if the plan provides that the maximum flat benefit will be accrued over a period of at least 25 years.

Those plans that do not satisfy any of the safe harbors must satisfy the general test for nondiscrimination with respect to the amount of benefits. This is accomplished only if no highly compensated employee has an accrual rate greater than that of any nonhighly compensated employee. The disparity permitted under sec. 401(l) may be taken into account by imputation for this purpose. The employer is generally required to determine accrual rates with respect to both the normal form of benefit and the most valuable form of benefit.

Nondiscriminatory Availability of Benefits, Rights, and Features—Optional forms of benefits, ancillary benefits, and other rights and features provided under the plan must be nondiscriminatory. Special rules exist for acquisitions, mergers, and similar transactions. An optional form of benefit is a distribution alternative that is available under a plan, an early retirement benefit, or a retirement-type subsidy. Each optional form of benefit must be currently available and effectively available to a nondiscriminatory classification of employees. Current availability focuses on the availability of the option to employees but assumes that certain conditions such as age or service under the plan's terms are currently satisfied. Effective availability examines whether actual availability of the option, taking into account the ability of employees to satisfy age and service requirements, substantially favors highly compensated employees.

Ancillary benefits include certain Social Security supplements, disability benefits, ancillary life insurance and health insurance benefits, death benefits under a defined contribution plan, preretirement death benefits under a defined benefit plan, and shut-down benefits.

Other rights or features are defined as any right or feature applicable to employees under the plan, other than a right or feature taken into account as part of an optional form of benefit or ancillary benefit provided under the plan and other than a right or feature that cannot reasonably be expected to be of more than insignificant value to an employee. For example, the following are specifically included in this definition:

- plan loan provisions;
- the right to direct investments;
- the right to a particular form of investment;
- the right to a particular class or type of employer securities;
- the right to make a particular rate of before-tax, after-tax, or matching contribution;
- the right to purchase additional retirement or ancillary benefits under the plan; and
- the right to make rollover contributions and transfers to and from the plan.

Nondiscriminatory Effect of Plan in Special Circumstances— Plan amendments and grants of past service credit must not have the effect of discrimination in favor of highly compensated employees. The regulations contain a safe harbor under which a grant of up to five years of past service credit is deemed to be nondiscriminatory. Restrictions on distributions are also prescribed to place a limit on the annual distributions received by the top-paid 25 employees. However, the distribution restrictions do not apply if the plan's funding ratio is at least 110 percent (measured on a current liability basis) or if the benefit payable is less than 1 percent of the current liability.

Employee Contributions—Generally, benefits derived from employer contributions and benefits derived from employee contributions must separately satisfy the nondiscrimination requirements. The regulations provide rules relating to the determination of the employer-derived benefit in a defined benefit plan that also includes employee contributions not allocated to separate accounts. It also provides rules for determining whether employee contributions under a defined benefit plan are nondiscriminatory.

Permitted Disparity—The regulations allow the disparity permitted by sec. 401(l) to be taken into account in showing that the amount of contributions or benefits satisfies sec. 401(a)(4). In many cases, this merely requires inspection of the plan benefit or contribution formula, e.g., where a plan is using one of the safe harbor rules for showing nondiscrimination in the amount of contributions or benefits. These safe harbors require that the plan formula satisfy 401(l) in form. Thus, for example, a single defined contribution plan that takes permitted disparity into account under a uniform formula satisfies sec. 401(a)(4) with respect to the amount of contributions if the disparity under the formula satisfies sec. 401(l) and the regulations thereunder. Similarly, a single defined benefit plan or target benefit plan that takes permitted disparity into account under a uniform formula satisfies sec. 401(a)(4) with respect to the amount of benefits if the disparity under the formula satisfies sec. 401(l) and the regulations thereunder.

If a plan does not use the safe harbor rules, or if two or more plans are combined for purposes of sec. 401(a)(4), permitted disparity is taken into account by using specified formulas that determine an adjusted allocation or accrual rate that reflects the amount of permitted disparity that may be taken into account.

In the case of a defined contribution plan, the plan's allocation rates are adjusted to take into account permitted disparity. This adjusted rate is used to determine whether the amount of contributions under the plan is nondiscriminatory under the general test and to apply the average benefit percentage test of sec. 410(b) (described later in this chapter). If an employee's compensation does not exceed the taxable wage base in effect as of the beginning of the plan year, the employee's adjusted allocation rate equals the sum of the employee's accrual allocation rate and maximum allocation rate that the plan could have used under the permitted disparity rules. If an employee's compensation exceeds the taxable wage base in effect as of the beginning of the plan year, the employee's adjusted allocation rate is the lesser of two rates provided in sec. 1.401(a)(4)-7(b)(3).

The process for a defined benefit pension plan is similar, although covered compensation is used to dichotomize employees instead of the taxable wage base. (For a definition of covered compensation, see chapter 13 on integrating pension plans with Social Security.) In this case, if an employee's compensation does not exceed the employee's covered compensation as of the beginning of the plan year, the employee's adjusted benefit accrual rate is the sum of the employee's actual accrual rate and the maximum excess allowance under the permitted disparity rules. (For a description of these rules, see chapter 13 on integrating pension plans with Social Security.) If an employee's compensation exceeds his or her covered compensation as of the beginning of the plan year, the employee's adjusted benefit accrual rate is the lesser of two rates provided in sec. 1.401(a)(4)-7(c)(3).

Minimum Participation Requirements

Overview—The Small Business Job Protection Act of 1996 eliminated the current law requirement that a defined contribution plan such as a 401(k) plan must benefit at least 50 employees or 40 percent of all employees, whichever is less. In addition, with respect to defined benefit plans, the 40 percent rule is modified to require that the greater of two employees or 40 percent of all employees must benefit under the plan.

Minimum Coverage Requirements

General Rule—In general, a plan must satisfy one of two requirements under IRC sec. 410(b) for both active and former employees on one day in each quarter.

Ratio Percentage Test—Under this test, the percentage of the employer's nonhighly compensated employees benefiting under the plan must equal at least 70 percent of the percentage of the employer's highly compensated employees benefiting under the plan. For example, if a plan benefits 60 percent of the employer's highly compensated active employees and 35 percent of the employer's nonhighly compensated active employees, it fails this test because the plan's ratio percentage is less than 70 percent (35 percent/60 percent =$58^1/_3$ percent).

Average Benefit Test—This test has two parts, both of which must be satisfied. Under the first, the nondiscriminatory classification test, the plan is required to benefit a classification of employees that does not discriminate in favor of highly compensated employees. Under the second, the average benefit percentage test, the average benefit percentage[1] of nonhighly compensated employees must equal at least 70 percent of the average benefit percentage of highly compensated employees.

Nondiscriminatory Classification Test—To satisfy the nondiscriminatory classification test under sec. 410(b), a plan must cover a classification of employees that is reasonable, reflecting a bona fide business classification such as salaried and hourly employees. Moreover, the plan must either

---

[1] The regulations provide detailed guidance concerning the calculation of the individual benefit percentages that are separately averaged for high paid and low paid employees. Benefit calculations are generally performed using the same actuarial techniques required by the nondiscrimination rules, with several important simplifications.

Table 12.1
Section 410(b) Nondiscriminatory Classification under the Safe Harbor/Unsafe Harbor Tests

Concentration Percentage	Safe Harbor Ratio Percentage	Unsafe Harbor Ratio Percentage
60.00% or less	50.00%	40.00%
62.00	48.50	38.50
64.00	47.00	37.00
66.00	45.50	35.50
68.00	44.00	34.00
70.00	42.50	32.50
72.00	41.00	31.00
74.00	39.50	29.50
76.00	38.00	28.00
78.00	36.50	26.50
80.00	35.00	25.00
82.00	33.50	23.50
84.00	32.00	22.00
86.00	30.50	20.50
88.00	29.00	20.00
90.00	27.50	20.00
92.00	26.00	20.00
94.00	24.50	20.00
96.00	23.00	20.00
98.00	21.50	20.00

- benefit at least a safe harbor percentage of nonhighly compensated employees or
- pass a facts and circumstances test and benefit at least an unsafe harbor percentage of nonhighly compensated employees.

Safe Harbor / Unsafe Harbor Tests—Under these tests, the plan's ratio percentage must be at least equal to the safe (or unsafe) harbor percentage. Mathematically, this is the same test as the ratio percentage test explained earlier, but it substitutes the safe (or unsafe) harbor percentage for 70 percent. The safe (or unsafe) harbor percentages are based on the concentration percentage[2] of all nonhighly compensated employees within the employer's work force. Table 12.1 illustrates the safe harbor and unsafe

---

[2] The concentration percentage is defined as the ratio of the nonhighly compensated employees to the employer's total work force (minus any excludable employees), whether or not they are covered by the plan.

harbor percentages for specific concentrations of nonhighly compensated employees. This still leaves a gray area for a plan if it has neither passed the safe harbor test nor failed the unsafe harbor test. In this case, it may be considered nondiscriminatory based on a review of all facts and circumstances.

Facts and Circumstances Test—The regulations indicate that the following factors, among others, may be considered in applying the facts and circumstances test:

- the employer's underlying business reasons for the classification;
- the percentage of the work force that benefits under the plan;
- whether the number of covered employees in each salary range is representative of the total number of employees in that salary range; and
- how close the classification comes to satisfying the safe harbor percentage.

Other Factors That Affect Testing—

Plans Deemed to Pass—The following plans are deemed to satisfy the minimum coverage requirements:

- frozen plans (i.e., plans in which no employees are accruing additional benefits);
- plans of an employer that employs only highly compensated employees;
- plans that benefit only nonhighly compensated employees; and
- plans that benefit only union employees (unless more than a de minimis number of professionals are included).

Excludable Employees—In general, all active and former employees are taken into account in applying the minimum coverage tests except:

- employees who have not satisfied the plan's minimum age and/or service requirements. (For further discussion of these requirements, see chapter 3 on ERISA.)
- nonunion employees who do not benefit under a plan because of a collective bargaining agreement (when testing a plan that benefits union employees);
- collective bargaining unit employees (when testing a noncollective bargaining unit plan);
- participants who fail to accrue a benefit or receive an allocation solely because of a minimum service requirement; and
- nonresident aliens with no U.S. source of income.

Mandatory Disaggregation of Plans—Certain single plans must be disaggregated into two or more separate plans, each of which must satisfy sec. 410(b). The following are examples.

- *Collectively Bargained Units*—The portion of a plan that benefits employees under a collective bargaining agreement and the portion of the plan that benefits nonunion employees must be treated as separate plans.
- *Employee Stock Ownership Plans*—For plan years after 1989, a plan with an ESOP and a non-ESOP feature is treated as two plans.
- *Sec. 401(k) and 401(m) Arrangements*—The portion of a plan that includes (1) a sec. 401(k) cash or deferred arrangement or (2) matching or employee contributions subject to sec. 401(m) rules are treated as separate plans. (For further discussion of 401(m) rules, see chapter 8 on 401(k) cash or deferred arrangements.)

Aggregation of Plans—For purposes of applying the ratio percentage test and nondiscriminatory classification test, two or more separate plans are permitted to be treated as a single plan. However, the aggregate plan would have to satisfy the nondiscriminatory benefit and contributions test of IRC sec. 401(a)(4). Also, an employer may not permissively aggregate plans that have been disaggregated on a mandatory basis (e.g., ESOPs and non-ESOPs, union plans, and nonunion plans). Generally, for purposes of the average benefit percentage test, all qualified plans of an employer, including qualified cash or deferred arrangements and matching or employee contributions subject to sec. 401(m), must be aggregated and treated as a single plan. However, union plans are tested separately from nonunion plans. Also, the new regulations permit separate testing of defined contribution and defined benefit plans.

Multiemployer/Multiple Employer Plans—Each separate employer's portion of a multiple employer plan that is maintained by more than one employer for nonbargained employees is tested separately. If one employer fails, the whole plan, for all employers, potentially could be disqualified. A multiemployer plan (a plan maintained by more than one employer for collectively bargained employees) is treated as one plan, and all participating employers are treated as one employer.

Former Employees—Former employees who currently benefit under the plan (e.g., are granted an ad hoc cost-of-living increase under a plan amendment) are tested separately from active employees. An employer may elect to disregard former employees who are not currently benefiting and who terminated prior to 1984 or more than 10 years before the year being tested. Under a special rule, if at least 10 former employees are currently benefiting under the plan and at least 60 percent of the former employees who are currently benefiting under the plan are nonhighly compensated, the plan will be deemed to pass with respect to former employees.

Compliance—A plan failing to meet the requirements of sec. 410(b) as previously described must be brought into retroactive compliance by the end of the applicable plan year. This may be accomplished either by extending coverage to a broader group of employees or modifying contribution allocations or benefit accruals.

Bibliography

Denbaum, Lewis H. *The 401(k) Handbook.* Washington, DC: Thompson Publishing Group, 1991.

Mamorsky, Jeffrey. D. *Employee Benefits Handbook.* Third edition. Boston, MA: Warren, Gorham & Lamont, Inc., 1992.

Additional Information

American Academy of Actuaries
1720 Eye Street, NW
Washington, DC 20006
(202) 223-8196

The 401(k) Association
1 Summit Square
Doublewoods Road and Rt. 413
Langhorne, PA 19047
(215) 579-8830

International Foundation of Employee Benefit Plans
P.O. Box 69
18700 West Bluemound Road
Brookfield, WI 53008-0069
(414) 786-6700

13. Integrating Pension Plans with Social Security

Introduction

Social Security taxes and benefits are a higher percentage of total compensation for lower paid employees than for higher paid employees. To allow employers to balance the benefit tilt toward lower paid employees inherent in the Social Security system, a system of pension integration rules evolved, culminating in 1971 with the release of Revenue Ruling 71-446, which was in effect until the enactment of the Tax Reform Act of 1986 (TRA '86). Integration allows the employer's pension to be combined with Social Security to result in an overall retirement scheme. While pre-TRA '86 integration rules no longer apply, it is useful to review their application as a basis for understanding the new rules.

Integration works differently for defined benefit and defined contribution plans. Under defined contribution plans, prior to TRA '86 an employer was allowed to make a total contribution (i.e., to the pension plan plus Social Security, exclusive of Medicare) that resulted in a constant percentage of compensation for all employees.

Integration rules for defined benefit pension plans represented the same logic, although the employer's contributions to Social Security first had to be translated into benefits for the employee. Recognizing that Social Security (exclusive of Medicare) represents more than just retirement benefits for the employee (e.g., spousal benefits as well as death and disability benefits), a value of 162 percent of the employee's retirement benefit was placed on the package of benefits received. Acknowledging the argument that the employer pays 50 percent of the payroll tax assessed for these benefits, pension integration rules for defined benefit pension plans were based on the concept that employers should be able to receive credit for approximately one-half of 162 percent (or 81 percent) of the primary retirement benefit for the employee.

In actual practice, this figure was increased up to 83.3 percent. Employers with defined benefit plans utilizing the offset approach to integrating their pension plans were allowed to subtract up to 83.3 percent of the initial primary Social Security benefit from the gross pension benefit.[1] A very large percentage of the employers adopting this approach concluded that it would be too difficult to communicate the rationale for taking credit for more than one-half of the Social Security retirement benefit actually received by the employee and chose to offset only 50 percent of the employee's primary Social Security benefit. Plans were allowed to offset by 83.3 percent of the entire Social Security benefit, even when the employee earned most of the benefit working for other employers.

Many employers chose to accomplish the same objective through an excess approach in which an employee would receive less benefit accrual (or none at all) for compensation below a threshold known as an integration level. The pre-TRA '86 mechanics of this approach were relatively complex and are no longer relevant for current pension plans. But it is important to recognize that, although the integrated pension plans of the past were actuarially equivalent to the other approaches, much of the controversy surrounding those plans resulted from the use of pure excess pension plans in which employees with compensation below the integration level could put in an entire career with an employer and receive no pension benefit.

One of the primary objectives of TRA '86 was to narrow the permitted integration spread and eliminate plans based solely on pay in excess of Social Security wages. This was accomplished (in principle) through the expansion of Internal Revenue Code (IRC) sec. 401(l), which essentially provides an exception for integrated plans to the general nondiscrimination rules that prohibit plans from providing highly compensated employees benefits that are greater, as a percentage of pay, than benefits provided to nonhighly compensated employees.[2] Although sec. 401(l) was the only specific exception available for integrated plans, regulations on general nondiscrimination (IRC sec. 401(a)(4)) provide additional rules that apply to integrated plans. (For further discussion of these rules, see chapter 12 on nondiscrimination requirements for pension plans.)

Integration after the Tax Reform Act of 1986

IRC sec. 401(l) and its related regulations explicitly allow for three different approaches to integration: defined benefit offset, defined benefit

---

[1] As explained in chapter 2, Social Security benefits receive automatic cost-of-living adjustments. Employers adopting this approach were not allowed to increase the offset as the retiree's Social Security benefit increased.

[2] The terms *highly compensated* employee and *nonhighly compensated* employee have specific statutory definitions. (For further discussion of these terms, see chapter 4 on pension plans.)

excess, and defined contribution. Regardless of which of these approaches is chosen, the employer must take into account three key elements in the design of an integrated plan:

- *Integration Level*—This is a threshold based on compensation that determines which participants will receive benefit accruals or contributions in excess of the basic rate and the proportion of their compensation that will benefit from the higher rate.
- *Maximum Offset or Spread*—This refers to the so-called "permitted disparity" between benefit accruals (in a defined benefit plan) or contributions (in a defined contribution plan). It places a limit on the difference that can exist between the accruals or contributions of employees who earn more than the integration level and those who earn less.
- *Two-for-One*—This is a constraint not found in pre-TRA '86 legislation that implicitly prevents employers from integrating a plan to prevent lower paid employees from receiving any pension benefits or contributions. For defined benefit excess and defined contribution plans, this is similar in concept to one of the nondiscrimination tests for 401(k) arrangements. (For futher discussion of nondiscrimination tests, see chapter 8 on 401(k) cash or deferred arrangements.) The two-for-one rule limits the maximum benefit or contribution for employees earning more than the integration level to twice the value (expressed as a percentage of compensation) below the integration level. Thus, if compensation below the integration level receives no benefit or contribution, no additional amount may be provided to compensation in excess of the threshold. For defined benefit offset plans, this rule is implemented (albeit in a complex manner) by limiting the dollar amount of the offset to one-half of the gross dollar benefit (before applying the offset).

Defined Contribution Plans

In general, an integrated defined contribution pension plan must be designed so that the maximum spread between the two contribution levels is 5.7 percent[3] and the contribution rate above the integration level is no more than twice the rate below. For example, a defined contribution plan

---

[3] This figure may increase in the future with increases in the Old Age portion of the employer's Social Security tax rate.

providing 5 percent of compensation for amounts below the integration level may not provide more than 10 percent for compensation in excess of the integration level. Anything more than 10 percent would violate the two-for-one rule. However, if a defined contribution plan provided a 7 percent contribution for compensation less than the integration level for the year, the maximum contribution for compensation greater than the integration level would be 12.7 percent. Anything greater than 12.7 percent would violate the 5.7 percent constraint. The integration level typically used for defined contribution plans is the Social Security wage base at the beginning of the current year.

An employer with a defined contribution plan may integrate the plan at a lower dollar threshold. In such cases, there are two alternatives. Under the first, an employer may choose an integration level less than or equal to 20 percent of the wage base of the current year or $10,000, whichever is greater. In 1995, this option would result in a maximum uniform dollar amount for all participants of $12,240 (because 20 percent of $61,200 (the 1995 Social Security wage base) is $12,240, which exceeds $10,000). This option allows an employer to adopt an integration level lower than the wage base, but it also results in a threshold so low that the vast majority of participants will receive the higher contribution rate on at least a portion of their compensation.

A second alternative allows the employer to designate an integration level at a point between the full wage base and the amount determined under the first alternative. Realizing that using such an interim integration level increases the possibility of discrimination, IRS requires that the 5.7 percent constraint mentioned above must be reduced if the second alternative is used.[4]

Defined Benefit Plans

An integrated defined benefit plan must be based on average annual compensation, defined as an average of at least three consecutive years' pay,[5] compared with nonintegrated plans, which may use different formulas. The employer is allowed to choose the averaging period, but in an

---

[4] A proportional reduction is also required in the old age portion of the Social Security contribution rate.

[5] If a participant has worked less than three years, compensation must be averaged over the entire period of service.

integrated plan the employer must use the years of an employee's career that produce the highest average. (Due to their systematic differences in benefit accruals, exceptions are granted for career average or unit benefit plans. These plans may determine each year's benefit using that year's compensation.) (For a discussion of pension plan formulas, see chapter 4 on pension plans.)

Integration Level—An important concept for determining the integration level used in defined benefit plans is the participant's covered compensation, defined as the average of the Social Security wage base for the 35 years up to and including the employee's Social Security retirement year. Although the Social Security normal retirement age is scheduled to increase in the future under a very detailed set of rules, for purposes of integration, the retirement age is determined as follows:[6]

Table 13.1	
Year of Birth	Social Security Retirement Age
1937 and Earlier	65
1938 through 1954	66
1955 and Later	67

Covered compensation amounts for 1995 are provided for selected years of birth in table 13.2. However, the actual integration level chosen for the plan must not exceed the wage base at the beginning of the year and may be either the covered compensation for each participant or one of four alternatives.

Excess Defined Benefit Plans—Under an excess defined benefit plan, the percentage of compensation at which benefits accrue with respect to compensation above the integration level may not be greater than 0.75 percent of compensation per year of service.[7] Moreover, this rate may not be more than twice the rate applied to compensation below the integration level.

Offset Defined Benefit Plans[8]—The limits for an offset plan are based

---

[6]The Small Business Job Protection Act of 1996 allows plans to use the official Social Security retirement age for discrimination testing.

[7]Only years of service during which benefits accrue may be counted.

[8]Prior to the Tax Reform Act of 1986, the allowable offset for an integrated defined benefit plan was based on the participant's Social Security benefit, but thereafter it is based on his or her compensation and service.

on final average compensation, defined as the average of a participant's annual compensation (excluding pay in any year above that year's wage base) for the three-consecutive-year period ending with the current plan year. (If a participant has worked fewer than three years, his or her compensation is to be averaged over the entire period of service.) The maximum offset is equal to 0.75 percent of final average compensation (up to the integration level) per year of service. As in the other two types of integration, the two-for-one rule is in effect and in this case specifies that the offset cannot be more than one-half the benefit that should be provided, prior to the application of the offset, with respect to the participant's average annual compensation not in excess of final average compensation (up to the integration level).

Career Cap—Both the excess and offset approaches for defined benefit (but not defined contribution) plans are subject to an additional constraint for long-term employees. The annual permitted differential of 0.75 percent is capped,at 35 years of service with the current employer.

Adjustments—The 0.75 percent factor mentioned above must be adjusted in the event of early retirement or integration levels that are outside specified boundaries. If benefits are paid before Social Security normal retirement age, the maximum 0.75 percent must be reduced in accordance with table 13.2 even if benefits under the pension plan are actuarially reduced for early retirement. Adjustments to the 0.75 percent factor may also be required for different integration levels.

Table 13.2
1996 Covered Compensation for Integration Purposes, Selected Years
1996 Wage Base = $62,700

Year of Birth	1996 Covered Compensation
1930	$25,926
1940	43,677
1950	56,589
1960	62,451
1963 or Later	62,700

Bibliography

Employee Benefit Research Institute. *EBRI Databook on Employee Benefits.* Third edition. Washington, DC: Employee Benefit Research Institute, 1995.

U.S. Department of Labor. Bureau of Labor Statistics. *Employee Benefits in Medium and Large Private Establishments, 1993.* Washington, DC: U.S. Government Printing Ofice, 1994.

Additional Information

Association of Private Pension and Welfare Plans
1212 New York Avenue, NW
Washington, DC 20005
(202) 289-6700

U.S. Department of Labor
Pension and Welfare Benefits Administration
Office of Public Affairs
200 Constitution Avenue, NW
Washington, DC 20210-0999
(202) 219-8921
(Publishes *What You Should Know About Your Pension Rights*)

14. Multiemployer Plans

Introduction

A multiemployer plan is typically an employee pension or welfare plan that covers the workers of two or more unrelated companies in accordance with a collective bargaining agreement. Contributions to support such plans are negotiated at the initiative of a labor union or a group of labor unions representing the workers of a number of companies, usually in a given geographic area. The workers are usually engaged in the same kind of employment (e.g., a skilled craft such as carpentry or acting).

There are two broad types of multiemployer plans. The first, a welfare benefit plan, may provide group life insurance; disability insurance; coverage for hospitalization, surgical, and/or medical costs; prepaid legal services; vacation; or unemployment benefits. The other, a pension plan, is designed to provide retirement income benefits. The multiemployer concept can also be used to provide other benefits. Its collective approach has been used effectively in areas such as employee training.

Multiemployer plans are set up under sec. 302(c)(5) of the Labor-Management Relations Act of 1947, commonly known as the Taft-Hartley Act. This law requires that the plans be governed by a board of trustees made up of employer and union representatives, each having equal representation.

The first multiemployer plan was probably an employer-funded pension plan started in 1929 by Local 3 of the Brotherhood of Electrical Workers and the Electrical Contractors Association of New York City. Subsequently, certain negotiated plans developed in the 1930s and 1940s in industries such as the needle trades and coal mining. Multiemployer pension plans grew after World War II with the passage of Taft-Hartley and a court ruling under federal labor law that established benefits as a mandatory subject of collective bargaining. By 1950, multiemployer pension plans covered 1 million workers. Participation under these plans rose to 3.3 million workers in 1960 and to 10.1 million active workers and retirees in 1991 (U.S. Department of Labor, 1995). The U.S. Department of Labor (DoL) estimates that there are approximately 2,994 multiemployer plans (U.S. Department of Labor, 1995). There is likely at least an equal number of multiemployer welfare plans and a growing number of multiemployer plans that provide annuity funds (individual account plans), supplementary unemployment insurance, and legal benefits.

There are also nonnegotiated multiemployer plans, which have been established by certain employers that have chosen, on their own initiative, to provide their employees with a benefit package. Nonnegotiated plans are common in the nonprofit area among religious, charitable, and educational institutions. They are categorized as multiple employer plans under the Employee Retirement Income Security Act of 1974 (ERISA) and the Internal Revenue Code (IRC), and are generally subject to the same legal rules as single employer plans.

Plan Characteristics

In a multiemployer plan, there must be at least two companies and at least two employees, but there is no maximum limit. Most participants in multiemployer pension plans are in large defined benefit plans. DoL reports that in 1987, the latest year for which data are available, nearly 92 percent of the 6.5 million active participants were in plans with 1,000 or more participants per plan, and over 80 percent of participants were in defined benefit plans (Turner and Beller, 1992).

Multiemployer plans are concentrated in certain industries, where there are many small companies with each too small to justify an individual plan. They are also found in industries in which, because of seasonal or irregular employment and high labor mobility, few workers would qualify under an individual company's plan if one were established. For example, construction workers are commonly hired by a given contractor for only a few weeks or months. When the job is completed, the worker may be unemployed until another contractor needs his or her particular skills or talent.

There is frequently more than one multiemployer plan within each large industry. Multiemployer plans may cover industry employees on a national, regional, or local basis, and some cut across several related industries (e.g., crafts or trades in one geographic area). Many plans cover a trade or craft rather than an entire industry. However, some plans that embrace whole industries or a large part of an industry include those of the American Federation of Television and Radio Artists, Communications Workers of America, International Ladies Garment Workers Union, United Paperworkers International Union, and Amalgamated Clothing Workers.

Many multiemployer plans exist in the following manufacturing industries, as defined by DoL: food, baked goods, and kindred products; apparel (or needle trades) and others; printing, publishing, and allied industries;

finished textile products; leather and leather products; lumber and wood products; furniture and fixtures; and metalworking.

In nonmanufacturing industries, multiemployer plans are common in mining; construction; motor transportation; wholesale and retail trades; services; entertainment; and communications and public utilities. The construction industry has the highest concentration of multiemployer plan participants. In 1987, 38 percent of all active multiemployer plan participants were in construction, followed by transportation at 14 percent (Turner and Beller, 1992).

Qualified Plan Rules

ERISA and the IRC set out rules that multiemployer plans, like single employer plans, must follow to qualify for preferential tax treatment. The rules govern fiduciary responsibility, disclosure and reporting, eligibility, vesting, benefit accrual, funding, coverage and participation, integration, and plan termination.

Some of the requirements—such as those for fiduciary responsibility and disclosure and reporting—are essentially the same for both types of plans, while other requirements differ. Benefits of the union-represented participants in multiemployer pension plans are generally deemed to meet the tax code's nondiscrimination standards, but the coverage for any other employees (e.g., the staff of the sponsoring union or of the fund itself) will have to meet the generally applicable nondiscrimination tests. (For further discussion of nondiscrimination requirements, see chapter 12; chapters 3, 12 and 13 address most of the multiemployer plan rules.)

Establishing the Plan

Once a union and various companies agree to set up a multiemployer plan, the first step is usually to negotiate how much each employer will contribute to the plan. Employer and union representatives then adopt a trust agreement that establishes a board of trustees, defines the board's powers and duties, and covers the affairs of both the trustees and the pension or welfare plan. An attorney and an accountant assist in establishing a trust fund to accept company contributions. Benefit and actuarial consultants assist the trustees in working out plan details and determining a supportable benefit level. The trustees probably will retain a professional investment advisor or portfolio manager to ensure competent asset management. The trustees may also hire a salaried plan administrator and staff or retain an outside administration firm to manage the plan and handle day-to-day details such as the collection of employer contributions and employee claims, payments, recordkeeping, and inquiries. Finally, the trustees must adopt a formal plan document and publish a booklet in lay language informing employees of plan benefits, eligibility rules, and procedures for filing benefit claims.

Like a corporation's board of directors, a board of trustees sets overall plan policy and directs the plan's activities. Trustees are responsible for proper fund management. They may delegate certain of their duties and functions, including the management of plan funds, but they bear ultimate responsibility for all actions taken in their names. Fund management is a serious responsibility, since vast sums of money may be involved and pensions or other benefits of hundreds or thousands of people are at stake. Trustees are bound by rigid fiduciary rules of honesty and performance. They are required by both ERISA and the Taft-Hartley Act to act on behalf of plan participants as any prudent person familiar with such matters (i.e., financial affairs) would act.

Contributions and Benefits

Plan contributions are normally made by the employers participating in the collective bargaining agreement. Occasionally, employees are required or permitted to make additional contributions to welfare plans (e.g., during short unemployment periods). The employer's contribution amount is determined through negotiations and fixed in the bargaining agreement. It is usually based on some measure of the covered employee's work (e.g., $1 for each hour worked by each employee). All the contributions are pooled in a common fund that pays for the plan benefits. Investment earnings augment the fund. A multiemployer plan by virtue of its size often can undertake certain forms of investment that are not available to a small fund or a plan established by a single company employing only a few workers.

Companies participating in the same multiemployer plan often make equal contributions. However, some large national or regional multiemployer plans provide several levels of benefits that require different levels of employer contributions. As a result of special circumstances, a company may be required to make higher contributions than other participating companies or its employees may receive lower benefits. For example, a company with a large number of older workers that brings the group into an established multiemployer pension plan might be required to make higher contributions because of the substantial past service liabilities of its older workers who are approaching retirement. However, in general, one hallmark of a multiemployer fund is the cross-subsidy among employers that usually contribute at the same rate for all their employees who are at the same benefit level regardless of their actuarial costs.

Reciprocity

Normally, pension credits cannot be transferred from one multiemployer plan to another unless the trustees of the various plans have negotiated reciprocity agreements. Under such agreements, a worker can shift from employer to employer and among different plans without losing pension credits. About 75 percent of the workers covered by multiemployer health, welfare, and pension programs in the construction industry were covered by reciprocity agreements in 1983. Many other multiemployer plans are also industrywide. Still others are adopting reciprocity agreements at an accelerating rate as international unions continue to encourage these arrangements.

Benefits

Benefit formulas under multiemployer plans may vary: they may be a flat-dollar amount for each year of service, or they may base benefits on earnings. (For further discussion of benefit formulas, see chapter 4 on pension plans.) About 75 percent of multiemployer plans (with 65 percent of multiemployer plan workers) base benefits on length of service and not on earnings level. This is partly because the range of earnings for workers covered by multiemployer plans tends to be narrower than that for workers covered by single employer plans. Under multiemployer plans that do not base benefits on pay, the need to keep individual earnings records is eliminated; the contribution rate for all employees at a given benefit level is usually identical.

Most multiemployer plans suspend pension benefit payments to retirees in their jurisdictions who work in the same trade or industry while receiving pensions. The restriction is intended to prevent retirees from competing for jobs with active workers or practicing their skills in the nonunion sector of the industry. Under rules issued by DoL, a multiemployer plan may suspend benefits for a retiree who completes 40 or more hours of service in one month under certain circumstances, such as: in an industry in which other employees covered by the plan were employed and accrued benefits under

the plan at the time benefit payments commenced or would have commenced if the retired employee had not returned to employment; in a trade
or craft in which the retiree was employed at any time under the plan; and
in the geographic area covered by the plan at the time benefit payments
commenced or would have commenced if the retired employee had not
returned to employment.

Advantages of Multiemployer Plans

Multiemployer plans offer attractive portability features. Employees
may carry pension credits with them as they move from company to company. Thus, they can earn pensions based on all accumulated credits, even if
some of their former employers have gone out of business or stopped making
plan contributions. Similarly, continuity of coverage can be assured for other
benefits, such as medical insurance, when the worker switches jobs within
the same industry. Multiemployer plans may also provide an incalculable
advantage to employees of small companies, who might not receive benefits
if multiemployer plans did not make benefit programs more affordable for
their employers.

There are several advantages for employers who participate in
multiemployer plans. First, economies can be achieved through group
purchasing and simplified administration. Second, benefit and labor costs
throughout a region or even an industry may be stabilized. This can help
reduce employee turnover, because workers will not be attracted to other
jobs by the promise of better benefits elsewhere. As with all benefit plans
qualified under the IRC, company contributions to a multiemployer plan are
generally tax deductible.

Conclusion

The years of heavy multiemployer plan growth are probably over. The
decline of unionized workers in many sectors is clearly one reason. Another
is the general leveling off of pension plan establishment among all employers. In the future, minimal growth will likely occur in the aggregate as
smaller numbers of new workers come under multiemployer plan protection.
Certain industries, such as entertainment, in which employees work
irregularly, and small manufacturers, retail trade, and transportation—
particularly mass transit—may experience heavier than average growth.

Bibliography

Employee Benefit Research Institute. *EBRI Quarterly Pension Investment Report.* Washington, DC: Employee Benefit Research Institute, 1986–1995.

_____. *Databook on Employee Benefits.* Third edition. Washington, DC: Employee Benefit Research Institute, 1995.

Pension Benefit Guaranty Corporation. *Annual Report to the Congress: Fiscal Years 1992 and 1993.* Washington, DC: Pension Benefit Guaranty Corporation, 1993 and 1994.

The Segal Company. *Survey of the Funded Position of Multiemployer Plans.* New York: Martin E. Segal Company, 1995.

Turner, John A., and Daniel J. Beller, eds. *Trends in Pensions.* Second edition. Washington, DC: U.S. Department of Labor, 1992.

U.S. Department of Labor. Pension and Welfare Benefits Administration. *Private Pension Plan Bulletin: Abstract of the 1991 Form 5500 Annual Reports.* Washington, DC: U.S. Department of Labor, 1995.

Additional Information

Construction Labor Research Council
1739 M Street, NW, Suite 900B
Washington, DC 20036
(202) 223-8045

International Foundation of Employee Benefit Plans
P.O. Box 69
18700 West Bluemound Road
Brookfield, WI 53008-0069
(414) 786-6700

National Coordinating Committee for Multiemployer Plans
815 16th Street, NW, Suite 603
Washington, DC 20006
(202) 347-1461

15. Section 403(b) Arrangements

Introduction

A unique type of tax-deferred retirement arrangement is available to certain nonprofit organizations and public school systems. Since 1942, the Internal Revenue Code (IRC) has permitted such employers to purchase annuities for their employees on a tax-deferred basis. However, it was not until 1958, through the Technical Amendments Act of 1958 and a later series of IRC amendments, that Congress established the ground rules for today's sec. 403(b) programs. In the university arena, two distinct retirement arrangements governed by IRC sec. 403(b) may be established. In the first, the employee is typically required to make a contribution if he or she chooses to participate, usually not exceeding 5 percent of salary. The employer then typically contributes a fixed percentage of salary for each participating employee. This arrangement is referred to in this chapter as a *sec. 403(b) pension plan*. The second provides a vehicle for voluntary employee tax-deferred savings, generally to supplement institutional plans. This arrangement is referred to in this chapter as a *tax-deferred annuity (TDA)*. In the public school arena, a voluntary employee tax-deferred arrangement is typically the only retirement plan offered to employees other than the state's retirement system.

To be eligible, nonprofit organizations must qualify as charitable under IRC sec. 501(c)(3). These organizations include hospitals, churches, social welfare agencies, and educational institutions. Publicly sponsored schools, colleges, and universities are also eligible. However, a number of nonprofit organizations do not qualify, including some federal, state, and local government offices; civic leagues; labor organizations; recreational clubs; fraternal societies; credit unions; business leagues; and cooperatives.

Until 1989, employers could establish sec. 403(b) arrangements for one or more employees on a selective basis; unlike other qualified retirement plans, these plans were not generally subject to nondiscrimination rules, although certain limited restrictions did apply. However, in plan years beginning after December 31, 1988, sec. 403(b) plans (except those maintained by churches) must satisfy essentially the same nondiscrimination rules as other qualified retirement plans, as changed by the Tax Reform Act of 1986 (TRA '86). (For further discussion of nondiscrimination rules, see chapter 12.) For plans involving employee salary reduction contributions, special coverage and participation rules apply, similar to those for 401(k) arrangements. (For further discussion of these rules, see chapter 8 on 401(k) cash or deferred arrangements.)

Since many organizations (e.g., hospitals) have contracts with professional persons, 403(b) plan sponsors must determine the true employer/employee relationship. If the employer is not paying Social Security taxes and is not withholding federal income taxes for a particular individual, it is likely that the individual is not considered an employee eligible for a sec. 403(b) plan. Radiologists, pathologists, and anesthesiologists working at a hospital, for example, might fall into this category.

Originally, 403(b) contributors were required to purchase an annuity contract or similar policy from a life insurance company. The IRC has been modified and now allows investment in mutual funds. Sec. 403(b) funding vehicles include: individual and group fixed and variable annuity contracts; custodial accounts held by registered investment companies, and for churches, certain retirement income accounts. Most employers specify the available funding arrangements, particularly in sec. 403(b) pension plans. Under TDA plans, some employers have no restrictions and permit employees to select the type of arrangement they prefer, as long as they meet the legal requirements of sec. 403(b).

Plan Features

Salary Reduction Agreement—Under sec. 403(b) pension plans providing employee salary reduction contributions, the employee and the employer enter into an agreement to reduce the employee's salary by a specified amount. The employer then remits these contributions, together with employer contributions, to an insurance company, custodian, or mutual fund. Under TDAs, the amount of the salary reduction is determined by the employee, as long as it falls within IRC limits. Instead of reducing current pay, employee TDA contributions may be derived from what otherwise would have become a pay increase. In this case, the employee agrees to forgo the pay increase in order for the employer to make TDA contributions of the same amount. In either situation, the language in the agreement must specifically state the level of the contribution, the date the contribution will become effective, and the investment vehicle in which the contribution will be placed.

A salary reduction agreement under a 403(b) pension plan or a TDA must follow the following requirements.

- The agreement must be in writing.
- Contributions can be derived only from money made available after the date of the agreement.[1]
- The agreement must specify the amount of the contribution (either as a dollar amount, percentage of pay, or as the maximum permitted by law).

Contributions—Annual contributions to a sec. 403(b) pension plan cannot exceed a maximum limit, referred to as the exclusion allowance. The exclusion allowance is generally equal to 20 percent of the employee's includable compensation from the employer, multiplied by the number of the employee's years of service with that employer, reduced by secs. 401(a), 403(a), 403(b), and 457 plan contributions paid in prior years through the same employer.

Because the employee's includable compensation is, in turn, based on taxable income (i.e., income after making a salary reduction), the specific calculation can be complex. In addition to the limit imposed by the exclusion allowance, employee contributions made by salary reduction are limited to $9,500 annually, coordinated with any contributions to a 401(k) arrangement and/or a simplified employee pension (SEP). (For further discussion of SEPs, see chapter 11.) The limit applies until the $7,000 limit for 401(k)s, adjusted annually for changes in the cost of living, reaches $9,500, at which time the 403(b) salary reduction limit will be indexed in the same manner. (In 1996, the annual limit for 401(k) arrangements reached $9,500.) If an employee is required to contribute a set percentage of compensation to an institutional pension plan by salary reduction as a condition of employment, or if the employee contribution is made as a one-time irrevocable election, this contribution is not necessarily applied toward the $9,500 annual limit.

A special annual catch-up election is available for employees of educational organizations, hospitals, home health agencies, health and welfare service agencies, and churches or conventions of churches. Under this provision, any eligible employee who has completed 15 years of service with the employer is permitted to make an additional catch-up salary reduction contribution equal to the lesser of:

- $3,000;
- $15,000 reduced by the total amount of prior contributions that, in any year, exceed $9,500; or

---

[1] The 403(b) participant may revoke the salary reduction agreement for amounts earned while the agreement is in effect, to the extent allowed under 401(k) plans.

- $5,000 multiplied by the number of years of service the individual has with the employer, minus an individual's lifetime elective deferrals under a 401(k), 403(b), or 457 plan and/or a SEP.

The Employee Retirement Income Security Act of 1974's overall limits on defined contribution plans under IRC sec. 415(c) also apply to total amounts that can be contributed on behalf of each employee in any one year. (For further discussion of these limits, see chapter 4 on pension plans.)

Employee Rights—A participant in a sec. 403(b) plan has a variety of rights and privileges. Some important rights provided to participants in 403(b) arrangements that are not generally required in other retirement plans include the right to select from a variety of settlement options at termination. If salary reduction is involved, participants must have the right to determine the contribution amount and the date contributions will begin.

Taxation

Employer contributions and employee salary reduction contributions to sec. 403(b) arrangements are excluded from reportable income at the time they are set aside. During the savings accumulation period, investment earnings on these funds are also exempt from current income taxes. When the employee withdraws funds, they are reported as ordinary income for federal tax purposes. However, the ultimate tax impact may be reduced for individuals who make withdrawals after retirement if their yearly retirement incomes are lower than their working year incomes.

Social Security—Employees' contributions that are attributable to voluntary salary reduction agreements are subject to Social Security taxes, even though they are excluded from employees' federal income taxes. Future Social Security benefits are then based on the higher income (i.e., not reflecting the salary reduction); thus, retired employees will not receive lower Social Security benefits as a result of participation in a sec. 403(b) plan.

Regular Distributions—Distributions from a 403(b) plan are generally taxed as ordinary income in the year received. If an employee rolls a lump-sum distribution into another 403(b) or into an individual retirement account (IRA) within 60 days, no tax applies until distribution. For benefits accrued after December 31, 1986, a 403(b) plan must generally comply with the standard distribution rules governing timing and payouts applicable to qualified retirement plans. (For further discussion of these rules, see chapter 4 on pension plans.)

Early Distributions—A 10 percent penalty tax is generally imposed on early distributions (those made before age 59 1/2) from all 403(b) plan accumulations. The tax is in addition to the regular income tax applicable for the year in which the distribution is taken. Some distributions are exempt from the additional tax, including amounts rolled over to an IRA or another 403(b) within 60 days, as are most distributions in the form of an annuity. Payments made on the participant's death or disability, made after the participant has separated from service on or after age 55, used for medical expenses to the extent deductible for federal income tax purposes (under IRC sec. 213), or made to or on behalf of an alternate payee pursuant to a qualified domestic relations order are also exempt from the penalty tax.

Until the end of 1988, the IRC permitted withdrawals at any age, for any reason, from TDAs funded through annuities (although not from those funded through custodial accounts such as mutual funds). As of January 1, 1989, TDAs funded through either annuity or custodial accounts must follow the same early withdrawal rules as 401(k) arrangements. Participants may not make withdrawals prior to age 59 1/2 from TDA accumulations attributable to salary reduction contributions except on account of separation from service, death, disability, or financial hardship. Withdrawals due to hardship are limited to contributions only; earnings may not be withdrawn. The limits on distributions are not applicable to amounts accrued in annuity contracts but are applicable to custodial accounts, prior to January 1, 1989. Hardship has been defined in IRS regulations, but at present these regulations only apply to sec. 401(k) arrangements. Although IRS may provide different regulations for sec. 403(b) plans, legislative history suggests that it intends to apply the same criteria for 403(b) hardship distributions. (For more information on hardship, see chapter 8 on 401(k) cash or deferred arrangements.)

Bibliography

Allen, Everett T., Jr., Joseph J. Melone, Jerry S. Rosenbloom, and Jack L. VanDerhei. *Pension Planning: Pension, Profit-Sharing, and Other Deferred Compensation Plans.* Seventh edition. Homewood, IL: Richard D. Irwin, Inc. 1992.

Employee Benefit Research Institute. *Fundamentals of Employee Benefit Programs for Education Employees.* Washington, DC: Employee Benefit Research Institute, 1993.

Additional Information

Association of Private Pension and Welfare Plans
1212 New York Avenue, Suite 1250
Washington, DC 20005
(202) 289-6700

Public Pension Coordinating Council
c/o Government Finance Officers Association
1750 K Street, NW, Suite 650
Washington, DC 20006
(202) 429-2750

16. Individual Retirement Accounts

Introduction

Through enactment of the Employee Retirement Income Security Act of 1974 (ERISA), Congress established individual retirement accounts (IRAs) to provide workers who did not have employment-based pensions an opportunity to save for retirement on a tax-deferred basis. U.S. tax law has substantially changed the eligibility and deduction rules for IRAs since then. The Economic Recovery Tax Act of 1981 (ERTA) extended the availability of IRAs to all workers, including those with pension coverage. The Tax Reform Act of 1986 (TRA '86) retained tax-deductible IRAs for those families in which neither spouse was covered by an employment-based pension but restricted the tax deduction among those with pension coverage to families with incomes below specified levels. In addition, TRA '86 added two new categories of IRA contributions: nondeductible contributions, which accumulate tax free until distributed, and partially deductible contributions, which are deductible up to a maximum amount less than the $2,000 maximum otherwise allowable. While TRA '86 made IRAs less advantageous for some individuals, most individuals may contribute the maximum amount on a tax-deductible basis. For all individuals, IRAs remain a tax-effective way to save for retirement. However, like any other financial arrangement, IRAs require careful planning and monitoring. And because their ultimate purpose is to provide retirement income, investments need to be directed toward long-term return. This chapter offers an introduction to IRA eligibility rules, contribution limits, distributions, taxation, and investment options.[1]

Eligibility

IRAs may be established under one or more of the following circumstances:

---

[1] The Small Business Job Protection Act of 1996 allows employers with 100 or fewer employees to set up a savings incentive match plan for employees (SIMPLE) IRA. Details of this new pension plan for small employers are provided in Appendix A. This chapter refers solely to IRAs other than those used in SIMPLE plans.

- *Individuals[2] who are not active participants in an employment-based retirement plan*—Regardless of income level, any part-time or full-time worker who is younger than age 70 1/2 and not an active participant in an employment-based plan may establish and contribute to a personal IRA. The Internal Revenue Service (IRS) defines active participant as a person who is covered by a retirement plan: i.e., an employer or union has a retirement plan under which money is added to the individual's account or the individual is eligible to earn retirement credits. An individual is considered an active participant for a given year even if he or she is not yet vested in a retirement benefit. In certain plans, the individual may be considered an active participant even if he or she was only with the employer for part of the year.

  IRA investors must have *earned* income, which can include: (a) wages, salaries, tips, professional fees, bonuses, and other amounts received for personal services; (b) commissions and income generated through self-employment; (c) payments from the sale or licensing of property created by authors, inventors, artists, and others; or (d) alimony. Unearned income derived from real estate rents, investments, interest, dividends, or capital gains cannot be used as the basis for IRA contributions.

- *Individuals who are active participants in an employment-based plan and whose adjusted gross income (AGI) does not exceed $25,000 (single taxpayers) or $40,000 (married taxpayers filing jointly)*—These taxpayers may make a fully deductible IRA contribution. Again, contributions can only be made from earned income.

- *Individuals who are active participants in an employment-based plan and whose AGI falls between $25,000 and $35,000 (single taxpayers) and between $40,000 and $50,000 (married taxpayers filing jointly)*— These taxpayers may make a fully deductible IRA contribution of less than $2,000 and a nondeductible IRA contribution for the balance, as follows. The $2,000 maximum deductible contribution is reduced by $1 for each $5 of income between the AGI limits. For example, a single taxpayer with AGI of $30,000 could make a $1,000 deductible IRA contribution and a $1,000 nondeductible contribution. Under a special rule, the deductible amount is not reduced below $200 if a taxpayer is

---

[2]Special rules apply to families with two wage earners. For more detail, see the discussion of maximum deductible contributions in the following section on contribution limits.

eligible to make any deductible contributions. Again, contributions can only be made from earned income.

- *Individuals who are active participants in an employment-based plan and whose AGI is at least $35,000 (single taxpayers) or at least $50,000 (married taxpayers filing jointly)*—These taxpayers may only make nondeductible IRA contributions of up to $2,000; earnings on the nondeductible contribution are tax deferred until distributed to the IRA holder. Again, contributions can only be made from earned income.
- *IRAs established as rollover vehicles for lump-sum distributions from employment-based pension plans or other IRAs*—A worker who receives a distribution from his or her employment-based retirement plan, an IRA, or a Keogh can generally place the distribution in a rollover IRA without tax penalty or current taxation (see section on rollovers).

Contribution Limits

Maximum Deductible Contributions—As stated earlier, IRA contributions may not exceed $2,000 per year. The amount that is tax deductible varies according to a worker's income tax filing status, AGI, and pension coverage status. Single workers may contribute up to $2,000 or 100 percent of earned income (whichever is lower) per year if they are not active participants in an employment-based plan or if they are covered and have AGI of not more than $25,000. For those with AGI between $25,000 and $35,000, the deductible amount is prorated (see section on eligibility).

- *Two-Earner Couples*—Where a husband and wife both have earned income, each may contribute up to $2,000 or 100 percent of earned income (whichever is lower) per year. This means that a two-earner couple may then make a combined annual deductible contribution of up to $4,000. If a husband and wife file a joint tax return and either spouse is covered by an employment-based plan, both are restricted in their eligibility to make deductible IRA contributions under the rules that apply to their combined AGI. Therefore, they are each allowed full $2,000 deductible contributions if their combined AGI does not exceed $40,000; a deductible IRA contribution of less than $2,000 and a nondeductible IRA contribution for the balance of the $2,000 if their combined AGI is between $40,000 and $50,000; and no deductible contribution if their AGI is $50,000 or above (a nondeductible IRA contribution of up to $2,000 would be allowed for each working spouse).

If a married individual files a separate tax return, the spouse's active participation does not affect the individual's eligibility to make deductible IRA contributions. But if a married individual files separately, the phase-out of the $2,000 deduction begins with $0 of AGI and ends at $10,000. Therefore, for each $5 of AGI above $0, the maximum $2,000 IRA deduction is reduced by $1, or 20 percent of income. For example, if a married person is an active participant, has $3,000 of income, and files a separate return, the maximum allowable IRA deduction would be $1,400 (i.e., $2,000 – $600 (0.20 x $3,000)). If the same individual had AGI of $10,000 or more, no deductible IRA contribution would be allowed.

- *One-Earner Couples*—The Small Business Job Protection Act of 1996 increased the amount that an individual may contribute to joint IRAs for the individual and the nonworking spouse, from $2,250 to $4,000 annually. The new limit equals the maximum combined IRA contributions allowable if both spouses work, which remains unchanged.
- *Nonworking Divorced Persons*—All taxable alimony received by a divorced person is treated as income for purposes of the IRA deduction limit. The regular IRA eligibility rules apply.[3]

Minimum Contributions—No minimum IRA contributions are required, and contributions are not required to be made in every year. However, the deductible amount is not reduced below $200, even if the individual's deductible contribution is less, until the deductible amount reaches zero.

Employment-Based IRAs

An employer may contribute to an IRA that has been set up by the employee or may set up an IRA for employees. The employee's interest must be nonforfeitable, and separate records showing the employee's contributions and the employer's contributions must be maintained. Although regular IRA contribution limits apply, the employer is also permitted to pay

---

[3]Contributions to spousal accounts are not permitted after the elder spouse reaches age 70½. If the employee-spouse is younger, he or she can continue only his or her own IRA after the other spouse reaches age 70½.

reasonable administrative expenses associated with the IRA.

Employers may also offer employees IRAs through payroll deduction arrangements. Automatic deductions from employees' earnings would be deposited in IRAs that are set up by the company. Some employers permit employees to select among a variety of investment options. This arrangement should not be confused with an employment-based retirement plan called a simplified employee pension (SEP), in which an employer establishes an IRA for each employee and makes contributions on their behalf. SEPs have different contribution limits from IRAs and are subject to some of the same rules as other qualified retirement plans (For further discussion on SEPs, see chapter 11 and for the new SIMPLE plans, see Appendix A).

Distributions

IRA distributions must begin by April 1 of the calendar year following the calendar year in which the individual reaches age $70^{1}/_{2}$. If an individual elects a lump-sum payment, the full amount must be distributed. If a distribution in the form of an annuity is elected, a minimum amount must be distributed to ensure full payout over the individual's expected life (or the expected life of the individual and a named beneficiary). The minimum distribution basically is computed by dividing the opening balance at the beginning of the year by the life expectancy of the individual (or the joint life expectancy of the individual and beneficiary), determined as of the date the individual attained age 70 and reduced by one for each taxable year elapsed after age $70^{1}/_{2}$. (As an alternative, life expectancies can be recalculated each year.) An individual who has multiple accounts may choose the account(s) from which he or she would like to take the required distribution, instead of taking distributions from each account (see section on penalties). Distributions can be paid in the following ways:

- *Lump-Sum Payments*—The entire account balance is distributed in one sum.
- *Periodic Certain*—The account balance is paid in a predetermined number of fixed payments over a specified period of time.
- *Life Annuity*—Payments are made to retirees for their remaining lifetimes and to their beneficiaries or estates on their death, usually on a monthly basis.
- *Joint and Survivor Annuity*—Payments are made for the IRA holder's remaining lifetime, usually on a monthly basis. After the IRA holder's death, the surviving spouse continues to receive lifetime payments.

The survivor usually receives only a portion (e.g., 50 percent) of the amount paid to the primary IRA holder. In addition, the monthly income to the primary holder will be lower than under an individual life annuity; this reflects the additional cost of insuring income over two lifetimes rather than one.

Rollovers

The law permits individuals to roll over account balances from one IRA to another and from a qualified retirement plan to an IRA. To avoid tax penalties, the transfer of assets from one account to another must be completed within 60 days.[4]

Rollovers between IRAs—Under this arrangement, the individual may roll over his or her account balance from one IRA to another, offering greater investment flexibility. This type of rollover can occur only once annually. A transfer of IRA funds from one trustee to another, either at the individual's request or at the trustee's request, is not a rollover—it is a transfer that is not affected by the one-year waiting period.

Rollovers between Employer Plans and IRAs—If employer retirement plans provide lump-sum distributions, the amounts corresponding to pretax employee and employer contributions may be transferred to a rollover IRA. Rollover IRAs were designed specifically to provide a savings vehicle for lump-sum distributions without imposing a tax penalty. Rollovers of lump-sum distributions may be made at any age. However, if the individual is aged 70$\frac{1}{2}$ or over, distributions must begin during the year in which the rollover is received. Lump-sum distributions from employer plans paid to a surviving spouse after an employee's death can also be rolled over into an IRA without penalty. An individual may also roll over a distribution from one employer plan into an IRA and at a later time roll over those same assets, plus any earnings, into another employer plan. In this case, the IRA acts as a conduit for the funds from one employer to another. However, the funds must be kept in a separate account and not mixed with any other funds.

---

[4] The Internal Revenue Service has ruled that IRA funds may be used for short-term loans provided they are redeposited in the same or another IRA within 60 days of withdrawal. Only one such transaction is permitted per IRA in any 12-month period.

Taxation

IRA taxation rules reflect the basic purpose of an IRA (i.e., to provide retirement income). Use of IRA savings for purposes other than retirement income, therefore, is discouraged through tax penalties. In general, penalty taxes will not apply to IRA distributions that begin no earlier than age 59¹/₂ and no later than April 1 of the calendar year following the calendar year in which the individual attains age 70¹/₂. Distributions in the case of death or disability and made in the form of an annuity can begin prior to age 59¹/₂ without penalty. Distributions are considered income in the year received and are subject to applicable marginal income tax rates.[5]

Income Taxes—Each year, tax-deductible contributions to new or existing IRAs must be made by the tax return filing date. Contributions can be made in one full payment or in installments throughout the year. The distributions are taxed as ordinary income in the year received, except for the portion of the total IRA distribution that is considered a return of the dollar amount of the nondeductible contributions, which is excludable from gross income. All IRAs (including rollover IRAs) are treated as a single contract, and all distributions from such plans in any taxable year are treated as a single distribution. If an individual withdraws an amount from an IRA that includes both deductible and nondeductible contributions, the amount excludable from gross income is determined by multiplying the withdrawal by a fraction, where the numerator is the individual's total nondeductible contributions and the denominator is the total balance (at the close of the calendar year) of all the individual's IRAs. For example, if an individual held four IRA accounts with a total value of $10,000, and $2,000 was the amount of the nondeductible contributions, then a withdrawal of, for example, $4,000 would be considered to consist of $800 attributable to excludable, nondeductible contributions ($4,000 x 2,000/$10,000 or 0.2) and $3,200 fully taxable as ordinary income.[6]

IRA lump-sum distributions are not eligible for income averaging or capital gains treatment.

Estate Taxes—The entire value of an IRA is included in the deceased participant's gross estate.

---

[5] The future tax treatment of IRA distributions is unclear in many state and local jurisdictions, although some have announced that they will follow federal tax law.

[6] Different, more complex, rules apply to amounts withdrawn as annuities.

Penalties—Under certain circumstances, tax penalties apply, as follows.

- Contributions in excess of the maximum limits described above are subject to a 6 percent excise tax on any excess contribution for each year the amount remains in the account. If an individual contributes more than the permissible amount, he or she can avoid the 6 percent tax penalty by withdrawing the excess, plus any earnings by the tax return due date in the year the contribution is made.
- Distributions prior to age 59½ are subject to a 10 percent penalty tax, unless they are taken as part of a series of equal payments made for the life (or life expectancy) of the employee or the joint lives (or joint life expectancies) of such employee and his or her beneficiary, or the IRA owner dies or becomes disabled. Neither a rollover between IRAs nor the portion of an early withdrawal that is attributable to nondeductible contributions is subject to the tax.[7]
- After April 1 of the calendar year following the year in which the individual turns age 70½, failure to make required minimum distributions will subject amounts that should have been withdrawn to a 50 percent excise tax.
- If total distributions from an IRA and any qualified employer retirement plan exceed $155,000 in 1996 (indexed to the consumer price index annually), a 15 percent excise tax is imposed on the excess with certain exceptions for lump sums and for grandfathered amounts.

Investments

IRA savings can be invested in retirement accounts and retirement annuities. The institutions that offer IRA investment vehicles include banks, brokerage houses, insurance companies, savings and loan associations, credit unions, mutual fund companies, other investment management organizations, and the federal government. IRA contributions can be placed in more than one account, provided the total annual contribution limits are not exceeded. Collectibles such as art, antiques, rugs, stamps, wines, and coins—other than certain U.S.-minted gold or silver coins and state-issued coins circulated after November 10, 1988—are not permissible IRA

---

[7]Effective for tax years beginning after December 31, 1996, individuals may make penalty free withdrawals from IRAs to pay for medical expenses in excess of 7.5 percent of adjusted gross income.

investments.

An IRA investor should understand the risks and limitations of the various investment options. Financial institutions are required to explain how their IRAs work and their financial ramifications. Before choosing an IRA, some important questions should be considered and answered. For example: What are the investor's retirement income needs?

- Should he or she invest in low-risk choices or can he or she afford to undertake potentially higher risks that may produce higher returns?
- What are the administrative fees or commissions charged on the type of IRA under consideration?
- Is there a minimum deposit requirement?
- What is the interest rate and how is it computed? Is it likely to fluctuate over the worker's lifetime?
- Can the investment be quickly converted into cash in an emergency? Is there a penalty charge for early withdrawal (separate from the income tax penalty)?
- Should IRA contributions be made early or late in the tax year? (If money is invested early, it accumulates interest longer. But if money is invested late, individuals have use of their money throughout the year and may have a better idea how much they can invest in an IRA.)

Conclusion

IRAs can be an important addition to retirement savings opportunities. They are particularly useful for persons who do not have employer pension coverage and for highly mobile workers with minimal or no pension benefits due to limited service in any one job. The amount of retirement income generated by an IRA will depend on a variety of factors, including contribution amounts, the participant's age when the IRA is established, the rate of investment return, and the participant's age at retirement.

Bibliography

Employee Benefit Research Institute. *EBRI Databook on Employee Benefits.* Third edition. Washington, DC: Employee Benefit Research Institute, 1995.

_____. "Retirement Confidence in America: Getting Ready for Tomorrow." *EBRI Special Report* SR-27/*Issue Brief* no. 156 (December 1994).

Gaudio, Peter E. *Your Retirement Benefit.* New York, NY: John Wiley & Sons, 1992.

Salisbury, Dallas L., and Nora Super Jones, eds. *Pension Funding & Taxation: Implications for Tomorrow*. Washington, DC: Employee Benefit Research Institute, 1994.

Salisbury, Dallas L. "Individual Saving for Retirement—The 401(k) and IRA Experiences." *EBRI Issue Brief* no. 95 (Employee Benefit Research Institute, October 1989).

Universal Pensions. *1994–95 IRA Fact Book*. Brainerd, MN: Universal Pensions, 1994.

U.S. Department of the Treasury. Office of the Secretary. Public Affairs Office. *Individual Retirement Arrangements*. Pub. no. 590. Washington, DC: U.S. Department of the Treasury.

Yakoboski, Paul, and Celia Silverman. "Baby Boomers in Retirement: What Are Their Prospects?" *EBRI Special Report* SR-23/*Issue Brief* no. 151 (Employee Benefit Research Institute, July 1994).

Yakoboski, Paul, et al. *Employment-Based Retirement Income Benefits: Analysis of the April 1993 Current Population Survey*. EBRI *Special Report* SR-25/*Issue Brief* no. 153 (Employee Benefit Research Institute, September 1994).

Additional Information

Association of Private Pension
and Welfare Plans
1212 New York Avenue, Ste. 1250
Washington, DC 20005
(202) 289-6700

International Foundation of Employee Benefit Plans
P.O. Box 69
18700 West Bluemound Road
Brookfield, WI 53008-0069
(414) 786-6700

U.S. Department of the Treasury
Public Affairs Information (Publications)
15th St. and Pennsylvania Ave., NW
Washington, DC 20220
(202) 622-2040

17. Retirement Plans for the Self-Employed

Introduction

Self-employment has long been part of the American dream. The continued willingness of entrepreneurs to accept the risks of starting their own business is testament to the strength of this dream.

Since 1962, federal policy has encouraged the provision of pensions for the self-employed and their employees through the Self-Employed Individuals Tax Retirement Act. This law created Keogh plans, named for U.S. Rep. Eugene J. Keogh of New York, who sponsored the original legislation. (Sometimes these plans are referred to as H.R. 10 plans, after the number assigned to an early version of the bill.) The act allowed unincorporated small business owners, farmers, and those in professional practice to establish and participate in tax-qualified plans similar to those of corporate employers. The self-employed may either be sole proprietors or members of a partnership.[1]

Prior to 1962, many small business owners found that their employees could participate in a tax-qualified pension plan, but the employers themselves could not. Self-employed individuals without employees also could not participate in a tax-qualified plan. Furthermore, where two people operated similar businesses and realized similar profits—but one was a sole proprietor and the other was incorporated—the corporate operator could benefit from a pension plan even though he or she was the only employee of the corporation, but the sole proprietor could not.

Legislative History

Keogh plans originally were subject to tighter limits on contributions and benefits and stricter rules governing plan operation than corporate retirement plans. Self-employed individuals were limited to a contribution of $2,500 per year, while (at that time) there was no limit imposed on corporate plans. This provision led to otherwise unnecessary incorporation by self-employed persons solely for the purpose of obtaining the tax benefits

---

[1] In addition to Keogh plans, the self-employed are also eligible for simplified employee pensions (SEPs). (For further discussion of SEPs, see chapter 11.)

for retirement savings. In addition, Keogh plans had stricter limits on vesting and contributions for owner-employees (those with a certain percentage ownership interest). To achieve somewhat greater equity with corporate plans, the Employee Retirement Income Security Act of 1974 (ERISA) increased the annual limit for deductible contributions to Keogh plans to 15 percent of earned income or $7,500, whichever was lower.

In 1981, Congress reviewed Keoghs at the same time that it expanded eligibility for individual retirement accounts (IRAs). The Economic Recovery Tax Act of 1981 retained the 15 percent of compensation deduction limit but increased the dollar maximum to $15,000, effective January 1, 1982.

In the Tax Equity and Fiscal Responsibility Act of 1982 (TEFRA), Congress established parity between corporate and noncorporate retirement plans. To this end, most of the special rules applicable to Keogh plans were eliminated. Maximum limits for a defined benefit or defined contribution Keogh plan were changed to be the same as those for corporate plans. And many of the provisions relating to owner-employees were repealed. By treating Keogh plans and corporate plans more equally, Congress intended to mitigate the tendency for professionals to incorporate simply to take advantage of the higher amounts that were tax deductible under prior law.

At the same time that many of the rules applicable specifically to owner-employees in Keoghs were repealed, TEFRA added new top-heavy rules for all qualified plans. The rules took the owner-employee concept, expanded it to include officers and other types of company owners, and applied stricter vesting and contribution limits to plans that benefited a certain proportion of key employees. (For further discussion of these rules, see chapter 4 on pension plans.)

The Tax Reform Act of 1986 made numerous changes in the rules governing all qualified retirement plans, which also affect Keoghs. (For further discussion of these rules, see chapter 4 on pension plans.)

Eligibility

The self-employed individual is treated as an employer as well as an employee for tax purposes in contributing to a Keogh plan. In addition, the self-employed individual must make contributions to the plan on behalf of his or her employees.

Keogh plans may be classified as either defined contribution or defined benefit plans. Defined contribution plans are those in which the contributions are defined, and the eventual benefit depends on the total amount of contributions and their investment performance. Defined benefit plans do not specify the amount of contribution but instead define the future retirement benefit in terms of a monthly pension. (For a discussion of the differences between defined benefit and defined contribution plans, see chapter 5.) Self-employed individuals are also eligible to contribute to an IRA but may only make deductible contributions to both an IRA and a Keogh plan if their taxable income is below the levels established for IRAs. (For further discussion of contribution levels, see chapter 16 on IRAs.)

Contributions and Benefits

Contributions made by self-employed individuals are not currently taxable to the self-employed individual, and the contributions by the self-employed individual on behalf of his or her employees are not currently taxable to employees. The contributions and any earnings accumulate tax free until distribution, when they are subject to normal income taxes. If distribution occurs prior to age $59\frac{1}{2}$, a penalty tax may be assessed (discussed in section on distributions).

Employee after-tax contributions are also permitted. These contributions, which are currently taxed, generate tax-sheltered earnings. However, special nondiscrimination rules for after-tax contributions may effectively reduce this limit for some employees (discussed in section on nondiscrimination). Keogh plans are subject to the same contribution and benefit limits as other corporate retirement plans under Internal Revenue Code sec. 415. For defined contribution plans, the maximum annual addition may not exceed the lesser of 25 percent of the employee's compensation (or earned income)[2] or $30,000 per year. The maximum annual benefit to a participant under a defined benefit plan is $120,000 or 100 percent of the participant's average compensation for his or her three consecutive highest-earning years. The $30,000 and $120,000 figures are scheduled to be adjusted in the future to reflect changes in the cost of living.

---

[2] For purposes of computing the limitations on deductions for contributions to a Keogh plan, earned income is computed after taking into account amounts contributed to the plan on behalf of the self-employed individual (i.e., the self-employed individual's earned income is reduced by the deductible contributions to the plan). Furthermore, earned income is computed after the deduction allowed for self-employment taxes.

Distributions

Keogh plan distributions can be paid in the same manner as other plans, namely in a lump-sum payment (where the entire account balance is distributed in one sum) or in periodic distributions from accumulated reserves as an annuity. The annuity can be in the form of a life annuity—in which a monthly payment is made to a retiree for his or her remaining lifetime and ceases on the retiree's death—or in the form of a joint and survivor annuity, in which the surviving spouse continues to receive monthly payments after the retiree's death. Plan distributions can also be paid out in regular installments for a fixed number of years. (For further discussion of plan distributions, see chapter 4 on pension plans.)

Taxation

At retirement, Keogh plan benefits are taxed as they are received. The tax treatment depends on the type of distribution—annuity or lump sum—and generally follows normal qualified plan rules. (For further discussion of taxation, see chapter 4 on pension plans.) A self-employed individual is limited in the use of income averaging[3] and capital gains treatment to distributions that are made after the attainment of age $59^{1}/_{2}$ or on account of death or disability. Distributions from a Keogh plan, like those from other qualified plans, prior to age $59^{1}/_{2}$ are penalized. Unless the distribution meets one of a limited number of exceptions, it is subject to a 10 percent excise tax in addition to regular income tax. (For further discussion of distribution rules, see chapter 4 on pension plans.)

Rollovers

Prior to the Deficit Reduction Act of 1984 (DEFRA), tax-free rollovers of lump-sum distributions could not be made by a self-employed individual from a Keogh plan to an employment-based pension plan or another Keogh plan. DEFRA permitted a tax-free rollover from one qualified plan to another of a distribution attributable to contributions made on behalf of a participant while he or she was self-employed. Tax-free rollovers of Keogh plan distributions can also be made to an IRA.

---

[3]This distinction will no longer exist for tax years beginning after December 31, 1999, when five-year averaging for qualified lump-sum distributions will be repealed.

Loans

Loans to participants in Keogh plans are permitted under the rules governing all qualified plans. (For further discussion of these rules, see chapter 4 on pension plans.) However, a Keogh plan may not make loans to self-employed individuals who are owner-employees.

Nondiscrimination

Keogh plans must satisfy the same nondiscrimination requirements as other qualified retirement plans. These are designed to guarantee that highly compensated employees do not disproportionately benefit in terms of participation in the plan or in benefits provided. (For further discussion of these requirements, see chapter 12 on nondiscrimination requirements for pension plans.)

Conclusion

Over the past two decades, Congress has passed a number of laws designed to provide tax incentives for self-employed individuals to supplement retirement income in addition to their Social Security benefit. Despite these incentives, the unincorporated self-employed have not participated in Keogh plans at a very high rate. However, there is some evidence of growth.

Bibliography

Allen, Everett T., Jr., Joseph J. Melone, Jerry S. Rosenbloom, and Jack L. VanDerhei. *Pension Planning: Pensions, Profit Sharing, and Other Deferred Compensation Plans.* Seventh edition. Homewood, IL Richard D. Irwin, Inc., 1992.

Cheeks, James E. *The Dow-Jones Guide to Keoghs.* Homewood, IL: Dow-Jones Irwin, 1989.

Employee Benefit Research Institute. *EBRI Databook on Employee Benefits.* Third edition. Washington, DC: Employee Benefit Research Institute, 1995.

Krass, Stephen J. *The Pension Answer Book.* Seventh edition. New York, NY: Panel Publishers, Inc., 1996.

Rosenbloom, Jerry S. *The Handbook of Employee Benefits: Design, Funding, and Administration.* Third edition. Homewood, IL: Business One Irwin, 1992.

Additional Information

American Academy of Actuaries
1720 Eye Street, NW, 7th Floor
Washington, DC 20006
(202) 223-8196

International Foundation of Employee Benefit Plans
P.O. Box 69
18700 West Bluemound Road
Brookfield, WI 53008-0069
(414) 786-6700

18. Planning for Retirement

Introduction

Retirement is a relatively new phenomenon. Until the decades following World War II, most men and many women worked throughout their lives. Those who were unable to continue working were either sustained by their family or by a public facility for destitute people. Since Social Security retirement benefits were first paid in 1940, age 65 has become the so-called normal retirement age, although many Americans retire well before age 65.[1] The growth of employment-based retirement plans and increased life expectancy have also contributed to present retirement trends. Since the "normal" retirement ages under Social Security, Medicare, and private plans have not adjusted to increasing life expectancies, current workers could potentially spend more time in retirement than retirees in the past. As a result, some analysts predict that many of today's young people probably will not be able to retire as early as those who have retired during the last decade or so, or their standard of living may fall in retirement. If this proves to be the case, later retirement and part-time jobs after retirement may be a fact of life for many individuals in the baby boom and later generations.[2]

On average, men who reach age 65 in 2000 are projected to live another 15 years (i.e., until about age 80); women who reach age 65 in 2000 are projected to live another 18.7 years (i.e., until about age 84).[3] Expanded life expectancy brings with it a new awareness of the aging process. Retirement is increasingly an important part of one's *total* life. However, many still view their retirement years with apprehension. Retirement is a challenging period that can bring rewards and new experiences. However, satisfying

---

[1] The current Social Security normal retirement age of 65 is scheduled to increase gradually to age 67, beginning with those who attain age 62 in the year 2000 and ending with those who attain age 62 in 2022 and later. For further discussion of Social Security, see chapter 2 on Social Security and Medicare.

[2] See Employee Benefit Research Institute, *Retirement in the 21st Century... Ready or Not...* (Washington, DC: Employee Benefit Research Institute, 1994).

[3] Based on the intermediate set of assumptions in the U.S. Social Security Administration, *1996 Annual Report of the Board of Trustees of the Federal Old-Age and Survivors Insurance and Disability Insurance Trust Funds* (Washington, DC: U.S. Government Printing Office, 1996).

retirement requires an adjustment period that is greatly aided by thoughtful, effective planning in earlier working years.

Ideally, one should begin planning for retirement early in one's career. The 1995 Retirement Confidence Survey, conducted by the Employee Benefit Research Institute (EBRI) and Mathew Greenwald & Associates, Inc., found that while three-quarters of American workers are confident regarding their retirement income prospects, many should probably evaluate their situation to determine whether their confidence is justified.[4] Many, but not all, American workers recognize the need to save (among those confident, 30 percent have nothing saved for retirement); however, most have not gone the next step and developed a saving plan based on a target. Among confident savers, 60 percent have not tried to calulate how much they will need to save to fund a comfortable retirement lifestyle. Advance planning can minimize the risk of not having enough retirement income to maintain a desired standard of living. Planning can also alleviate some of the psychological problems that may accompany retirement.

The first part of this chapter identifies some areas on which those who are preparing for retirement need to focus. It is not intended to provide all the necessary information. Instead, it poses certain questions that need early consideration. Discussion is provided on: financial planning, preventive health, health care costs, living arrangements, use of leisure time, interpersonal relationships, and estate planning. A worksheet provided in this section can help individuals estimate a retirement savings goal, where they are in relation to that goal, and how much needs to be saved on their behalf to reach that goal. The second part of the chapter discusses the potential role of employers in helping employees to prepare for retirement.

Considerations for the Employee

Financial Planning Considerations—A difficult aspect of retirement planning is ensuring adequate household income. A common misconception is that financial planning is only necessary for wealthy people. Retirement income planning may be even more important for average or low income people due to the complexities of taxation, the sophistication of financial markets and instruments, and increasing longevity. Workers

---

[4]Paul Yakoboski, "Are Workers Kidding Themselves? Results of the 1995 Retirement Confidence Survey," *EBRI Issue Brief* no. 168 (Employee Benefit Research Institute, December 1995).

should be saving and investing large amounts at the peak of their earning power. Additionally, they should understand that certain options existing at one point in time may not be available later.

Throughout their career years, workers should give careful consideration to the following questions: At what age should I retire? What kind of retirement do I want? Where will I live? How much money will I need in retirement? What are my assets and liabilities now? What will they be at retirement? What are my health care costs likely to be? Will I have long-term care needs? How can I cope with inflation? And, for those who are married, if I should die before my spouse, will my family be left with an adequate income?

Retirement income is generally derived from three sources: Social Security, pensions, and personal savings. In addition, retirees may have access to life insurance, home equity, welfare programs, or new forms of employment. Following are some sources of retirement income.

Social Security—Social Security replaces a portion of covered earnings that may be lost as a result of a person's old age, disability, or death. Various requirements must be met before benefits are payable. For those who qualify, benefits are paid to workers and their spouses, widows, widowers, divorcees, dependent children, and dependent parents. Social Security benefits are automatically adjusted for inflation.

Social Security replaces a portion of preretirement income. It is not intended to provide income sufficient to satisfy *all* retirement needs. For individuals in all income quintiles—but especially for individuals in the higher income quintiles—Social Security must be supplemented by pensions, personal savings, and other investments if individuals hope to maintain their preretirement standards of living. For example, the Social Security replacement rate for an individual aged 65 with final annual earnings of $15,000 in 1996 was 50 percent, while the replacement rate for an individual aged 65 with final annual earnings of $62,700 was 24 percent. The design of Social Security helps assure these results with a benefit formula that delivers larger benefits, as a percentage of final compensation, to those earning the least and a maximum salary cap for taxes and benefit calculation.

Today, most workers qualify for reduced retirement benefits at age 62 or full benefits at age 65. Social Security has no minimum age or service requirements for participation, thus all covered workers are also program participants. Workers with covered earnings of $2,560 (indexed) or more in 1996 earned four quarters of Social Security coverage. For those reaching age 62 after 1990, 40 quarters are required for retirement benefits. An overwhelming majority of the work force ultimately qualifies for benefits. Social Security payments are not automatically provided; workers must apply for benefits. The Social Security Administration advises people to file claims about three months before they want the benefits to begin.

Workers should determine whether they will qualify for Social Security benefits. At least once every three years they should also obtain a Personal Earnings and Benefit Estimate Statement (PEBES) from the Social Security Administration. Answers to questions concerning Social Security can be obtained from local Social Security offices; the address and phone number are listed in the telephone directory under Social Security Administration. The administration also has a nationwide toll-free number: (800) 772-1213. (For further discussion of Social Security, see chapter 2 on Social Security and Medicare.)

Private Pension Programs—There are several methods of payment for private pensions, although not every plan provides all of these options. One way in which a private pension can be paid to a retiree is the straight-life annuity—a periodic payment for the life of the retiree, with no additional payments to survivors. For married employees, the standard benefit prescribed by law is the joint-and-survivor annuity, which provides payments to a surviving spouse after a retiree dies. The Employee Retirement Income Security Act of 1974 (ERISA), as modified by the Retirement Equity Act of 1984, stipulates that an employee may reject a surviving spouse's benefit only with the written consent of the spouse. Before retirement, workers and their spouses should confirm the status of their survivor benefits. Another method of payment that may be available to a retiree is the lump-sum payment, which provides the employee with the "actuarial equivalent"[5] of an annuity. Particular care is required when considering a lump-sum distribution from an employer's plan. Important considerations include the health of the employee and spouse, the ability and willingness to manage a significant amount of money, the availability of this money for nonretirement purposes, and the complex rules governing the tax treatment of lump sums (e.g., five-year averaging until the turn of the century and individual retirement account (IRA) transfer and rollover rules).

Full private pensions (normal retirement benefits) in annuity form are usually offered at a specified age—frequently age 65. Often, it is possible to

---

[5] Two different benefit amounts are considered to be actuarially equivalent if the present value of the two benefits, considering mortality and interest, is the same.

retire before normal retirement age and receive reduced pension benefits. Under the Tax Reform Act of 1986 (TRA '86), individuals receiving pension payments in a lump sum prior to age 59$\frac{1}{2}$ will generally incur a 10 percent nondeductible tax penalty (in addition to the regular income tax already required) on the distribution if the distribution is not transferred to an IRA or another qualified retirement plan within 60 days. However, the 10 percent tax does not apply to certain distributions (a) made in the form of substantial equal periodic payments over the life or life expectancy of the participant (or the joint lives or life expectancies of the participant and his or her beneficiaries); (b) made during or after the year in which the participant has attained age 55, separated from service, and satisfied the conditions for early retirement under the plan; (c) used for payment of medical expenses to the extent deductible under federal income tax rules;[6] (d) made to or on behalf of an alternate payee pursuant to a qualified domestic relations order; (e) made on account of death or disability; or (f) made before January 1, 1990, from an employee stock ownership plan (ESOP).

In addition, the Unemployment Compensation Amendments Act of 1992 imposed a mandatory 20 percent withholding on lump-sum distributions that are not directly transferred as rollovers into an IRA or other qualified retirement plan. Mandatory withholding occurs even if the distribution is rolled over within the permitted 60-day period. The 20 percent withheld is applied toward any income tax, including the 10 percent penalty tax on distributions before age 59$\frac{1}{2}$ that is owed on distribution amounts not rolled over into a tax-qualified vehicle.

Most private pension plans do *not* provide automatic cost-of-living adjustments, although some provide ad hoc pension supplementation on a discretionary basis. This is an important consideration in retirement planning, since inflation reduces the value of fixed pension income. Some pension plans permit employees to voluntarily contribute to the plan; these contributions may result in higher retirement income.

Private pension plan participants should thoroughly understand their plans. By doing this, they can develop reasonable estimates of future pension benefits. ERISA sets minimum funding, participation, and vesting standards for private pension plans. ERISA also requires reporting and disclosure of pension plan financial and operations information to plan participants and beneficiaries. Reports to participants must be written in a

---

[6] Medical expenses must exceed 7.5 percent of adjusted gross income.

manner that can be understood by the average participant or beneficiary. (For further discussion of ERISA requirements, see chapter 3.)

Federal Pensions—The Civil Service Retirement System (CSRS) covers most federal employees hired before 1984. Full civil service pension benefits are generally provided to retirees who satisfy one of several possible age and service criteria: age 55 with 30 years of service, age 60 with 20 years of service, or age 62 with 5 years of service. In accordance with the Omnibus Budget Reconciliation Act of 1983, pension benefits under this program are automatically adjusted for inflation.

Changes in the federal pension program were implemented as a result of the 1983 Social Security Amendments. Effective January 1, 1984, Social Security participation became mandatory for all newly hired federal employees. Before the 1983 amendments, federal employees generally did not participate in Social Security.

Federal employees who first became covered on or after January 1, 1984, are covered by the Federal Employees' Retirement System (FERS). FERS is a three-part pension program that uses Social Security as a base and provides an additional defined benefit and a voluntary thrift savings plan. FERS provides for full immediate or deferred retirement benefits at the minimum retirement age (MRA) for employees with 30 years of service, at age 60 for those with 20 years of service, or at age 62 for those with 5 years of service. The MRA is 55 for those born before 1948 and gradually increases to 57 for those born in or after 1970. Generally, retirees who are aged 62 or over receive cost-of-living adjustments. (For further discussion of federal pensions, see chapter 40 on public-sector defined benefit plans and chapter 41 on public-sector supplemental savings plans.) Information may also be obtained by contacting the U.S. Office of Personnel Management, listed under Additional Information at the end of this chapter.

Military Plans—Since 1957, all members of the U.S. Armed Forces have been covered by the Social Security program. Individuals with 20 or more years of service are also eligible for retirement benefits under the military retirement system. This system covers members of the Army, Navy, Marine Corps, and Air Force, although most of its provisions also apply to retirement systems for members of the Coast Guard, the Commissioned Corps of the Public Health Service, and the Commissioned Corps of the National Oceanic and Atmospheric Administration. The system is a funded, noncontributory defined benefit plan that includes nondisability retirement pay, disability retirement pay, retirement pay for reserve service, and survivor annuity programs.

Veterans' Pensions—Veterans with service-connected disabilities may be eligible for disability compensation from the Veterans Administration if their disabilities are a result of injuries or diseases incurred or aggravated by active military duty, whether in wartime or in peacetime. These benefits are paid regardless of other income or resources. On a veteran's death, benefits are paid to the eligible spouse and children. Pensions for nonservice-connected disabilities may be paid to wartime veterans with limited income and resources who are totally and permanently disabled because of conditions not attributable to their military service. Pensions for nonservice-connected death may also be paid, on the basis of need, to surviving spouses and dependent children of deceased veterans of certain wartime periods. More information can be obtained by contacting a local Veterans Administration office.

The Uniformed Services Employment and Reemployment Rights Act of 1993 guaranteed a veteran's right to pension benefits that would have accrued during military service. Pension plans would not have to pay earnings or forfeitures on make-up contributions. Repayment of employee contributions can be made over a period of three times the period of military service, not to exceed five years. If the service member elects not to be reemployed, no pension rights accrue for the period of military service, but the person's vested interest prior to entering military service would remain intact.

State and Local Government Pensions—Most employees of state and local governments are covered by retirement systems maintained by the states and localities. Plan provisions vary from one jurisdiction to another, and many require contributions from employees. Benefits are usually guaranteed to at least equal the amount of the employee contributions.

Workers normally must meet age and service requirements, but employees in high-risk jobs (e.g., police and firefighters) may be eligible for retirement based on any length of service, regardless of age. Most state and local plans permit retirement because of disability or age and provide for early retirement at a reduced benefit. State and local government employees may also be covered by Social Security. (For further discussion of state and local government employee pensions, see chapter 40 on public-sector defined benefit plans and chapter 41 on public-sector supplemental plans.)

Keogh Plans and IRAs—Keogh plans for the self-employed and IRAs are voluntarily established by individuals. Keoghs and IRAs offer tax deferral on personal contributions and their investment earnings. According to current law, those eligible for IRA participation may contribute the lesser of

$2,000[7] or 100 percent of earned income. Persons eligible to deduct IRA contributions may claim the deduction for the tax year in which contributions are made. However, TRA '86 restricts the deductibility of IRA contributions for families in which either spouse is covered by an employment-based retirement plan and for families with income above specified levels. Distributions from IRAs are taxed in the year they are received, with a 10 percent additional tax imposed on distributions received before age 59$\frac{1}{2}$, unless the distribution meets one of the exceptions included in the tax code. (For further discussion of IRAs and Keoghs, see chapter 16 on individual retirement accounts and chapter 17 on retirement plans for the self-employed.)

The self-employed and employees of unincorporated businesses can save for retirement through Keogh plans. Keogh plans can be established either on a defined benefit or a defined contribution basis. The maximum annual contribution for a defined benefit Keogh plan is the lesser of the amount needed to fund either a $120,000 (indexed) annual benefit or 100 percent of the employee's average compensation for the highest three years. For a defined contribution Keogh plan, the annual contribution maximum is $30,000 (indexed) or 25 percent of earned income, whichever is less. (These limits are identical to those found in corporate plans.) Distributions from Keoghs are taxed in the year they are received, with a 10 percent penalty imposed on those who take a distribution before age 59$\frac{1}{2}$, unless the distribution meets one of the statutory exceptions.

Personal Savings—Personal savings are an important part of retirement income, supplementing pensions and Social Security benefits. In determining how much money you will need from savings to maintain your standard of living throughout your retirement years, it is important to factor in the effect inflation has on purchasing power. The worksheet at the end of this chapter provides a series of calculations that can be used to determine a worker's total retirement savings goal and how much the worker must save each year to reach that goal.

Individuals who have access to a personal computer may also consider using one of the many retirement planning software packages available. Most packages contain an introductory section that discusses basic retirement concepts, a work sheet section that looks at retirement goals and current savings, and a strategy section that helps individuals determine

---

[7] The maximum annual combined contribution to both a regular and a spousal individual retirement account is $2,250.

how to achieve their retirement goals. Although the software programs range from $15–$60, a number of the organizations may provide retirement planning work sheets/booklets free of charge. (For a list of some of the retirement planning software packages available, see the Software Programs section at the end of this chapter.) Individuals may also want to check with the benefits representative at their place of employment, since many employers provide software packages for use by employees. Often the employer-provided packages have a retirement factor specific to the employer built into the programs.

Homeownership—Often individuals accumulate their largest share of personal wealth in home equity. A substantial proportion of homes owned by the aged do not have outstanding mortgages. At retirement, individuals can convert their home value into income-generating assets, or they can continue to enjoy the financial and personal advantages of owning residential property. Many elderly persons have a financial incentive to continue living in their homes, since normal maintenance costs and taxes may be less than the amount of rent required for comparable facilities.

Two basic types of home equity conversion are reverse mortgages and sale leasebacks.

A *reverse mortgage* is a loan made against home equity that provides cash advances and requires no repayment until a future time. The cash advances may be paid to the homeowner in a variety of ways, including: a single lump sum, monthly advances, or a line of credit. Repayment of all loan advances (plus interest) is required when the homeowner dies, sells the home, or permanently moves. When a homeowner takes out a reverse mortgage, he or she keeps the title to the property and any ownership responsibilities (including making repairs, doing maintenance work, paying property taxes, and paying homeowners' insurance). New variations of reverse mortgages occur regularly. Careful review of the reverse mortgage documents by a qualified independent advisor is critical prior to entering an arrangement.

In a *sale leaseback* plan a homeowner sells the home and then rents it from the buyer on a long-term lease. The buyer gives the former homeowner a down payment and pays off the rest of the purchase price over time. The buyer is responsible for taxes, insurance, and maintenance. On the former homeowner's death or change of residence, all rights associated with the house belong to the investor. As with reverse mortgage arrangements, consulting with a tax and legal advisor prior to entering a sale leaseback plan is important.

For more information on home equity conversion, contact a savings and loan institution or see listings under Additional Information at the end of this chapter.

Life Insurance—One major purpose of life insurance is to produce an immediate income for surviving dependents when working spouses or pensioners die. As a source of retirement income, life insurance assures that benefits will be paid to surviving beneficiaries according to the policy's stated conditions. However, the rate of return on savings invested in some policies may be lower than that of other investment alternatives.

Employees may purchase individual life insurance and pay premiums out of personal income. Sometimes employers pay group life insurance premiums for active and retired employees. Employees should inquire whether employer plans will continue to provide coverage after retirement and whether there are conversion privileges if coverage will not be continued. (For further discussion of life insurance, see chapter 32 on group life insurance plans and chapter 43 on life insurance in the public sector.)

Other Savings Alternatives—There are many other types of investment instruments that produce retirement income (e.g., stocks, bonds, mutual funds, and savings accounts). Workers should understand their alternatives and weigh the advantages and disadvantages of each against their individual needs. They should also consider the different tax aspects of these various investment instruments.

Employment—Many older persons who are eligible for retirement continue working—at least part time. Aside from the financial advantages, employment provides a productive and structured activity. Currently, there is a Social Security earnings test limiting the amount that can be earned before Social Security benefits are partially or fully reduced. In 1996, beneficiaries aged 65 through 69 can earn up to $12,500 without a reduction in benefits.[8] For beneficiaries under age 65, the 1996 earnings limitation is $8,280. For a beneficiary aged 65–69, one benefit dollar will be withheld for every three dollars in earnings above the limit; the reduction is one dollar for every two dollars earned over the limitation if the beneficiary is under age 65. The earnings test does not apply once an individual reaches age 70.

Some employment agencies now specialize in placing older workers, and some employers sponsor job-search seminars for retiring workers.

---

[8]Increases in the earnings limit for retirees aged 65 through 69 will be phased in gradually until the limit reaches $30,000 in 2002. After 2002, increases in the earnings limit will be based on the growth in average wages.

Public Welfare Programs—For those who reach retirement age without adequate income, public welfare programs are available. These assistance programs offer economic support based on demonstrated need.

Supplemental Security Income (SSI) is a federally administered program that went into effect in 1974. It provides monthly cash assistance to low income aged, blind, and disabled persons who have assets below specified limits. Benefits are indexed to Social Security cost-of-living increases. Additionally, most states supplement the basic federal benefit. Income from other sources reduces available SSI benefits.

More information on SSI can be obtained by contacting a Social Security Administration office.

Health Care Cost Considerations—Health care costs have risen dramatically. It has become imperative to plan ahead for potential large costs associated with unexpected illness. Without insurance assistance, few people have adequate financial resources to cover catastrophic illnesses, particularly for long-term care associated with a chronic illness.

The availability of health insurance for retired individuals is a growing concern. Ever-increasing health care costs and the Financial Accounting Standards Board's Statement No. 106[9] have caused many employers to reexamine their role in providing health benefits for current and future retirees. In addition, federal government budgetary constraints will limit the growth of Medicare benefits. Both of these situations will leave retirees with more health care costs and expenditures.

Preventive Health Care Considerations—Many of the problems associated with old age result from years of poor health habits. To enhance the chances of good health in later years, doctors recommend eating properly, exercising, and having regular physical examinations.

A number of special programs have been developed to encourage good health habits at affordable prices. Programs that provide low-cost nutritional meals to older people can be located by contacting an area senior center. To encourage exercise, the YMCA and other athletic facilities offer reduced membership rates for people over age 65.

Medicare—Medicare was established by the Social Security Amendments of 1965. Medicare consists of two parts: Part A (Hospital Insurance,

---

[9] In December 1990, the Financial Accounting Standards Board approved Statement No. 106 (FAS 106), requiring many employers to record a liability for retiree health benefits on their balance sheet in order to comply with generally accepted accounting standards, beginning with fiscal years after December 15, 1992.

or HI) helps pay for inpatient hospital care and certain post-hospital care, home health care, and hospice care; Part B (Supplementary Medical Insurance, or SMI) helps pay for physicians' fees, most outpatient hospital services, and certain related services. Those eligible for HI benefits at age 65[10] include: individuals eligible for Social Security or Railroad Retirement benefits as well as workers and their spouses in federal, state, or local government employment with a sufficient period of Medicare-only coverage.[11]

An individual automatically applies for Medicare when he or she applies for Social Security benefits. If planning to work past age 65, he or she should apply for Medicare separately about three months before reaching age 65. Those who are enrolled in Part A are automatically enrolled in Part B, unless they choose not to be. There is a monthly premium for Part B ($42.50 in 1996). Those who are not eligible for premium-free Part A can almost always enroll in Part B at age 65. (For further discussion of Medicare deductibles and copayments, see chapter 27 on retiree health benefits.)

Since Medicare does not cover all expenses, it is important that employees planning their retirement develop a sound understanding of what is and is not covered by Medicare. Employees should ascertain whether their group health coverage will continue after retirement. If not, many retirees purchase additional health insurance coverage on their own. Group health plans sometimes can be converted to individual policies. If this option is not available, some policies (known as Medicare supplement, or Medigap, policies) are designed specifically to fill in the gaps not covered by Medicare. In addition to the Medigap policies, there is an experimental managed care option, available only in 15 states, called Medicare Select. Medicare Select is a preferred provider arrangement in which lower premiums may be charged if the participant agrees to use the services of particular health care providers. To assure that major medical expenses will be covered, retirees must understand their private insurance coverage and how it coordinates with Medicare.

Health Maintenance Organizations (HMOs)—Participants in an HMO make fixed monthly payments to the HMO. In turn, the HMO provides most

---

[10] For further discussion of the various groups covered by Hospital Insurance (HI), see chapter 2 on Social Security and Medicare.

[11] These individuals are covered, regardless of Social Security coverage, if they have sufficient earnings credits.

or all of the needed health care services. Such fixed-price arrangements permit retirees to estimate future health care costs more accurately. Many Medicare beneficiaries receive all Medicare-covered health services through enrollment in HMOs. (For further discussion of HMOs, see chapter 23.)

Medicaid—Medicaid, established in 1965, offers health assistance to people with low incomes. It is jointly financed by federal and state governments. Each state that elects to participate administers its own program. Medicaid reimburses health care providers for specified services rendered to older and disabled persons, as well as members of families with dependent children, who satisfy income tests. Covered services and the amount of deductibles (i.e., an amount an individual is required to pay before receiving any Medicaid payments) differ from state to state.

Long-Term Care—Many chronically ill and functionally impaired older persons require ongoing health and social services known as long-term care (LTC). A report released in 1995 by the U.S. General Accounting Office indicated that about 7.3 million elderly persons in the United States required LTC. Of the 7.3 million requiring care, about 1.6 million were in institutions, and the remaining 5.7 million were either at home or in community settings. Aside from informal care provided in the community, the current system of financing LTC depends largely on the Medicaid program and individual financing. Medicaid is the single largest source of public financing for formal LTC, accounting for 71.3 percent of nursing home and home health care financed through public programs in 1993.[12] Private insurance now finances only a small portion of LTC needs. However, many leaders regard private long-term care insurance (LTCI) as a way to increase access to financing and as a potential alternative to Medicaid and out-of-pocket financing. (For more information on long-term care insurance, see chapter 31.)

Even as they approach their own retirement, many persons are confronted with the prospect of providing financial, emotional, and often physical support to their parents and other older relatives. This added responsibility, sometimes referred to as elder care, can make it difficult to plan for retirement effectively. Some individuals may be forced to delay their retirement or to postpone travel or relocation plans.

Independent Living Considerations—Choosing an appropriate living

---

[12] See Sarah Snider, "Long-Term Care and the Private Insurance Market," *EBRI Issue Brief* no. 163 (Employee Benefit Research Institute, July 1995).

environment after retirement requires careful thought and planning. Many options are available and should be considered before making a decision. For example, a retired couple may choose to stay in their present home or move into an apartment, smaller house, mobile home, or continuing care community. They may buy or rent a home. They may stay in the same geographic area or move—possibly to an area with a more comfortable climate. Some older people choose to share homes with others as an alternative to living alone. There are many considerations that people should keep in mind as they plan for living arrangements in retirement. For example, if they plan to stay in the homes that they have lived in most recently and have paid off the mortgage, they must not forget that budgeting for home maintenance, taxes, and possible remodeling is still necessary—especially as the home gets older. If moving to a new area is an option, costs of moving and changes in the cost of living should be considered when making a decision. Deciding on living arrangements in retirement should be based on financial considerations as well as individual needs and desires.

Financial Considerations—Capital gains on the sale of a home that has been a principal residence are offered as a once-in-a-lifetime tax break for older homeowners. If a homeowner is aged 55 or over and if the home has been his or her principal residence for at least three of the last five years prior to the date of sale, he or she may sell the home and enjoy a one-time exclusion of taxes on gains of up to $125,000. For more information, contact the Internal Revenue Service (IRS) and request the IRS publication, *Tax Benefits for Older Americans*.

Property taxes should also be considered when choosing a retirement home, as states vary widely in the amount of this tax and the rate at which it can be expected to increase. Some states offer deferral programs that let older homeowners put off payment of their property taxes until they sell the property or die. Others offer credits or homestead exemptions that reduce property taxes outright. Residents of other states can get either a tax deferral or a credit, depending on the amount of their income and assets. For more information, contact local IRS offices.

Housing Assistance—Under the 1937 Housing Act and subsequent amendments, several programs have been developed to provide direct and indirect housing assistance to older people. Such assistance can be separated into four basic categories: homeownership, rental, rental subsidy, and nursing home/intermediate care facility programs. There are often long waiting periods for housing assistance, so individuals should inquire and apply early. These programs are subject to change, and interested parties should keep abreast of new developments. Many of these programs are limited to older people with low incomes. More information on housing assistance can be obtained through local housing authorities or social services offices.

Physical and Social Considerations—Before moving to a new home, individuals should consider such issues as the accessibility of public transportation. A time may come when driving a car is not possible. Retirees should be in close proximity to grocery stores, doctors' offices, and other frequently used places. Isolation and loneliness are common concerns for retirees; they should locate where it is easy to establish and maintain contact with others.

Use of Leisure Time—One of the greatest challenges to workers facing retirement is the satisfactory use of a dramatic increase in leisure time. Discovering positive ways to use free time requires energy and imagination. People who develop outside interests and commitments in their working years are more likely to adjust well in retirement. Retirement frequently provides an opportunity for more active involvement in the community, travel, an avocation, and/or further education.

Interpersonal Relationships—Work provides an environment for meeting people and sharing common interests; thus, retirement can result in less interaction with people. Finding new ways to meet people and develop friendships is important. Those who develop strong friendships and family relationships in earlier years usually have a happier, more productive retirement.

Adjustments are also necessary in spousal relationships. Developing friendships and outside interests before retirement reduces the strain of retirement on a marriage. Another area that needs attention is that concerning the death of one's spouse. Early discussion of coping methods that can be used after a spouse dies may reduce present and future anxieties. Psychological and financial adjustments must be considered.

Estate Planning—A decedent's estate is made up of assets minus liabilities at death. Many people put off estate planning because they do not want to face the unpleasant thought of death. Lack of qualified legal assistance in estate planning can cause unnecessary hardship and expense to a decedent's surviving family and friends. For tax considerations, it is often recommended that individuals who potentially have over $600,000 in their estate consult a financial planner for tax-oriented estate planning. Those who die without a will leave the distribution of their property according to rules set by the state. No estate is so small that it eliminates the need for a formalized will.

Wills may be prepared by a lawyer, although some states encourage statutory "do-it-yourself" wills. To ensure legality, they must be properly witnessed and signed. Handwritten or spoken wills are usually not valid. States have differing probate laws; therefore, it is advisable to have all important documents reviewed by a lawyer when relocating to another state. If there is a major change in family circumstances, such as a death, divorce, or marriage, the will should again be reviewed by a lawyer.

Considerations for the Employer

Employers can also play an important role in helping employees prepare for retirement. Growing numbers of employers are beginning to recognize the value of educating employees about retirement planning. The remainder of this chapter will focus on retirement planning programs.

Retirement planning programs have varied widely. Some employers have offered programs since the 1960s. More recently the trend is growing. The more assistance employees receive in preparing for retirement, the more likely it is that they will adapt successfully.

Interest in Retirement Planning Programs—Reasons for the increased interest in retirement counseling programs include:

- Retirees are living longer and represent the fastest-growing segment of the population. There is a growing appreciation of their problems. The 1978 Amendments to the Age Discrimination in Employment Act have heightened awareness of the importance of the decision to retire.
- The spread of pension plans has resulted in greater dissemination of information about benefit plans. As more information becomes available, interest in retirement planning programs is increasing.
- Concerns about high rates of inflation have contributed to employees' uneasiness about their financial security during retirement. They have been forced to recognize the problems of living on relatively fixed incomes.
- Employees nearing retirement age often experience feelings of insecurity and anxiety; this can lead to a reduction in productivity. By offering retirement counseling, employers have learned they can alleviate anxieties and reduce the decline in productivity. Research shows that employees who believe their employers care about them tend to produce better quality work.
- Studies show that employees who receive employer retirement coun-

seling adapt better to retirement. By providing retirement counseling, employers invest in the goodwill of their workers and create a positive public image.

Program Content—Retirement planning programs generally include counseling in some or all of the areas such as financial planning, health, interpersonal relationships living arrangements, leisure time, new careers.

Program Design—Individual counseling is a popular way of providing benefit information to employees. Some organizations combine individual interviews with group sessions, while others conduct only group meetings. Much of the retirement planning information is similar for all employees, and group meetings can be efficient. Although attendance is encouraged, participation is usually voluntary.

Packaged programs are available from firms with retirement planning expertise. Custom-tailored programs are available from employee benefit consulting firms, accounting firms, and others. Some employers use a combined approach, starting with a packaged program and conforming it to their employees' needs. Other methods of retirement planning include the use of expert speakers, printed materials, interactive software, and videos. The majority of counseling seminars enlist the assistance of outside professionals to hold sessions on topics such as real estate, health care, Social Security, and psychological adjustment.

Timing and Length of Counseling Sessions—Topics can be covered in separate weekly sessions; however, a session of two to three consecutive days may be preferable. Some employers schedule sessions during nonworking hours. Others hold sessions during working hours to reinforce the importance given to retirement planning. Sessions are usually conducted away from the work site. Participants should be encouraged to devote sole attention to the retirement counseling session; the session should not be interrupted by work. If a weekly format is adopted, two-hour sessions are generally advisable. Usually, in this period of time, one retirement topic can be discussed with a question-and-answer period.

Group Size—Because the success of a counseling program depends on attendee participation in group discussions, it is wise to limit attendance at each meeting to 40 participants. Assuming that most employees bring a spouse or friend, 20 to 25 employees should be invited.

Who Should Attend—Employees, their spouses, and other close family members or friends generally attend retirement planning meetings. Inclusion of spouses and friends helps to alleviate an employee's anxieties about retirement. Additionally, it provides the employee with access to other informed persons. These persons can discuss future problems with the employee if and when they occur.

Participants' Ages—Generally, employees who are aged 55 or over are invited to participate in retirement planning programs. The 10-year period before normal retirement age is an appropriate time for an employee's financial and attitudinal preparation. Increasing numbers of employers are reducing the age of eligibility to attend these programs, often recasting them as long-range planning programs instead of focusing solely on retirement.

Conclusion

Increasing life expectancies and increasing health care costs make the need for retirement planning even more crucial today than it was in the past. Through individual and company retirement planning efforts, employees can prepare more effectively for a happy, healthy, and productive retirement.

Bibliography

Addicott, James P., and Charles F. Butler. *Can You Afford to Grow Old?: Solving the Crisis of Money and Healthcare in Retirement and Old Age.* Chicago, IL: Probus Publishing Company, 1992.

Allen, Everett T. Jr., Joseph J. Melone, Jerry S. Rosenbloom, and Jack L. VanDerhei. *Pension Planning: Pensions, Profit-Sharing, and Other Deferred Compensation Plans.* Seventh edition. Burr Ridge, IL: Irwin, 1992.

Arnold, Suzanne, et al. *Ready or Not: Your Retirement Planning Guide, 1994.* Twenty-first edition. Bronx, NY: Manpower Education Institute, 1994.

Brenner, Lynn. *Building Your Nest Egg with Your 401(k): A Guide to Help You Achieve Retirement Security.* Washington Depot, CT: Investors Press, Inc., 1995.

Comberiate, Leonard B., and Bonnie Gellas. *Educating Employees About Retirement Planning and Investment Choices.* New York, NY: The Segal Company, Inc., 1993.

Employee Benefit Research Institute. *Retiree Health Benefits: What Is the Promise?* Washington, DC: Employee Benefit Research Institute, 1989.

_____. *Retirement in the 21st Century...Ready or Not... .* Washington, DC:

Employee Benefit Research Institute, 1994.

Fidelity Investments, *Retirement Planning Guide*. Dallas, TX: Fidelity Distributors Corporation, 1994.

Garnitz, R. N. *It's Your Future: Midlife and Preretirement Planning*. Third edition. Brookfield, WI: International Foundation of Employee Benefit Plans, Inc., 1992.

Gaudio, Peter E., and Virginia S. Nicols. *Your Retirement Benefits*. New York: John Wiley & Sons, Inc., 1992.

McCarthy, John T. *Financial Planning for a Secure Retirement*. Second Edition. Brookfield, WI: International Foundation of Employee Benefit Plans, 1996.

Milne, Deborah, Jack VanDerhei, and Paul Yakoboski. "Can We Save Enough to Retire?: Participant Education in Defined Contribution Plans." *EBRI Issue Brief* no. 160 (Employee Benefit Research Institute, April 1995).

Nielson, Norma L., Rodolfo Camacho, Mary Ellen Phillips, and Carol E. Brown. *Financial Planning as an Employee Benefit*. Brookfield, WI: International Foundation of Employee Benefit Plans, 1992.

Rosenbloom, Jerry S., ed. *The Handbook of Employee Benefits: Design, Funding, and Administration*. Vol. 1. Third Edition. Homewood, IL: Business One Irwin, 1992.

Scholen, Ken. *Retirement Income on the House: Cashing in on Your Home with a "Reverse" Mortgage*. Marshall, MN: National Center for Home Equity Conversion Press, 1992.

Snider, Sarah. "Long-Term Care and the Private Insurance Market." *EBRI Issue Brief* no. 163 (Employee Benefit Research Institute, July 1995).

U.S. Department of Defense. Office of the Actuary. *Valuation of the Military Retirement System: September 30, 1993*. Washington, DC: U.S. Department of Defense, n.d.

U.S. Social Security Administration. *Social Security Bulletin Annual Statistical Supplement, 1995*. Washington, DC: U.S. Government Printing Office, 1995.

U.S. Department of Health and Human Services. Social Security Administration. "Social Security Programs in the United States, 1993." *Social Security Bulletin* (Winter 1993). Washington, DC: U.S. Government Printing Office, 1993.

U.S. Department of Labor. Bureau of Labor Statistics. *Employee Benefits in Medium and Large Private Establishments, 1993*. Washington, DC: U.S. Government Printing Office, 1994.

U.S. General Accounting Office. *Long-Term Care: Current Issues and Future Directions.* GAO/HEHS-95-109. Washington, DC: U.S. General Accounting Office, 1995.

U.S. Office of Personnel Management. *Civil Service Retirement and Disability Fund Report for the Year Ended September 30, 1994.* Washington, DC: U.S. Office of Personnel Management, 1995.

U.S. Social Security Administration. *1996 Report of the Board of Trustees of the Federal Old-Age and Survivors Insurance and Disability Insurance Trust Funds.* Washington, DC: U.S. Government Printing Office, 1996.

Walsh, Patricia, ed. *Lifelong Retirement Planning for Local Government Employees.* Washington, DC: International City Management Association, 1988.

Wang, Penelope. "How to Retire with Twice As Much Money." *Money* (October 1994): 77–87.

Williamson, Gordon K. *Sooner Than You Think: Mapping a Course for a Comfortable Retirement.* Homewood, IL: Business One Irwin, 1993.

Yakoboski, Paul. "Are Workers Kidding Themselves? Results of the 1995 Retirement Confidence Survey." *EBRI Issue Brief* no. 168 (Employee Benefit Research Institute, December, 1995).

Yakoboski, Paul, et al. "Employment-Based Retirement Income Benefits: Analysis of the April 1993 Current Population Survey." *EBRI Issue Brief* no. 153/*Special Report* no. 25 (Employee Benefit Research Institute, September 1994).

Additional Information

American Association of Homes and Services for the Aging
901 E Street, NW, Suite 500
Washington, DC 20004-2037
(202) 783-2242

Home Equity Information Center
American Association of Retired Persons
601 E Street, NW
Washington, DC 20049
(202) 434-2277

International Foundation of Employee Benefit Plans
P.O. Box 69
18700 West Bluemound Road
Brookfield, WI 53008-0069
(414) 786-6700

National Center for Home Equity Conversion
7373 147th Street
Suite 115
Apple Valley, MN 55124
(612) 953-4474

U.S. Department of Labor
Pension and Welfare Benefits Administration
200 Constitution Avenue, NW
Washington, DC 20210
(202) 219-8776

U.S. Office of Personnel Management
1900 E Street, NW
Washington, DC 20415
(202) 616-1212

U.S. Social Security Administration
6401 Security Boulevard
Baltimore. MD 21235
(800) 772-1213
TTY: (800) 325-0778

Pension Rights Center
918 16th Street, NW, Suite 704
Washington, DC 20006
(202) 296-3779

Software Programs

Fidelity Retirement Planning Thinkware
Fidelity Investments
(800) 457-1768

Harvest-Time Personal Edition
The Computer Lab
(800) 397-1456

Price Waterhouse Retirement Planning System
Price Waterhouse
(800) 752-6234

Quicken Financial Planner
Intuit
(800) 816-8025

Rich and Retired
DataTech
(800) 556-7526

T. Rowe Price Retirement Planning Kit
T. Rowe Price Investment Services
(800) 541-5350

The Vanguard Retirement Planner
The Vanguard Group
(800) 876-1840

Chapter 18 Worksheet

On completion of this worksheet, you will have an estimate of your total retirement savings goal, where you are in relation to that goal, and how much needs to be saved on your behalf—by you, your employer, or by you and your employer—to reach that goal. By determining how much should be put aside for retirement on an annual basis, you give yourself a more meaningful target. It is also easier to save regularly, which may increase the probability of achieving your retirement goals. For a more complete analysis, you may want to contact a financial planner.

A 4 percent annual rate of inflation is assumed. It is also assumed that you will be in the same tax bracket after retirement as before retirement. Couples retiring at the same time may want to pool their income, expected retirement benefits, and savings for this worksheet. If they plan to retire at different times, they should do the worksheet separately.

All Amounts Should Be Entered in Current Dollars.

Retirement Age and Years in Retirement
Estimate the number of years until your retirement and how long you expect to be retired.
- Determine the number of years until your retirement, and enter it on line 1 below. Recall that the Social Security normal retirement age (currently age 65) is scheduled to increase incrementally to age 67 for those who attain age 62 in 2022 and later.
  1. Number of years until retirement:

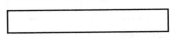

- Determine the number of years you expect to spend in retirement, and enter this number on line 2 below. Currently, at age 65, the average female lives for another 19 years (age 84), while the average male lives for another 15 years (age 80). For a conservative estimate, you may want to assume a longer time span (i.e., living into your 90s), which may result from unknown but expected improvements in medical technology.
  2. Expected years in retirement:

Return on Investments Before and After Retirement
Estimate the rate of return on your investments both before retirement and after retirement.

Over the 68-year period 1926–1994, Treasury bills had a compound nominal annual return of 3.7 percent; long-term government bonds, intermediate government bonds, and long-term corporate bonds had compound nominal annual returns of 4.8 percent, 5.1 percent, and 5.4 percent, respectively; and large company stocks and small company stocks had compound nominal annual returns of 10.2 percent and 12.2 percent, respectively.

- Determine the nominal annual rate of return from your investments that you expect *from the present until retirement* and enter the rate on line 3 below. (Many individuals choose to invest in less conservative investments during their working years since they have a number of years until they will be in need of their personal retirement savings.)
  3. Assumed nominal annual rate of return from your investments *prior to* retirement:

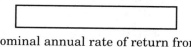

- Determine the nominal annual rate of return from your investments that you expect *during* retirement and enter the rate on line 4 below. (Many individuals choose to invest in more conservative investments during their retirement years since they are in need of their retirement savings.)
  4. Assumed nominal annual rate of return from your investments *during* retirement:

Annual Retirement Expenses
Estimate or budget what you expect your annual expenses to be in retirement.

- To budget your annual retirement expenses, compare what you spend annually for various categories today with what you expect to spend each year after you retire. For example, costs likely to increase in retirement include travel, medical, and insurance; costs likely to decrease include housing, Social Security taxes, savings, work expenses, and federal, state, and local taxes. If you are not sure how your expenses will be budgeted in retirement, a quick way to estimate your annual expenses is to multiply your current annual income by

60 percent to 80 percent. (Financial analysts suggest you will need 60 percent to 80 percent of your current annual income *each year* in retirement if you wish to maintain your present standard of living.) Enter your estimated or budgeted annual expenses in retirement on line 5 below.

5. Anticipated annual retirement expenses:

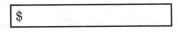

Retirement Income from Annuities
Estimate the annual income you expect to receive from various sources in retirement.

Retirement income comes primarily from three sources: Social Security, employment-based retirement plans, and personal savings.

- Annual Social Security benefit in retirement—Contact the Social Security Administration at 1-800-772-1213 and ask for a Personal Earnings and Benefit Estimate Statement (PEBES). Four to six weeks after you complete and mail back the form, you will receive an estimate of your future benefit. Enter this amount on line 6 below.

  6. Amount you expect to receive annually in Social Security benefits:

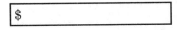

On this worksheet, the annual retirement income you expect to receive from defined benefit pension plans will be considered separately from the retirement income you expect to receive from defined contribution pension plans.

- Annual retirement income from defined benefit plans—To estimate your pension benefits, ask the employee benefits departments of your current employer and all former employers to estimate your annual pension benefits in current dollars. This information may also be available as part of your most recent annual benefits statement or summary plan description from your employer. You should also receive estimates for vested pensions from all of the companies for which you have worked. Enter the total of all expected pension benefits from your current employer and all former employers on line 7 below.

  7. Amount you expect to receive as your annual pension benefit from all employers:

- Determine your total estimated annual annuity income in retirement by summing the amounts on lines 6 and 7 and entering the result on line 8 below.

  8. Total estimated annual annuity income in retirement:

  $

Total Retirement Savings Goal
Estimate how much needs to be saved on your behalf by the time you retire.

- Determine the amount of annual income you will need in retirement that will not be covered by Social Security or your current or former defined benefit plan(s) by subtracting line 8 from line 5 and entering the result on line 9 below. (If you plan to retire early, the amount on line 9 should be increased in order for you to be able to cover your expenses before you begin receiving Social Security and pension benefits, or to offset the reduction in benefits if you begin to receive them early. If you plan to work during retirement, the amount on line 9 could probably be decreased to compensate for your earnings.)

  9. Amount you will need annually in retirement in addition to annuity income:

  $

- Determine your annuity factor using table 18.1. Find the row corresponding to the number of years you expect to live in retirement (from line 2) and the column corresponding to the assumed annual rate of return from your investments *during* retirement (from line 4). The figure in the box where the row and column intersect is your annuity factor. Enter the annuity factor on line 10 below.

  10. Annuity factor from table 18.1:

- Determine the amount that will need to be saved on your behalf by the time you retire in order to generate the amount on line 9 by multiplying your annuity factor (line 10) and the amount you will need annually in retirement in addition to annuity income (line 9). Enter the result on line 11 below.

  11. Retirement savings goal at retirement age:

  $

Retirement Savings Goal Shortfall
Estimate how much needs to be saved on your behalf after accounting for money in employment-based defined contribution plans and personal savings.

- Determine your current retirement savings accumulated (in tax-deferred accounts) by counting any money (both employer and employee contributions) in employment-based defined contribution plans, (e.g., 401(k)s, 403(b)s, and profit-sharing accounts), and funds you have set aside in individual retirement accounts, simplified employee pensions, and Keoghs. Enter the result on line 12 below.
  12. Current retirement savings accumulated in defined contribution plans and personal retirement savings:

  $

- Determine your savings growth factor using table 18.2. Find the row corresponding to the number of years until your retirement (from line 1) and the column corresponding to the assumed annual rate of return from your investments *prior to* retirement (from line 3). The figure in the box where the row and column intersect is your savings growth factor, which you should enter on line 13 below.
  13. Savings growth factor from table 18.2:

  $

- Determine the projected value of your current retirement savings by multiplying your current retirement savings accumulated (line 12) and your savings growth factor (line 13). This is what your current savings will be worth when you retire, assuming you do not add to them and that you earn the return you expect. Enter the result on line 14 below.
  14. Projected value of current retirement savings:

  $

- Determine your retirement savings goal shortfall by subtracting the projected value of your current savings (line 14) from your retirement savings goal (line 11). Enter the result on line 15 below.
  15. Retirement savings goal shortfall:

  $

Annual Retirement Savings Target
Estimate how much needs to be saved *each year* on your behalf to reach your retirement savings goal.

- Determine your annual payment factor using table 18.3. Find the row corresponding to the number of years until your retirement (line 1) and the column corresponding to the assumed annual rate of return from your investments prior to retirement (line 3). The figure in the box where the row and column intersect is your annual payment factor, which should be entered on line 16 below.
16. Annual payment factor from table 18.3:

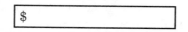

- Determine how much needs to be saved on your behalf every year (by you, your employer, or both) to make up the retirement savings goal shortfall by multiplying the annual payment factor (line 16) and the savings shortfall (line 15). Enter the result on line 17 below.
17. Additional annual retirement savings needed to meet retirement savings goal:

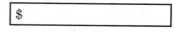

The amount on line 17 will have to increase every year to keep up with inflation. It is important that the amount saved on your behalf increases each year by at least the annual inflation rate so your retirement savings reflect the impact of inflation.

If the result on line 17 seems unreasonable, redo the calculation using different assumptions. Maybe you will earn a higher rate of return on your investments before retirement and/or after retirement. Perhaps you can retire a few years later. Reconsider your expected living expenses in retirement—perhaps you could live more modestly.

Sources: Lynn Brenner, *Building Your Nest Egg with Your 401(k): A Guide to Help You Achieve Retirement Security* (Washington Depot, CT: Investors Press, Inc., 1995); Fidelity Investments, *Retirement Planning Guide* (Dallas, TX: Fidelity Distributors Corporation, 1994); and Penelope Wang, "How to Retire with Twice As Much Money," *Money* (October 1994): 77–87.

Table 18.1
Annuity Factor

Number of Years in Retirement	Expected Return on Savings in Retirement				
	4%	6%	8%	10%	12%
20	20.00	16.79	14.31	12.36	10.82
25	25.00	20.08	16.49	13.82	11.80
30	30.00	23.07	18.30	14.93	12.48
35	35.00	25.79	19.79	15.76	12.95
40	40.00	28.26	21.03	16.39	13.28

Source: Employee Benefit Research Institute.

Table 18.2
Savings Growth Factor

Number of Years until Retirement	Expected Return on Savings until Retirement				
	4%	6%	8%	10%	12%
5	1.00	1.10	1.21	1.32	1.45
10	1.00	1.21	1.46	1.75	2.10
15	1.00	1.33	1.76	2.32	3.04
20	1.00	1.46	2.13	3.07	4.40
25	1.00	1.61	2.57	4.06	6.38
30	1.00	1.77	3.10	5.38	9.24
35	1.00	1.95	3.75	7.12	13.38
40	1.00	2.14	4.52	9.43	19.38

Source: Employee Benefit Research Institute.

Table 18.3
Annual Payment Factor

Number of Years until Retirement	Expected Return on Savings until Retirement				
	4%	6%	8%	10%	12%
5	0.200	0.189	0.178	0.168	0.159
10	0.100	0.090	0.081	0.073	0.065
15	0.067	0.057	0.049	0.041	0.035
20	0.050	0.041	0.033	0.026	0.021
25	0.040	0.031	0.024	0.018	0.013
30	0.033	0.024	0.018	0.012	0.009
35	0.029	0.020	0.013	0.009	0.006
40	0.025	0.017	0.011	0.006	0.004

Source: Employee Benefit Research Institute.

PART THREE
HEALTH BENEFITS

19. Health Insurance

Introduction

As the cost of health care continues to climb, health insurance is becoming an increasingly valuable employee benefit. Employers view it as an integral component of the overall compensation packages that allow them to attract and retain workers. In addition to health protection for themselves and their family members, health insurance is viewed by many employees as a sometimes substantial source of income protection. Depending on the nature of an illness and the benefits provided, an employee's financial well-being could be jeopardized by unanticipated medical expenses.

In 1993, an estimated 82 percent of full-time employees in medium and large private establishments were covered by an employment-based health insurance plan. Among these 29 million persons, approximately 40 percent had medical care benefits that were fully financed by their employer; approximately 20 percent had family coverage fully financed by their employer (U.S. Department of Labor, 1994a). In 1994, 62 percent of full-time employees in small private establishments participated in a group health plan (U.S. Department of Labor, 1996).

There are two primary types of health plans that may be offered by an employer: prepaid plans, such as those provided through health maintenance organizations (HMOs), and traditional fee-for-service plans. This chapter describes fee-for-service plans, including basic, major, and comprehensive medical insurance. (For more information on health insurance, see chapter 23 on HMOs, chapter 24 on preferred provider organizations, and chapter 25 on managing health care costs.)

Employee Participation

Many employers cover all eligible employees under a single health plan, although different employee groups may have different plans (e.g., union members and nonunion members may have separate plans). Most employees are covered at the time they are hired or after they satisfy a waiting or service period. In 1993, 44 percent of full-time employees in medium and large private establishments participating in medical plans were subject to a service requirement. The most common service period was three months (Employee Benefit Research Institute, 1995).

Many plans cover employees and their dependents. All or part of the cost of the coverage for an employee or for his or her dependents may be paid by the employer. However, in many plans, the employer contributions for employee coverage may differ from the employer contribution for dependents' coverage. Employee and dependent costs for coverage are generally paid through payroll deduction and may be paid with pre-tax dollars.

Plan Operators

Employment-based health benefits may use any of a variety of plan operators: commercial insurance plans, Blue Cross and Blue Shield plans, or self-insured plans.

Commercial Insurance Plans—Insurance companies are a major source of health insurance. Generally, the premium for such insurance protection is calculated to cover the benefits that will be paid, administrative costs, insurance sales commissions, state premium taxes, and surplus (i.e., profit). Generally, for employee groups of 50 or more, the insurer maintains separate claims records for the group and periodically adjusts the premium to reflect the group's claims experience; these are called experience-rated plans.

Blue Cross and Blue Shield Plans—Blue Cross plans cover hospital services; Blue Shield plans cover medical and surgical services. Although many plans operate under the Blue Cross and Blue Shield name, each plan is independent; each generally operates in a specific geographic area; the various plans may offer different benefit structures.

Blue Cross and Blue Shield plans must comply with certain standards established by the Blue Cross and Blue Shield Association. In addition, in some states, Blue Cross and Blue Shield plans are required to enroll all applicants regardless of health status.

Self-Insured Plans—In a self-insured plan, the employer, or a trust to which the employer contributes, pays employee health care claims directly. Thus, the employer essentially acts as its own insurance company and bears the financial risk of making payments to providers. Some employers both self-insure and self-administer their medical plans. Other employers self-insure their plans but purchase administrative services contracts to take care of their administrative needs. Additionally, some insurers offer stop-loss insurance to employers, which covers catastrophic health expenses above a maximum and, therefore, limits a self-insured plan's liability.

Employers that self-insure do so for a number of reasons. Some employers self-insure in order to retain control of the plan reserves, others self-insure in an attempt to manage health care costs more directly. Some employers prefer to self-insure because these plans are not subject to state mandated benefit laws and insurance premium taxes.[1]

Health Insurance Benefits

Insurance plans calculate fee-for-service payments to providers in different ways: based on usual, customary, and reasonable (UCR)[2] charges; a fixed schedule of fees; or a combination of the two.

---

[1] On April 26, 1995, the U.S. Supreme Court ruled that the Employee Retirement Income Security Act of 1974 (ERISA) does not preempt New York state surcharges on hospital bills paid by commercial insurance companies and health maintenance organizations (HMOs) (*Travelers Insurance Inc. v. Pataki*). The ruling did not address self-insured plans.

Under the New York hospital rate system, a 13 percent surcharge (retained by the hospital) is imposed on hospital bills covered by commercial insurers and HMOs. Commercial insurers are subject to an additional 11 percent surcharge (retained by the state), while HMOs that do not enroll a specified percentage of Medicaid patients face up to an additional 9 percent surcharge.

The Supreme Court determined that although the surcharges may have an indirect effect on ERISA plans with respect to the cost of providing the benefit, the state regulation does not restrict an administrator's plan choice or structure, thus the surcharges are not preempted by ERISA. In a footnote to the Supreme Court decision, the court stated that it specifically did not address the surcharge statute insofar as it applies to self-insured funds because neither the District Court nor the Court of Appeals expressly addressed the issue. The issue of self-insured plans was left to the lower courts.

On August 15, 1995, the U.S. Court of Appeals for the Second Circuit handed down a ruling that states the Supreme Court's decision in the *Traveler's* case leaves no room for claiming self-insured plans are exempt from New York's hospital surcharges.

Thus, New York state can impose its surcharges on all payers, including self-insured plans. The ramifications of the decision on self-insured plans are still unclear. The Second Circuit Court decision could lead to increased costs for employers in New York that self-insure their health care benefits, and it may also lead to other states adopting similar statutes. (For more information on self-insured health benefit plans and ERISA, see chapter 3 on ERISA or Employee Benefit Research Institute *Special Report*/SR-31/*Issue Brief* no. 167, "ERISA and Health Plans" (Employee Benefit Research Institute, November 1995).

[2] Usual, customary, and reasonable means that the charge is the provider's usual fee for the service, does not exceed the customary fee in that geographic area, and is reasonable based on the circumstances. A fee may be considered reasonable when special circumstances require extensive or complex treatment, even though it does not meet the standard UCR criteria.

The UCR approach recognizes all usual, customary, and reasonable charges for covered services. Plans that use fixed schedules recognize charges for covered services only up to a fixed dollar limit. This limit can take many forms; e.g., a plan may limit hospital benefits to a fixed dollar amount per day and reimburse surgical charges according to a schedule of payment by procedure.

Some plans combine elements of UCR and fixed payment. An example would be a hospital plan that recognizes the UCR amount for room and board and a scheduled amount for surgical procedures. Most fee-for-service plans use UCR to determine payments for covered services.

Prepaid Plans—Whereas fee-for-service plans reimburse insured persons for covered charges they incur, prepaid plans promise to deliver needed health care and require that care be obtained from a prepaid plan provider. Because care is paid for before, rather than after, it is provided, there are no UCR or fixed dollar limitations. (For a discussion of prepaid plans, see chapter 23 on HMOs.)

Premium Contributions, Deductibles, Coinsurance, Out-of-Pocket Limits, and Maximum Coverage Limits

Virtually all covered services in non-HMO health care plans are subject to employer payment limitations and require the employee to share in the costs of coverage.[3] These cost-sharing features generally include premium contributions, deductibles, coinsurance, and maximum caps on benefits. These plan features are intended to reduce plan costs, encourage employee cost consciousness, and reduce administrative expenses.

A deductible is a specified amount of initial medical costs that would otherwise be treated as covered expenses under the plan, which each participant must pay before any expenses are reimbursed by the plan. Deductibles typically range from $100 to $500. Under a plan with a $200 individual deductible, for example, a participant must pay the first $200 in recognized expenses for covered health care expenses according to the plan

---

[3] Non-HMO plans include both fee-for-service and preferred provider organization plans. Although cost-sharing features may be included in HMOs, cost sharing is less prevalent in this type of delivery system due, in large part, to restrictions outlined in the Health Maintenance Organization Act of 1973 (P.L. 93-222). For example, deductibles for basic benefits are prohibited in federally qualified HMOs. In addition, allowable copayments are limited.

provisions.

The deductible must be satisfied periodically (generally every calendar year) by each participant, sometimes with a maximum of two or three deductibles per family. However, some plans contain a three-month carryover provision. If so, any portion of the deductible that is satisfied during the last three months of the year can be applied toward satisfaction of the following year's deductible.

Coinsurance provisions require the plan participant to pay a portion of recognized medical expenses; the plan pays the remaining portion. Commonly, the employee pays 20 percent, with the plan paying the remaining 80 percent of recognized charges. Most major medical plans include both deductibles and coinsurance provisions. Thus, once the plan participant pays the deductible (e.g., the first $200 in medical expenses), the plan pays 80 percent of all other covered charges. Some services may have special coinsurance provisions (e.g., 50 percent coinsurance).

Because 20 percent of a large medical claim may pose a significant financial burden for many individuals and families, most plans limit participants' out-of-pocket expenditures for covered services. In this case, once a participant has reached the out-of-pocket maximum, covered expenses are reimbursed in full for the remainder of the year. The out-of-pocket limit may be renewed at the start of the calendar year for each individual participant. In 1993, the average dollar maximum on family out-of-pocket expenses for full-time, medium and large private establishment employees participating in non-HMO medical plans was $2,642. The average dollar maximum on individual out-of-pocket expenses for full-time, medium and large private establishment employees participating in non-HMO medical plans was $1,319 in 1993 (Employee Benefit Research Institute, 1995).

Most medical plans impose a maximum dollar limit on the amount of health insurance coverage provided. Plans may impose an annual or lifetime maximum on payments for all covered services. Individual lifetime maximums are set usually at very high levels, such as $250,000 or $1 million. Separate lifetime maximums may be set for specific coverages such as psychiatric care. Although less common, plans that impose limits may do so on an episode basis, such as per hospital admission or per disability.

As health care plan costs continue to escalate, employers are increasingly changing the design of these cost-sharing features. Employees are more often required to contribute toward routine health care plan cost expenses such as premiums and deductibles. However, a growing proportion of employees are protected against catastrophic loss by out-of-pocket limits on the overall amount they must pay toward health care costs. Moreover, U.S. Department of Labor data indicate that plans increasingly include higher plan maximums, further protecting employees.[4]

Preexisting Conditions

A preexisting condition is a condition for which care or treatment was recommended or received during the six months prior to coverage under a health plan and does not include genetic information. Group health plans are prohibited from applying preexisting condition limits for periods greater than 12 months (or 18 months for late enrollees). The preexisting condition limit cannot be applied in cases involving pregnancy or in cases involving newborns or newly adopted children who become covered under the plan within 30 days.[5] Group health plans are required to take into account an individual's prior creditable coverage when applying any preexisting condition limit. A plan must reduce the duration of its preexisting condition limit for one month for every month of prior creditable coverage, so long as the individual does not have a break in coverage exceeding 63 days. Waiting periods are not counted as a break in coverage.

Basic Health Insurance Plans

Basic health insurance plans primarily cover health care services associated with an episode of hospital care, including hospitalization, in-hospital physician care, and surgery and generally also cover outpatient surgery. Basic health insurance plans typically pay for hospital room and board, physician care, and surgery on a UCR basis but may pay other charges in full.

Hospitalization— Hospitalization coverage pays for inpatient hospital charges, such as room and board, intensive care, necessary medical sup-

---

[4] See Sarah Snider, "Features of Employer-Sponsored Health Plans," *EBRI Issue Brief* no. 128 (Employee Benefit Research Institute, August 1992). A plan maximum is the dollar limit on the amount of health insurance provided. Plans that impose limits may do so on a per episode basis or on an annual and/or lifetime basis.

[5] HMOs are allowed to substitute a 60-day affiliation period (90 days for late enrollees) for a preexisting condition limit.

plies, general nursing services, and inpatient drugs. Some outpatient services (such as preadmission testing or emergency treatment as a result of an accident) may also be covered. The plan may have separate limits for certain types of care (e.g., room and board benefits may be limited on a per admission basis).

Physician Care—Physician care coverage pays for in-hospital visits by a physician. Medical care obtained in a physician's office or at home is usually excluded from the basic plan. A major medical plan will cover these types of services. Benefit limits often apply, such as a dollar amount per visit or a limited number of visits (e.g., for mental health care) per calendar year.

Surgical—This type of coverage pays for surgical procedures performed by a licensed physician. The surgery can be performed in a hospital, outpatient facility, or physician's office. Additionally, the services of an assistant surgeon, anesthesiologist, and anesthetist may also be covered. Surgical procedures often are reimbursed according to a fee schedule.

Major Medical Insurance

Major medical insurance plans are of two types—supplemental and comprehensive. Supplemental major medical plans cover some services that are excluded under basic plans and may also cover the same services but with higher coverage limits. Comprehensive major medical plans provide the combined coverage of a basic plan and a supplemental plan. Unlike basic medical plans, major medical plans cover a broad range of health care services and are designed to protect against large medical expenses.

Comprehensive Plans—Comprehensive major medical plans provide coverage for the same types of services covered under combined basic supplemental plans and have replaced many combination plans. Comprehensive plans also include deductible and coinsurance requirements but may provide first dollar coverage for emergency accident benefits or waive out-of-pocket expenses for certain types of benefits altogether.

Other Health Care Plans

Medical plans generally exclude services that are predictable or not considered medically necessary, including most types of dental, vision, and hearing care. As a result, stand-alone plans providing these benefits are growing in popularity. Because of their highly elective nature, various limits are placed on the benefits provided. (For more information on these benefits, see chapter 20 on dental care plans and chapter 22 on vision care plans.)

Continuation of Coverage

The Consolidated Omnibus Budget Reconciliation Act of 1985 (COBRA) requires public and private employers with health insurance plans to offer continued access to group health insurance to former employees and their dependents:

- for up to 18 months (29 months for the disabled) if employment is terminated (other than for gross misconduct) or if hours of work are reduced below the level at which coverage is normally provided: or
- for up to 36 months if coverage is lost as a result of cessation of dependent status, death of the employee, divorce or legal separation, or entitlement to Medicare.

The coverage offered must be identical to that actually provided prior to the change in employment status. The qualifying employee or dependent may be required to pay up to 102 percent of the premium (102 percent of the average cost if the plan is self insured). The employer may charge disabled employees 102 percent for the first 18 months and up to 150 percent during the 19th through 29th months. At the end of the 18- or 36- month period, the employer must offer conversion to an individual policy if the group plan includes a conversion privilege (an option required in some states). Also, some states may require a longer coverage period and/or include groups with fewer than 20 employees.

Group health plans for public and private employers with fewer than 20 employees are excluded from these provisions, as are church plans (as defined in sec. 414(e) of the Internal Revenue Code), the District of Columbia, and any territory, possession, or agency of the United States.

Prior to the enactment of the Omnibus Budget Reconciliation Act of 1989 (OBRA '89), coverage could be terminated prior to the end of the maximum required period if the qualified beneficiary became covered under another group health plan. OBRA '89 provides that COBRA may not terminate before the maximum period if the qualified beneficiary becomes covered under another group health plan that excludes or limits a preexisting condition of the qualified beneficiary. However, the Health Insurance Portability and Accountability Act of 1996 allows COBRA coverage to be cut off as soon as any preexisting condition limit in the new plan has been satisfied.

Conclusion

For many decades, health insurance plans have played a significant role in employee benefit planning. Modern technology, increased longevity, and a growing emphasis on good physical and mental health make these plans even more important today. The development of managed care plans, and dental, prescription drug, vision, and hearing care plans attests to the dynamic nature of this employee benefit area, as does the development of wellness and employee assistance programs. Future innovative efforts in plan design will be influenced strongly by the continuing need for health care cost management as well as by constantly changing government regulations.

Bibliography

Employee Benefit Research Institute. *EBRI Databook on Employee Benefits.* Third Edition. Washington, DC: Employee Benefit Research Institute, 1995.

Health Insurance Association of America. *Source Book of Health Insurance Data: 1993.* Washington, DC: Health Insurance Association of America, 1993.

Rosenbloom, Jerry S. *The Handbook of Employee Benefits.* Third Edition. Homewood, IL: Dow Jones-Irwin, 1992.

Snider, Sarah. "Features of Employer-Sponsored Health Plans," *EBRI Issue Brief* no. 128 (Employee Benefit Research Institute, August 1992).

U.S. Department of Labor. Bureau of Labor Statistics. *Employee Benefits in Medium and Large Private Establishments, 1993.* Washington, DC: U.S. Government Printing Office, 1994a.

_____. *Employee Benefits in Small Private Establishments, 1994.* Washington, DC: U.S. Government Printing Office, 1996.

Additional Information

American Association of Health Plans
1129 20th Street, NW, Suite 600
Washington, DC 20036
(202) 778-3200

Center for Health Policy Research
American Medical Association
515 North State Street
Chicago, IL 60610
(312) 464-5022

International Foundation of
Employee Benefit Plans
P.O. Box 69
18700 West Bluemound Road
Brookfield, WI 53008-0069
(414) 786-6700

Self-Insurance Institute of America, Inc.
17300 Red Hill Avenue, Suite 100
Irvine, CA 92714
(714) 261-2553

Washington Business Group on Health
777 North Capitol Street, NE, Suite 800
Washington, DC 20002
(202) 408-9320

20. Dental Care Plans

Health authorities agree that many Americans' dental care could be improved substantially. Among the deterrents to better care are the public's perception that dental care costs are high and the fact that correction of many dental problems is often postponed for long periods. Surprisingly, the majority of workers have dental care coverage but do not utilize it. In 1993, 62 percent of full-time employees in medium and large private establishments had employment-based coverage for dental care (U.S. Department of Labor, 1994a).

A 1993 survey of over 3,000 employers indicated that large employers (87 percent) were more likely to offer dental coverage than small employers (47 percent) (A. Foster Higgins & Co., Inc., 1993). Employee sharing of dental costs has also increased, with 72 percent of plans requiring employee contributions in 1993, compared with 63 percent in 1988, according to another recent survey (Hewitt Associates, 1994).

A sound dental insurance plan has two primary objectives: to help pay for dental care costs and to encourage people to receive regular dental attention, which can prevent potentially serious problems.

The three major dental care plans are the traditional fee-for-service plans, preferred provider organizations (PPOs), and health maintenance organizations (HMOs). In 1993, the majority of full-time employees (87 percent) were enrolled in the traditional fee-for-service plan, while 7 percent were in HMOs, and 6 percent were in PPOs. Although HMOs and PPOs currently represent only 13 percent of the market, it is widely believed that interest in these two options is increasing, and enrollment in these plans is expected to grow.

With fee-for-service plans, dentists are usually paid on a service-to-service basis. Fee-for-service plans usually include deductibles, coinsurance levels, and annual plan maximums. (For more information on HMOs and PPOs, see chapters 23 and 24).

Services

A dental insurance plan should specify the types of services that are and are not covered. Typically, the least expensive procedures (i.e., examinations and x-rays) are most likely to be 100 percent covered; fillings, endodontics, periodontics, and dental surgery are most likely to be

80 percent covered; and the more expensive procedures (i.e., crowns, prosthetics, and orthodontia) are most likely to be 50 percent covered.

Services that are usually not covered include hospitalization due to necessary dental treatment; cosmetic dental work (e.g., closing a gap between two front teeth); cleaning and examinations performed more often than twice a year; and services covered by workers' compensation or other insurance programs.

Payment of Benefits

There are several methods used by dental care plans to cover dental services. The plan may pay a certain percentage of the participant's dental charges; pay a fixed dollar amount per procedure; require the participant to pay an initial copayment, after which the plan will pay the remaining charges; or the plan may pay a certain percentage of dental charges based on the participant's use of dental services.

Dental insurance plans may also require payment of a *deductible* (i.e., an amount a participant must pay before receiving any insurance payments). Some dental plans require copayments (participant's share of the dentist's fee after the benefits plan has paid) as well. Copayments for preventive care may be as low as $5 or $10 per procedure. As the procedures become more expensive, the copayment increases.

In addition, in 1993, most dental plan participants (83 percent) were subjected to a yearly maximum benefit. The most common (applicable to 45 percent of participants) yearly maximum benefit was $1,000, followed by $1,500 (13 percent) (U.S. Department of Labor, 1994a).

Other Dental Plan Features

Predetermination of Benefits—Before beginning dental treatment, a plan participant may want to know how much he or she will be charged for the treatment and how much the plan will pay. A plan may require the participant's dentist to fill out a predetermination-of-benefits form describing the proposed treatment and its cost. The participant would then send the form to the claims office, which would, in turn, advise the participant and the dentist of the amount the plan would pay. Some dental plans require this procedure when anticipated charges exceed a stated amount (e.g., $200).

Alternative Benefits—Dental problems can often be successfully treated in more than one way. When this situation occurs, many dental plans base payments on the least expensive treatment that is customarily used for the condition in question. For example, a decayed tooth may often be satisfactorily repaired with a crown or a filling. In this case, a dental plan bases its payment on the filling, which is the less expensive treatment. The participant and the dentist may proceed with the more expensive crown only if the participant agrees to pay the difference.

Cost Sharing—Most dental plans are designed with cost-sharing features that require the participant to pay some portion and the plan to pay the remaining portion of the charges for dental services. Two common cost-sharing features are deductibles and copayments.

As noted earlier, a deductible is an amount a participant must pay before receiving any insurance payments. Depending on a plan's design, deductibles must be satisfied once annually or once in a lifetime. Consider a hypothetical example in which a participant's first dental bill for the year is $75; the bill covers the filling of several cavities. The yearly deductible under this plan is $50. Thus the participant pays the first $50. The remaining $25 is covered, either partially or fully, by the plan. No other deductible is required this year. The participant will have to pay another $50 deductible in the following year, however. In 1993, 64 percent of dental plan participants had to meet a separate deductible. The most common deductible (applicable to 34 percent of participants) was $50 per year, followed by $25 per year (19 percent).

If a plan has a coinsurance feature, the plan and the participant share the costs of each covered dental service. The plan pays a specified percentage of covered services (e.g., 80 percent), and the participant pays the balance (in this case, 20 percent). Additionally, a plan may offer a number of coinsurance schedules, depending on the treatment. For example, a plan may pay 80 percent of a dentist's bill for filling a cavity but only 50 percent of a bill for orthodontic work.

In some plans, coinsurance is used in conjunction with a deductible. Under such a plan, after a yearly deductible (for example $50) has been paid by the participant, the plan will pay some stated percentage (e.g., 80 percent) of additional dental expenses.

Some plans require a deductible and/or coinsurance for some types of treatment but not for preventive care services. These features are intended to encourage regular dental visits and preventive care.

Claims Payment—Payment of claims under a group dental plan generally follows the same procedure as payment of claims under a group medical plan. The participant and the dentist fill out and submit claim forms. Payments for covered services may be sent to the dentist or to the participant. Dental insurance plans usually experience heavy claims the first year because of a backlog of unmet dental needs in a newly covered employee group.

Continuation of Coverage—The Consolidated Omnibus Budget Reconciliation Act of 1985 (COBRA) requires employers with dental plans to offer continued access to group dental insurance for former employees and their dependents. (For an explanation of these rules, see chapter 19 on health insurance).

Deciding on a Dental Care Plan

Effective and economical use of a group dental plan requires close interaction among the employee, the employer, and the service provider. It requires that all parties work together to achieve the plan's goal of maintaining good dental health at a reasonable cost.

Bibliography

Brown, Christopher. "Dental Benefits: Setting Objectives, Picking a Plan." *Employee Benefit Plan Review* (March 1995): 30–33.

Employee Benefit Research Institute. *EBRI Databook on Employee Benefits.* Third edition. Washington, DC: Employee Benefit Research Institute, 1995.

Foster Higgins. *National Survey of Employer-Sponsored Health Plans / 1993.* New York, NY: Foster Higgins, 1993.

Hewitt Associates. *Salaried Employee Benefits Provided by Major U.S. Employers in 1994.* Lincolnshire, IL: Hewitt Associates, 1994.

Mayes, Donald S. *Managed Dental Care: A Guide to HMOs.* Brookfield WI: International Foundation of Employee Benefit Plans, 1993.

U.S. Department of Labor. Bureau of Labor Statistics. *Employee Benefits in Medium and Large Private Establishments, 1993.* Washington, DC : U.S. Government Printing Office, 1994a.

_____. *Employee Benefits in Small Private Establishments, 1992.* Washington DC: U.S. Government Printing Office, 1994b

Additional Information

American Academy of Dental Group Practice
5110 North 40th Street, Suite 250
Phoenix, AZ 85018
(602) 381-1185

American Board of Quality Assurance and Utilization Review Physicians
890 West Kennedy Blvd., Suite 260
Tampa, FL 33609
(813) 286-4411

American Dental Association
211 East Chicago Avenue
Chicago, IL 60611
(312) 440-2500

21. Prescription Drug Plans

Introduction

Expenditures on prescription drugs have been rising over the last several years. In 1993, the nation spent $48.8 billion on prescription drugs, compared with $38.2 billion in 1990 (Levit, et al., 1994). The average total prescription drug cost per employee in 1993 was $386, compared with $334 in 1992 (Employee Benefit Research Institute, 1995). While total expenditures for prescription drugs have increased less rapidly than those for other medical services, the prices of these drugs have risen at a greater rate. According to a recent survey, prices of the 20 top-selling drugs increased more than one and one-half times faster than the general rate of inflation between 1993 and 1994 (Families USA, 1995).

Coverage for prescription drugs encourages participants to complete prescribed drug therapy in order to avoid more costly medical complications later. Although most medical plans cover prescription drugs, some employers and joint funds prefer to provide separate drug plans for the following reasons:

- Employees may not otherwise know that their medical plans cover the cost of prescription drugs.
- Participants covered under health care insurance plans that require payment of large or separate deductibles may not submit prescription drug claims.
- Employees may be confused by the paperwork required by typical medical plans (e.g., saving drug store receipts and filing claims).
- The influx of prescription drug claims at the end of a medical year can cause problems for plan administrators.
- Price discounts are available in separate mail order programs.

Employers may cover employees under prescription drug plans after a brief waiting period and pay part or all of the employees' premiums. In addition, some plans cover employees' dependents. As is the case with health insurance, some employers pay the full cost of dependent coverage, while others require payroll deductions to cover part or all of the cost.

Services

Prescription drug plans provide coverage for out-of-hospital prescription drugs. Generally, these plans do not cover proprietary medicines, medical appliances or devices, nonprescription drugs, in-hospital drugs, blood and blood plasma, immunization agents, and any drugs or medicines lawfully obtained without prescription (with the exception of insulin). Plans may also exclude contraceptive drugs.

Many plans place limits on the quantity of a drug that may be dispensed at any one time. A typical limitation is a 34-day supply or 100 doses, whichever is greater. A higher limitation usually applies to maintenance drugs. Most plans do not place a maximum on the overall covered quantity of a drug. However, some plans may limit the total dollar cost of prescription drugs that will be reimbursed in a plan year.

Prescription drug plans typically require only a small copayment, such as $3 to $8 per prescription, from the participant for drugs provided under the plan. Many plans encourage the use of generic drugs in an effort to contain costs. Cost containment can also be accomplished through employee education and/or plan design.

Payment of Benefits

The most common types of plans include *open panel plans, closed panel plans, mail order plans,* and *nationwide panel plans.*

Open panel plans permit employees to choose the pharmacies they use. Participants pay for prescriptions and send the receipts, with claim forms, to the plan administrator for reimbursement. If a plan has a deductible, receipts are usually accumulated until the deductible is satisfied and then are submitted to a claims office at one time.

Closed panel plans generally employ a number of pharmacies, ranging from a few to several thousand. These pharmacies dispense drugs to plan members at prices agreed upon by the plan provider and the pharmacy. Sometimes the price is the pharmacy's cost plus a dispensing fee. The plan administrator pays the panel pharmacies directly. Plan members pay only the applicable deductible and are not required to submit claims forms. If plan participants use a nonpanel pharmacy (e.g., in an emergency situation), they must submit a claim form as though they were in an open panel plan.

To contain prescription drug costs, employees may be encouraged to obtain prescription drugs through mail order pharmacies. In mail order plans, employees send their prescriptions to specified mail order firms. Because of volume, mail order pharmacies frequently offer prescriptions at lower prices than other pharmacies. Under mail order arrangements, all claims are processed at one location; thus, the use of a claim form is eliminated most of the time. Their "door-to-door" service also makes these plans attractive. However, they are not designed for drugs that are needed immediately.

Nationwide panel plans, also known as prescription card service plans, are popular. They use a network of pharmacies, usually through a *prepaid drug plan administrator* (i.e., a firm administering plans for insurance companies, employers, joint funds, and others) and negotiate price discounts. These carriers provide participating employees a plastic identity card, similar to a credit card, that is presented at the time of purchase. The cards are recognized by participating pharmacists, who then submit a claim for payment from the carrier. Sometimes a nationwide panel plan includes a mail order option; this approach achieves savings on maintenance drugs while maintaining access to a community pharmacy for emergency situations.

In addition to these plans, many pharmacy chains negotiate discounts with employers under a type of preferred provider arrangement.

Bibliography

Betley, Charles. "Prescription Drugs: Coverage, Cost, and Quality." *EBRI Issue Brief* no. 122 (Employee Benefit Research Institute, January 1992).

Boston Consulting Group, Inc. *The Changing Environment for U.S. Pharmaceuticals: The Role of Pharmaceutical Companies in a Systems Approach to Health Care.* New York, NY: The Boston Consulting Group, Inc., 1993.

Employee Benefit Research Institute. *Databook on Employee Benefits.* Third edition. Washington, DC: Employee Benefit Research Institute, 1995.

Families USA. *Worthless Promises: Drug Companies Keep Boosting Prices.* Washington, DC: Familes USA, 1995.

Foley, Jill. "The Role of Health Care in the U.S. Economy." *EBRI Issue Brief* no. 142 (Employee Benefit Research Institute, October 1993).

Foster Higgins. *National Survey of Employer-Sponsored Health Plans / 1994.* New York, NY: Foster Higgins, 1994.

Levit, Katherine R., et al. "National Health Expenditures." *Health Care*

Financing Review (Fall 1994): 247–294.

Rosenbloom, Jerry S., ed. *The Handbook of Employee Benefits: Design, Funding and Administration.* Third edition. Homewood, IL: Dow Jones-Irwin, 1992.

U.S. Congress. Office of Technology Assessment. *Pharmaceutical R&D: Costs, Risks and Rewards.* Washington, DC: U.S. Government Printing Office, 1993.

U.S. Department of Labor. Bureau of Labor Statistics. *Employee Benefits in Medium and Large Private Establishments, 1993.* Washington, DC: U.S. Government Printing Office, 1994.

_____. *Employee Benefits in Small Private Establishments, 1992.* Washington, DC: U.S. Government Printing Office, 1994.

Additional Information

American Pharmaceutical Association
2215 Constitutional Avenue, NW
Washington, DC 20037
(202) 628-4410

Nonprescription Drug Manufacturers Association
1100 Connecticut Avenue, NW, Suite 1200
Washington, DC 20036
(202) 429-9260

Pharmaceutical Research and Manufacturers of America
1100 15th Street, NW
Washington, DC 20005
(202) 835-3400

22. Vision Care Plans

Introduction

Vision problems are common in the United States; more than one-half of the population requires optometric care. It is estimated that 74 percent of all employees wear corrective lenses, although only 33 percent of all Americans receive an eye exam every year. Vision problems are often chronic and require regular attention.

Except for medical and surgical treatment and, in some cases, contact lenses after cataract surgery, traditional health insurance plans have provided little or no vision care coverage. Employment-based vision care plans are designed to insure vision care services.

Similar to most medical plans, vision care benefits are usually available to a group of covered employees after a nominal waiting period; the employer often pays the cost for employee coverage. In addition, most plans provide for coverage of employees' dependents. Coverage for dependents can be extended in a number of ways; the employer may pay for dependent protection, the employee may pay, or the employer and the employee may share the cost.

A variety of organizations offer vision care plans to employee groups. These include jointly managed funds, health maintenance organizations (HMOs), administrators of Blue Cross and Blue Shield plans, vision care corporations, optometric associations, closed-panel groups of vision care providers, and insurance companies. In addition, some employers self-fund and self-administer their plans.

The principal providers of vision care are:

- *Ophthalmologists*—Medical doctors specializing in eye examination, treatment, and surgery. Some ophthalmologists dispense eyeglasses and contact lenses.
- *Optometrists*—Health care professionals who are specifically educated and licensed at the state level to examine, diagnose, and treat conditions of the vision system. Optometrists may not operate on the eye and, in most states, may not administer therapeutic drugs. Most optometrists dispense eyeglasses and contact lenses.
- *Opticians*—Persons who make and/or sell lenses and eyeglasses.

Extent of Coverage

Vision plans may cover eye exams, eyeglasses, contact lenses, and orthoptics (exercises for the eye muscles). In 1993, among employees in medium and large private establishments who participated in medical plans, 26 percent had vision care benefits. Of the employees participating in a vision care plan, 72 percent were enrolled in a traditional fee-for-service plan, 17 percent were enrolled in an HMO, and 10 percent were enrolled in a preferred provider organization. Ninety-four percent of these plans covered eye exams, 100 percent had eyeglass coverage, and 91 percent had contact lens coverage (U.S. Department of Labor, 1994a).

Services

The typical vision care plan covers eye examinations, lenses, frames, and the fitting of eyeglasses. Eye examinations provide the information needed for lens prescriptions and may reveal eye diseases such as glaucoma or cataracts. (They may also reveal evidence of diabetes or high blood pressure.) Many plans cover some portion of the costs for contact lenses; however, other plans only cover contact lenses following cataract surgery.

Nearly all vision care plans impose limitations on the frequency of covered services and glasses. Typically, they limit participants to one eye examination within a 12-month period, one set of lenses within a 12-month period, and one set of frames within a 2-year period. Most plans do not cover the additional cost of oversized, photosensitive, or plastic lenses, nor do they cover prescription sunglasses.

Payment of Benefits

Similar to other types of health insurance, vision care plans cover services in a variety of ways. For example:

- Some plans pay the full cost of services, provided they satisfy the *usual, customary, and reasonable* cost criteria. In other words, the covered amount is the provider's usual fee for the service, the customary or prevailing fee for the service or product in that geographic area, and a reasonable amount based on the circumstances involved. A fee may be considered reasonable when circumstances necessitate extensive or complex treatment, even though it does not meet the usual, customary, and reasonable criteria.

- Sometimes vision care plan participants are required to pay *deductibles*. The deductible is a specified amount of vision care costs that the participant must pay before any costs are paid by the plan. Under a plan with a $50 individual deductible, for example, a participant must pay his or her first $50 in vision care expenses. The plan then pays for additional vision care expenses in accordance with other plan provisions.
- Plans may have a *coinsurance* arrangement in which the plan participant pays some portion of the vision care expenses and the plan pays the remainder. The plan participant, for instance, may pay 20 percent and the plan may pay 80 percent.
- Other plans specify a covered dollar amount for each service. Under the *schedule-of-benefits* approach, the plan participant pays any amount over the scheduled dollar limit. The schedule is usually adjusted at intervals to keep it consistent with changes in the cost of care.
- Vision care costs are often covered by employers through a health reimbursement account. Under such arrangements, the employee chooses how much money to contribute to the account at the beginning of the year, and pretax contributions to the account are deducted from each paycheck. The employee pays for any medical expenses (including vision care) and is then reimbursed by the employer. Any unused balances are forfeited by employees at the end of the plan year. (See chapter 25 on managing health care costs.)
- Plans may also use a *closed-panel arrangement*, in which a designated group (i.e., a closed panel) of vision care professionals provide services to an employee group. The full cost of services is paid when plan participants go to providers specified by the plan. Employers pay a premium for such services, which may cover a fixed cost per beneficiary. The providers are reimbursed for their cost of materials plus a dispensing fee. If participants go to providers who are not in the closed-panel, the plan pays only a specified amount; the participant must pay any excess amount.
- Plans commonly use a combination of the approaches described above. A plan that covers services based on usual, customary, and reasonable charges may also require payment of a deductible or coinsurance. Coinsurance may also be included in a schedule-of-benefits approach.

Continuation of Coverage

The Consolidated Omnibus Budget Reconciliation Act of 1985 (COBRA) requires employers with vision and other health care plans to offer continued access to group health insurance for former employees and their dependents. (For an explanation of these rules, see chapter 19 on health insurance.)

Deciding on a Vision Care Plan

When considering the cost of a vision care plan, a potential plan sponsor should be aware that such plans have a high incidence of claims in the first year because there may be a backlog of unmet needs in a newly covered employee group. An employment-based vision care plan should include a program to increase employee awareness and understanding of vision care and the plan; effective communication among all involved parties (i.e., employee, employer, and service providers); and an efficient claims filing and payment system.

Bibliography

Employee Benefit Research Institute. *Databook on Employee Benefits.* Third edition. Washington, DC: Employee Benefit Research Institute, 1995.

Rosenbloom, Jerry S., ed. *The Handbook of Employee Benefits: Design, Funding, and Administration.* Third edition. Homewood, IL: Dow Jones-Irwin, 1992.

Rosenthal, Jesse, and Mort Soroka. *Managed Vision Benefits.* Brookfield, WI: International Foundation of Employee Benefit Plans, 1995.

U.S. Department of Labor. Bureau of Labor Statistics. *Employee Benefits in Medium and Large Private Establishments, 1993.* Washington, DC: U.S. Government Printing Office, 1994a.

_____. *Employee Benefits in Small Private Establishments, 1992.* Washington, DC: U.S. Government Printing Office, 1994b.

Additional Information

American Optometric Association
243 North Lindbergh Blvd.
St. Louis, MO 63141
(314) 991-4100

Vision Service Plan
7711 Carondelet, Suite 807
St. Louis, MO 63105
(314) 725-6500

23. Health Maintenance Organizations

Introduction

Since the 1980s, enrollment in health maintenance organizations (HMOs) has greatly increased. HMO advocates believe HMOs offer great potential for controlling health care costs while maintaining quality medical care. HMOs provide a wide range of services to subscribers and their dependents on a prepaid basis. Subscribers purchase HMO coverage for a contract period by paying a fixed periodic fee (typically annual). HMOs generally emphasize preventive care and early intervention. Because HMOs are contractually obligated to provide all covered medical services for a fixed dollar amount, they have an incentive to provide care early, before illnesses become more serious. At the same time, HMO members tend to have lower rates of hospitalization than persons covered by traditional fee-for-service insurance plans.

The first HMO was established in 1929. The number of HMOs has risen dramatically since then. As of July 1, 1995, there were an estimated 593 pure and open-ended[1] HMOs covering 53.4 million people (InterStudy, 1995). InterStudy projects that by 1997 the number of individuals enrolled in a pure HMO will increase from 58.5 million to 66.0 million. According to the Bureau of Labor Statistics' employee benefit surveys, in survey years 1992 and 1993, 20 percent of full-time employees in private industry and state and local governments who participated in an employment-based health plan were enrolled in an HMO (U.S. Department of Labor, 1994a and 1994b). As of July 1, 1995, 3.4 million older Americans were enrolled in HMOs through Medicare (Marlowe and Childress, 1995).

How HMOs Work

HMOs both finance and deliver health care services. Instead of paying a health care provider each time a service is delivered, HMO subscribers

---

[1] A pure health maintenance organization (HMO) is an organization that offers prepaid, comprehensive health coverage for both hospital and physician services. Members are required to use participating providers and are enrolled for specified periods of time. An open-ended HMO, also known as an HMO point-of-service, is an organization in which the patients are prepaid enrollees who may receive services from providers who are not members of the HMO's panel. There usually is a substantial deductible, copayment, or coinsurance requiirement for use of nonpanel providers. These products are governed by state HMO regulations (InterStudy, 1995).

agree to pay periodic fees (typically annual). In turn, HMOs provide for virtually all of their subscribers' covered health care needs. (Subscribers may be required to make a modest copayment for some HMO services.) Each HMO develops its own rates and benefits, although certain HMOs that are regulated by federal law must provide at least the basic health services required by law. HMOs accept the risk of providing covered health care services. Thus, they have an economic incentive for monitoring utilization and costs.

HMOs' basic functions are to provide comprehensive health care services to subscribers, contract with or employ physicians and other health care professionals who will provide the covered medical services, and contract with one or more hospitals to provide covered hospital care (a few HMOs own and operate hospitals).

Because HMOs both finance and provide health care services, their role is different from that of commercial insurers or a Blue Cross and Blue Shield plan. Conventional insurance plans simply reimburse health care providers whom the patient has to locate, usually under a fee-for-service arrangement. However, commercial insurers, self-insured employers, and Blue Cross and Blue Shield plans are increasingly using preferred provider organization (PPO) arrangements and other managed care arrangements to encourage employee use of certain designated health care providers.

Types of HMOs

Currently, there are five different HMO models: staff, group, network, independent practice association, and mixed model. Each of these models differs with respect to its rules for patients and the financial incentives it imposes on health care providers to manage services and costs.

- *Staff Model*—In a staff model, the HMO owns its health care facility and employs health care providers on a salaried basis. Patient choice is limited: enrollees are restricted to network providers and are required first to see a primary care physician, who then refers them to specialists within the HMO when it is considered medically necessary and appropriate.
- *Group Model*—In a group model, the HMO contracts with a single independent group practice to provide services to the HMO participants. The practice is managed independently and is usually paid on a capitated basis. Group model HMO providers usually spend most of

their time with HMO participants but may spend some time in private practice.

- *Independent Practice Associations (IPAs)*—IPAs are groups of physicians in private practice who provide some services to HMO participants but primarily provide services to patients not enrolled in an HMO. The IPA may contract with more than one insurer or HMO. The non-HMO patients are treated on a fee-for-service basis. IPA providers working with HMOs are generally paid on a fee-for-service basis; therefore, they do not have strong incentives to provide cost-effective care. However, there has been a movement toward reimbursing IPAs on a discounted fee-for-service basis or on a capitated basis. The advantage of an IPA is that contracting with physicians practicing in their own offices allows the HMO to offer services in a broader geographic area, requires less capital investment than a staff or group model HMO of similar size, and generally offers patients more choice among providers.
- *Network Model*—In the network model, the HMOs contract with two or more independent physician groups that often provide general and specialty services. These groups are typically paid on a capitated basis by the HMO, but they also spend some time in private practice operating on a fee-for-service basis.
- *Mixed Model*—A mixed model HMO initially adopts one type of model, such as a staff model, and then expands its capacity and/or its geographic region later by adding another type of model such as an IPA.

Health Maintenance Organization Act of 1973

The Health Maintenance Organization Act of 1973 was intended to encourage the growth of HMOs. In addition, it established requirements for an entity seeking designation as a federally qualified HMO. Under these requirements, HMOs must offer certain benefits and satisfy federal regulations for administrative, financial, and contractual arrangements. The U.S. Department of Health and Human Services administers the act and oversees federal qualification of HMOs. A federally qualified HMO must meet uniform standards for service delivery, quality assurance, marketing practices, and financial standing.

The federal HMO law and regulations also include the following provisions. The HMO's solicitation to the prospective employer customer must be in writing, and it must be directed to a managing official at the solicited location. The written request must be extended at least 180 days before renewal or expiration of the employer's regular health benefit contract or collective bargaining agreement. Additionally, the HMO must satisfy other requirements before it will be considered as an optional employer plan (e.g., information must be available on the HMO's ownership and control, facilities, hours of operation, service areas, and rates). In actual practice, most employers who offer HMOs do so voluntarily (i.e., not as a result of the formal solicitation process). For more information on federal legislation, see section on Dual Choice Requirement.

Services that federally qualified HMOs must provide include primary and specialty physician care, inpatient and outpatient hospital care, emergency care, short-term outpatient mental health care, medical treatment and referral for alcohol/drug abuse and addiction, diagnostic laboratory services, diagnostic and therapeutic radiology services, home health care, and preventive health care. At its discretion, a federally qualified HMO may also provide a broad range of supplemental health care services, such as intermediate and long-term care (e.g., institutional or home health care); adult vision care; dental care; long-term or inpatient mental health care; long-term physical therapy and rehabilitation services; and prescription drugs. These supplemental services can be offered on a fee-for-service basis. For more information on dental care, prescription drug, and vision care plans, see chapters 20, 21, and 22, respectively.

Employers who offer HMOs must provide for annual group enrollment periods, during which employees can choose either the HMO or the regular health insurance plan without waiting periods, exclusions, or restrictions due to health status. As of January 1, 1995, 270 HMOs were federally qualified; these HMOs provided health care services to 70.3 percent of all HMO subscribers (InterStudy, 1995).

Some HMOs are not federally qualified because they do not meet the HMO act's requirements or because they have not applied for qualification. However, all HMOs must be state certified. HMOs generally provide more comprehensive services than are covered by commercial insurance plans or Blue Cross and Blue Shield plans. For example, federally qualified HMOs must provide routine examinations, and their allowable copayments are limited.

HMO Act Amendments of 1988

Responding to employer concerns about selection bias and HMO pricing,

Congress enacted the 1988 amendments to the HMO Act (P.L. 100-517) on October 24, 1988. The new law relaxed some regulations applying to federally qualified HMOs, allowing employers to negotiate HMO rates and coverage more easily.

Dual Choice Requirement—One of the major provisions of the 1973 HMO act was a requirement that most employers offer their employees a qualified HMO, in addition to a traditional health plan, if requested to do so by such an HMO. The 1988 amendments repealed the dual choice requirement, effective October 24, 1995.

Equal Contribution Requirement—Regulations provided under the original act had interpreted the dual choice provision to require that mandated employers contribute the same dollar amount to federally qualified HMOs as they contribute to their highest cost non-HMO health plan. The 1988 law eases this requirement and states that any contribution made by a mandated employer to a qualified HMO must be in an amount that does not "financially discriminate" against an employee enrolled in the qualified HMO. A contribution is considered not financially discriminatory "if the employer's method of determining the contributions on behalf of all employees is reasonable and is designed to assure all employees a fair choice among health benefit plans."

Community Rating Requirement—The original HMO act required that federally qualified HMOs community rate their services. A community rating system determines rates based on the HMO's total membership experience rather than on the experience of each subscriber group. The 1988 amendments allow employers to negotiate group rates on the basis of an estimate of how much it is likely to cost to provide services to the employee group. This type of pricing is similar to the experience rating used in fee-for-service insurance plans, except that HMOs are not permitted to adjust premiums retroactively if the estimates prove inaccurate. Employers with fewer than 100 employees can be charged no more than 110 percent of the community rate.

HMO Growth and Competition

Since the passage of the 1973 HMO act, some observers have indicated that HMOs have been an important influence in restructuring the U.S. health care system and slowing rising health care costs. However, the growth of HMOs was relatively slow during the 1970s for a number of reasons, including physician reluctance to leave fee-for-service medical practice and beneficiary reluctance to accept restrictions on freedom of provider choice. Additionally, there was some initial confusion over the 1973 HMO act. The act has been amended several times, in part to alleviate this confusion and, in 1988, to promote competition among HMOs for employers' business, which in turn could lower employers' cost of providing health coverage to employees.

Sustained growth in HMO membership since the 1980s suggests increasing employer, consumer, and government interest in HMO arrangements and increased acceptance by providers and employees. Employers, unions, and insurance companies have been more involved as direct sponsors and organizers of HMOs. Government policies increasingly encourage enrollment in managed care programs of Medicare/Medicaid populations and government employees. Also, hospital managers and private practice physicians have become more interested in HMOs as well as other types of alternative health care delivery systems.

Conclusion

Despite HMOs' growth and increasing acceptance, some observers question their ability to stem rising health care costs. Several studies have been conducted on the impact of HMOs on health care costs. More recent studies have shown that, in markets with a high penetration of HMOs, hospital costs are lower than in markets with low HMO penetration. (Gaskin and Hadley, 1995). One of the main points on which HMOs are criticized is that their cost savings result primarily from selection bias, i.e., healthy, young individuals are more likely to enroll in HMOs than relatively older unhealthy individuals. Yet research into the selectivity bias in HMOs has shown little or no conclusive evidence of selectivity bias.

Recent studies do indicate that, while HMO costs continue to increase, they are increasing at a slower rate than traditional fee-for-service plan costs. One study indicates that between 1992 and 1995, HMO medical plan costs increased from $3,075 to $3,255 per employee, an average annual growth rate of 1.9 percent, while traditional fee-for-service medical plan costs increased from $3,268 to $3,650 per employee, an average annual growth rate of 3.8 percent.[2] Thus, despite continued debate regarding the optimal system for health care delivery, given continued health care cost inflation, the role of HMOs is likely to grow.

---

[2] Foster Higgins, *Foster Higgins National Survey of Employer-Sponsored Health Plans / 1995* (New York, NY: Foster Higgins, 1996).

Bibliography

Employee Benefit Research Institute. "The Changing Health Care Delivery
System: An EBRI/ERF Policy Forum." *EBRI Special Report* SR-21/*Issue
Brief* no. 148 (Employee Benefit Research Institute, April 1994).

_____. *Databook on Employee Benefits.* Third edition. Washington, DC:
Employee Benefit Research Institute, 1995.

_____. "The Future of Employment-Based Health Benefits." *EBRI
Special Report* SR-29/*Issue Brief* no. 161 (Employee Benefit Research
Institute, May 1995).

Foster Higgins. *Foster Higgins National Survey of Employer-Sponsored
Health Plans/1995.* New York, NY: Foster Higgins, 1996.

Fronstin, Paul. "The Effectiveness of Health Care Cost Strategies: A Review
of the Evidence." *EBRI Issue Brief* no. 154 (Employee Benefit Research
Institute, October 1994).

_____. "Physician Practice in a Dynamic Environment: Implications for
the Health Care System." *EBRI Issue Brief* no. 162 (Employee Benefit
Research Institute, June 1995).

Gaskin, Darrell J., and Jack Hadley. *The Impact of HMO Penetration on the
Rate of Hospital Cost Inflation, 1984–1993.* Washington, DC:
Georgetown University Medical Center, Institute for Health Care
Research and Policy, 1995.

Group Health Association of America. *HMO Industry Profile: 1995 Edition.*
Washington, DC: Group Health Association of America, 1995.

_____. *Patterns in HMO Enrollment.* Fourth edition. Washington, DC:
Group Health Association of America, 1995.

Health Insurance Association of America. *Source Book of Health Insurance
Data: 1994.* Washington, DC: Health Insurance Association of America,
1995.

InterStudy. *The InterStudy Edge: Managed Care: A Decade in Review, 1980–
1990.* Excelsior, MN: InterStudy, 1991.

_____. *The InterStudy Competitive Edge Part II: Industry Report.* Excelsior, MN: InterStudy, 1995.

Marlowe, Joseph F., and H. Kathleen Childress. "Medicare Risk HMOs:
Careful Consideration Can Yield Rewards." *Employee Benefits Journal*
(September 1995): 2–11.

Olsen, Reed Neil. "The Impact of Health Maintenance Organizations on
Health Care Costs." *Applied Economics* (November 1993): 1451–1465.

U.S. Department of Labor. Bureau of Labor Statistics. *Employee Benefits in*

Medium and Large Private Establishments, 1993. Washington, DC: U.S. Government Printing Office, 1994a.

_____. *Employee Benefits in Small Private Establishments, 1992.* Washington, DC: U.S. Government Printing Office, 1994b.

Additional Information

American Association of Health Plans
1129 20th Street, NW, Suite 600
Washington, DC 20036
(202) 778-3200

Health Insurance Association of America, Public Affairs
1025 Connecticut Avenue, NW
Washington, DC 20036
(202) 223-7783

International Foundation of Employee Benefit Plans
P.O. Box 69
18700 West Bluemound Road
Brookfield, WI 53008-0069
(414) 786-6700

InterStudy, Incorporated
P.O. Box 4366
St. Paul, MN 55104
(612) 858-9291

RAND
P.O. Box 2138
1700 Main Street
Santa Monica, CA 90406-2138
(310) 393-0411

24. Preferred Provider Organizations

Introduction

Preferred provider organizations (PPOs) are not actually organizations but rather are contractual arrangements, generally between health care providers and an employer or insurance company, to provide fee-for-service health care, usually at a discount. The term PPO refers to a variety of arrangements among employers, insurers, health care providers, and entrepreneurial organizations. Employers may offer a PPO benefit plan instead of, or in addition to, a traditional indemnity plan and/or health maintenance organization (HMO).

Under a PPO arrangement, health care providers (e.g., physicians and hospitals) agree to rates that they have prenegotiated with those who contract for their services (e.g., employers and insurance companies) in return for an increased pool of patients, faster claims processing, or both. Arrangements are based on a percentage of charges, a specific cost per day, or the cost of treating specific diagnostic groups. PPOs are sometimes used for a specific type of medical care such as mental health, vision, or dental services.

PPO arrangements have been developed in response to employer concern over rising health care costs and to provider concern about growing competition from alternative health delivery systems, such as HMOs, that promise lower cost services. PPO arrangements not only offer reduced prices for health care services but, according to their proponents, can reduce costs by selecting cost-efficient providers and implementing utilization review (UR) and control. Savings of at least 15 percent reportedly are typical.

According to the American Managed Care and Review Association, there were 895 PPOs operating in 1993, covering an estimated 54.4 million lives (American Managed Care and Review Association, 1994). The number of employees participating in a PPO has steadily increased. According to the Bureau of Labor Statistics, among full-time employees of medium and large private establishments who participated in a group health plan, the portion who participated in a PPO increased from 1 percent in 1986 to 26 percent in 1993 (U.S. Department of Labor, 1994).

Types of PPO Arrangements

There are three primary types of PPO arrangements: provider based, entrepreneur based, and purchaser based. They differ according to their sponsors.

- Provider-based PPO sponsors include hospitals, physician groups, joint hospital/physician arrangements, dentists, podiatrists, and other health professionals.
- Entrepreneur-based PPO sponsors include private investors, third-party administrators, and UR organizations.
- Purchaser-based PPO sponsors include Blue Cross and Blue Shield plans, commercial insurers, employers, and community groups.

One type of PPO benefit plan is an exclusive provider organization (EPO), a plan established by self-funded employers. In an EPO benefit plan, employees use EPO providers exclusively to receive coverage, in contrast to PPO benefit plans, which merely offer a financial incentive for employees to use the preferred providers. PPO benefit plans are subject to state insurance regulations, unless they are established or purchased by self-funded employers. Such employers consequently can establish EPO benefit plans, agreeing to reimburse only for services of the exclusive providers. For further information on self-funded group plans, see chapter 3 on ERISA.

Sometimes employment-based PPO benefit plans are known as negotiated provider agreements because they allow an employer to negotiate pricing and determine how health care utilization will be monitored.

Most existing PPO benefit plans were formed by hospitals, physicians, and investors, but those sponsored by Blue Cross and Blue Shield plans and commercial insurers represent the largest share of PPO enrollment.

Relatively few employers have organized their own PPO benefit plans, although some employers have created associations that sponsor plans within geographic areas. Employers sometimes use insurance carriers as intermediaries in a PPO arrangement, but more often they purchase a PPO benefit product developed by a Blue Cross and Blue Shield plan or other insurer.

Physicians who provide services through PPOs may have their own practices, belong to small groups that participate in independent practice associations, or belong to multispecialty group practices. A PPO may contract with a combination of these physician practice arrangements and offer subscribers a choice among groups. PPO arrangements usually include both primary care physicians and specialists. In a large metropolitan area, a PPO may have agreements with as many as 10 or 15 hospitals and thousands of physicians.

Incentives

In most cases, employees covered by a PPO benefit plan (subscribers) are free to choose any physician or hospital they wish but are given financial incentives to use the services of preferred providers. These incentives may include expanded benefits and lower costs for certain services. Financial incentives for employees might include no deductible and only minimal copayments, while employees who choose nonparticipating physicians may be required to pay a deductible and larger copayments. For example, subscribers who use a preferred provider may have no deductible and a copayment of only $5 or $10 per office visit, plus extra services such as well-baby care and diabetes testing. Those who use nonparticipating physicians may be subject to a $200 or $500 deductible and/or 20 percent coinsurance and receive no extra coverages.

Differences between HMOs and PPOs

Although HMOs existed 50 years ago, the rapid growth of both HMOs and PPO arrangements has occurred relatively recently. It is important to understand the major differences between them.

- HMOs are organizations that are responsible for the provision of care, while PPO arrangements are contractual relationships between the purchasers and the providers of care.
- HMOs are prepaid systems, while PPO providers operate on a fee-for-service basis.
- HMO members must use the services of HMO physicians and affiliated hospitals to be covered, while PPO benefit plan subscribers generally are not restricted to preferred providers (with the exception of EPOs).
- HMOs must bear the financial risk for their operations, while in most PPOs the purchaser (the insurer, the employer, etc.), rather than the health care provider, bears the risk.

As new variations of PPO arrangements emerge, many are assuming the characteristics of HMOs. For example, risk sharing between provider and purchaser is taking place in some PPOs. Also, some PPOs have begun to require primary care physicians to refer patients only to specific hospitals or specialists.

Managing Costs

The primary cost management option that PPOs offer to subscribers is discounted prices for medical services. While PPOs rely on these discounted prices, they are increasingly adopting other cost management techniques such as UR and quality management.

PPO sponsors may monitor claims, require prior authorization for certain types of treatment, and examine physician case records. Effective UR may also incorporate quality assurance measures. UR is often handled by the PPO health care providers, as is the case with many PPOs sponsored by hospitals, or by using an outside professional peer review organization. Hospitals or physician groups that conduct their own internal reviews are susceptible to the criticism that it is difficult for an organization to police its own behavior.

Employers who establish their own PPO arrangements, as well as Blue Cross and Blue Shield plans and insurance carriers that offer PPO benefit products, often develop their own UR systems to ascertain whether they are receiving cost-efficient services from the providers with whom they contract.

Self-insured employers or insurers who want to reduce their risk of incurring large losses are in many cases able to negotiate risk-sharing agreements with providers. Risk sharing includes splitting costs in catastrophic cases, paying bonuses to health care specialists for keeping costs under certain dollar limits, and setting fees for certain procedures. If the procedure turns out to be more costly, the hospital absorbs the difference.

Provider-based PPOs that accept responsibility for a share of financial risk may establish expenditure targets. If expenditures fall below the target, the savings may go to the physicians or be shared by the physicians and the employer. If expenditures exceed the target, the losses may be shared by the PPO and the employer or absorbed by the PPO, but only up to certain limits.

Legal Issues

There is currently no direct federal legislation pertaining to PPOs.

However, many states regulate PPO benefit plans to varying degrees in such areas as provider selection, rate differentials, provision of emergency care, and reporting and disclosure requirements.

In addition, the Federal Trade Commission has stated that it would consider enforcing antitrust laws against plans that impede or prevent other plans from entering the market. Thus, plans shown to have a significant anticompetitive effect that is not balanced by an equal or greater procompetitive effect may be considered unlawful. For example, antitrust issues could arise if a plan restricted its participating physicians from practicing in other managed care arrangements, thereby making it difficult for other plans to form and compete.

Questions concerning the legal status of PPOs are complicated by the many structural differences among them. However, although PPO arrangements in general are open to legal review, their dramatic growth is expected to continue.

Conclusion

Changes in health care delivery systems present employers with new possibilities for cost management. The rapid growth of PPO arrangements during the last decade suggests that they are finding acceptance among employers and insurers that are searching for alternatives to traditional indemnity plans in an effort to control rising health care costs.

PPOs are seen as having the potential to bring about price competition among providers. They also hold out the promise that they can provide more than discounted prices. However, to ensure both cost-effective and quality care, PPO sponsors must be energetic in searching out efficient and competent providers and vigilant in discouraging excessive or inappropriate treatment by those providers.

Although there is ancedotal evidence of PPOs' ability to hold down health care costs, few scientific studies have been conducted to assess their cost effectiveness. Many PPOs have been in existence for too short a time for conclusive data to be available. Nevertheless, some trends, including the increasing surplus of physicians and hospital beds, favor PPOs' continued growth.

PPO benefit plans may also find greater acceptance by employees because they permit a broader choice of physicians than HMOs and other managed care plans. However, some PPOs are moving closer to the HMO model by using a primary care physician as a so-called gatekeeper who controls referral to specialists and hospitals.

In today's changing medical marketplace, different types of PPO arrangements continue to emerge in response to competition and the search for successful cost management strategies. If studies show that the PPO is a successful strategy for limiting increases in health care costs, its use is likely to continue to grow.

Bibliography

American Association of Preferred Provider Organizations. *Summary of State Legislation in Health and Managed Care: 1993.* Chicago, IL: American Asssociation of Preferred Providers, 1994.

_____. *1994 National Directory of PPOs and PPO Industry Profile.* Tenth edition. Chicago, IL: American Association of Preferred Provider Organizations, 1994.

American Managed Care and Review Association. *1993/95 Managed Health Care Directory.* Washington, DC: American Managed Care and Review Association, 1994.

Dowell, Michael A. "Have PPOs Lost the Right to Choose?" *Business and Health* (April 1994): 100–101.

Foster Higgins. *Foster Higgins National Survey of Employer-Sponsored Health Plans/1994.* New York, NY: Foster Higgins, 1995.

Kang, Sam, and Jim Stumpsel. "PPOs: Moving from Fee-for-Service to Accepting Financial Risk." *Medical Interface* (November 1994): 141–142, 144, 150.

Kertesz, Louise. "PPOs Diversify, Accept Some Risk to Ensure Survival." *Modern Healthcare* (May 1, 1995): 41, 42, 44, 46, 48.

Margolis, Robin Elizabeth. "ERISA Does Not Preempt State Insurance Law Regulating Preferred Provider Organizations." *Managed Care Quarterly* (Autumn 1993): 41–45.

Marion Merrell Dow. *Marion Merrell Dow Managed Care Digest: PPO Edition.* Kansas City, MO: Marion Merrell Dow, 1994.

Poynter, William L. *The Preferred Provider's Handbook.* New York, NY: Brunner/Mazel Publishers, 1994.

"PPOs Are Changing Managed Care." *Employee Benefit Plan Review* (March 1993): 59–60.

"PPOs Have Become a Dominant Force in Health-care Delivery." *Medical Economics* (October 24, 1994): 16.

Rodin, Barbara. "PPO and HMO Performance Factors: Insurance Company Evaluation Criteria." *Managed Care Quarterly* (Winter 1993): 46–52.

Romeo, Nancy C. "Making the PPO Connection: National vs. Regional." *Journal of Health Care Benefits* (January/February 1993): 22–25.

U.S. Department of Labor. Bureau of Labor Statistics. *Employee Benefits in Medium and Large Private Establishments, 1993*. Washington, DC: U.S. Government Printing Office, 1994.

Wagner, Eric R. "Types of Managed Care Organizations." In Peter R. Kongstvedt, *The Managed Health Care Handbook*. Second edition. Gaithersburg, MD: Aspen Publishers, Inc., 1993.

Additional Information

American Association of Preferred Provider Organizations
601 13th St., NW, Suite 370S
Washington, DC, 20005
(202) 347-7600

American Association of Health Plans
1129 20th Street, NW, Suite 600
Washington, DC 20036
(202) 778-3200

25. Managing Health Care Costs

Introduction

Health care spending in the United States has grown rapidly, reaching nearly $884 billion, or 13.9 percent of Gross Domestic Product (GDP), in 1993 and is projected to reach $2.2 trillion, or 17.9 percent of GDP, by 2005 (Burner et al., 1995). This growth is largely a consequence of the rising cost of delivering health care resulting from the introduction of new technology; the expanded scope of covered health benefits (which, by lowering the relative price of health care services to insured individuals, increases demand for them); the rapid expansion of treatment options without concurrent research on their relative efficacy; demographic factors such as the aging of the population; and general price inflation.

In the United States in 1994, about 64 percent of the civilian population under age 65 received health insurance coverage through employment-based plans. Employers' contributions to employment-based health plans and Medicare on behalf of employees and their insured family members have risen dramatically, reaching nearly $263 billion (6.6 percent of compensation) in 1994, up from $12 billion (2.0 percent of compensation) in 1970[1] (U.S. Department of Commerce, 1996).

The use of cost management strategies in health care has become more prevalent as a result of health care cost increases. Employers have made sweeping changes in benefit plans as a whole as well as within the framework of existing health plans. While such measures are designed to contain individual employer spending, they also serve the broader goal of managing the increase in overall health care costs.

Plan design changes that have been adopted by employers can be grouped into three categories:

- Changes that encourage employees to use health care more economically, including the imposition of higher deductibles and coinsurance

---

[1] When calculating health benefit costs as a percentage of total compensation, the number used for total compensation includes all employers that pay wages and salaries. This number includes employers that provide health insurance benefits as well as those employers that do not. It is not possible to separate out only the employers that offer health insurance benefits because no data exist on the number of employers that offer health insurance benefits.

levels for all or for some services covered by a plan and the expansion
of covered services to include less expensive alternatives to inpatient
hospital care.

- Changes that specifically limit the inappropriate use of services, such
as requiring a formal review of hospital utilization, case management,
second opinions, and same day surgery.
- Changes that restructure the delivery and/or financing of health care
services within a plan, including incentives for employees to select
prepaid health plans such as health maintenance organizations
(HMOs) and the establishment of preferred provider organization
(PPO) arrangements, which encourage employees to seek services from
providers who have agreed to accept lower negotiated rates.

Changes most commonly initiated by employers include: imposing or
increasing cost-sharing requirements such as deductibles, coinsurance, and
employee contribution to the premium; utilization review (UR) techniques
such as requiring that tests be performed prior to hospital admission and
second surgical opinions; and managed care plans such as HMOs and PPOs.
Other changes include the use of lower cost alternatives such as ambulatory
surgical care, treatment in extended care facilities, home health and hospice
care, case management, and wellness or health promotion programs. (For
more information on health insurance, HMOs, PPOs, and health promotion
programs, see chapters 19, 23, 24, and 28, respectively).

In addition to these changes within the framework of existing employer
health insurance plans, some employers have initiated a much more sweeping reorganization of their health insurance benefits. Other employers have
more fundamentally reorganized their plans within the framework of
flexible benefit or cafeteria plans. Employers have adopted flexible benefit
plans to induce employees to share more of, and take greater responsibility
for controlling, their health care costs.

Improving Incentives To Use Health Care Economically

Plan design changes that encourage employees to use health care
services more economically include increasing employee cost sharing and
redesigning service coverage under the plan. Increased cost sharing required by a plan involves the portion of the cost—copayment, deductible, or
coinsurance[2] —paid by the employee for services actually used. Cost sharing
under employer group plans may be increased by raising copayments,

deductibles, and/or coinsurance levels for all or some services covered by a plan or by raising employee contributions to the premium for their own or their dependents' coverage.

Because changes in the level of cost sharing, and sometimes the range of covered services, reduce real compensation levels by raising employees' out-of-pocket health care costs, they have generally been resisted by employees, particularly by those with collectively bargained health plans. Therefore, it is important for employers to effectively communicate to employees the reasons for changes in their health plans and for employees to fully understand their role in the health care partnership: that of being efficient consumers of health care. This may be accomplished through in-house newsletters and other literature, audio-visual presentations, meetings, telephone hotlines, and benefit summaries that identify the health coverage component of an employee's annual total compensation.

Despite some employee resistance to greater cost sharing, many employers report having raised the deductible or copayment provisions of their group health plans in recent years. As a result, first dollar coverage for inpatient hospital expenses has become much less common.[3] First dollar coverage pays initial expenses (a specified amount, depending on the plan) for hospital care, with no deductible or coinsurance provisions on the first dollar of care delivered.

Changes in the range of services covered by a plan may redirect patient use of health care services toward less expensive substitutes for inpatient hospital care. For example, some employers have expanded the range of group health plans to include coverage for home health care services; hospice services; and outpatient hospital care, including preadmission testing, outpatient surgery, or surgery performed in a free-standing surgical center. Coverage of these services is aimed at providing the most appropri-

---

[2] Copayment refers to a flat payment (e.g., $10 per office visit). A deductible is a fixed amount for insured medical services, usually expressed in dollars, that must be paid by the beneficiary before a health insurance plan begins to pay for any costs. Coinsurance refers to a percentage of payment (e.g., 20 percent of total covered expenses).

[3] Despite the growth of many cost-sharing provisions, studies indicate that, in the aggregate, individuals are paying a smaller percentage of total health care costs. In 1960, 69 percent of private health care expenditures were paid for out-of-pocket, and 31 percent were paid for by private health insurance. In 1995, only 32 percent of private health care expenditures were paid out-of-pocket, compared with 60 percent paid for by private insurance.

ate care in the most appropriate setting and discouraging the unnecessary use of inappropriate inpatient hospital care or prolonged hospital stays.

Cost-sharing features are intended to reduce health plan expenditures, encourage workers to be cost conscious, and reduce administrative expenses; however, the evidence of their effectiveness is inconclusive. Some proponents of cost sharing have argued that it gives the patient an incentive to shop around for the lowest cost health care provider or to forgo care when it is not absolutely necessary. Others argue that, when cost sharing is increased, some of the care forgone by employees may include preventive or other necessary care, the lack of which may result in higher long-term costs.

Restricting Inappropriate Use of Benefits

Another technique for managing employer health care costs is to intervene in the health care utilization decision in order to limit the inappropriate use of certain benefits under the plan. This is most commonly done through UR programs. UR programs are used on a case-by-case basis to monitor the progress and appropriateness of care. Ninety-five percent of fee-for-service health plans now include UR programs and can be considered managed indemnity plans. Consequently, a UR industry has developed to provide UR services. Besides large national insurers, approximately 200 national and local companies offer only UR services (Fronstin, 1994). These companies provide numerous UR strategies, including preadmission certification, concurrent review, retrospective review, and mandatory second opinion. Preadmission certification requires that patients receive prior authorization for certain procedures, nonemergency hospital admissions, and elective surgery or the insurer may not pay for the full cost of care. Under concurrent review, care is monitored as it is provided and may include the prior determination of the length of hospital stays and the scope of the treatment during the stay. Under retrospective review, care is reviewed after it is given. This strategy is used primarily by insurers to address the UR of future cases. It is also used to give an incentive to providers to carefully assess the amount of care provided in order to avoid the potential of a retroactive denial of payment. Under mandatory second opinion, the patient must receive a second opinion about the appropriateness of a proposed treatment from a health care provider other than the one making the original recommendation.

UR appears to reduce inpatient charges, but there is some evidence suggesting that treatment is shifted to an outpatient basis. As a result, UR is now being extended to the outpatient setting and over time may lead to reductions in outpatient utilization rates. Previous Employee Benefit Research Institute studies have found the effectiveness of UR in reducing health care costs varies by region. Houston employers found that inpatient charges were significantly lower in plans with UR, but outpatient charges were significantly greater in plans with it. UR did not affect total plan costs among Rhode Island employers. Among Los Angeles employers, UR had the effect of decreasing total plan costs by decreasing total charges per admission, without lowering the admission rate. UR was also associated with lower outpatient costs in Los Angeles (Custer, 1991).

Restructuring Service Delivery

The health care delivery system has changed in recent years in response to health care cost inflation. One of the most notable changes is the expansion of a managed care industry. Prepaid group practices have been in existence since the 19th century in the mining and lumbering industries but did not become a major alternative to traditional fee-for-service health plans until the Health Maintenance Organization Act of 1973, which encouraged the growth of HMOs. Many individuals typically view HMOs as the only type of managed care arrangement. However, managed care can be thought of as any type of intervention in the provision of health care services or reimbursement of health care providers that is intended to ensure that the most appropriate care is provided in the most appropriate setting. In general, managed care arrangements range from fully integrated models, such as staff and group model HMOs, which require members to receive care from a panel of "in-house" providers, to less restrictive arrangements such as independent practice association (IPAs), which contract with groups of independent providers, PPOs, and point-of-service (POS) plans (chart 25.1) . Traditional indemnity plans have also begun to incorporate features of managed care into their plans. Nearly 95 percent of employees in traditional fee-for-service plans were subject to some form of UR. Basically, managed care uses groups or networks of providers, has explicit criteria for selecting primary care providers, and/or subjects providers to UR. Participants in managed care plans are given financial incentives to use the network-based health care providers.

The most recent form of a managed care plan to evolve is the physician/hospital organization (PHO), an innovation developed by the providers of medical services. PHOs are providers' response to new competitive pres-

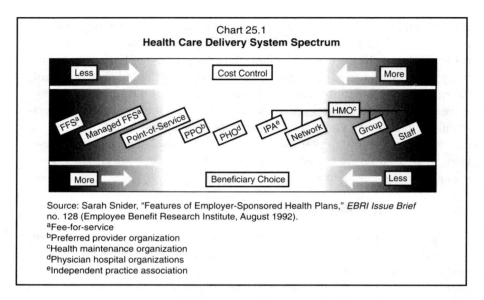

Chart 25.1
Health Care Delivery System Spectrum

Less → Cost Control ← More

FFSa Managed FFSa Point-of-Service PPOb PHOd IPAe Network HMOc Group Staff

More → Beneficiary Choice ← Less

Source: Sarah Snider, "Features of Employer-Sponsored Health Plans," *EBRI Issue Brief* no. 128 (Employee Benefit Research Institute, August 1992).
aFee-for-service
bPreferred provider organization
cHealth maintenance organization
dPhysician hospital organizations
eIndependent practice association

sures from employers and other payers of medical services. Under a PHO arrangement, physicians and hospitals form group practice arrangements to contract directly with employers to provide services based on customized benefit packages. These arrangements can include a full range of medical services, e.g., in/out patient services and prescription drugs. These arrangements also take on a range of risk-bearing arrangements—some are fully capitated, while others simply provide services to self-funded employers. As the health care delivery system evolves, some analysts believe that PHOs are a transitional stage in the development of a more integrated health delivery system.

Adopting Flexible Benefit Plans

A flexible benefit or cafeteria plan is an employee benefit plan that gives employees some choice among cash or nontaxable benefits provided by an employer. Internal Revenue Code (IRC) sec. 125, created by the Revenue Act of 1978, formally introduced tax-qualified flexible benefit plans. Flexible benefit plans typically include two or more health plans. They may also include, for example, dental coverage, group life insurance, dependent care benefits, and a cash account—sometimes called a reimbursement account or flexible spending account (FSA)—from which employees may be reimbursed on a pretax basis for out-of-pocket health care or dependent care expenditures.

Employer goals in establishing a flexible benefit program are complex. They often include:

- managing the cost of group health benefits by inducing employees to share more of the health care costs covered by the plan;
- offering employees new, specialized benefits tailored to the needs of individuals in a demographically changing work force, without substantially raising total benefit costs;
- enhancing employee perceptions of the value of employment-based benefits; and
- limiting employer contributions to a defined dollar amount.

From the employee's perspective, cafeteria plans include both advantages and disadvantages. A cafeteria plan gives each individual the opportunity to determine (within employer-defined limits) the proportion of his or her total compensation that will be allocated to wages versus benefits. Thus, employees may be able to make their total compensation more valuable by choosing their desired combination of pay and benefits. However, implementation of a cafeteria plan may require that employees absorb most or all of health care cost increases because this type of plan allows employers to use a defined contribution approach to health benefits. Under this approach, employers can determine the level of funding for the flexible program annually rather than providing the same level of benefits coverage regardless of cost increases. This approach is often used in funding retirement plans and has the advantage of shifting part or all of cost increases to employees. Employers can use this approach to limit rising health care expenditures, although these savings may come at the employees' expense.

Flexible Spending Accounts—Employers may offer premium conversion options and FSAs in order to provide employees with a simple and inexpensive way of paying for health care premiums, uncovered dependent care expenses, and/or uncovered health care expenses. FSAs are usually funded through employee pretax contributions, which are designated prior to the plan year and withheld in equal amounts from the employee's paycheck. When employees incur expenses, they are reimbursed with pretax dollars. Some employers also contribute to these accounts. There is no statutory limit on annual contributions to medical care FSAs.[4] An individual

---

[4] Dependent care accounts have a legal contribution limit of $5,000.

benefit or the plan itself may have established contribution limits. In practice, most employers set an upper limit. Employees must be careful when designating annual contributions because unused portions are forfeitable at the end of the plan year. FSA participants can increase their disposable income because pretax salary contributions are exempt from both federal income tax and Social Security (FICA) tax.[5]

Employers can also realize tax savings from employees' salary reduction contributions to an FSA because they are not required to pay FICA tax on employee salary reduction contributions to these accounts. The tax savings realized through an FSA may be used to at least partially offset the cost of plan administration.

Despite legal restrictions on the use of flexible benefits plans, these plans offer employers an opportunity to reduce their benefit costs and their overall expenditures for health coverage and other benefit programs. Employers are able to fix their contribution to health insurance benefits—either absolutely or as a percentage of a lower cost health insurance option—rather than automatically raise their contribution as plan costs rise. With or without a FSA, a flexible benefits plan gives employees an incentive to opt for lower cost health coverage: choosing a more generous, and more costly, health insurance plan reduces the employee's ability to elect alternative benefits (including pretax savings) or higher cash earnings.

Adjusting the price of alternative health insurance plans offered in a flexible benefits program is important to its success in managing health insurance costs. Providing more than one health plan runs the risk of "adverse selection" by employees. That is, employees who foresee few medical needs during the year are most likely to choose a low-cost, less generous health insurance plan. Employees remaining in the most generous—and most costly—health insurance plan are likely to have greater health care costs, on average, than those who choose a less generous health plan. The average cost of the most generous plan is likely to rise much faster than the average cost of the least generous plan. Therefore, there is a need to adjust or "reprice" the health plans to reflect the cost history subsequent to the initial offering of alternative plans. (For more information on this issue, see chapter 31 on flexible benefits plans).

---

[5] Contributions are excluded from state income taxes in states with an income tax except in the Commonwealth of Pennsylvania as of 1995.

Employer Health Care Coalitions and Cooperatives

Not only have networks of providers taken steps to manage health care costs, but employers have also been able to affect the evolution of the managed care system by using their bargaining power to effectively reduce health care expenditures. Coalitions have been formed for this purpose in Cedar Rapids, IA; Chicago, IL; Cincinnati, OH; Cleveland, OH; Denver, CO; Houston, TX; Kingsport, TN; Memphis, TN; Minneapolis, MN; and other cities. The activities of these coalitions have varied greatly but include the selection of preferred providers on the basis of efficiency, assistance in the purchase of cardiovascular care, the provision of mental health and substance abuse programs at reduced rates, the enactment of healthy lifestyle programs for adults and children, and the provision of small business insurance options.

Health coalitions are concerned as much with maintaining quality standards as with managing costs. For example, the major goal of the Business Health Care Action Group in Minneapolis, MN, is to cut back on the use of specialists and increase the use of primary care physicians; however, the coalition will do business only with providers that maintain high standards of quality.

These coalitions are successful in reducing expenditures on health care because they create a competitive market, with sound business principles such as volume purchasing and competitive bidding. It is also possible that the groups with the highest costs, i.e., higher risk groups, are most likely to form coalitions. As long as pro-competitive benefits accrue to consumers, anti-trust legislation supports the formation of health care coalitions. The Federal Trade Commission and the Justice Department believe that it is economically efficient for providers of health care to share information on outcomes and costs with purchasers of health care in order to influence the terms of any agreement between them. These laws are based on the economic principle that increased competition in the health care industry should result in the production of more health care services and goods at a lower price. Pro-competitive benefits will also accrue to consumers of health care in the form of higher quality services.

Conclusion

Public and private efforts to manage health care costs more effectively are likely to continue to accelerate changes in the health care delivery and financing system. Overall, health care cost inflation has slowed recently, reaching a 21-year low at 4.1 percent in 1995. This is likely in large part to be a result of three underlying factors: managed care is reducing costs; overall inflation in the economy fell to 2.5 percent in 1995, the lowest increase in 28 years except for 1986; and the threat of health care reform accelerated cost saving changes designed to make health care reform appear unnecessary. As efforts to manage health care costs continue, we are likely to see a continued movement of Americans into managed care arrangements, an increase in the number of physicians forming networks, a reduction in the number of insurers, an increase in the number of employers joining coalitions to purchase health care services for their employees, and a health care system that is generally more concentrated and vertically integrated.

Bibliography

Boland, Peter. *Making Managed Healthcare Work: A Practical Guide to Strategies and Solutions.* Gaithersburg, MD: Aspen Publishers, Inc., 1993.

Burner, Sally, et al. "Projections of the National Health Expenditures 1994–2005." *Health Care Financing Review* (Summer 1995).

Custer, William. "Health Reform: Examining the Alternatives." *EBRI Issue Brief* no.147 (Employee Benefit Research Institute, March 1994).

————. "Issues in Health Care Cost Management." *EBRI Issue Brief* no. 139 (Employee Benefit Research Institute, September 1991).

————"Measuring the Quality of Health Care." *EBRI Issue Brief* no. 159 (Employee Benefit Research Institute, March 1995).

Employee Benefit Research Institute. "The Changing Health Care Delivery System: An EBRI/ERF Policy Forum." *EBRI Special Report* SR-21/*Issue Brief* no. 148 (Employee Benefit Research Institute, April 1994).

————. *EBRI Databook on Employee Benefits.* Third edition. Washington, DC: Employee Benefit Research Institute, 1995.

————. "The Future of Employment-Based Health Benefits," *EBRI Special Report* SR-29/*Issue Brief* no. 161 (Employee Benefit Research Institute, May 1995).

————. "Making Choices: Rationing in the U.S. Health System." *EBRI Special Report* SR-17/*Issue Brief* no. 136 (Employee Benefit Research Institute, 1993).

Foster Higgins. *Foster Higgins National Survey of Employer-Sponsored Health Plans / 1995* New York, NY: Foster Higgins, 1996.

Fronstin, Paul. "The Effectiveness of Health Care Cost Strategies: A Review of the Evidence." *EBRI Issue Brief* no. 154 (Employee Benefit Research Institute, October 1994).

Fronstin, Paul and Edina Rheem. "Sources of Health Insurance and Characteristics of the Uninsured: Analysis of the March 1995 Current Population Survey." *EBRI Issue Brief* no. 170 (Employee Benefit Research Institute, February 1996).

Levit, Katharine R., et al. "National Health Expenditures, 1993." *Health Care Financing Review* (Fall 1994): 249–294.

Morrisey, Michael A. "Hospital Pricing: Cost Shifting and Competition." *EBRI Issue Brief* no. 137 (Employee Benefit Research Institute, May 1993).

Panel Publishers, Inc. *Driving Down Health Care Costs, Strategies and Solutions 1995.* New York, NY: Aspen Publishers, Inc., 1995.

Snider, Sarah. "Features of Employer-Sponsored Health Plans." *EBRI Issue Brief* no. 128 (Employee Benefit Research Institute, August 1992).

U.S. Department of Commerce. Bureau of Economic Analysis. *The National Income and Product Accounts of the United States: Statistical Supplement, 1959–1988.* Vol. 2. Washington, DC: U.S. Government Printing Office, 1992.

_____. *Survey of Current Business, Jan. / Feb. 1996.* Washington, DC: U.S. Government Printing Office, 1996.

U.S. Department of Labor. Bureau of Labor Statistics. *Employee Benefits in Medium and Large Private Establishments, 1993.* Washington, DC: U.S. Government Printing Office, 1994.

_____. *Employee Benefits in Small Private Establishments, 1992.* Washington, DC: U.S. Government Printing Office, 1994.

_____. *Employee Benefits in State and Local Governments, 1992.* Washington, DC: U.S. Government Printing Office, 1994.

Additional Information

American Association
of Health Plans
1129 20th Street, NW, Suite 600
Washington, DC 20036
(202) 778-3200

International Foundation of
Employee Benefit Plans
P.O. Box 69
18700 West Bluemound Road
Brookfield, WI 53008-0069
(414) 786-6700

26. Mental Health and Substance Abuse Benefits

Introduction

The cost of treating mental illness and substance abuse is an issue of growing concern to employers and society because it has been increasing more rapidly than the cost of other types of health care. However, the consequences of lack of treatment for these problems may also be costly. The National Institute of Mental Health estimates that one in three American adults will experience at least one acute mental disorder or chemical dependency problem at some time in his or her life. Yet only about 20 percent of those in need seek any mental health services. The total cost of mental illness and substance abuse due to lost productivity, property damage, and treatment is estimated to have been as high as $273 million in 1988. Mental health problems have been shown to be an important factor in the decision to retire and a factor in worker productivity. Moreover, there is some evidence that the diagnosis and treatment of mental health problems lower the costs of other types of health care. However, the nature of mental health care makes it difficult to insure and makes the efficacy of cost management techniques problematic. Employers and society face the difficult question of how to finance appropriate treatment without incurring unmanageable increases in health care costs.

Mental Health Care Costs

In 1994, employers spent an average of $209 per employee in an indemnity plan and $264 per employee in a preferred provider organization (PPO) for behavioral health care benefits. Employers are finding the costs of an episode of mental health care to be two to three times the cost of an episode of care for other types of ailments. Mental health care costs accounted for about 4 percent of employers' total health care expenditures in 1995.[1] Moreover, the costs of mental health care and substance abuse treatment for

---

[1] Mental health and substance abuse benefits have declined as a percentage of employers' total health plan costs from 6 percent in 1993 to 4 percent in 1995. Part of the reason for this decline is that carve-out mental health plans are not included in the total health care plan calculation.

employees' dependents are often greater than those for the employees themselves. Corporate Health Strategies has found that the average expense per hospital admission for mental disorders is $9,400 for an employee or an employee's spouse but more than $18,000 for other dependents. Likewise, a substance abuse treatment costs between one-third and one-half more for dependents than for employees and their spouses. This difference is due in part to the screening effect of employment. Individuals who are able to obtain and retain employment are less likely to have serious mental illnesses than others. No such screening exists for employees' dependents.

The Market for Mental Health Care

Three factors have shaped the market for mental health care and substance abuse treatment: the subjectivity in the demand for mental health care, the intensity of treatment, and the uncertainty in the efficacy of treatment. These factors have led to a large variation in the cost of care; limits on the applicability of peer review as a cost management technique; an increase in the number and types of providers; and reduced responsiveness of the demand for mental health care to out-of-pocket costs, in terms of both the demand for care and the site of care.

Subjectivity of Treatment—The failure of the market for health care services lies in the inability of consumers of health care to evaluate the quality of the services they purchase. The market for mental health care and substance abuse treatment suffers from these defects more than the market for other forms of health care. The nature of mental illness makes it difficult for insurers to develop actuarial estimates of the risk associated with extending coverage for mental health care. The subjectivity in diagnosis, uncertainty concerning the efficacy of treatment, and indefinite determination of recovery result in large variations in the costs of an episode of care. Employers often find that their highest health expenses are for cases involving mental health.

Intensity of Treatment—Treatment for mental illness and substance abuse differs from that for other ailments in a number of ways that have profound implications for the financing and delivery of mental health care. First, personal assessment of the need for treatment is obviously much different for mental health care than for other types of health care. Individuals may be unaware or deny that they need treatment, or they may view treatment as a luxury even when they feel it is needed.

Second, the treatment of mental illness and substance abuse is, in most cases, much more intensive than the treatment of other illnesses, especially in an outpatient setting. On average, episodes involve 12 visits and last 18 weeks. This intensity of treatment means that individual episodes of care are likely to be costly in relation to other types of care.

Appropriateness of Treatment—The appropriateness and efficacy of competing treatments have not been well established. Individuals seeking treatment must choose among several types of providers and settings and among more than 150 types of therapies, with little information about the efficacy of treatment or the quality of care. While there is evidence that mental health treatment, in general, and individual therapies, in particular, are effective, little conclusive evidence exists of the relative effectiveness of various therapies.

Employer Plan Design

When employers began to provide health insurance benefits to their employees, they extended coverage to include mental health benefits under the same terms as other health care services. They quickly found that, while only a small proportion of the beneficiaries used mental health care services, the costs associated with this care were very high. As a result, employers placed limits on mental health benefits relative to other health benefits in an attempt to make the insurance risk more manageable.

In 1993, while 98 percent of participants in a medical plan had inpatient hospital coverage for mental health care, only 14 percent had coverage that was the same as that for other illness. For outpatient care, only 3 percent had equivalent coverage. A lower percentage of participants had coverage for substance abuse than had coverage for mental health care. Ninety-eight percent of medical plan participants were covered for inpatient detoxification for alcohol and drug abuse in 1993, but only 28 percent to 29 percent of these participants had coverage that was the same as for other illnesses. Coverage for inpatient rehabilitation and outpatient care for alcohol and drug abuse was lower, extending to approximately 80 percent of medical plan participants, with only 7 percent to 8 percent having coverage equivalent to that for other illnesses.

Federal legislation adopted in 1996 requires all health plans to offer identical lifetime and annual limits for mental and physical health benefits. However, this legislation is somewhat limited in scope. It does not take effect until January 1, 1998. It exempts employers with 50 or fewer workers and also exempts health plans that experience premium increases of

1 percent or more. It does not apply to substance abuse or chemical dependency treatment. Most significantly, it does not require plans to offer mental health benefits and does not require mental health benefits to be offered under the same terms and conditions that apply to physical health care. In other words, a health plan may offer no mental health benefits or it may apply different cost-sharing requirements.

Employee Assistance Programs and Carve-Outs of Mental Health/Substance Abuse Benefits

Realizing that placing limits on allowable reimbursement for mental health care services may hinder employees' ability to receive adequate care, some employers have carved out their mental health and substance abuse benefits. This carve-out generally involves contracting with a managed care network that specializes in these services. Managed mental health care networks function differently from medical care networks. Because an individual in need of mental health care services may be reluctant to admit that he or she needs them, the managed care network secures and coordinates these services, making access easier. Twenty percent of employers carved out their mental health and substance abuse benefits in 1995, up from 7 percent in 1993 (Foster Higgins, 1996).

Another way to facilitate an employee's access to mental health care services is through an employee assistance program (EAP). EAPs are generally counseling services directed toward acute problems that affect job performance, such as drug and alcohol abuse and emotional and financial problems. The EAP can function as a gatekeeper and guide to the managed care network. (For further information on EAPs, see chapter 29.)

Conclusion

One problem with behavioral health care is that its benefits are difficult to quantify, while its costs are all too obvious. The evidence is clear that any mental health care is better then none, but there has been little research assessing the relative merits of the numerous treatments available for each symptom of mental illness. A number of studies show that the specific therapy chosen is much less important in determining effectiveness than the characteristics of the therapist and the context of the treatment.

Because of the social stigma attached to mental health care and the subjectivity inherent in the patient's assessment of the need for this care, the demand for it is much more price sensitive than that for other forms of health care. The price sensitivity is apparent not only in the overall demand for care but also in the demand for specific providers and sites of care.

Bibliography

Caldwell, Bernice. "Focus on Behavioral Benefits." *Employee Benefit Plan Review* (December 1995): 38–39.

Custer, Bill. "Issues in Mental Health Care." *EBRI Issue Brief* no. 99 (Employee Benefit Research Institute, February 1990).

Foster Higgins. *Foster Higgins National Survey of Employer-Sponsored Health Plans: Report 1995*. New York, NY: Foster Higgins, 1996.

The George Washington University. "Managed Care Carveouts for Mental Health and Substance Abuse: Private Sector Strategies in Public Programs." National Health Policy Forum. *Issue Brief* no. 681 (November 1995).

Glazer, William M., and Nancy N. Ball. *Mental Health Benefits: A Purchaser's Guide*. Brookfield, WI: International Foundation of Employee Benefit Plans, 1993.

Lueger, Robert J. *Assessing Quality in Outpatient Psychotherapy: Implications for Designing and Selecting Cost-Efficient Mental Health Care Benefits*. Brookfield, WI: International Foundation of Employee Benefit Plans, 1993.

Mechanic, David, Mark Schlesinger, and Donna D. McAlpine. "Management of Mental Health and Substance Abuse Services: State of the Art and Early Results." *The Milbank Quarterly*. Vol. 73, no. 1 (1995): 19–55.

"Mental Health: In the Age of Managed Care." Special Issue. *Health Affairs* (Fall 1995).

National Association of Private Psychiatric Hospitals. *Minding America's Mental Health: Trends in Mental Health Coverage*. Washington, DC: National Association of Private Psychiatric Hospitals, 1991.

National Association of Psychiatric Health Systems. *Trends in Psychiatric Health Systems: 1995 Annual Survey: Final Report*. Washington, DC: National Association of Psychiatric Health Systems, 1995.

Additional Information

The George Washington University
Intergovernmental Health Policy Project
2021 K Street, NW, Suite 800
Washington, DC 20006
(202) 872-1445

International Foundation of Employee Benefit Programs
P.O. Box 69
18700 W. Bluemound Road
Brookfield, WI 53008
(414) 786-6700

National Association of Psychiatric Health Systems
1319 F Street, NW Suite 1000
Washington, DC 20004
(202) 393-6700

27. Retiree Health Insurance

Introduction

Retiree health benefits were originally offered on a very limited basis in the late 1940s and 1950s. The number of employers offering these benefits expanded in the late 1960s in conjunction with the creation of the Medicare program. The benefits were provided as part of the health plan for active workers, generally without a separate premium structure or separate accounting. In subsequent years, the changing demographics of the work force, coupled with increasing life spans and rising health care costs, left many employers with higher retiree-to-active-worker ratios, increasing the costs and liabilities of retiree medical benefits. In 1989, the Financial Accounting Standards Board issued Statement No. 106 (FAS 106), which required companies to account for these benefits and report liabilities for the future value of all promised benefits on their corporate balance sheets, beginning in December 1992. For the first time, the true cost of the benefits was understood (Employee Benefit Research Institute, 1989). In response to these cost pressures, some employers have eliminated retiree health benefits, and others continue to reevaluate them. Currently, employers need to consider the evolution of Medicare when shifting costs to retirees.

Retiree Health Participation and Cost

Among workers aged 45 and over whose employer offered a health care plan in 1993, 41.4 percent worked for an employer that offered a health plan in retirement (Yakoboski et al., 1994). Seventeen percent of workers whose employer offered a retiree health plan had coverage available until age 65. The average annual cost per retiree among firms with 500 or more employees in 1995 was $3,131, compared with the average cost for an active employee of $3,795 (Foster Higgins, 1996). The average cost for a retiree under age 65 was $5,242; for a retiree aged 65 and over (the Medicare eligible group), the average cost was $1,803.

Retiree Health Benefits Design

There are two basic designs for retiree health benefit plans: one for plans covering retirees under age 65 and one covering retirees aged 65 and over. The reason for this age distinction is that eligibility for the Medicare program begins at age 65. For retirees under age 65, the benefit plan is usually a continuation of the coverage they received while working. For retirees aged 65 and over, the benefit plan is coordinated with Medicare.

Medicare—The Medicare program is the critical component of any employment-based retiree health benefit plan. Medicare is the primary payer for medical services for all enrollees. All employer plans that extend health insurance coverage to retirees aged 65 and over are coordinated with Medicare.

Medicare is composed of two parts. Part A covers hospital and post-hospital skilled nursing care facility services, and Part B covers physician and outpatient services and medical devices. Both parts cover home health care services. The following discussion highlights some of the services that Medicare does not cover and Medicare's deductibles and copayments. (For a detailed discussion of participation, eligibility, plan design, and financing, see chapter 2 on Social Security and Medicare.)

The most important medical service for the elderly not covered by Medicare is maintenance prescription drugs, i.e., medications used to treat a chronic ailment such as insulin for diabetes. (Prescription drugs that are given to hospitalized patients are covered by Medicare.) Another important service to the elderly not covered by Medicare is long-term care. Long-term care includes nonmedical services, such as help with activities of daily living, that may nevertheless require the assistance of a medical professional. Both prescription drugs and long-term care can be expensive. Prescription drugs, for example, represent one of the fastest growing components of health care costs. The elderly are usually large users of both services.

Medicare's deductibles and copayments can become quiet expensive. For a hospital stay of up to 60 days, the deductible is $736 in 1996. For hospital stays of 61–90 days, the deductible is $184 per day (a maximum of $5,520) in 1996, and for stays of 91–150 days, it is $368 per day (a maximum of $22,080) in 1996. Medicare does not cover hospital stays beyond 150 days. For outpatient and physician services, Medicare requires a $100 deductible and a 20 percent copayment. Medicare calculates the use of its benefits in benefit periods and reserve days. The benefit period is the block of time used to determine how much of a deductible and/or copayment the beneficiary owes. It begins on the day a beneficiary enters the hospital and ends when he or she has been out of the hospital for 60 consecutive days. For example, if a beneficiary enters the hospital on November 10, 1996, and is released on November 25, 1996, he or she is liable for $736. If the beneficiary is readmitted to the hospital on December 20, 1996 and released on December 26, 1996, he or she does not have to pay another $736. The beneficiary is liable to pay the deductible per benefit period, not per admission.

Integration with Medicare—Because Medicare does not cover some vital medical services and the copayments, and deductibles can become quite expensive, a continuation of health benefits into retirement can be a great financial bonus to a retiree. Employers use various methods to integrate their retiree health plans for retirees aged 65 and over with Medicare. Some of the more common methods are:

- *Medicare carve-out*—used by 40 percent of employers that offered health insurance to Medicare eligible retirees in 1994. With this method, Medicare's payment is subtracted from the employer plan's normal benefit.
- *Exclusion or nonduplication*—used by 21 percent of employers in 1994. With this method, Medicare benefits are deducted from a covered expense before normal employer plan benefits are calculated.
- *Medigap*—used by 21 percent of employers in 1994. With this method, the employer plan pays for services not covered by Medicare (Foster Higgins, 1995).

Medicare HMOs—The Medicare program is under increasing financial strain. According to the Social Security board of trustees' report for 1995, the Medicare trust fund is expected to be bankrupt in 2001. In an attempt to slow the growth of Medicare spending, the federal government has introduced three types of HMOs for Medicare recipients: risk HMOs, cost HMOs, and health care prepayment plans (HCPPs). These HMOs are also proving beneficial to employers by reducing an employer's overall FAS 106 retiree health liability. (For a further discussion of FAS 106, see the following section.)

- Risk HMOs completely replace Medicare Parts A and B. The HMO agrees to accept a fixed monthly capitated amount, paid by the Health Care Financing Administration, set at 95 percent of the adjusted average per capita cost of treating a Medicare enrollee in a traditional fee-for-service setting, adjusted for age, sex, institutional status, and county of residence. Risk HMOs offer all Medicare services and usually offer expanded benefit packages, precluding the need for individual Medigap policies or employer retiree health plans for beneficiaries aged 65 and over. Enrollees must receive their care from network providers, except for emergency situations. Risk HMO enrollees are not liable for any of Medicare's deductibles or copayments. The risk

HMO assumes all financial risk for providing care to the enrollees. As of June 1995, there were 164 risk HMOs in operation, serving 2,674,095 Medicare enrollees.

- Cost HMOs offer the same services that Medicare Parts A and B cover. Cost HMOs are paid on a monthly interim per capita rate based on the HMO's operating budget and enrollment forecasts. Enrollees may receive care from providers outside of the network but are then liable for all of the deductibles and copayments Medicare normally charges. The cost HMO is not at financial risk for providing care to the enrollees. As of June 1995, there were 30 cost HMOs operating, serving 180,989 Medicare enrollees.

- HCPPs operate similarly to cost HMOs but are not subject to the same regulatory oversight for composition of the provider network and quality of care delivered as risk and cost HMOs. HCPPs are not at financial risk for providing care to the enrollees (Marlowe, 1995). As of June 1995, there were 56 HCPPs operating, serving 549,078 Medicare enrollees.

Medicare HMOs are the most recent cost-saving technique implemented by Congress to slow the Medicare program's expenditure growth rate. However, growth in expenditures continues to outpace increases in revenue. As the Medicare Part A trust fund approaches insolvency, members of Congress have been unable to agree on a comprehensive strategy for long-term Medicare reform. Competing Republican and Democratic budget proposals have differed in how much they would cut spending growth. In addition, there are fundamental disagreements over the increased use of managed care, medical savings accounts, increased Part B premiums, and a number of other issues. A sweeping redesign of the Medicare program is not likely to occur until the program is closer to bankruptcy.

FAS 106

In addition to the proposed changes in Medicare, employers are faced with FAS 106, "Employers' Accounting for Postretirement Benefits Other Than Pensions," which requires companies to record unfunded retiree health liabilities explicitly on their financial statements, effective for fiscal years beginning after December 15, 1992. Companies may elect to recognize the "transition obligation" immediately and take a one-time charge against earnings on their financial statements, or they may amortize the costs over a 20-year period or over a period representing the future service to the participants. FAS 106 applies to current and future retirees, their beneficiaries, and qualified dependents. The U.S. General Accounting Office estimated employer retiree health liabilities to be $412 billion in 1993 (U.S. General Accounting Office, 1993). FAS 106 has forced employers to confront the issue of funding for their retiree health plans.

Prefunding the retiree health liability is one option open to employers, with some tax advantages and limitations. Funds must be segregated and restricted (usually in a trust) to be used as an asset against the FAS 106 liability. Vehicles that can be used for this purpose include 501(c)(9) trusts, or voluntary employees' beneficiary associations (VEBAs), and 401(h) plans. Alternatively, some plans can be used to help employers and employees set aside monies to help plan for the purchase of retiree health insurance, although these funds are not specifically reserved for this purpose. Such plans include 401(k) plans, corporate-owned life insurance, and employee stock ownership plans. Not all are tax-deductible means of funding or setting money aside, and each has specific limits. Table 27.1 outlines these differences.

Because of the limited tax preferences of the available funding vehicles, employers are looking to reduce their FAS 106 liability by redesigning their

Table 27.1
Funding Vehicles for Postretirement Medical Benefits
(Those Specifically in Tax Law and Examples of Other Arrangements)

	Deductible Contributions	Limited Contributions	Tax-Exempt Earnings for Company	Benefits Excludable from Retiree Tax	Benefit Security for Retirees	Applies as Financial Accounting Standards Board Asset
401(h)	●	●	●	●	●	●
501(c)(9) (Voluntary Employee Benefit Associations)	●	●	◖	●	●	●
401(k)	●	●	●	○	○	○
Corporate-Owned Life Insurance	○	○	●	○	◖	○
Employee Stock Ownership Plan	●	●	●	○	○	○

Source: Employee Benefit Research Institute. ● Applies ◖ Partially Applies ○ Does Not Apply

retiree health benefit plans. As with health plans for active employees, the most common design changes have been increased cost sharing with retirees; increased retiree contribution to the premium (30 percent of employers since 1992); increased deductible, co-insurance; and/or decreases in the lifetime maximum (16 percent of employers since 1992) (Foster Higgins, 1995). A few employers have dropped their retiree health coverage for future retirees.

Any changes that are made to a retiree health benefit plan should be made with great care in order to avoid a class action lawsuit. Any ambiguity in plan documents can be interpreted in favor of retirees.

Conclusion

The future of retiree health benefits is likely to be tied to health care costs. Employers will continue to require more cost sharing from retirees and will enroll more retirees in managed care plans. Few employers will drop their retiree health plan altogether, but the days of free medical care benefits for retirees are gone. The future of retiree health benefit plans is uncertain because these plans will be greatly affected by the future design of the Medicare program, to which they are closely tied.

Bibliography

Brenner, Lynn. "Radical Surgery." *Plan Sponsor* (June 1994): 18–25.

Davis, Jennifer. "Retiree Health Benefits: Issues of Structure, Financing, and Coverage." *EBRI Issue Brief* no. 112 (Employee Benefit Research Institute, March 1991).

Employee Benefit Research Institute. *EBRI Databook on Employee Benefits.* Third edition. Washington, DC: Employee Benefit Research Institute, 1995.

_____ *Retiree Health Benefits: What Is the Promise? An EBRI-ERF Policy Forum.* Washington, DC: Employee Benefit Research Institute, 1989.

_____. "Retirement Security in a Post-FASB Environment." *EBRI Special Report* SR-15/*Issue Brief* no. 124 (Employee Benefit Research Institute, March 1992).

Fronstin, Paul. "Retiree Health Benefits: What the Changes May Mean for Future Benefits." *EBRI Issue Brief* no. 175 (Employee Benefit Research Institute, July 1996).

Foster Higgins. *Foster Higgins National Survey of Employer-Sponsored Health Plans/1995*. New York, NY: Foster Higgins & Company, Inc., 1996.

_____. *Foster Higgins National Survey of Employer-Sponsored Health Plans—Tables 1994*. New York, NY: Foster Higgins & Company, Inc., 1995.

Marlowe, Joseph F., and H. Kathleen Childress. "Medicare Risk HMOs: Careful Consideration Can Yield Rewards." *Employee Benefits Journal* (September 1995): 2–11.

Mazo, Judith F., Anna M. Rappaport, and Sylvester J. Schieber, eds. *Providing Health Care Benefits in Retirement: Ralph H. Blanchard Memorial Endowment Series*. Vol. V. Philadelphia, PA: Wharton School, University of Pennsylvania, 1994.

Snider, Sarah. "Features of Employer-Sponsored Health Plans." *EBRI Issue Brief* no. 128 (Employee Benefit Research Institute, August 1992).

U.S. Government Accounting Office. *Retiree Health Plans: Health Benefits Not Secure Under Employer-based System*. Washington, DC: U.S. Government Printing Office, 1993.

Yakoboski, Paul et al. "Employment-Based Health Benefits: Analysis of the April 1993 Current Population Survey." *EBRI Special Report* SR-24/ *Issue Brief* no. 152 (Employee Benefit Research Institute, August 1994).

Additional Information

American Association of Retired Persons
601 E Street, NW
Washington, DC 20049
(202) 434-2277

The Conference Board
845 Third Avenue
New York, NY 10022-6679
(212) 759-0900

International Foundation of Employee Benefit Plans
18700 West Bluemound Road
Brookfield, WI 53008-0069
(414) 786-6700

28. Health Promotion Programs

Introduction

Employer-sponsored health promotion programs gained prominence in the early 1980s. Originally, these programs focused on physical fitness and often encouraged employees to exercise, eat well, quit smoking, and moderate alcohol consumption. Employers hoped that by initiating these programs they would increase productivity and morale, reduce absenteeism and turnover, and manage health care costs.

Health promotion programs, also called "wellness" or "fitness" programs, have changed considerably over the years. Today, programs are emphasizing prevention of physical and emotional illness by using self-care and targeted strategies to encourage healthier lifestyles. Employers are trying to motivate and educate employees on healthy living as well as provide opportunities for employees to participate in healthy activities. Employee assistance programs (EAPs) are also being used to address the physical and mental health of employees. EAPs are generally counseling services directed toward acute problems that affect job performance, such as drug and alcohol abuse and emotional and financial problems. (For more information on employee assistance programs, see chapter 29.)

It is estimated that 81 percent of companies with 50 or more employees offered at least one health promotion activity in 1992, compared with approximately 66 percent in early 1985 (U.S. Department of Health and Human Services, 1993). In showing concern for employees' physical and mental health, employers might provide information on such problems as substance abuse, smoking, and stress through seminars, classes, or written materials and/or start programs to assist employees in changing patterns of behavior that can lead to poor health.

Health promotion programs are being developed and offered by employers to address a number of issues. According to a 1992 survey of work site health promotion programs, improving employee health is the most frequently cited reason for initiating a health promotion program (41 percent of work sites initiated a program for this reason), followed by reducing employee health insurance costs (27 percent), improving employee morale (17 percent), and responding to employee requests (13 percent) (U.S. Department of Health and Human Services, 1993).

Types of Health Promotion Programs

Health promotion programs range from modest efforts (e.g., the distribution of pamphlets on health issues or the provision of showers or changing facilities for employees who exercise) to individually targeted strategies for intervention and health improvement to major initiatives such as elaborate, well-equipped gymnasiums and a full package of physical fitness activities.

One type of health promotion program—health screening—encourages good health through early detection and intervention for medical problems. Under a group health plan, employers may waive deductibles or copayments for specific screenings. Common screenings include high blood pressure, breast cancer, diabetes, high cholesterol levels, and annual physical examinations. Screenings are sometimes followed by education or counseling on how to reduce identified risks. Other programs involve classes and seminars on such topics as good nutrition and ways to stop smoking, lose weight, and manage stress.

Another type of health promotion program rates the employee's lifestyle and determines the cost of that particular employee's health care based on his or her personal lifestyle choices. An unhealthy lifestyle may include smoking, excessive alcohol consumption, overeating, and not exercising. Based on the belief that employees who participate in such activities have higher health plan claims, employers will use a reward/penalty system that will discourage these unhealthy behaviors.

Some companies have their own exercise facilities for employees (and sometimes for family members as well), with swimming pools, jogging tracks, saunas, racquetball/handball courts, and workout rooms. If they do not have their own facilities, employers sometimes pay a share of an employee's health club membership.

Many companies and unions have initiated one or more of these wellness programs. The most common programs were basic screening for blood pressure and cholesterol (91 percent of companies that initiated a program offered this service), information on nutrition and healthy lifestyles (78 percent), smoking cessation (74 percent), weight loss (67 percent), and health club discounts (41 percent) (William M. Mercer, 1993). Other programs addressed disease prevention, medical self-care materials, and safety.

Planning a Health Promotion Program

Careful planning helps to ensure high levels of employee participation.

This planning should include:
- involving employees at all levels in the planning process,
- tailoring the program to the company and its work force,
- communicating the company's commitment to the program and belief in its importance,
- providing a variety of options and developing incentives for employee participation,
- conducting periodic health assessments for employees to measure progress in achieving goals, and
- evaluating the program.

Employers have adopted a variety of incentives to encourage employee participation. Some employers are encouraging employee participation by allowing employees to use official company time to participate in these programs (72 percent of work sites allow this) and/or allow the use of flex-time (45 percent) (U.S. Department of Health and Human Services, 1993). Others pay a portion of the cost for employees to attend outside clinics to stop smoking or pay a higher percentage of medical expenses for employees who do not smoke or who regularly participate in an exercise program. Others set up competitions among employees, with prizes awarded to winners, or offer bonuses to employees who complete a specified number of hours of exercise.

Health promotion programs provide extra benefit options to employees through on-site or employer-owned fitness facilities, educational pamphlets or videos, and physical examinations. Depending on the program's design, employees may pay a fee for participation in certain activities.

Evaluating Health Promotion Programs

Companies with health promotion programs generally report lower absenteeism rates, lower health care costs, and more productive and satisfied employees. Some companies evaluate their programs by comparing exercise program participants' fitness with that of a control group, in terms of such factors as weight control, smoking cessation, elevated blood pressure, and the number of sick days used. However, in many cases data have not been collected over a long period of time. Some studies suggest that younger employees who are already fit, and who exercised regularly before joining a company program, are the ones most likely to join and remain in employer-sponsored fitness programs.

To make a health promotion program cost effective, an employer must communicate the program to employees, encourage broad participation, and regularly assess the program's effectiveness. Dropout rates can be high unless employers are innovative in their choice of programs and in the incentives they offer employees to participate. Health promotion programs can be valuable in providing early detection of health problems and offering employees the means to reduce the risks from such problems. As employers modify and tailor programs to their employees' needs and desires, the programs' potential to improve productivity and reduce health care costs may increase.

Conclusion

To establish whether health promotion programs can be credited with health care cost savings, employers and researchers must track a large number of employees over a long period of time. Regardless of the results, many employers believe that the mere existence of these programs is beneficial in that they demonstrate employers' concerns for their employees and the value that they place on employees' well-being and good health.

Bibliography

Hewitt Associates. *Health Promotion Initiatives / Managed Health Provided by Major U.S. Employers in 1994*. Lincolnshire, IL: Hewitt Associates, 1995.

Kerber, Beth-Ann. *How Employers Are Saving through Wellness and Fitness Programs*. Wall Township, NJ: American Business Publishing, 1994.

O'Donnell, Michael. *Health Promotion in the Workplace*. Albany, NY: Delmar Publishers Inc., 1994.

Panel Publishers. *Driving Down Health Care Costs: Strategies and Solutions 1995*. New York, NY: Panel Publishers, 1995.

U.S. Department of Health and Human Services. *1992 National Survey of Worksite Health Promotion Activities*. Washington, DC: U.S. Government Printing Office, 1993.

U.S. Department of Labor. Bureau of Labor Statistics. *Employee Benefits in Medium and Large Private Establishments, 1993*. Washington, DC: U.S. Government Printing Office, 1994.

William M. Mercer. Wellness Programs. A William M. Mercer Survey (October 1993).

Additional Information

American Business Publishing
3100 Brinley Professional Plaza
Hwy 138, P.O. Box 1442
Wall Township, NJ 07719-1442

National Wellness Institute, Inc.
1045 Clark Street, Suite 210
Stevens Point, WI 54481

U.S. Department of Health and Human Services
Public Health Service
Office of Disease Prevention and Health Promotion
Mary E. Switzer Bldg., Rm. 2132
330 C Street, SW
Washington, DC 20201

PART FOUR
OTHER BENEFITS

29. Employee Assistance Programs

Introduction

Employee assistance programs (EAPs) are increasingly being used by employers as a health care cost management measure and as a tool for improving employee productivity, morale, and job satisfaction; reducing absenteeism and turnover; and improving the corporate image.

EAPs provide counseling services directed toward acute problems that affect job performance. These programs were originally designed to identify and address the problem of employee alcoholism (and then drug abuse). Today, alcoholism and drug abuse continue to be a major focus of many EAPs. However, counseling is also being offered on stress management, family and marital problems, work place violence, pressures from child and elder care responsibilities, and coping with the effects of company downsizing.

Today, more and more employers are offering EAPs. In 1993, 62 percent of workers in medium and large private establishments were eligible for these programs, compared with 43 percent in 1988 (U.S. Department of Labor, 1994). Employers concerned with their employees' physical and mental health may offer in-house or outside counseling services and/or provide information on such problems as substance abuse, smoking, and stress through seminars, classes, or written materials.

Employers often provide coverage in their company medical plans for the treatment of substance abuse and mental health problems in addition to offering EAPs. Often, this coverage is provided within the framework of an integrated program that includes an EAP as well as a network of behavioral health providers.

Like health promotion programs, EAPs are being developed and offered by employers to address three basic issues: rising health care costs, increasing concern about how employees' personal problems affect job productivity, and growing awareness of the benefits of good health and fitness. EAPs offer employees, and in most cases their families, the opportunity to receive confidential professional counseling and assistance. (See chapter 28 for more information on health promotion programs.)

Types of EAPs

All EAPs differ. A basic EAP may offer informational pamphlets, while a more comprehensive EAP may offer diagnostic, counseling, and referral services.

EAPs can be provided internally or externally. An internal EAP is an in-house program that offers employees direct assistance through the employer's own staff counselors. Most EAP counseling services that are provided in-house are free of charge to the employee.

Some employers provide external EAPs by contracting with specialists such as psychologists, counselors, or social workers to provide services for their employees. Employers may also contract with a community agency to provide services to employees. An employee who is referred to an outside counselor may be required to pay a fee.

Some EAPs utilize telephone hotlines. Employees can use the hotlines to talk with trained counselors who make assessments and provide referrals to sources of professional help or services.

Today, in addition to addressing the "traditional" problems such as alcoholism and drug abuse, EAPs offer a broad range of services. According to a William M. Mercer survey, the most prevalent counseling service offered through EAPs (besides chemical dependency) is for family or marital problems (94 percent), followed by stress management (92 percent) and work place concerns (i.e., downsizing and reorganizations) (73 percent).

Planning an EAP

If employees are to seek out the services of an EAP, the program must be structured to guarantee confidentiality and trust. Communication with employees about the program needs to emphasize the EAP's role in assisting those who need help.

Confidentiality of records is very important. Employees need to be assured that, by participating in the EAP, they are not jeopardizing their jobs. Confidentiality makes the collection of information for evaluating the EAP difficult. However, employers will need a way to measure the EAP's use, the program's effects on job performance, and how employees feel about the program.

Supervisors and managers must be formally trained to refer employees to the EAP for problems that are affecting their job performance. Supervisors who label employees as alcoholics or drug abusers and who try to coerce them into treatment programs could cause legal problems for the employer.

Conclusion

As EAPs have grown, they have lost their stigma as a resource for alcoholics and drug abusers. These programs have become a valuable employee benefit for all workers. Employees are able to utilize the counseling services for problems ranging from those of everyday life to very serious issues.

It is estimated that employers spent close to $4,200 on health benefit costs per employee in 1995 (A. Foster Higgins & Co., Inc., 1995). EAPs may help employees deal with problems that could be interfering with their work performance and costing employers several billion dollars in productivity each year. It is estimated that EAPs cost employers approximately $25 per employee but that they recover $4 to $5 for every $1 spent. Many employers believe they have achieved significant cost savings through the initiation of employee assistance and health promotion programs. Moreover, they point to employee satisfaction with such programs.

Bibliography

Bureau of National Affairs. *Employee Assistance Programs; Focusing on the Family.* Washington, DC: Bureau of National Affairs, 1988.

Employee Benefit Research Institute. *EBRI Databook on Employee Benefits.* Third edition. Washington, DC: Employee Benefit Research Institute, 1995.

Foster Higgins. *National Survey of Employer-Sponsored Health Plans, 1995.* New York, NY: Foster Higgins, 1995.

Hewitt Associates. "Keeping Employees Healthy: A New Approach to Managing Health Care Costs." News release, 16 February 1990.

U.S. Department of Labor. Bureau of Labor Statistics. *Employee Benefits in Medium and Large Private Establishments, 1993.* Washington, DC: U.S. Government Printing Office, 1994.

William M. Mercer. "EAPs." *A William M. Mercer Survey* (24 March 1995).

Additional Information

EAP Digest
2145 Crooks Road, Suite 103
Troy, MI 48084
(313) 643-9580

Employee Assistance Professionals Association, Inc.
4601 N. Fairfax Drive, Suite 1001
Arlington, VA 22203
(703) 522-6272

30. Disability Income Plans

Introduction

Unexpected illness or injury can result in a person's inability to work, creating serious financial problems for the individual and his or her family. The costs of necessary medical treatment can exacerbate these financial problems. Health insurance plans may help to pay for medical care costs, while private and public disability income plans may replace a portion of a disabled worker's lost income.

Industry and government studies suggest that total disability-related costs now represent 6 percent to 12 percent of payroll for the average company. Studies have also found that 1 out of 7 individuals will become disabled for 5 or more years before reaching age 65, and that 3 out of every 10 workers between age 35 and age 65 will be disabled for 90 or more days.[1] In 1994, the average age of a disabled worker receiving Social Security disability benefits was 50 (U.S. Social Security Administration, 1995b).

A survey by the U.S. Bureau of the Census found that 17.5 percent of persons aged 15 and over—including 11.5 percent of those aged 15–64 and 49.6 percent of those aged 65 and over—had difficulty with or were unable to perform one or more functional activities.[2] The survey also found that the proportion of women with disabilities was 20.2 percent, compared with 18.7 percent for men. (The difference occurs largely because women outnumber men in the elderly age groups.) Among people aged 16–67, the report indicated that about 19.5 million, or 11.6 percent, had a work disability, and 8.6 million (5.1 percent) had a disability that prevented them from working.

In the past, many employers offered informal pay-continuation arrangements when disability occurred—especially for salaried employees. Today, formal disability income programs have gained wide acceptance. According to the U.S. Bureau of Labor Statistics (BLS), 87 percent of full-time employees in medium and large private establishments were covered by short-term disability protection in 1993; 41 percent were covered by long-term disabil-

---

[1] UNUM Corporation, *Disability Management: Costs and Solutions* (Portland, ME: UNUM Corporation, 1993).

[2] U.S. Department of Commerce, Bureau of the Census, *Americans with Disabilities: 1991–92, Data from the Survey of Income and Program Participation*, Current Population Reports Household Economic Studies: P 70–33 (Washington, DC: U.S. Government Printing Office, 1993).

ity insurance in that same year. Virtually all jobs are covered by mandatory public disability plans (e.g., Social Security[3] and workers' compensation). Disability income plans include both public and private programs and can be categorized as short term or long term and as partial or total.[4]

Public Programs

Social Security—Monthly disability insurance benefits are payable to a disabled worker under the normal retirement age (NRA)—currently age 65[5]—and his or her spouse and children, provided the worker is fully insured[6] and has 20 credits (formerly called quarters of coverage) in the 40 calendar quarters ending with the quarter of disability onset.[7] Monthly disability benefits are payable to a *blind* worker under the NRA and his or her spouse and children, provided the worker is fully insured.[8]

For purposes of entitlement to monthly benefits, disability is defined as being so severely impaired, mentally or physically, that an individual cannot

---

[3] For further information regarding Social Security, see chapter 2 on Social Security and Medicare and the section on Public Sector Benefits.

[4] A disability is considered partial if some kinds of work can be performed while others cannot. For example, an individual may be able to perform clerical tasks but unable to perform more strenuous forms of work, such as lifting. If he or she can perform no profitable work, the disability is considered to be total.

[5] Disability benefits are not paid to persons who have reached the normal retirement age (NRA), which is scheduled to increase gradually from age 65 to age 67, beginning with those who attain age 62 in 2000 and ending with those who attain age 62 in 2022 and later. When a disabled individual attains the NRA, he or she is transferred to the retirement rolls.

[6] The number of credits (formerly called quarters of coverage) needed for a worker to be fully insured is equal to the number of full calendar years elapsing between age 21 and either age 62, disability, or death, whichever occurs first. For workers who attained age 21 before 1951, the requirement is one credit for each year after 1950 and before the year of attainment of age 62, disability, or death.

[7] The special alternative insured status requirement for young workers disabled before age 31 is one-half the credits (or calendar quarters) after age 21 up to date of disability, or, if disabled before age 24, one-half the credits (or quarters) in the three years ending with the quarter of disability.

[8] A person must be *insured* under the Old-Age, Survivors, and Disability Insurance (or Social Security) program before retirement, survivors, or disability insurance benefits can be paid to the person or to the person's family. A person's insured status is determined by the number of Social Security credits earned.

perform any substantial gainful work. In addition, the impairment must be expected to result in death or to last for a continuous period of not less than 12 months. Initial determinations of disability are generally made by State Disability Determination Services (DDS) under regulations established by the Secretary of Health and Human Services.

Monthly disability benefits are payable to a disabled worker under the NRA after a waiting period of five full calendar months. A disabled worker receives a monthly benefit equal to what his or her primary insurance amount (PIA)[9] was at the time that the disability occurred. The benefit is not reduced because it begins before the NRA. If an individual becomes disabled after age 62 and had been receiving a reduced retirement benefit, his or her disability benefit will be reduced to take into account the number of months he or she received the retirement benefit. Like other Social Security benefits, disability benefits are increased each year to reflect changes in the cost of living. If a disabled worker receives workers' compensation (see section below) or certain other disability benefits under federal, state, or local law, the total of all such disability benefits may not exceed 80 percent of the worker's recent earnings before disability began.

Benefits to a disabled worker's family members are paid on the same basis as those to a retired worker's family. The maximum family benefit is somewhat more stringent for disabled-worker families than for retired-worker or survivor families. Although the earnings limitation[10] does not apply to disabled-worker beneficiaries, it does apply to working spouses and children who receive benefits as the dependents of disabled beneficiaries.

In order to encourage a return to work, a disabled person who has not recovered but who returns to work is allowed a nine-month (not necessarily consecutive) trial-work period during which his or her benefits are continued.

As of December 1994, 5.6 million beneficiaries were receiving payments on the basis of disability—an increase of 31 percent from December 1990. Of the 5.6 million disability beneficiaries in December 1994, 4.0 million were disabled workers, 0.3 million were spouses of disabled workers, and

---

[9] The primary insurance amount (PIA) is derived from the worker's annual taxable earnings, averaged over a time period that encompasses most of the worker's adult years. For more information on the PIA, see chapter 2 on Social Security and Medicare.

[10] For more information on the earnings limitation, see chapter 2 on Social Security and Medicare.

1.4 million were children of disabled workers (U.S. Social Security Administration, 1995a).

Workers' Compensation—Disability income plans differ from workers' compensation in that disability plans cover *nonwork*-related injury or illness, while workers' compensation covers only *work*-related injury or illness. Disability plans are public and private programs that cover temporary or permanent illness. Workers' compensation is a public program that pays wage loss benefits and medical benefits. Workers' compensation was the first form of social insurance to develop in the United States.

Today, each of the 50 states, the District of Columbia, Puerto Rico, and the Virgin Islands have their own workers' compensation program. In addition, two federal workers' compensation programs cover federal government employees and longshore and harbor workers throughout the country. A federal program also protects coal miners suffering from black lung disease.

Before the passage of workers' compensation laws, to recover damages for a work-related injury, employers ordinarily had to file suit against their employers and prove that the injury was caused by the employer's negligence. As a result of workers' compensation legislation, the usual condition for entitlement to benefits is that the injury or death arise out of and in the course of employment.

Close to 90 percent of the nation's employed wage and salary labor force is covered by state and federal workers' compensation laws. Among the most common exemptions are domestic service, agricultural employment, and casual labor. Many programs also exempt employees of nonprofit, charitable, or religious institutions, and some programs limit coverage to workers in hazardous occupations. Still other programs exempt employers with fewer than a stipulated number of employees, typically fewer than 3–5 employees (U.S. Department of Health and Human Services, 1993).

Compensation laws are either compulsory or elective. Under an elective law, the employer may accept or reject coverage under the law. If coverage is rejected, the employer loses the customary common-law defenses[11] against suits by employees in private industry. Only three states still have elective coverage: New Jersey, South Carolina, and Texas. A compulsory law requires each employer within its scope to accept its provisions and provide for benefits specified.

---

[11] The three common-law defenses are contributory negligence, assumption of risk, and negligence of fellow employees.

Workers' compensation programs also vary in their methods to assure that compensation will be paid when it is due. In most states, coverage is provided through private insurance or through employer self-insurance arrangements. However, in eight jurisdictions, commercial insurance is not allowed. In four of these areas, employers must insure with an exclusive state insurance fund, and in four others, they must either insure with an exclusive state insurance fund or self-insure. In 17 jurisdictions, state funds have been established that compete with private insurance carriers.

Workers' compensation benefits include periodic cash payments and medical services to the worker and death and funeral benefits to the worker's survivors. Most programs also have lump-sum settlements. The cash benefits for temporary total disability, permanent total disability, permanent partial disability, and death of a breadwinner are usually calculated as a percentage of weekly earnings at the time of accident or death—usually 66 2/3 percent. In some states, the percentage varies with the worker's marital status and the number of dependents. All programs place dollar maximums on the weekly amounts payable to a disabled worker or to survivors. Compensation is generally payable after a waiting period of three to seven days.

Nonoccupational Temporary Disability Insurance (TDI) Plans—
Nonoccupational TDI plans (so called because payments have a durational limit) cover disabilities that are not job related and that are short term in nature. Most of these plans are voluntary. However, five states (California, Hawaii, New Jersey, New York, and Rhode Island), Puerto Rico, and the railroad industry require employers to provide short-term or temporary disability insurance under rules set by law. Workers in states that do not have compulsory TDI laws are often protected by their employers or unions through group disability insurance or formal paid sick-leave plans established through collective bargaining or the employer's initiative.

In 1991, approximately 22 percent of the nation's wage and salary workers in private industry were covered by TDI laws. The five state TDI laws and the Puerto Rico law cover most commercial and industrial wage and salary workers in private employment if the employer has at least one worker. Occupational groups generally exclude domestic workers, family workers (parent, child, or spouse of the employer), government employees, and the self-employed. Hawaii includes state and local government employees, and the other state programs generally provide elective coverage for some or all public employees (U.S. Department of Health and Human Services, 1993).

The methods used for providing this protection vary depending on the state. Coverage may be provided through a state-operated fund into which all contributions are paid and from which all benefits are disbursed. Some states provide coverage through a state-operated fund but give employers the option of contracting out of the state fund by purchasing group insurance from commercial insurance companies, by self-insuring, or by negotiating coverage through a union-employer benefit plan. Still other states require employers to provide their own TDI plans for their workers by setting up an approved self-insurance plan, by an agreement with employees or a union establishing a labor-management benefit plan, or by purchasing group insurance from a commercial carrier.

In order to limit benefits to individuals with a substantial attachment to the covered labor force, a worker must have a specified amount of past employment or earnings to qualify for benefits. The claimant must also be unable to perform regular or customary work because of a physical or mental condition. All the laws restrict payment of TDI benefits if the claimant is also receiving workers' compensation payments or unemployment benefits.

In all seven TDI systems, weekly benefits are related to a claimant's previous earnings in covered employment. In general, the benefit amount for a week is intended to replace at least one-half the weekly wage loss for a limited time (between 26 and 52 weeks). All of the laws specify minimum and maximum amounts payable for a week. A noncompensable waiting period of a week or seven consecutive days of disability is generally required before the payment of benefits for subsequent weeks. Both employers and employees (through payroll taxes) may be required to contribute to the cost of TDI benefits. In general, the government does not contribute.

Employment-Based Private Programs

Individual employers, jointly managed (Taft-Hartley) trust funds, and employer associations may offer private disability income plans. Before a private plan is adopted, a number of plan design and administrative questions must be answered. For example: What benefit level should be provided? How long should benefits be provided? What portion of the benefits should be paid by employers, and what portion should be paid by employees?

Employers are legally required to contribute to the public disability plans discussed in the previous section. To avoid costly duplication, private plan sponsors should recognize all sources of disability income when determining benefit levels. This is usually accomplished by a benefit integration provision. Integration is intended to limit combined disability benefits to a reasonable income replacement level (i.e., the portion of a worker's income prior to disability that is replaced after disability).

There are two primary types of private disability income plans: short-term disability plans (in which benefit payments usually are provided for 26 weeks or less) and long-term disability plans (in which benefit payments are usually provided after short-term benefits have ended).

Short-Term Disability Plans—A short-term disability is usually defined as an employee's inability to perform the duties of his or her current position. Paid sick leave and sickness and accident insurance protect workers against loss of income during temporary absences from work due to illness or accident. Sick leave is provided to most full-time employees and sickness and accident insurance to a significant but smaller number of full-time workers. Some workers have both sick leave and sickness and accident insurance, with the two benefits coordinated. The duration of short-term disability benefits ranges from 13 weeks to 52 weeks, although most workers are covered for up to 26 weeks. Short-term disability plans usually specify when successive periods of disability are considered to be separate disabilities and when they are considered to be a continuous disability.

Often, paid sick leave is available to the employee without any waiting period, and it may be used during the interim before sickness and accident insurance payments begin. Under most sickness and accident insurance plans, the disability must exist for at least one week before a worker becomes eligible for benefits. This waiting period is intended to control plan costs.

Sick leave usually provides 100 percent of a worker's normal earnings, and the plan frequently specifies a number of covered days each year that are permitted for paid sick leave (e.g., 13 days). Other plans provide sick leave benefits (e.g., 30 days) per illness instead of per year. When used in conjunction with sick leave plans, sickness and accident plans provide benefits after sick leave benefits are exhausted. The level of sickness and accident benefits for short-term disability may be expressed as a flat dollar amount or as a percentage of employee earnings. The level and duration of benefits may increase with service. Generally, benefits replace between one-half and two-thirds of a person's predisability gross weekly income. Many believe that a higher replacement rate would create a disincentive for employees to return to work.

Employers usually pay for short-term disability plans. These plans may be financed under a group insurance contract with a private insurance carrier, an employer self-insurance arrangement, an employer-established employee benefit trust fund, a Taft-Hartley multiemployer welfare fund, or general corporate assets (e.g., for a sick leave plan). Short-term disability plans may be administered by an employer, an insurance carrier, or the board of trustees of a Taft-Hartley plan.

Data from BLS indicate that in 1993, 87 percent of full-time employees in medium and large private establishments had some form of short-term disability protection. Of those workers with short-term disability coverage, 25 percent had sickness and accident insurance only, 49 percent had paid sick leave only, and 26 percent had combined sickness and accident insurance/paid sick leave.

Long-Term Disability Plans—In most long-term plans, disability for the first two years is defined in the same way as disability under short-term plans (e.g., an employee's inability to perform the duties of his or her current position). If the disability continues for more than two years, the definition of disability usually changes to the inability to perform any occupation that the person is reasonably suited to do by training, education, and experience. Some plans use the payment of Social Security disability benefits as the sole test for ascertaining whether a participant should receive long-term disability benefits under the plan.

Private sources of long-term disability benefits include disability provisions under long-term disability plans, group life insurance, employer-sponsored pension plans, and other insurance arrangements (e.g., individual insurance protection). Like short-term benefits, long-term disability benefits are integrated with benefits from other sources to produce reasonable replacement rates and to control costs.

Long-term benefits generally begin after short-term disability benefits (sick leave and sickness and accident insurance) expire. Although some long-term disability plans may limit benefits to a specified number of months (depending on the employee's age at the time of disability), most plans provide benefits for the length of a disability, up to a specified age (e.g., age 65, when Social Security and employer-provided retirement benefits usually begin). Under the 1986 Amendments to the Age Discrimination in Employment Act, which abolished mandatory retirement, plans that provide disability benefits cannot impose an upper age limit on active employees' eligibility for these benefits. The benefits may be paid to employees age 65 or over who become disabled, based on age-related cost considerations. Employers must either provide equal benefits to employees regardless of age, or—as is usually the case—provide benefits that are equal in cost to employees of all ages. Because disability costs rise with age, this means that employees who are disabled at older ages may be paid disability benefits for a shorter duration or lower benefits for the same duration, relative to younger employees.

Typically, long-term disability plans pay benefits amounting to approximately 60 percent of a person's predisability monthly pay. However, some plans provide as much as 70 percent or more of predisability pay. Additionally, some plans contain a provision stating that private-sector long-term disability benefits, plus Social Security disability benefits, cannot exceed a stated amount (e.g., 75 percent of predisability salary). Most plans set a limit on monthly payments, e.g., between $4,000 and $10,000. The cost of long-term disability benefits may be financed by employer contributions, employee contributions, or employer/employee cost sharing.

Similar to short-term disability plans, long-term plans usually specify when successive periods of disability are considered to be separate disabilities and when they are considered to be a continuous disability. Also, some long-term plans provide for continued payment of at least some disability benefits when long-term disabled persons engage in rehabilitative employment.

BLS data indicate that in 1993, 11.8 million full-time employees in medium and large private establishments had long-term disability insurance. Eighty-nine percent of these employees received their benefits as a fixed percentage of predisability earnings, with the most prevalent benefit being 60 percent of monthly pay. The majority of workers with percentage of earnings benefits were subject to a monthly dollar maximum, averaging $6,861 per month. Twenty-eight percent of workers with long-term disability benefits were subject to a maximum imposed on all sources of disability income—such maximums were generally 70 percent or more of predisability earnings.

Conclusion

The possibility of disability threatens everyone. When a family's primary supporter becomes disabled, the financial impact can be devastating. Although nothing can eliminate the suffering caused by disabling injuries or illnesses, disability plans can provide some needed economic security for disabled persons and their families.

Bibliography

Detlefs, Dale R., Robert J. Myers, and J. Robert Treanor. *Mercer Guide to Social Security and Medicare, 1996.* Louisville, KY: William M. Mercer, Inc., 1996.

Mamorsky, Jeffrey D., ed. *Employee Benefits Handbook.* Third edition. Boston, MA: Warren, Gorham & Lamont, 1992.

Rosenbloom, Jerry S., ed. *The Handbook of Employee Benefits: Design, Funding, and Administration.* Third edition. Vol. 1. Homewood, IL: Business One Irwin, 1992.

Rosenbloom, Jerry S., and G. Victor Hallman. *Employee Benefit Planning.* Third edition. Englewood Cliffs, NJ: Prentice Hall, 1991.

Soule, Charles E. *Disability Income Insurance: The Unique Risk.* Third edition. Burr Ridge, IL: Business One Irwin, 1994.

The Bureau of National Affairs, Inc. *Life, Accident, and Disability Benefits.* Personnel Policies Forum Survey No. 150, December 1992. Washington, DC: The Bureau of National Affairs, 1992.

U.S. Chamber of Commerce. *1994 Analysis of Workers' Compensation Laws.* Washington, DC: U.S. Chamber of Commerce, 1994.

U.S. Department of Commerce. Bureau of the Census. *Americans with Disabilities: 1991–92, Data from the Survey of Income and Program Participation.* Current Population Reports. Household Economic Studies: P 70-33. Washington, DC: U.S. Government Printing Office, 1993.

U.S. Department of Health and Human Services. Social Security Administration. *Social Security Programs in the United States, 1993. Social Security Bulletin* (Winter 1993). Washington, DC: U.S. Government Printing Office, 1993.

U.S. Department of Labor. Bureau of Labor Statistics. *Employee Benefits in Medium and Large Private Establishments, 1993.* Washington, DC: U.S. Government Printing Office, 1994.

U.S. Social Security Administration. *1995 Annual Report of the Board of Trustees of the Old-Age and Survivors Insurance and Disability Insurance Trust Funds.* Washington, DC: U.S. Government Printing Office, 1995a.

———. *Social Security Bulletin Annual Statistical Supplement, 1995.* Washington, DC: U.S. Government Printing Office, 1995b.

Additional Information

American Federation of Labor and Congress of Industrial Organizations
815 16th Street, NW
Washington, DC 20006
(202) 637-5000

Institute for Rehabilitation and Disability Management
Washington Business Group on Health
777 North Capitol Street, NE, Suite 800
Washington, DC 20002
(202) 408-9320

International Foundation of Employee Benefit Plans
P.O. Box 69, 18700 West Bluemound Road
Brookfield, WI 53008-0069
(414) 786-6700

National Academy of Social Insurance
1776 Massachusetts Avenue, NW, Suite 615
Washington, DC 20036
(202) 452-8097

National Association of Manufacturers
1331 Pennsylvania Avenue, NW, Suite 1500
Washington, DC 20004
(202) 637-3000

Workers' Compensation Research Institute
101 Main Street
Cambridge, MA 02142
(617) 494-1240

31. Long-Term Care Insurance

Introduction

Increased life expectancy and the aging of the baby boom generation will bring rapid growth in the number of people at risk of needing long-term care (LTC). Relative to those who can provide physical and financial assistance, the proportion in need of long-term care will increase dramatically over the next several decades. Continuing trends of more two worker families, more single workers, and the increased geographic spread of family members means that there will be fewer family members available to provide care on an informal basis.

Long-term care—or long-term services—refers to a broad range of health, social, and environmental support services and assistance provided by paid and unpaid caregivers in institutional, home, and community settings to persons who are limited in their ability to function independently on a daily basis. Functional dependency can result from physical or mental limitations and is generally defined in terms of the inability to independently perform essential activities of daily living (ADLs) such as dressing, bathing, eating, toileting, transferring (e.g., from a bed to a chair), walking, and maintaining continence or to perform instrumental activities of daily living (IADLs) such as shopping, cooking, and housekeeping.[1]

The majority of LTC services are provided by the private sector but are financed through the public sector. LTC can be provided in many different settings and for many different kinds of support services. For example, care may be provided at home, in an adult day care center, or in a nursing facility. It may include both skilled medical care (care that can only be provided by a registered nurse on a doctor's orders) and custodial care (e.g., assistance with bathing and dressing), or it may include only custodial care. Skilled care for an acute temporary medical condition is different from LTC. Treatment for a temporary medical condition by a licensed provider generally is covered by private medical insurance plans and Medicare, while custodial care generally is not.

---

[1] The index of independence in activities of daily living was developed by Sidney Katz and colleagues as a measure of function that could be used to objectively evaluate the chronically ill and aging. Results were first published in 1963. For a further discussion of the index, see Katz et al., 1963 and Katz et al., 1970.

Long-Term Care Market

The population in need of LTC has become increasingly diverse. A growing proportion of those in need of services are under age 65. A recent study by the U.S. General Accounting Office indicates that, of the 12.8 million people needing assistance with everyday activities, 5.1 million (39.6 percent) are working-age adults and approximately 420,000 (3.3 percent) are children under age 18 (U.S. General Accounting Office, 1994). Chronic conditions such as mental retardation and AIDS affect individuals of all ages. In addition, due to advances in medical technology and treatments, individuals are increasingly likely to survive—although not necessarily free from disability—what may in the past have been a fatal accident or childhood ailment. However, the likelihood of requiring long-term care increases with age.

Individuals, employers, and public policymakers have all begun to focus on the impact of these trends. Among the general population, recognition that neither Medicare nor most private health insurance plans cover LTC has come slowly. Nevertheless, many retirees and workers have now begun to understand their exposure to the risk of needing costly community or institutional LTC as an increasing number have faced the necessity of caring for a parent, spouse, or child needing chronic (and often increasing) assistance for personal care. Employers have also begun to realize that not only must many of their employees now care for young children, but many are being called on to care for elderly parents. Recognizing and meeting the needs of these individuals by assisting them in providing for their children, parents, and grandparents may have the potential to reduce absenteeism and improve morale, company loyalty, and ultimately productivity.

The private sector long-term care insurance (LTCI) market has evolved significantly in recent years, growing from 815,000 policies sold by 1987 to a total of 3.4 million by 1993 (Coronel and Fulton, 1995).[2] Improvements in plan design have helped to fuel this growth. For example, many plans now include protection against inflation and loss of benefits due to policy lapses. Perhaps the most significant change has been in the increased flexibility that is now built into many policies, which in some cases even allows individuals to customize the use of their benefits package to meet their long-term care needs at the time care becomes necessary. This flexibility enables

---

[2] These data represent the total number of policies sold as of the date indicated. Due to policy lapses, the number of policies actually in force is lower.

plans to keep pace with the continually evolving LTC market.

While private insurance now finances only a small portion of LTC needs, it is expected to grow as plan design improves and as an increasing number of individuals recognize the possibility of needing LTC and the associated costs. In addition, with the passage of the Health Insurance Portability and Accountability Act of 1996, employer-based LTC insurance plans are likely to expand because of favorable tax treatment. In general, qualified LTC insurance would be treated like accident and health insurance, and benefits paid would be excluded from taxable income, up to a limit.

Medicaid and Medicare

Medicaid, the federal/state health insurance program for certain categories of poor individuals, is the single largest source of public financing for formal LTC, accounting for 71 percent of nursing home and home health care financed through public programs in 1993 (Levit et al., 1994). In addition to an array of medical services, Medicaid covers all levels of institutional care and provides limited coverage for home care and formal community-based LTC. No other public program provides comprehensive coverage for LTC.

Although Medicare, the publicly financed health insurance program for the elderly and certain disabled individuals, does not cover LTC, it accounted for 15 percent of national nursing home and home health care expenditures, or just over one-quarter (26 percent) of public expenditures, in 1993 (Levit et al., 1994). This figure represents Medicare's coverage for recuperative medical care in Medicare-certified skilled nursing facilities (SNFs) for individuals who require skilled nursing after a hospital stay. Medicare may also provide limited coverage for home health or hospice care, but only in certain situations. Medicare does not cover custodial care, intermediate nursing care, or long-term home health care costs.

Employment-Based LTC Insurance

Private insurance now finances only a small portion of LTC needs. However, as an increasing number of individuals recognize the possibility of needing LTC and the costs associated with such care, private initiatives to provide for this need have grown, both through individually purchased and employment-based plans. Private policies include individual, group association, continuing care retirement communities (CCRC), employment-based, and accelerated death benefits specifically for LTC. While the majority of these plans were sold to individuals or through group associations, employment-based plans accounted for a significant proportion of this growth (increasing from 20,000 policies sold and 7 employers offering LTCI in 1988 to over 400,000 policies sold and 968 employers offering LTCI in 1993).

Employment-based plans are marketed to individual employers and are typically available to a firm's employees, their spouses, parents of employees and spouses, and retirees on a beneficiary-pay-all basis. These insurance plans have grown significantly over the past few years but are still uncommon relative to other types of employment-based insurance. For example, analysis of the April 1993 Current Population Survey indicates that 73 percent of workers aged 18–64 worked for an employer that offered a health insurance plan in 1993 (Yakoboski, et al., 1994). A separate Bureau of Labor Statistics study indicates that 6 percent of full-time employees in medium and large private establishments in 1993 were eligible for LTCI (U.S. Department of Labor, 1994). However, these policies have the potential to reach a large number of people because they are marketed not only to older retirees and parents of active workers but also to younger active workers and their spouses.

Although the LTCI market is currently dominated by policies that are sold individually and through associations, employment-based plans offer several benefits over individual policies and could potentially dominate the market in the future. Group insurance can be less costly because of potential economies of scale in marketing and administration.[3] Employment-based groups generally have a particular advantage in this respect because there is a central mechanism for collecting premiums (i.e., payroll deduction). These factors, together with the reduced likelihood of adverse selection[4] when enrolling younger groups, can make group plans less expensive

---

[3] However, employment-based long-term care insurance is not yet as heavily subscribed to as other types of employment-based insurance such as health and life insurance. Thus, group size may be small—even among large employers offering such coverage—and the advantages of economies of scale may not be able to be fully realized.

[4] Adverse selection refers to a phenomenon whereby people who believe they are likely to experience a certain event (in this case functional dependency) find insurance against the costs of that event more attractive than people who believe they are not likely to experience that event. Generally speaking, the risk of adverse selection decreases as the proportion of the group enrolled increases because enrollment begins to approximate random selection. This is less true for long-term care insurance than for health insurance since individuals voluntarily choose and pay for group long-term care insurance, while health insurance is often mandatory.

than comparable coverage offered on an individual basis (Friedland, 1990).

In addition to the potential of group insurance to be less expensive, employment-based LTCI policies may make employees, retirees, and their families aware at an earlier age of the possible liabilities associated with LTC, when they can better afford to plan for LTC needs. Moreover, employment-based LTCI policies are generally negotiated by a benefits professional, who may be better informed than a lay person about the nuances of policy provisions and coverage limitations.

Plan Design

Private LTCI plans have changed significantly since their inception in the early and mid 1980s. LTCI policies have become less restrictive as they have evolved, and many of today's policies have additional provisions that make them more valuable to employees and other individuals than earlier policies. For example, many plans no longer require that the insured experience a medical event to become eligible for benefits, and several insurers now offer policies that adjust the benefit for inflation. Many policies also now offer an optional rider that ensures that policyholders who have stopped paying premiums will nevertheless retain some of the benefit. These and other innovations give an indication of how much the private LTCI market has evolved. However, the most significant development relates to the flexibility included in current plan design.

LTCI is evolving in an environment of continuously changing regulations and uncertainty regarding the future direction of LTC policy, the cost of LTC, which services are most cost effective, and which design features are best suited to meet individuals' needs—especially given the increasingly diverse population in need of LTC services. The market has responded by creating plans that have several options and that, in some cases, can be custom tailored at the time care is needed.

Eligibility and Benefit Eligibility Triggers—Many employment-based plans guarantee issue of insurance to active workers with limited or no medical underwriting required during an enrollment period. Other enrollees (e.g., retirees, spouses, parents, and parents-in-law) are generally medically underwritten.

Benefit eligibility is generally triggered when the insured is unable to perform or needs assistance with two out of five or three out of six or seven ADLs, depending on the insurer and insurer's definition of ADL. Eligibility may also be triggered based on cognitive impairment such as the need for supervision due to Alzheimer's disease.

Benefit waiting periods generally require the individual to wait between 20 days and 100 days from the time of meeting the criteria to the time of receiving payment for services received. The waiting period (often called the elimination period) may be based on a set number of days regardless of the receipt of services or may be based on services received.

Sites of Care—Most plans now offer coverage for nursing home care and home- and community-based care. In addition, coverage is often now available in many nontraditional types of settings, such as in adult day care centers.

Some plans give potential insureds the option of selecting a nursing home only provision or a more comprehensive plan that lets the individual decide on where care will be provided at the time care is needed. However, even though a policy may indicate that care at home is covered, there will be restrictions.

Many plans also now include a case management or care advisory provision. Case management is a form of utilization review. In some plans, it is mandatory that the plan of care be followed in order for benefits to be paid. More often, plans include a care advisory provision. In this case, the plan of care does not need to be followed in order that benefits be paid but is there to assist the individual in identifying and sorting through care options.

Benefit Amounts—Private LTCI plans now generally base benefit amounts on a *daily benefit maximum* with a corresponding *lifetime benefit maximum*. A benefit maximum is the amount of money or number of days of care beyond which a long-term care insurance policy will not pay benefits. Generally, an individual is given several options regarding level of coverage. For example, an individual may select a daily benefit maximum of $50, $100, or $150 per day for five years with corresponding lifetime benefit maximums of $91,250, $182,500, or $273,750. Once the individual becomes eligible for benefits, the insurer would pay based on charges incurred up to the daily benefit maximum and based on site of care.[5] Nursing home care is

---

[5]However, some plans pay based on disability rather than on services received. With this type of policy, policyholders may use the money "as they see fit." For example, while many policies do not cover care provided by family members, a policyholder with a contract based on disability, rather than on service, would be able to use his or her per diem funds to pay a family member for care (Aetna Life Insurance Company, 1995).

generally paid at 100 percent of the daily benefit amount, while charges incurred for home health care and adult day care are generally paid at 50 percent of the daily benefit amount. Most plans now also include a *coordination of benefits* feature to prevent duplication of benefits.

Inflation Protection—Several insurers now offer policies that adjust the daily benefit maximum and lifetime benefit maximum for inflation. One type of inflation protection feature results in an automatic adjustment in the benefit, commonly 5 percent per year. Premiums for a policy with this feature will be considerably higher than for a policy without such a feature.

A second type of inflation protection feature allows policyholders the option of increasing their benefit every so many years (e.g., every three to five years) (Teachers Insurance and Annuity Association, 1993; The Prudential, 1994). In this case, premiums are lower from the outset, but the cost of any additional coverage purchased is based on age at the time the increase is selected.

Premiums—Premiums for LTCI vary substantially based on age and plan design. Other plan features, such as categories of care covered (nursing home care, home care, community care), daily benefit amount, maximum benefit duration, and deductible periods can also significantly affect premium amounts (National Association of Insurance Commissioners, 1993b). Because premiums are based on age at enrollment, the younger the individual, the lower the premium. Insurers generally attempt to set premiums such that they will remain level over the individual's lifetime. Thus, premiums do not increase based on aging or use of benefits. In addition, policies are guaranteed renewable; thus, as long as premiums are paid, coverage cannot be canceled.

However, premiums may rise over time because rates generally can be increased on a class basis if claims are higher than expected. And, because the LTCI market is such a new market, it is difficult to set premiums accurately. Little long-term care insurance claims experience yet exists, and it may not be available for many years to come since many of those who currently hold LTCI will likely not use it for many years.

Nonforfeiture—As is increasingly common in private disability insurance, many LTCI policies now include optional nonforfeiture features. Nonforfeiture provisions prevent the policyholder from forfeiting his or her full benefit in the event of a voluntary policy lapse.

Nonforfeiture provisions can take many different forms and may vary with an insured's age, claims history, and the duration the policy has been in force. These benefits may be included in the policy on a voluntary basis, with a higher premium assessed for those purchasing the option.

One type of nonforfeiture provision continues coverage at a reduced benefit level if a minimum number of payments has been made. Another type of nonforfeiture benefit allows partial recovery of premiums paid in the event of a voluntary lapse of the policy. While a nonforfeiture provision may be effective for the person who does not want another LTCI policy, for the buyer who wants to exchange one policy for another, a nonforfeiture provision is of only limited value (McNamara, 1995). Some larger employers may be able to negotiate when establishing their plan to provide for upgrades and to ensure that funds will be transferred to another insurer on request. If this is not done, the insurer may refuse to transfer reserves. Then, if the employer does decide to move to a new insurer, individuals in the plan are required to decide whether they want to pay the higher premium or leave the group plan in order to remain with the original insurer.

The Taxation of Long-Term Care Insurance

The Health Insurance Portability and Accountability Act of 1996 provides favorable tax treatment for LTC insurance and noninsured LTC expenses for contracts issued (or exchanged) after December 31, 1996. Qualified LTC insurance is generally treated like accident and health insurance. Employer-paid premiums are fully excludable from employee taxable income. Employee-paid premiums are treated as unreimbursed medical expenses. To the extent that employee-paid premiums and other unreimbursed medical expenses exceed 7.5 percent of an individual's adjusted gross income, the premiums would be deductible up to an age-weighted dollar amount. In addition, employee-paid unreimbursed LTC expenses are treated as unreimbursed medical expenses potentially deductible from income. LTC insurance could not be offered through a cafeteria plan, and LTC expenses could not be reimbursed through a flexible spending arrangement. Employer-provided LTC insurance is not subject to the continuation of coverage requirements of the Consolidated Omnibus Budget Reconciliation Act of 1985 (COBRA). LTC insurance premiums may also be funded through a tax-exempt medical savings account, for individuals who qualify.

Because of previous ambiguities in the tax treatment of LTC insurance premiums and benefits, many employers have not sponsored a LTC policy or have offered the coverage on an employee-pay-all basis. Opponents of the tax incentives for private LTCI contend that such incentives benefit only those with higher incomes, as they are the people who have assets to protect, and that the federal revenue lost to tax deductions might be better spent on, for example, a LTC home care block grant to the states (American Association of Retired Persons, 1995; Weiner, 1995).

The Health Insurance Portability and Accountability Act of 1996 also provides an exclusion from gross income for amounts received by terminally ill or chronically ill individuals under a life insurance contract, or upon the sale or assignment of such a contract to a qualified viatical settlement provider, for amounts received after December 31, 1996. A terminally ill individual must be certified by a physician as having an illness or physical condition where death is likely within 24 months. For chronically ill individuals, the amount excludable is subject to the same dollar limitations that apply under the long-term care provisions. Insurance companies that issue qualified accelerated death benefit riders are permitted to treat these riders as life insurance for income tax purposes.

Regulation of Long-Term Care Insurance

The Health Insurance Portability and Accountability Act of 1996 establishes consumer protection requirements for LTC insurance policies for contracts issued (or exchanged) after December 31, 1996. LTC policies would be required to comply with various provisions of the model LTC act and regulation adopted by the National Association of Insurance Commissioners (NAIC) in January 1993. The NAIC models address guaranteed renewal, prohibitions on limitations and exclusions, extension of benefits, conversion coverage, discontinuance and replacement of policies, unintentional lapses, underwriting, disclosure, post-claims underwriting prohibitions, inflation protection, preexisting condition limitations, and prior hospitalizations. The provisions would impose a $100 penalty per contract for each day an insurer fails to satisfy these requirements or to properly disclose information related to the contract.

Insurers that sell the majority of LTC policies have adjusted their policies to reflect many of the NAIC standards. However, not all states have adopted NAIC standards as law, and some insurers may not have voluntarily conformed to NAIC standards.

Conclusion

The need for LTC services is most prevalent among the elderly. However, individuals of all ages may need LTC services. Moreover, demographic

trends such as an aging population, an increased female labor force participation rate, and delayed childbearing may mean a reduction in traditional
sources of informal LTC. Individuals, employers, and policymakers have all
begun to focus on the impact of these trends in terms of providing and
financing long-term care services.

As an employee benefit, long-term care insurance has grown substantially since the late 1980s, but it is still relatively less common than other
types of insurance provided through the work place. However, there are
certain advantages that can be achieved by offering long-term care insurance through the work place that cannot be achieved through individual
policies.

The future growth of long-term care insurance is likely to depend on an
increase in public readiness to use assets to insure against the relatively
low probability of need.

Bibliography

Aetna Life Insurance Company. Written and personal communication. April
1995.

American Association of Retired Persons. "Long-Term Care Tax Clarification." Testimony before the House Ways and Means Subcommittee on
Health. 20 January 1995.

Coronel, Susan, and Diane Fulton. "Long-Term Care Insurance in 1993."
Managed Care & Insurance Operations Report. Washington, DC: Health
Insurance Association of America, 1995.

Friedland, Robert, B. *Facing the Costs of Long-Term Care*. Washington, DC:
Employee Benefit Research Institute, 1990.

IBM. Written communication, 1994.

Katz, Sidney, et al. "Progress in Development of the Index of ADL." *The
Gerontologist* (Spring 1970) Part 1: 20–30.

_____. "Studies of Illness in the Aged: The Index of ADL, a Standardized
Measure of Biological and Psychosocial Function." *Journal of the
American Medical Association* (September 21, 1963): 914–919.

Levit, Katharine R., et al. "National Health Expenditures, 1993." *Health
Care Financing Review* (Fall 1994): 247–294.

McNamara, Cheryl. CNA Insurance Companies. Written communication,
1995.

National Association of Insurance Commissioners. Long-Term Care Insurance Model Act, Model #640-1. Kansas City, MO: National Association of

Insurance Commissioners, 1993a.

_____. Long-Term Care Insurance Model Regulation, Model #641-1. Kansas City, MO: National Association of Insurance Commissioners, 1994.

_____. *Shoppers Guide*. Kansas City, MO: National Association of Insurance Commissioners, June 1993b.

The Prudential. Written communication, 1994.

Snider, Sarah. "Long-Term Care and the Private Insurance Market." *EBRI Issue Brief* no. 163 (Employee Benefit Research Institute, July 1995).

Teachers Insurance and Annuity Association. *Long-Term Care: A Guide for the Education and Research Communities*. New York, NY: Teachers Insurance and Annuity Association, 1993.

Transamerica Life Companies. Personal and written communication, April 1995.

University of Maryland. Center on Aging. *Partnership Update*. College Park, MD: University of Maryland, December 1994.

U.S. Department of Labor. Bureau of Labor Statistics. *Employee Benefits in Medium and Large Private Establishments, 1993*. Washington, DC: U.S. Government Printing Office, 1994.

U.S. General Accounting Office. *Long-Term Care: Diverse, Growing Population Includes Millions of Americans of All Ages*. GAO/HEHS-95-26. Washington, DC: U.S. General Accounting Office, 1994.

Wiener, Joshua M. "Long-Term Care Tax Clarification." Testimony before the House Ways and Means Subcommittee on Health. 20 January 1995.

Yakoboski, Paul, et al. "Employment-Based Health Benefits: Analysis of the April 1993 Current Population Survey." *EBRI Issue Brief* no. 152 (Employee Benefit Research Institute, August 1994).

Additional Information

American Association of Retired Persons
901 E Street, NW, Suite 500
Washington, DC 20004
(202) 783-2242

Health Insurance Association of America
1025 Connecticut Avenue, NW
12th Floor
Washington, DC 20036
(202) 223-7783

National Association for Home Care
519 C Street, NE
Washington, DC 20002
(202) 547-7424

United Seniors Health Cooperative
1331 H Street, NW
Washington, DC 20005
(202) 393-6222

32. Group Life Insurance Plans

Introduction

Many employers provide death benefits for survivors of deceased employees. There are two types of plans designed specifically for this purpose: *group life insurance plans,* which normally make lump-sum payments to a designated beneficiary or beneficiaries, and *survivor income plans,* which make regular (usually monthly) payments to survivors. Additionally, benefits may be paid to survivors from other employee benefit plans (e.g., profit-sharing, thrift, and pension plans). Survivor benefits are also available through the Social Security program. This chapter discusses group life insurance plans. (See chapter 33 for information regarding survivor benefits other than group life insurance plans.)

The concept of *individual* life insurance was developed centuries ago, but *group* life insurance developed more recently. In 1911, the first known group life insurance contract was created at the Pantasote Leather Company in Passaic, NJ. The contract was called the *yearly renewable term employees' policy* and included many features that are standard in today's group term life policies. According to the American Council of Life Insurance (ACLI), by the end of 1920, there were 6,000 group life insurance master policies[1] in force, providing total coverage of $1.6 billion; by 1940, there were 23,000 master policies providing total coverage of $15 billion; and by 1945, there were 31,000 master policies providing total coverage of $22 billion.

In the years after World War II, the wage freeze spurred a boom in group life insurance. Employees, knowing they could not get wage increases, requested additional benefits. Employment-based life insurance coverage was one of the most demanded benefits. As a result, in 1950, there were approximately 56,000 group life insurance master policies in force, providing total coverage of $48 billion.

Employment-based life insurance has continued to grow. At the end of 1994, approximately 143 million group life insurance certificates were providing $4.6 trillion of coverage to Americans—most of it employer sponsored. This group coverage accounted for 39 percent of *all* life insurance coverage in force in the United States at the end of 1994. There were

---

[1] A master policy is a policy issued to an employer or trustee establishing a group insurance plan for designated members of an eligible group.

864,000 group life insurance master policies at the end of 1993 (American Council of Life Insurance, 1994 and 1995).

Among full-time employees in medium and large private establishments in the United States in 1993, 91 percent had employer-provided life insurance protection in 1993 (U.S. Department of Labor, 1994). Thirteen percent were required to contribute toward coverage, and 58 percent were covered by a multiple-of-earnings formula (usually one or two times earnings).

The Insurance Contract

The contract between the insurance company and the employer is usually for *group term* life insurance. Many associations and multiemployer plans also provide group term life benefits.[2] The word *term* means that the coverage is bought for a specific time period (usually one year), with a renewable provision, and remains in effect only as long as premiums are paid. It may be referred to as *yearly* or *annual renewable term.* Term insurance has no savings features and no buildup of cash value. It is pure insurance protection, paying a benefit only at death.

The cost of providing group life coverage varies, depending on the insurer and the covered group. For small groups, charges usually are taken from a *standard rates table.* Monthly premiums typically range from $0.08 per $1,000 of coverage for employees under age 30 to $1.17 per $1,000 of coverage for employees in their early sixties. For large groups, the initial premium might also be taken from a standard rates table; however, in the second and subsequent years of coverage, plans are often designed such that the premium varies according to the group's claims experience. After the first year, the net premium for a large group is essentially the sum of claims incurred plus the insurer's administrative costs and an amount to provide for profit and risk.

Plan Provisions

Eligibility—Most group term life plans allow permanent full-time employees to be eligible for coverage on the first day of active employment. Some plans require that participants work a minimum period (typically one

---

[2] Other major types of group life insurance are *permanent* forms, including *paid-up* and *ordinary* life insurance. For more information on these two other types, see Rosenbloom, 1992. Since *term* insurance is the most popular group coverage, this chapter will focus primarily on group *term* life insurance.

to three months) to qualify for the plan.

Amounts of Insurance—Employers provide varying levels of coverage. The amount of coverage can be based on one or more factors (e.g., occupation and/or salary). According to the Bureau of Labor Statistics (BLS), the most common method of determining basic coverage for full-time employees in medium and large private establishments in 1993 was the multiple-of-earnings benefit. Fifty-eight percent of the employees in the BLS survey had basic life insurance determined by the multiple-of-earnings method. A dollar amount benefit, which occasionally varies with earnings or service, was the other prevalent means of providing life insurance protection. Thirty-six percent of the employees in the BLS survey had basic life insurance determined by a flat dollar amount (i.e., not varying with earnings or service), often $5,000–$15,000, and five percent had a dollar amount benefit that varied with earnings or service. Although it typically provides smaller amounts of insurance than earnings-based formulas, flat-amount coverage has improved considerably over the years.

Employee Cost—Employers typically pay the entire cost of basic life insurance. When life insurance benefits are offered as part of a cafeteria plan or reimbursement account, employee contributions may be required. Another form of employee contribution is a specified flat dollar amount (e.g., $0.20 per $1,000 of coverage per month). In supplemental plans, the cost is usually paid entirely by the employee. Supplemental coverage is more prevalent for employees who have their basic insurance determined by a multiple-of-earnings formula than for those with a flat dollar amount of coverage.

Dependent Life Insurance—As part of the group life insurance plan, some employers offer insurance coverage for dependents. The cost of dependent coverage is usually paid by employees who elect such protection. Dependent life insurance usually provides a flat dollar benefit for a worker's spouse and an equal or smaller benefit for children (usually between the ages of 14 days and 19 years), although the benefit may vary by employee option or may be a percentage of employee coverage. Spousal coverage typically provides benefits of $5,000 or more, while coverage for children usually offers benefits of $1,000, $2,000, or $5,000 per child.

Accidental Death and Dismemberment (AD&D) Insurance—Frequently, group life insurance plans include AD&D insurance. This insurance provides additional benefits if a worker dies in an accident or loses an eye or a limb in an accident. In the case of accidental death, the AD&D benefit commonly equals the basic life insurance benefit, whereas in the case of dismemberment, the AD&D benefit is usually equal to only a portion of the basic life insurance benefit.

In 1993, 69 percent of full-time employees of medium and large private establishments had AD&D insurance. For 85 percent of workers with AD&D protection, benefits were determined as a multiple of life insurance benefits (most commonly one times the life insurance benefit). Ten percent had flat dollar benefit amounts, and four percent had a multiple-of-earnings benefit.

Beneficiary Provisions—Under a typical group plan, employees may designate and change the beneficiaries who are to receive their group life insurance proceeds. At an insured employee's death, the stipulated benefit is paid directly to the named beneficiary. If payment cannot be made to a designated beneficiary, group contracts usually permit payment by the insurance company to one or more of a group of the employee's surviving relatives.

Benefits for Retired Persons and Older Active Workers—Most group life policies are designed to cover active employees. Coverage for active older employees can be reduced to reflect the increase in the cost of life insurance as a result of age. This practice will not violate the Age Discrimination in Employment Act as long as the reduction for an employee of a particular age is justified by the increased cost of coverage for that employee's specific age bracket, encompassing no more than five years. Plans that reduce coverage typically make their first reduction at age 65 or 70. Many plans reduce coverage for older workers only once, but other plans reduce coverage in several stages. At retirement, basic life insurance coverage may continue (often for the rest of the retiree's life), but the amount of the benefit is usually reduced at least once during retirement. In 1993, of the 26.2 million full-time employees in medium and large private establishments with basic life insurance, 42 percent were in plans with reductions for older active workers, and 41 percent were in plans with retiree coverage.

Conversion Privileges—If an employee's insurance ceases under certain situations (e.g., employment termination or retirement), the employee may usually convert his or her group coverage to an individual policy. Under state law, the employee is generally permitted to obtain an individual ordinary life insurance policy of an amount equal to the amount of the employee's previous coverage. Application must be made and a premium (based on the employee's age, type of insurance, and the class or risk involved) paid within 30 days after termination of group coverage. A second conversion situation exists when the group master policy itself is terminated or amended so as to terminate the insurance on all employees or on the class of employees to which the employee belongs. In this situation, the conversion privilege is available for employees who have been insured at least five years, and the maximum amount that may be converted on any one life is $2,000. In some states, the employee has the option to purchase a one-year term policy instead of the ordinary life policy; the purpose of this option is to allow an employee to continue insurance between jobs or after retirement.

Disability Benefits—Group plans generally continue to provide some life insurance protection for a covered employee who becomes totally and permanently disabled. Although group term life plans contain three basic types of provisions regarding the continuation of coverage in the event of a covered person's disability, the most common is a *waiver-of-premium disability benefit*.[3] Under such a provision, coverage is continued at no cost to the disabled employee, providing:

- the employee is under a specified age (such as 60 or 65) at the onset of disability;
- the employee is covered under the plan at the onset of disability;
- disability continues until death; or
- proof of total and continuous disability is presented as required by the plan.

Optional Forms of Payment—The standard payment method for group life insurance claims is a lump-sum distribution. However, virtually all insurers permit other settlement arrangements at the insured employee's option (or the beneficiary's option, if the employee did not make an election before death). Alternative payment arrangements include installment payments and life income annuities.

Taxation

The employer's premiums for group term life insurance are tax deductible as a business expense, and the benefits paid to beneficiaries are exempt from federal income taxation up to a limit. However, the proceeds are generally subject to estate taxes.

Employees may receive up to $50,000 in employer-provided life insurance coverage without paying income tax on the amount. On coverage

---

[3] The two other provisions are a *maturity value benefit* and an *extended death benefit*. For more information on these provisions, see Rosenbloom and Hallman, 1991.

beyond $50,000, the employee is taxed on the cost[4] of the balance. In cases where an employee contributes toward the cost of the insurance, that part of the contribution is credited to any coverage in excess of $50,000.

Group Universal Life Programs

Group universal life programs (GULPs) were first introduced in 1985 and developed from individual policy universal life (UL). UL is issued on an individual basis, whereas GULP coverage is available on a group basis. GULP plans may supplement a regular group term life insurance plan or may exist as stand-alone plans.

GULPs combine group term life insurance with a savings element or cash accumulation feature. This investment element can be used to create nontaxable permanent insurance or to accumulate savings. GULPs are made available to employees by an employer to which a master policy has been issued, and employees pay the entire premium. According to ACLI, in 1993, life insurance companies issued 741 master policies for group universal life insurance.

Participation by employees is voluntary. A formula in the plan is used to establish the amount of life insurance coverage available to employees (e.g., one or two times compensation). Employees may choose to contribute only to the cost of term protection and administrative expenses, but many also contribute to the savings element. All employee contributions (including those to the cash value) are withheld from after-tax pay, although the investment earnings on the cash value are not taxed until coverage is surrendered or until the cash values are taken as income or withdrawn. This tax-deferred buildup of the cash values is an attractive feature for the employees.

Another feature important to employees is the portability of GULPs. When a participating employee terminates employment (e.g., to change jobs or to retire), he or she may make premium payments directly to the insurance company and hence continue coverage. Employees may withdraw cash values at any time and may take loans against their cash values.

Some GULPs limit coverage to employee life insurance, but others allow employees to include accidental death and dismemberment insurance and dependent coverage for spouses and children. Children are usually only

---

[4] Cost is determined by a table in the Internal Revenue Code, although this cost may differ somewhat from the actual cost of the insurance.

covered for term insurance, whereas spouses may be able to accumulate cash values. Some plans also allow employees to add coverage payable in the event of the employee's disability.

Premium rates for the term insurance portion of each employee's group coverage are stated in the plan and usually increase with the employee's age. These rates are usually guaranteed for some amount of time (e.g., one, three, or five years) and may be lower than individual term rates. The interest credited to cash values is set periodically by the insurance company. Once a rate is set, it may be guaranteed for a limited period of time (e.g., one year). There is also a guaranteed minimum interest rate that is set for purposes of state insurance and federal tax laws.

Living Benefits

Living benefits, also known as viatical settlements, allow the insured to receive the proceeds payable on death while still living. The amount received is the actuarially discounted value based on the individual's expected remaining lifetime and is paid by a third party (a living benefits company) rather than by the insurance company that issued the life insurance policy. The living benefit company typically takes an irrevocable absolute assignment of the life insurance policy and in return pays (in cash) 50 percent to 80 percent of the face amount of an individual life insurance policy of a terminally ill individual (and sometimes of an individual who has attained a specified age, such as 83 or over). As terminally ill patients reach lifetime health benefit limits in an employment-based health benefit plan, they may find living benefits attractive since they allow individuals to access the cash value of the life insurance policy while still living, usually to help pay medical bills.

Conclusion

The death of a worker can be financially devastating to his or her family. Employer-sponsored life insurance benefits can ease the ensuing financial difficulties. The number of employer-sponsored life insurance plans has grown significantly, attesting to their importance. To design effective programs and to ensure an adequate amount of compensation for family members in the case of the covered employee's death, employers and employees should consider how these plans fit in with other potential private and public sources of life insurance, survivor benefits, and death benefits.

Bibliography

American Council of Life Insurance. *1994 Life Insurance Fact Book*. Washington, DC: American Council of Life Insurance, 1994.

———. *1995 Life Insurance Fact Book Update*. Washington, DC: American Council of Life Insurance, 1995.

Combe, Cynthia M., and Gerard J. Talbot. *Employee Benefits Answer Book*. Fourth edition. New York, NY: Panel Publishers, 1996.

Mamorsky, Jeffrey D., ed. *Employee Benefits Handbook*. Third edition. Boston, MA: Warren, Gorham & Lamont, 1992.

Rosenbloom, Jerry S., ed. *The Handbook of Employee Benefits: Design, Funding, and Administration*. Third edition. Vol. 1. Homewood, IL: Business One Irwin, 1992.

Rosenbloom, Jerry S., and G. Victor Hallman. *Employee Benefit Planning*. Third edition. Englewood Cliffs, NJ: Prentice Hall, 1991.

U.S. Department of Labor. Bureau of Labor Statistics. *Employee Benefits in Medium and Large Private Establishments, 1993*. Washington, DC: U.S. Government Printing Office, 1994.

Additional Information

American Council of Life Insurance
1001 Pennsylvania Ave., NW
Washington, DC 20004-2599
(202) 624-2000

International Foundation of
Employee Benefit Plans
P.O. Box 69
18700 West Bluemound Road
Brookfield, WI 53008-0069
(414) 786-6700

Life Insurance Marketing &
Research Association (LIMRA)
300 Day Hill Road
Windsor, CT 06095
(203) 688-3358

National Organization of Life and
Health Guaranty Associations
13873 Park Center Road, Suite 329
Herndon, VA 22071
(703) 481-5206

33. Survivor Benefits

Introduction

Most employers, regardless of size, offer survivor or death benefits to their employees. The classic and most prominent source of employer-provided death benefits is group term life insurance, which pays a lump sum to a designated beneficiary or beneficiaries. (For more information on group life insurance plans, see chapter 32.) However, benefits are also payable to the survivors of deceased employees through other sources, including Social Security, employer-sponsored survivor income plans, and employer-sponsored pension plans. This chapter offers an overview of these three survivor benefit sources.

Social Security Survivor Benefits

In order for the survivors of a deceased worker to receive monthly Social Security survivor benefits or the lump-sum death benefit, the worker must have been either currently insured or fully insured.[1] (Survivors of a currently insured deceased worker are eligible for some, but not all, survivor benefits.) The amount of survivor benefits payable to family members is based on the worker's primary insurance amount (PIA)[2] at the date of death. Like other Social Security benefits,[3] survivor benefits are increased each year to reflect changes in the cost of living.

Currently Insured Status—In order to be currently insured, a worker must have earned at least six credits[4] (previously called quarters of cover-

---

[1] A person must be *insured* under the Old-Age, Survivors, and Disability Insurance (or Social Security) program before retirement, survivor, or disability insurance benefits can be paid to the person or to the person's family. A person's insured status is determined by the number of Social Security credits earned.

[2] The primary insurance amount (PIA) is derived from the worker's annual taxable earnings, averaged over a time period that encompasses most of the worker's adult years. For more information on the PIA, see chapter 2 on Social Security and Medicare.

[3] For a detailed discussion of these benefits, see chapter 2 on Social Security and Medicare.

[4] For more information on Social Security credits, see chapter 2 on Social Security and Medicare.

age) during the 13 calendar quarters ending with the quarter in which he or she died.

When a currently insured individual dies (regardless of whether or not he or she was retired), a lump-sum death benefit of $255, intended to help the deceased worker's family pay the costs associated with the worker's last illness and death, is payable to the spouse who was living with the worker at the time of death. The lump-sum death benefit is also payable to the spouse if he or she was eligible to receive benefits at the time of death based on the deceased worker's earnings record. If there is no qualified spouse, the lump-sum death benefit may be payable to the child or children of the deceased worker. Otherwise, the benefit is not payable.

In addition to the lump-sum death benefit, certain survivors of a deceased worker who was currently insured are eligible for *monthly* benefits. A currently insured worker's surviving spouse (or surviving divorced spouse[5]) *who is caring for a child* under age 16 (or for a child disabled before age 22) is eligible to receive monthly survivor benefits equal to 75 percent of the deceased worker's PIA. Remarriage of the surviving spouse (or surviving divorced spouse) terminates this benefit. An eligible child, including the deceased worker's natural child (legitimate or illegitimate), adopted child, stepchild, or dependent grandchild (if the grandchild's parents are deceased or disabled), also qualifies for monthly survivor benefits. An eligible child must be unmarried and must also meet one of the following three requirements in order to receive benefits: under age 18, age 18 and in high school, or any age but disabled before age 22. If both parents are deceased, a child can qualify for benefits on the earnings record of either parent, whichever gives the larger benefit.

Fully Insured Status—The number of credits needed for a worker to be fully insured so that dependents qualify for *all* survivor benefits is equal to the number of full calendar years elapsing between age 21 and either age 62 or death, whichever occurs first. For workers who attained age 21 before 1951, the requirement is one credit for each year after 1950 and before the year of attainment of age 62 or death.

If the deceased worker was fully insured, the survivors noted in the previous section continue to qualify for benefits. Other survivors, including spouses, divorced spouses, and parents, also qualify for benefits. Except for

---

[5] A surviving divorced spouse is not required to have been married to the deceased worker for a specified length of time for *this type* of benefit.

disabled individuals, anyone receiving survivor benefits is subject to the earnings limitation.[6]

A fully insured worker's surviving spouse aged 60 or over qualifies for survivor benefits if (a) the couple had been married for at least nine months (if death is due to an accident or military duty, no length of marriage is required) or (b) the surviving spouse is the parent of the deceased worker's child (natural or adopted). If the worker dies either before being entitled to retirement benefits or after retiring at the normal retirement age (NRA),[7] the surviving spouse benefit is equal to 100 percent of the worker's PIA, provided the surviving spouse has reached the NRA. If the deceased worker retired before reaching the NRA and hence had a reduced benefit, the surviving spouse will receive the smaller of either 100 percent of the worker's PIA (an amount that will be reduced if the surviving spouse is under the NRA) or the reduced benefit that the worker was receiving (but not less than 82.5 percent of the worker's PIA). If the deceased worker retired after the NRA, the surviving spouse will receive the same benefit (including the delayed retirement credit[8]) as that formerly received by the deceased worker, provided the surviving spouse has reached the NRA.

In all cases noted above, if the surviving spouse begins receiving benefits before reaching the NRA,[9] a reduction applies. With an NRA of 65, the reduction factor applied to the PIA of the deceased worker is 19/40 of 1 percent for each month that commencement is prior to the surviving spouse's NRA. (The maximum reduction is 28.5 percent.)

A surviving *divorced* spouse qualifies for the same benefit as that

---

[6] For more information on the earnings limitation, see chapter 2 on Social Security and Medicare.

[7] The current normal retirement age (NRA) of 65 is scheduled to increase gradually to age 67, beginning with those who attain age 62 in 2000 and ending with those who attain age 62 in 2022 and later.

[8] For individuals reaching age 65 in 1996, the delayed retirement credit is 5 percent for each year between ages 65 and 70 that a worker does not receive retirement benefits either because the worker did not claim benefits or because of the worker's earnings. The credit will increase gradually (0.5 percent every two years) until it reaches 8 percent for those attaining age 62 in 2005 and later.

[9] The NRA for a surviving spouse (currently age 65) is scheduled to increase at a slightly different rate than that for living workers and spouses. The surviving spouse NRA is scheduled to increase gradually to age 67, beginning with those who attain age 62 in 2002 and ending with those who attain age 62 in 2024 and later.

payable to a spouse, provided he or she was married to the deceased worker for at least 10 years.

A surviving spouse or surviving divorced spouse generally loses the right to benefits when he or she remarries before age 60, unless the subsequent marriage ends. Remarriage after attaining age 60 does not prevent or stop entitlement to benefits.

If a fully insured worker's surviving spouse is disabled and aged 50–59, he or she qualifies for a benefit equal to 71.5 percent of the deceased worker's PIA. The disabled surviving spouse must be unable to perform any substantial gainful work, and the disability must have lasted five full months.

A disabled divorced spouse qualifies for the same benefit as that payable to a disabled spouse, provided the marriage to the deceased worker lasted at least 10 years. Remarriage by a disabled spouse or a disabled divorced spouse after age 50 and after the date of disability does not affect benefits.

A fully insured worker's father or mother aged 62 or over qualifies for a survivor benefit equal to 82.5 percent of the deceased worker's PIA if, at the time of the worker's death, the parent was receiving at least one-half of his or her support from the worker. If both parents are entitled to benefits, each receives 75 percent of the worker's PIA.

An individual eligible for more than one type of Social Security benefit receives, in effect, the larger of the two benefits.

The total amount of benefits that all members of one family may receive based on the earnings record of one worker is limited by the maximum family benefit (MFB), an amount that varies with the deceased worker's PIA. If the sum of the individual benefits based on one worker's earnings exceeds the MFB, the benefits of the family members are reduced proportionately to bring the total within the limit. The amount payable to a surviving divorced spouse is not included in figuring the MFB unless the qualification is on the basis of caring for a child of the worker. The MFB assures that the family is not considerably better off financially after a worker dies than it was while he or she was working.

Survivor Income Benefit Plans

Survivor income benefit plans are a type of employment-based death benefit plan. These plans typically pay benefits to specified dependents rather than to designated beneficiaries (who may or may not be dependents) of deceased employees. These benefits are generally paid in equal monthly installments. They are related to survivors' needs and are intended to provide continuing income support. Advocates of survivor income plans believe this need is greatest when the employee is young and has young children rather than when the employee has reached his or her peak earning years and probably has substantial life insurance protection.

When designing survivor income plans, employers typically consider the income level necessary to maintain the survivors' living standard; additional benefit sources that survivors may receive (i.e., other employer-provided death benefits and Social Security benefits); and inflationary effects on benefits. Some plans are designed to provide income for specified lengths of time; these plans enable survivors to make financial adjustments during a transition period; they may pay benefits for periods as short as 2 years or as long as 20 years.

Insurance companies are commonly used as providers of survivor income coverage. However, employers may also self-insure this coverage. Survivor income plans may be entirely employer paid or they may be contributory. Employee contributions are generally made through payroll deductions.

Employee Eligibility—Survivor income plans may cover employees immediately on employment or after a specified waiting period.

Survivor Eligibility—The definition of qualified survivor varies among plans. Typically, qualified survivors who are defined by the terms of the plan and are not named by the individual employee include an employee's spouse and any unmarried dependent children under age 19 (or age 23 if they are still students). Less frequently, eligible survivors include parents or other relatives. In some instances, coverage depends on whether the survivors are truly dependent on the employee for support.

Benefits—Survivor income plans are generally designed to supplement Social Security survivor benefits. Usually, survivor income plans base benefits on the employee's salary at the time of death. The spousal benefit is typically 20 percent to 30 percent, and children's benefits 10 percent to 20 percent, of an employee's salary before death. However, the family's combined benefit may be limited to an overall maximum (e.g., 40 percent).

The amount of a survivor's monthly benefit can also be a fixed dollar amount (specified for all employees) or an amount designated according to an employee's position.

Duration of Benefits—Some plans are designed to pay benefits for time periods related to survivors' ages. Other plans pay benefits for survivors' remaining lifetimes. Generally, children's benefits stop once they reach the plan's age limit or if they marry before reaching the limit. Spouses' benefits may continue until age 60, when a widow(er) becomes eligible for Social Security survivor benefits. Other plans continue widow(er) benefits until the date when the deceased employee would have reached normal retirement age.

Spousal benefits may cease when the widow(er) remarries. However, some plans continue benefits for a specified period regardless of whether the widow(er) remarries. Other plans pay a dowry benefit—i.e., a lump-sum benefit payable on remarriage—to encourage reporting of the marriage.

Taxation—The cost of survivor income benefit plans is tax deductible to the employer. Employer contributions to these plans are generally tax free to employees. If the employer provides the employee with coverage that exceeds $50,000 in life insurance value, the employee may be required to pay taxes on the cost—as determined by a table in sec. 79 of the Internal Revenue Code (IRC)—of the insurance coverage above $50,000. Life insurance proceeds are exempt from federal income tax. But if the beneficiary receives payment in installments over time instead of in a lump sum, a portion of the installment payments that represents the interest is considered to be taxable income. Life insurance proceeds from an unfunded, self-insured plan are taxable if the lump-sum benefit exceeds $5,000.

The portion of the survivor benefit that is taxable qualifies for taxation at a joint-return rate provided the survivor meets the qualifications for a surviving spouse:

- the survivor's spouse died during one of the two immediately preceding taxable years;
- the survivor did not remarry before the close of the taxable year;
- the survivor was able to file jointly in the year the spouse died; and
- the survivor maintained a home (i.e., furnished at least one-half of the cost of maintaining the household) that was the principal place of abode of a dependent of the survivor (as defined by IRC sec. 152) and for whom the taxpayer is entitled to a deduction in the current taxable year.

Pension and Other Qualified Retirement Plan Death Benefits

Most pension and other qualified retirement plans contain provisions for death benefits payable when a participant dies. The Internal Revenue Service requires that these benefits be *incidental* to the plan's main purpose, which is to provide retirement benefits.

Although the Employee Retirement Income Security Act of 1974 (ERISA) and the Retirement Equity Act (REA) of 1984 impose certain requirements, there is still a considerable amount of flexibility in designing pension plan death benefits. Plans may provide both preretirement death benefits and postretirement death benefits.

The REA requires that once a married participant in a pension plan becomes vested, he or she is covered by a qualified preretirement survivor annuity (QPSA) unless the participant and spouse elect otherwise.[10] This protection will provide an annuity to a surviving spouse in the event the participant dies before the retirement annuity commences. This is true whether the participant stays with the employer until retirement or terminates employment sooner.

The minimum amount of the required QPSA is equal to the survivor portion of a joint and survivor annuity (discussed below). If the participant dies before reaching the earliest age at which annuity payments could begin, the annuity is determined by assuming that the participant terminated employment instead of dying, elected commencement of benefits at the earliest date allowed by the plan (usually age 55), and died immediately thereafter. The plan could provide that no annuity payments be provided to the surviving spouse until the date the participant would have reached the earliest retirement age had he or she survived. If the participant dies after the earliest retirement age, the survivor annuity is generally determined by assuming that the participant had retired, elected commencement of a joint and survivor annuity at the time of death, and died on the day after retirement.

The REA also requires that retirement benefits to married persons be paid as a qualified joint and survivor annuity (QJSA), unless the participant and spouse elect to receive benefits in some other form or unless the plan meets one of the exceptions granted under the Tax Reform Act of 1986.[11]

Under a QJSA, the retired worker receives a benefit during his or her retirement years; after death, benefits continue to be paid to the surviving spouse. The survivor annuity cannot be less than 50 percent or more than

---

[10] These automatic survivor benefits apply to participants who have been married at least one year.

[11] Under the Tax Reform Act of 1986, a plan is exempt from the qualified joint and survivor annuity law if, for example, the plan was established before January 1, 1954, as a result of an agreement between employee representatives and the

100 percent of the annuity payable during the joint lives of the retired worker and his or her spouse. The retired worker's benefit is usually reduced to reflect the cost of survivor protection and the ages of the retiree and spouse at the time of retirement. However, some plans pay an unreduced amount to the retired worker. If a married participant wants to reject the joint and survivor annuity, his or her spouse must agree to this rejection in writing before a notary public or plan representative.

ERISA also requires that, as a minimum, all *employee* contributions be paid with interest to a beneficiary if a participant dies before receiving benefits.

Examples of other forms of death benefits under pension plans include the lump-sum value of a participant's accrued benefit, a life insurance contract with a face value equal to 100 times the monthly pension benefit the decedent would have received at normal retirement, monthly payments in the amount the decedent would have received as a pension, and lump-sum death benefits designed to meet final illness and funeral expenses (usually such benefits range from $1,000 to $3,000).

Eligibility for survivor benefits may require a couple to have been married for a specified length of time, or the beneficiary may be required to be a parent of a dependent child. When there is no surviving spouse, benefits may be paid to dependent children. Some plans pay benefits to other dependent relatives.

Taxation—A death benefit from a qualified pension plan paid as a lump-sum distribution may be eligible for five-year forward averaging if it is received after the date on which the participant would have attained age 59 1/2. Lump-sum distributions are generally taxed as ordinary income and are eligible for five-year forward averaging; they may also be eligible for a $5,000 death benefit exclusion. This provision permits beneficiaries to exclude up to $5,000 in employer-provided death benefits from gross income. If the distribution is in the form of periodic payments, this exclusion may not apply.[12]

---

federal government during a period of government operation (under seizure powers) of a major part of the productive facilities of the industry; and if participation in the plan is substantially limited to participants who ceased employment covered by the plan before January 1, 1976.

[12] For a further discussion of taxation of periodic payments, see Everett T. Allen, Jr., et al., *Pension Planning: Pensions, Profit-Sharing, and Other Deferred Compensation*, Seventh edition (Homewood, IL: Richard D. Irwin, 1992).

Under certain circumstances, a lump-sum distribution to a surviving spouse may be eligible for rollover to an individual retirement account (IRA) or another qualified plan. Also, if a spouse inherits an IRA, he or she may roll over that account into his or her own IRA without being taxed on the amount.

Conclusion

The death of a worker or pensioner can be financially devastating to the surviving family. Awareness of this problem has resulted in increasing interest in survivor benefit plans. However, in designing survivor benefit plans one must consider the different public and private programs that currently provide survivor protection. Careful benefit planning can produce effective protection while reducing costly benefit overlaps.

Bibliography

Detlefs, Dale R., Robert J. Myers, and J. Robert Treanor. *1996 Mercer Guide to Social Security and Medicare*. Louisville, KY: William M. Mercer, Inc., 1996.

Mamorsky, Jeffrey D., ed. *Employee Benefits Handbook*. Third edition. Boston, MA: Warren, Gorham & Lamont, 1992.

Martorana, R. George. *Your Pension and Your Spouse—The Joint and Survivor Dilemma*. Third edition. Brookfield, WI: International Foundation of Employee Benefit Plans, 1994.

Rosenbloom, Jerry S., ed. *The Handbook of Employee Benefits: Design, Funding, and Administration*. Third edition. Vol. 1. Homewood, IL: Business One Irwin, 1992.

Rosenbloom, Jerry S., and G. Victor Hallman. *Employee Benefits Planning*. Third edition. Englewood Cliffs, NJ: Prentice-Hall, Inc., 1991.

U.S. Department of Health and Human Services. Social Security Administration. *Social Security Bulletin (Winter 1993)*.

U.S. Department of Labor. Bureau of Labor Statistics. *Employee Benefits in Medium and Large Private Establishments, 1993*. Washington, DC: U.S. Government Printing Office, 1994.

U.S. Social Security Administration. Office of Research and Statistics. *Social Security Bulletin: Annual Statistical Supplement, 1995*. Washington, DC: U.S. Government Printing Office, 1995.

_____. *Social Security Handbook, 1995*. Twelfth edition. Washington, DC: U.S. Government Printing Office, 1995.

Additional Information

International Foundation of Employee Benefit Plans
P.O. Box 69
18700 West Bluemound Road
Brookfield, WI 53008-0069
(414) 786-6700

U.S. Department of Labor
Employee Benefits Survey
200 Constitution Avenue, NW
Washington, DC 20210
(202) 606-6222

U.S. Social Security Administration
6401 Security Boulevard
Baltimore, MD 21235
(800) 772-1213

34. Educational Assistance Benefits

Introduction

During the last 50 years, participation in higher education has grown. One reason has been the demand for more skilled workers to meet the challenges of high technology industries. Another factor was passage of the World War II GI bill, which entitles World War II veterans to a higher education—previously virtually an impossibility for low income veterans. In the late 1950s and in the 1960s, higher education also became more accessible to minorities and low income individuals as a result of government grants, job, and loan programs, most of which were established under the Higher Education Act of 1965.

Higher education is more expensive today than it has been during any previous period in U.S. history. Many individuals who cannot afford to finance their education in full look to federal loan grant programs for financial assistance. However, some of these programs are only available to students who are enrolled at least half time. Many part-time students, therefore, may not receive government assistance. For these individuals, employment-based educational assistance is an important benefit.

Program Design and Types of Assistance

Employers can design their educational assistance plans in a variety of ways. They may reimburse for job-related courses only, for courses relating to future jobs within the company, for degree-related courses, and/or for non job-related courses.

Some employers pay all of the educational expense, most pay only a portion. Employers usually limit benefits in some way, either by reimbursing less than one hundred percent of expenses, by setting a dollar maximum on the reimbursement, or by limiting the number of courses an employee may take per semester or year. Many employers require the employee who receives educational assistance to obtain a certain grade on completion of the course he or she is taking before the cost will be reimbursed. Others reimburse a greater proportion of the cost for a higher grade. Some employers require the employee to stay with the firm for a certain number of years after completing the course or to repay the course costs.

Taxation of Benefits—Originally legislated through the Revenue Act of 1978, Internal Revenue Code (IRC) sec. 127 educational assistance benefits were made explicitly nontaxable from December 31, 1978, through December 31, 1983. Subsequently, Congress extended the provision several times and added dollar limits on excludable amounts. The latest extension was provided through the Omnibus Budget Reconciliation Act of 1993. Through this act, tax-favored treatment of educational benefits was temporarily extended retroactively from years ending after June 30, 1992, through December 31, 1994. The Small Business Job Protection Act of 1996 retroactively extended this income exclusion from January 1, 1995 through May 31, 1997. An overview of the tax benefits is given below.

Under IRC sec. 127, the following requirements must be met in order for employment-based educational benefits to receive preferential treatment.

- The program is required to be a "separate written plan of an employer for the exclusive benefit of his employees to provide such employees with educational assistance."
- The plan cannot discriminate in favor of officers, shareholders, or the highly compensated, or their dependents, who are also employees.
- No more than 5 percent of annual educational assistance benefits can be paid out to shareholders or owners (or their dependents) who own more than 5 percent of the company.
- A plan cannot provide employees with a choice between educational benefits and other *taxable* benefits.
- Reasonable notification must be provided to the employees regarding the terms and availability of the program.

Educational assistance expenses are defined to include tuition, fees, books, certain supplies, and equipment. Meals, lodging, transportation, and courses involving sports, games, or hobbies cannot be included.

Any amounts provided over $5,250 are taxable to the employee. When an employee has multiple jobs, the annual limit applies to educational assistance from all employers.

Employers offering sec. 127 educational assistance benefits are required to file an information return with the U.S. Department of the Treasury, including: the number of employees in the firm; the number of employees eligible to participate in the plan; the number of employees participating in the plan; the program's total cost during the year; and the name, address, and taxpayer identification number of the employer and the type of business in which the employer is engaged.

Availability and Assistance Through the Work Place

Despite the tenuous tax status of educational assistance benefits, many employers continue to offer them. In 1993, 72 percent of medium and large private establishments provided job-related educational assistance, compared with 72 percent and 69 percent in 1991 and 1989, respectively (Employee Benefit Research Institute, 1995). According to a survey conducted by the U.S. Chamber of Commerce, employment-based educational assistance accounted for only a small proportion (0.2 percent) of total employee wages and salaries in 1993.

The provision of these benefits can facilitate career advancement for employees at all income levels. In addition, surveys have shown that educational benefits can contribute to reduced employee turnover, increased productivity, and bolstered morale and motivation. One survey of the restaurant industry—which experiences high turnover and labor shortages—found that the turnover rate of employees participating in educational assistance programs dropped from a preprogram high of 180 percent to 58 percent after the program. The industry norm for turnover ranges from 200 percent to 300 percent.[1]

Scholarships, Loans, and Leave—These are other ways employers can assist in furthering employees' education. Scholarships are nontaxable, loans are generally low-interest, and leave may be paid or unpaid.

Federal Educational Assistance Programs

The U.S. Department of Education offers six major student financial aid programs: Pell grants, Supplemental Educational Opportunity Grants (SEOG), College Work-Study (CWS), Perkins loans (formerly known as National Direct Student Loans), Stafford loans, and PLUS Loans/Supplemental Loans for Students (PLUS/SLS).

Pell Grants—Pell grants help undergraduates finance their college education. This is the largest federal student aid program. If a student is enrolled in two different schools, he or she may not receive Pell grants for duplicative costs. For these grants, each participating school (i.e., one that meets requirements) is guaranteed to receive enough money to pay for the Pell grants for each qualifying student. A student must show financial need to qualify.

[1]Enterprise Communications, "Part-Timers Eat Up Education Program," *Employee Benefit News* (February 1989): 14–15.

Supplemental Educational Opportunity Grants—SEOGs are also financial awards for college undergraduates. Unlike Pell grants, however, the SEOG program allocates a set amount of money each year to an institution. Thus, there is no guarantee that each qualified applicant will receive an award. Like Pell grants, these awards are based on financial need.

College Work-Study—The CWS program, which is for both undergraduate and graduate college students, pays students to work on- or off-campus. It is a combined contribution program sponsored by the government and an employer, college, institution, or off-campus agency. A CWS job must always be with a public or private nonprofit organization.

Perkins Loans—Perkins loans are low-interest loans available to undergraduate and graduate college students through a school's financial aid office. Repayment begins six months after the student graduates, leaves school, or drops below half-time student status. The definition of half-time status is determined by the college or institution. The amount a student may borrow depends on his or her need, the availability of Perkins loan funds at the school, and the amount of other aid received. A Perkins loan is generally repaid monthly over a total repayment period of 10 years, with some exceptions.

Stafford Loans—Stafford loans (formerly guaranteed student loans) are also low-interest loans—financed through banks, credit unions, savings and loan associations, and other eligible lenders—that are available to undergraduate and graduate students attending school at least half time. The amount a student can borrow depends on his or her financial need and student status, not to exceed certain limits.

PLUS/SLS Loans—PLUS loans are available to parents of dependent students; SLS loans are available for student borrowers. PLUS/SLS loans are similar to Stafford loans, but they are available at higher interest rates. Unlike Stafford borrowers, PLUS/SLS borrowers do not have to show need for their loan.

Stafford and PLUS/SLS programs are administered by a state or private nonprofit agency referred to as a "guarantee agency." Each state has its own guarantee agency, which usually charges an origination fee and an insurance premium at the time the loan is disbursed. Interest repayments for an SLS begin within 60 days unless the applicant has qualified for a deferment and the lender agrees to allow the interest to accrue until the deferment ends. There are no deferments for a parent borrower. (For more information on grant, job, and loan programs and state guarantee agency information, contact the U.S. Department of Education, Office of Student Financial Assistance, Washington, DC 20202.)

State Student Incentive Grant Program

The State Student Incentive Grant Program is a combination state and federal tuition assistance program. The government allocates funds to each state guarantee agency based on its enrollment of students in postsecondary education. The state agency must contribute at least 50 percent of the total grant awards made available to students.

Other Federal Assistance Programs

The Veterans Administration offers three types of educational assistance programs: the Montgomery G-1 Bill for active duty service men and women, reservists, and their dependents on duty after June 30, 1995; the Montgomery G-1 Selected Reserve Program for those with a six-year obligation to serve in the selected reserve after June 30, 1985; and the Post Vietnam Veterans' Educational Assistance program, for those on active duty after December 31, 1976 and before July 1, 1985. The latter is a contributory program with a government match. For more information on these programs, contact the Veterans Administration, Washington, DC 20420.

Conclusion

Like most other employee benefits, educational assistance is often a combined effort of employers, the federal government, and individuals. Employers usually provide educational assistance that can enrich their employees' skills and careers. The federal government provides grants, loans, and work-study programs to undergraduate students and loans and work-study programs for graduate students seeking a degree or certificate. Employees, with or without federal or employer assistance, also enrich their job skills and careers by pursuing education on their own.

Bibliography

Combe, Cynthia, and Gerald Talbot. *Employee Benefits Answer Book.* New York, NY: Panel Publishers, 1994.

Employee Benefit Research Institute. *EBRI Databook on Employee Benefits.* Third edition. Washington, DC: Employee Benefit Research Institute, 1995.

Enterprise Communications. "Part-Timers Eat Up Education Program."
Employee Benefit News (February 1989): 14–15.

Hewitt Associates. *Educational Reimbursement Programs, 1990.*
Lincolnshire, IL: Hewitt Associates, 1990.

U.S. Chamber of Commerce. Research Center. *Employee Benefits: 1994
Edition Survey Data from Benefit Year 1993.* Washington, DC: U.S.
Chamber of Commerce, 1994.

Additional Information

American Society for Training and Development
1630 Duke Street
Alexandria, VA 22313
(703) 683-8100

National Institute for Work and Learning
1200 18th Street, NW
Suite 316
Washington, DC 20036
(202) 887-6800

35. Legal Services Plans

Introduction

According to an American Bar Association (ABA) survey, 80 percent of the public is uncertain about how to obtain legal advice. Employed persons usually do not qualify for legal aid or the services of public defenders. Most people tend to postpone seeking legal information and assistance until their needs become acute and, typically, more costly. Thus, wills go unwritten and legal documents go unchecked. Legal services plans can provide affordable legal representation and consultation for many who would otherwise not obtain such services.[1]

Legal services plans are arrangements between a group of people and one or more lawyers to obtain legal assistance. Although such plans have been in existence since the late 1800s, their development was hindered well into the 1900s by bar associations, which opposed the plans out of concern that they constituted a form of client solicitation. However, four U.S. Supreme Court decisions between 1963 and 1971 recognized the constitutional right to obtain legal advice, and the court ruled that bar associations could not interfere with the establishment of legal services plans.

The U.S. Department of Labor reports that 7 percent of full-time employees in private-sector medium and large establishments, or 2.0 million workers and their family members, were eligible for employer-sponsored legal services benefits in 1993 (U.S. Department of Labor, 1994).

Legal services plans primarily provide preventive assistance by making legal information and advice readily available. By preventing questions or simple legal matters from becoming serious problems, they offer the potential for reducing legal expenses; in addition, plan members often receive discounted rates.

Plan Design and Cost

Legal services plans encompass a broad spectrum of designs and costs, ranging from plans that offer free consultations and discounts to those that cover a wide range of legal services. Most plans are group plans.

---

[1] Legal services plans are sometimes known as prepaid legal services plans or group legal services plans.

Plan Types—*Access plans* provide members access to legal advice and services. They typically include in-office or telephone consultation with a lawyer; followup services, such as correspondence; a review of legal documents; self-help counseling; referrals to participating attorneys for further legal assistance; and fee discounts for more complex matters.

In addition to the services provided in the access plans, *comprehensive plans* provide other services such as legal representation for domestic matters; will and estate planning; traffic matters; and consumer, debt, and real estate issues.

Enrollment—In group plans, enrollment may be *automatic* or *voluntary*. In an automatic enrollment plan, all members of the group are automatically members of the plan. In a voluntary enrollment plan, only those members who choose to enroll are covered, on a prepaid basis. Household members typically are also covered.

Both comprehensive plans and access plans seldom cost more than $150 per family per year. According to the National Resource Center for Consumers of Legal Services, the average cost for a qualified group legal service plan is less than $100 per family per year. In addition to group plans offered to members of defined groups, *individual* enrollment plans may be offered by businesses to their customers, also on a prepaid basis.

Delivery of Benefits

The structures for delivering benefits vary as much with legal services plans as with health insurance plans, but they can be classified under three broad categories: open panel plans, closed panel plans, and modified panel (or combination) plans.

Open Panel Plans—Under open panel plans (the least common), a member may use any licensed attorney. Payment for services is usually made according to an established fee schedule, with fees varying depending on the type of service provided. The plan participant is responsible for attorney fees in excess of the scheduled amount. Open panel plans may also use legal services trust funds.

Open panel plans offer advantages and disadvantages. While a participant is able to choose his or her own attorney, the attorney selected is never obligated to accept the case, particularly if the attorney's caseload is heavy or the case is outside his or her area of expertise. Administrative costs are generally higher in open panel plans. Since the sponsoring employer has no control over the attorneys' fees, sponsors often restrict coverage to selected services and/or impose maximum coverage limits.

Closed Panel Plans—There are two types of closed panel plans: staff plans and participating attorney plans. *Staff plans* provide benefits through a full-time, salaried staff of lawyers who are hired specifically to handle the group's needs. In *participating attorney plans*, a plan sponsor contracts with one or more law firms to provide access to legal services to a group of participants who are geographically dispersed. A closed panel can pay lawyers a per capita amount or pay according to a fee schedule. The plan usually pays the entire cost, but some plans may allow the client to be billed for costs in excess of a certain amount or require a percentage payment by the client, as in many health plans.

Administrative costs under closed panel plans are generally lower than open panel plans. Since a smaller number of attorneys is involved, there are fewer records to manage and payments for services may be easier. The lawyers in a closed panel plan often acquire special expertise in areas associated with the covered group's most common problems. Unions usually favor closed panel plans, under which they are able to control the quality of the legal work by controlling the selection of attorneys. Closed panel plans frequently can offer more efficient legal services at lower rates than open panel plans.

Scope of Services

Types of Services Covered— Four broad service categories that may be covered under a comprehensive service plan are consultation, general nonadversarial, domestic relations, and trial and criminal.

- *Consultation*—Legal services plans are used most frequently for legal information and advice (most legal matters require no more). They may deal with virtually any type of legal issue, including consumer matters, landlord-tenant disputes, and domestic disputes (e.g., overdue child support payments and visitation rights). Here, the attorney counsels the participant, either by telephone or in the office, on appropriate legal action or may provide self-help information so the plan participant can resolve the problem on his or her own.
- *General Nonadversarial*— These services are generally performed in an attorney's office. They deal with such matters as review of documents, wills, and adoption papers; guardianship; name changes; personal bankruptcy; real estate transfers; estate closings; and Social

Security, unemployment, and other benefit claims.

- *Domestic Relations*— Legal separations and divorces are the most frequently used services covered by legal services plans. Most plans that cover these services also cover the costs of modifying divorce and separation agreements (such as changes in the terms of child custody agreements, visitation agreements, child support, or separate mainte-nance arrangements). Due to the high cost that is often associated with domestic relations legal problems, many plans limit these types of services.
- *Trial and Criminal*— This type of service includes adversarial legal matters, such as contested adoptions and guardianship, civil suits, and contested domestic relations matters, and minor criminal matters, such as suspension or revocation of driver's licenses, juvenile court proceedings, and misdemeanors. Although infrequently utilized, these services usually incur the highest plan cost per claim; thus, many plans do not cover them.

Exclusions and Limitations— In order to avoid excessive attorney fees and unnecessary services, plan sponsors may build in cost controls by excluding coverage for certain types of services such as actions against employers and unions; services for legal problems existing before the plan's effective date; lawyers' contingency fees; and court expenses such as fines, court costs, filing fees, subpoenas, assessments, penalties, and expert witness fees.

Plans may also use closed lists of eligible procedures, which automati-cally exclude some legal services from the schedule of benefits; limit the number of hours or dollar amount of services rendered; limit the frequency of coverage for a particular service over a specified time; or place maximum limits on the attorneys' hourly fees, which are usually less than the prevail-ing rate.

Taxation

Initially, legal services plan contributions were counted as gross income to the employee. However, employers were allowed to take a tax deduction for their contributions. Subsequent legislative changes removed many of the initial deterrents to the establishment of these plans, particularly their explicit exclusion from taxation under the Tax Revenue Act of 1976, which added sec. 120 to the Internal Revenue Code (IRC). The original law expired at the end of 1981, but subsequent tax laws in 1981, 1984, 1986, 1988, 1989, and 1990 extended the tax exclusion, sometimes retroactively. The extension included in the 1990 law expired on June 30, 1992. Currently, the tax exclusion for legal services plans under IRC sec. 120 is still "expired"; however, there is active lobbying to make it a permanent part of the tax code. Some observers believe that the impermanence of the tax exclusion for legal services plans may discourage their widespread development and use.

In the past, in a qualified plan under IRC sec. 120, employer contributions for legal services benefits of up to $70 per year were excludable from income tax. To qualify for favorable tax treatment, the plan had to meet the following requirements.

- An application for qualification must be filed with the Internal Revenue Service.
- The employer must establish a separate written plan for the exclusive benefit of employees (and their spouses or dependents); the plan must provide only legal services.
- The plan must provide personal legal services; it cannot provide legal services related to an employee's trade or investment property.
- The plan cannot discriminate in favor of shareholders, officers, or highly paid employees. In determining whether the plan is discriminatory, certain employees may be excluded from consideration—specifically, those covered under an agreement determined by the Secretary of Labor to be a collective bargaining agreement, providing there is evidence that group legal services benefits were the subject of good faith bargaining. Certain limits also apply to contributions made on behalf of shareholders and owners who have more than a 5 percent interest in a firm.
- The employer must transmit its plan contributions to designated recipients (e.g., insurance companies, tax-exempt trusts, or authorized service providers).

All legal services plans maintained by a private employer or employee association are classified under the Employee Retirement Income Security Act of 1974 (ERISA) as employee welfare plans and are subject to certain requirements (discussed in chapter 3). Legal services plans sponsored by public employers are not subject to ERISA.

Bibliography

International Foundation of Employee Benefit Plans. "Group Legal Services Plans." In *Employee Benefit Basics: Third Quarter 1995*. Brookfield, WI: International Foundation of Employee Benefit Plans, 1995.

U.S. Department of Labor. Bureau of Labor Statistics. *Employee Benefits in Medium and Large Private Establishments, 1993*. Washington DC: U.S. Government Printing Office, 1994.

Additional Information

American Prepaid Legal Services Institute
1155 E. 60th Street
Chicago IL 60637
(312) 988-5751

National Resource Center for Consumers of Legal Services
6596 Main Street
P.O. Box 340
Gloucester, VA 23061

36. Dependent Care

Introduction

The labor force has changed dramatically over the past few decades. One of the most significant changes is the increase in the number of women in the work force. In 1965, only 37.1 percent of women were in the labor force, compared with 55.3 percent in 1994 (U.S. Department of Labor, 1995). The increasing labor force participation among women means that men are no longer the sole wage earners in many families. Differences in employment patterns for women according to marital status and the presence and age of children have almost disappeared.

In 1993, the husband was the sole earner in only 25 percent of married-couple families, down from 36 percent in 1980. At the same time, husband and wife two-earner couples have increased from 38 percent of all married-couple families in 1980 to 48 percent in 1993 (U.S. Department of Commerce, 1994a). The number of working mothers with children is also increasing. In 1960, approximately 19 percent of women with children under age 6 were in the labor force; in 1993, close to 60 percent of these women were employed (U.S. Department of Commerce, 1994a).

At the same time, the U.S. population is aging. Between 1980 and 1992, the percentage of the population over age 65 increased by more than 21 percent, compared with an 11 percent increase for the total population (U.S. Department of Commerce, 1994a).The growth of the elderly population will be even more dramatic with the aging of the baby boomers.

In response to changing work force and family patterns, dependent care—both child and elder—is emerging as a valuable employee benefit that is offered by a growing number of employers.

Children of Working Parents

The types of child care arrangements available to working parents vary by locality but often include in-home care, in which a person, sometimes a relative, comes to the child's home; family care, in which a child is taken to another home where the provider often takes care of several children; or child care centers, which are organized facilities that care for many children. Most children are cared for in the child's home. The U.S. Bureau of the Census reported that in 1991, among children under age 5 of working mothers, 37.5 percent were cared for in the child's home; 31.0 percent were cared for in another home; 23.0 percent attended a day care center, pre-school, or kindergarten; and 8.7 percent were cared for by their mothers at work.

Child care arrangements vary over the course of a year, especially for school age children. Parents often use multiple arrangements and providers to try to guarantee supervision through the day. The cost of child care varies widely, averaging $64.00 per week in 1990. On average, 7 percent of total family income went toward child care costs (Employee Benefit Research Institute, 1995).

Child Care and the Employer

Studies show that when employees experience child care difficulties, the results are absenteeism, tardiness, decreased morale, and unproductive work time. Employers are beginning to respond to these problems. Many employers have become involved in child care, especially those with a high proportion of younger employees and women and those with high turnover rates and problems with absenteeism.

Types of Assistance—Employer-sponsored child care programs may take a variety of forms. Examples range from company-sponsored day care centers to access to child care information to direct financial assistance to flexibility in work scheduling.

- *Child care centers* at or near the work place are the most visible form of assistance. They usually are company operated or contracted out. Sometimes employers contract with other employers or municipal governments to establish facilities. However, startup costs for centers are high, and continuing labor costs can be higher.

  Some firms support community child care programs. When an employer chooses to finance a community day care center rather than to create an on- or near-site service, the employees of the participating company may receive preferential admission, reduced rates, or a reserved space in the day care center in exchange for the employer's financial support to the center. In this way, the employer avoids the administrative and legal responsibilities but still offers support services. However, support or maintenance of child care centers is not as common as other forms of employer-provided assistance.

- *Resource and referral services* are more common. These services can help parents obtain information on child care and, in many cases, refer them to the most appropriate form in their community. Most companies that offer child care services contract with an existing federal referral agency in the community; others have an in-house hotline capacity. A growing number of employers sponsor educational seminars on parenting issues. Although this form of assistance may not include access to a child care center, it can help the employer estimate the potential demand for child care services before investigating other forms of child care support.

- *Direct financial assistance* with child care expenses is typically provided through employers' flexible benefit plans. Sometimes called "cafeteria plans," these arrangements allow employees to choose among a variety of benefit options paid for by employer contributions, employee contributions, or both. There are various approaches to design, but often flexible benefit plans provide credits that employees can use to purchase benefits of their own choice. When child care benefits are offered in this type of arrangement, those employees who need and want them can purchase them; those who do not may choose other benefits. Flexible benefit plans allow employers flexibility to meet the needs of different lifestyles and at the same time satisfy equity considerations among a diverse work force.

- *Flexible spending accounts*—also known as reimbursement accounts—provide a way to finance child care and other benefits, either within flexible benefit plans or separately as stand-alone plans. These accounts are funded by employee salary reduction arrangements, employer contributions, or both. Under a salary reduction arrangement, the employee makes a pretax contribution to a spending account, which reduces the amount of salary subject to federal income and Social Security taxes. Employees must determine how much they wish to contribute in advance and forfeit any unused dollars at the end of the year. (For more information, see chapter 37 on flexible benefits plans.)

Elder Care

As workers experience conflicts and complications between work and the demands of aging relatives, elder care becomes an increasingly important benefit to employees. When it comes to elder care, workers are requiring information and resources as well as flexible work arrangements from their employers.

Several practical factors differentiate elder care from child care. Elder care may be defined as any assistance given to an elderly person. Cooking a meal, setting up medical appointments, and contributing to rent payments can be forms of elder care (Bureau of National Affairs, 1991). Unlike the birth of a child, the need for elder care often comes suddenly, leaving little time for planning by potential caregivers. Similarly, costs for elder care may be much less predictable than those for child care.

Twenty-four percent of the 1,035 employers surveyed by Hewitt Associates in 1994 offered elder care benefits. Resource and referral service was the most common type of assistance offered (78 percent of employers who offered elder care benefits offered this type of assistance), followed by counseling (21 percent), long-term care insurance (21 percent) and other, e.g., financial support of outside facility (9 percent) (Hewitt Associates, 1994).

The number of employers offering elder care benefits is expected to grow. There is a consensus that the issues surrounding elder care cannot be overlooked; they are expected to gain increasing attention in the coming years. There are two possible reasons for such interest. First, the issue has long-term implications for increasing numbers of employees. As working women delay childbearing into their 30s and 40s, while their parents live longer and longer, increasing numbers of women will join the "sandwich generation," with simultaneous responsibilities for children and dependent adults. Second, corporate executives who are themselves caring for elderly parents identify with the needs of their caregiving employees.

Flexible Work Options

Flexible work schedules have become another form of child and elder care support. Flexible work schedules refer to any adjustment in the hours worked that is different from a traditional fixed daily schedule of five days per week. Certain flexible work schedule policies such as flextime, job sharing, compressed work week, and part-time work have become valuable to many working parents. According to Hewitt Associates, 66 percent of employers offered flexible schedules. Of those employers that offered flexible scheduling, flextime was the most prevalent option, with 71 percent of employers offering this benefit to employees (Hewitt Associates, 1994).

Flextime—This work schedule allows employees to vary the times their work day begins and ends. Variations can occur in the number of hours worked each day or the total number of hours worked each week or pay period. Flextime plans usually have a required core time each day or specified days of the week.

Part-Time—Part-time workers are those who work on a temporary basis or those who work part-time on a continuous or so-called permanent basis. Temporary part-time work helps employers meet their peak time or seasonal needs but generally offers employees lower wages, a somewhat lower job status, and no company benefits. However, some employers may prefer to hire someone they know and trust on a permanent part-time basis rather than hire a new full-time employee. In some cases, permanent part-time workers are offered some benefits as well. Despite the loss of some traditional benefits, permanent part-time employment may afford the worker advantages similar to those offered by flextime.

Job Sharing— Job sharing refers to a structured arrangement that merges the efforts of two or more (part-time) workers into one job. Employees involved in the sharing usually complement each other by having different strengths. The incidence of workers actually using this scheduling practice is low relative to other types of flexible benefits.

Compressed Work Weeks— Compressed work weeks are made up of several long work days on a fixed or rotating basis. Many federal government agencies offer employees the option of working nine hours a day for eight days in a two-week period, followed by one eight-hour day and then the next day off. This scheduling provides a day off every other week.

Taxation

The Economic Recovery Tax Act of 1981 (ERTA) provided tax incentives for employer-sponsored child and dependent care benefits. Dependent care assistance programs (DCAPs), qualified by the Internal Revenue Service under Internal Revenue Code (IRC) sec. 129, provide tax incentives to both employers and employees.

Employers may deduct from income tax the cost of providing child care benefits. Employees may exclude the value of child care benefits from taxable income. The cost of service is not treated as part of employee wages, so neither the employee nor the employer pays FICA or other payroll taxes on this amount. An employee (single or married) may exclude from income up to $5,000 annually or $2,500 for a married individual filing separately, but the amount of dependent care assistance cannot exceed the income of the employee or spouse, whichever is lower. The limits are applicable to the taxable year in which the service occurs, not the year in which the employee is billed or reimbursed. Eligible expenses are limited to dependents under age 13, disabled spouses, and disabled dependents.

To qualify for tax-free status under IRC sec. 129, the program, regardless of the type—child care center, direct payment to a child care provider, or resource and referral service—must be available to all employees and cannot discriminate in favor of employees who are officers, owners, or highly compensated.

An employer must also prepare a written plan setting forth eligibility requirements and the method of payment. Eligible employees must be notified of the plan's availability and terms. On or before January 31 of each year, the employer must give each employee a written statement showing the amounts paid or expenses incurred by the employer in providing dependent care assistance to the employee during the previous calendar year.

IRC sec. 21 permits a federal income tax credit for qualified child care expenses not covered or paid for by an employer-sponsored DCAP. A credit is allowed for eligible children when both spouses work full time or when one spouse is a student and the other is employed. A single parent must be employed or be a student. Qualified expenses are limited to $2,400 for one child and $4,800 for two or more children and cannot exceed the earned income of the individual, if single, or the income of the lesser-earning spouse of a married couple.

A credit equal to 30 percent of eligible expenses is available to individuals with adjusted gross incomes of $10,000 or less. The credit is reduced by one percentage point for each $2,000 of income between $10,000 and $28,000. For individuals with adjusted gross incomes above $28,000, the credit is limited to 20 percent of qualified expenses.

Employees claiming a tax credit or excluding employer DCAP expenses must provide the name, address, and Social Security number or other taxpayer identification number of the care provider on their tax forms. Nonprofit 501 (c)(3) organizations, such as day care centers operated by nonprofit religious or educational organizations, are not required to provide a taxpayer identification number.

The use of both the federal tax credit and employer-sponsored DCAP for child care expenses is restricted. Expenses claimed for the tax credit are reduced dollar for dollar by the amounts excluded under an employer's DCAP. Prior to 1989, an individual could use one form of tax relief (either the tax credit or income exclusion) up to its maximum, then use the other for expenses exceeding that amount. The ability to use either provision independently has not been changed.

Parental Leave

The Family and Medical Leave Act of 1993 requires employers to provide up to 12 weeks of unpaid, job-protected leave each year to eligible employees for the birth or adoption of a child or for the serious illness of the employee or the employee's child, parent, or spouse. Employers are required to maintain the same health care coverage for the duration of the employee's leave that was provided when he or she was actively employed. Employers with fewer than 50 employees are exempt from the law.

The Pregnancy Discrimination Act (PDA) of 1978 requires that employers who choose to offer disability insurance plans treat pregnancy and childbirth as any other disability, with the same employee benefit programs. PDA covers employers with 15 or more employees.

In 1993, 59 percent of full-time employees in medium and large private establishments were eligible for unpaid maternity leave, 52 percent were eligible for unpaid paternity leave, and a small percentage (about 1 percent) were eligible for paid leave (U.S. Department of Labor, 1994a). The length of leave (maternity or paternity) allowed under an employer's plan ranged from under 1 month to 24 months, with an average of 4.3 months.

Adoption Benefits

Adoption benefits include direct financial assistance or reimbursement for expenses related to the adoption of a child and/or the provision for paid or additional unpaid leave (other than what is required by the Family and Medical Leave Act of 1993) for the adoptive parent employee. Such benefits are increasing in popularity but are only available in a limited number of companies. In the Hewitt Associates survey, 21 percent of employers offered employees financial adoption assistance. Among those offering this assistance, 33 percent offered a $2,000 maximum per adoption (Hewitt Associates, 1994). ERTA allowed for the first time a deduction of up to $1,500 for the adoption of a "special needs" child (i.e., one who is aged 5 or over or handicapped) or children belonging to a sibling set. Since this tax revision, a number of legislative proposals have been considered to broaden tax deductibility for cash assistance and/or expenses related to adoption. Currently, the tax status of such cash awards made by employers remains an issue.

Conclusion

In the years ahead, employers are likely to continue to provide a range of child care and elder care assistance. This assistance supports the changing employment relationship between employers and employees, which is evolving from one based on employment guarantees and paternalistic benefits to a partnership based on shared responsibilities. As the standard benefits package changes to support the new employment relationship, assistance will likely broaden beyond dependent care. Some employers are already expanding the scope of their programs to meet the needs of a more diverse group of employees—not just those with families. Among the broader "work/life" benefits they now offer are convenience benefits (on-site dry cleaning, convenience stores, etc.); housing assistance; health promotion programs (health fairs, free flue shots, etc.); and time off with pay.

Bibliography

Bureau of National Affairs, Inc. *Eldercare: A Maturing Benefit.* Bureau of National Affairs Special Report Series on Work and Family, no. 48. Washington DC: Bureau of National Affairs, Inc., 1991.

Catalyst. *Child Care Centers: Quality Indicators.* New York, NY: Catalyst, 1993.

Employee Benefit Research Institute. *EBRI Databook on Employee Benefits.* Third edition. Washington, DC: Employee Benefit Research Institute, 1995.

Hewitt Associates. *Salaried Employee Benefits Provided by Major U.S. Employers in 1994.* Lincolnshire, IL: Hewitt Associates, 1994.

Levitan, Sar A., and Elizabeth A. Conway. *Families in Flux: New Approaches to Meeting Workforce Challenges for Child, Elder, and Health Care in the 1990s.* Washington, DC: Bureau of National Affairs, Inc., 1990.

Neal, Margaret B., et al. *Balancing Work and Caregiving for Children, Adults, and Elders.* Newbury Park, CA: Sage Publications, Inc., 1993.

Sachar, Sally J., et al. *From Homes to Classrooms to Workrooms: State Initiatives to Meet the Needs of the Changing American Family.* Washington, DC: National Governors' Association, 1992.

Saltford, Nancy C. "The Changing Environment of Work and Family." *EBRI Issue Brief* no. 138 (Employee Benefit Research Institute, June 1993).

Saltford, Nancy C., and Ramona K.Z. Heck. "An Overview of Employee Benefits Supportive of Families." *EBRI Special Report* SR-6 (Employee Benefit Research Institute, February 1990).

Smith, Dayle M. *Kin Care and the American Corporation: Solving the Work /
Family Dilemma*. Homewood, IL: Business One Irwin, 1991.

U.S. Department of Commerce. Bureau of the Census. *Statistical Abstract of
the United States, 1994*. Washington DC: U.S. Government Printing
Office, 1994a.

_____. *Who's Minding the Kids? Child Care Arrangements; Fall 1991
(Data from the Survey of Income and Program Participation)*. Current
Population Survey, P-70-36. Washington DC: U.S. Government Printing
Office, 1994b.

U.S. Department of Labor. Bureau of Labor Statistics. *Employee Benefits in
Medium and Large Private Establishments, 1993*. Washington, DC: U.S.
Government Printing Office, 1994a.

_____. *Employee Benefits in Small Private Establishments, 1992*. Wash-
ington, DC: U.S. Government Printing Office, 1994b.

_____. *Employment and Earnings, January 1995*. Washington DC: U.S.
Government Printing Office, 1995.

Additional Information

Catalyst
250 Park Ave. South, 5th Floor
New York, NY 10003
(212) 777-8900

Families and Work Institute
330 Seventh Avenue
New York, NY
(212) 465-2044

37. Flexible Benefits Plans

Introduction

The characteristics of the U.S. labor force and population have changed substantially in the last 25 years. Family relationships, lifestyles, and increased longevity have raised questions about the efficacy of conventional benefit plans. The work force has experienced an influx of young workers and female workers whose lifestyles and values are different from those of 25 years ago. Changes in social and economic circumstances have affected workers' needs and preferences.

Most employee benefit programs are designed to satisfy the traditional family's needs. Workers' benefit needs are largely determined by their age, marital and family status, and compensation levels. Traditional programs may not reflect the circumstances of single workers with no dependents, two-earner couples, and single-parent workers; additionally, they may not anticipate changes in workers' needs over time.

Some employers have implemented flexible benefit plans to respond to their workers' differing needs. The central idea in flexible plans is that they allow employees to make choices about their benefits that previously were made by their employers. Within the plan's rules, some flexible plans allow an employee to determine how the employer's contributions will be allocated among the benefits offered. Depending on plan specifications, employees may also elect to reduce their salaries to purchase additional benefits.

Flexible benefit plans are attracting great interest among employees and employers. According to a recent survey of full-time employees in private medium and large establishments, 12 percent had flexible benefit plans, and 52 percent were covered by employer-sponsored reimbursement accounts in 1993, compared with 9 percent and 23 percent, respectively, in 1989 (U.S. Department of Labor, 1994). Furthermore, the number of employers offering flexible benefit plans is growing. A 1993 survey of flexible compensation found that an estimated 1,444 flexible benefit plans were in effect, compared with 19 in 1981 (Hewitt Associates, 1993).

Tax Status

Flexible benefit or cafeteria plans are governed by sec. 125 of the Internal Revenue Code (IRC). Prior to the enactment of this section in 1978, employees could not choose between taxable forms of compensation (including cash) and nontaxable benefits without rendering the latter taxable. Sec. 125 provided that the opportunity to choose would not alter the tax status of the benefit chosen. Thus, its enactment made a choice between cash and nontaxable benefits and between taxable and nontaxable benefits feasible. Employee choice in benefit programs had previously been limited to a choice among options without a benefit category, such as health insurance.

Types of Plans

As the term implies, flexible plans present a variety of design alternatives. Premium conversion plans, flexible spending accounts (FSAs), and cafeteria plans are each a specific type of flexible benefit plan.

Premium Conversion Plans—These plans may exist within a cafeteria plan or separately. If an employer's health care plan requires an employee premium contribution, premium conversion allows employees to make their contribution with pretax dollars.

Flexible Spending Accounts—Typically, FSAs may exist as stand-alone plans or within cafeteria plans. FSAs allow employees to set money aside for qualified unreimbursed medical or dependent care expenses through pretax salary reduction in separate accounts. Employees choose how much money they want to contribute to an FSA at the beginning of the plan year within limits (see chapter 36 on dependent care). To the extent that these funds are not used for expenses incurred during the plan year, they are forfeited.

Cafeteria Plans—Technically, a cafeteria plan is an employee benefit plan that offers an employee certain choices in accordance with IRC sec. 125. Cafeteria plans must offer a combination of qualified nontaxable benefits (health insurance, sickness and accident insurance, long-term disability, etc.) and taxable benefits (or cash).

Cafeteria plans and flexible benefit plans are often used interchangeably. However, a flexible benefit plan does not necessarily need to be an IRC sec. 125 (tax advantaged) cafeteria plan—but a cafeteria plan is a type of flexible benefit plan.

Benefits That May Be Included in a Flexible Benefit Plan

In March 1989, the Internal Revenue Service (IRS) released proposed regulations on cafeteria plans that update and supplement the regulations issued in 1984. Under the 1989 proposed regulations, the following nontaxable and taxable benefits (including cash) may be offered under a cafeteria plan:

- accident and health plans, including health care spending accounts;
- group term life insurance (including taxable coverage over $50,000) and dependent coverage;
- disability benefits and accidental death and dismemberment plans;
- employee contributions to sec. 401(k) plans or thrift savings plans, either pretax or after tax;
- dependent care assistance plans, including dependent care spending accounts;
- otherwise qualified benefits that are taxable because they fail to satisfy nondiscrimination requirements;
- vacation days;
- group legal services (although these plans are usually offered separately);
- any taxable benefit that is purchased by the employee with after-tax dollars, such as group automobile insurance.

Flexible plans may not be used to defer compensation or to defer benefits from one year to another, except for 401(k) deferrals. Benefits that may not be included under a cafeteria plan include scholarships, defined benefit plans, education assistance benefits, employee discounts, and other employee benefits, whether or not taxable.

Funding

Flexible benefit plans may be funded by employer contributions, employee contributions, or both. Some plans utilize salary reduction, which enables employees to use pretax dollars to fund certain benefits. (When an employee agrees to a salary reduction, the reduction amount is not part of his or her taxable income).

Salary reduction is frequently used to fund health care and dependent care spending (reimbursement) accounts and to convert the contributions employees make to health insurance premiums to employer contributions, thus rendering them nontaxable. Salary reduction amounts under flexible plans are excluded from Social Security (FICA) and unemployment (FUTA) taxes unless the amounts are contributed to 401(k) plans. Flexible benefit plans may also permit employees to purchase benefits with after-tax dollars.

Impact on Cost

Some employers have used flexible benefit plans to reduce their benefit costs or the rate of increase in these costs. When flexible credits are used, the amount of credits accorded each employee does not necessarily increase each year or move in tandem with the most inflation prone benefit (health care). Thus, the full impact of inflation may not be reflected in the employer's costs. Flexible plans may also encourage cost conscious behavior on the part of employees. Employees have more control over employer contributions under flexible plans than they have when benefits are offered on a "take it or leave it" basis, and they may opt for less expensive coverage in one area (health) in order to release funds for another desired benefit or cash. Salary reduction arrangements can produce savings for both employees and employers. Employees "save" the amount of the tax they would have paid on the salary reduction amount, while both employees and employers save on FICA taxes associated with the amount. The employee's savings are counterbalanced by the fact that benefits based on pay (e.g., Social Security) may also be reduced.

IRS Requirements

The design of cafeteria plans is constrained by a number of requirements in the IRC and its implementing regulations. A few of the more important requirements are listed below.

- In order to obtain favorable tax status, flexible benefit plans must not discriminate in favor of highly compensated or key employees (as defined in law and regulation). Three tests are applied. The first requires that no more than 25 percent of the tax-favored benefits provided under the plan be provided to key employees. The second requires that the flexible plan be available to a classification of employees that does not discriminate in favor of the highly compensated. The third requires that the flexible program must not discriminate in favor of the highly compensated employees with regard to contributions and benefits. In addition, specific benefits offered under a flexible plan may be subject to special nondiscrimination rules applicable to that benefit.
- Employees must make their elections under flexible benefit plans before the coverage period begins. Generally, these choices cannot be revoked after the start of the plan year. The 1989 proposed regulations

clarify and expand the circumstances under which an employee may make election changes. However, a plan is not required to allow these election changes. In general, election changes may be made when a change in family status occurs (provided the change is consistent with the altered family status) and when a health plan provided by an independent third party undergoes significant change in cost or coverage. Also, to the extent that an employee is allowed to make changes in contributions to a 401(k) plan, these changes are permissible under a cafeteria plan. Elections may be revoked when an employee separates from service or stops making premium payments.

- To assure that the regulations are satisfied, the coverage period for each benefit should be a full year, and all coverage periods should coincide with the cafeteria plan year.
- Flexible plans must not be used to defer compensation (except in the case of sec. 401(k) arrangements). Unused credits or benefits, including unused vacation days, may be carried over to a subsequent plan year. However, unused funds in FSAs must be forfeited.
- Funds allocated to one FSA, such as a health care reimbursement account, cannot be used to reimburse other types of claims, such as dependent care expenses.
- In the case of health care reimbursement accounts, the coverage must be uniform throughout the year (i.e., the full amount for the benefit year must be available regardless of how much has actually been contributed at a particular point during the year).
- Claims for reimbursement from FSAs must be documented with a written statement from an independent third party (i.e., physician or day care center) specifying that the expense has been incurred and the amount. The employee must certify that the claim has not been reimbursed through any other coverage (or, in the case of dependent care, that the charge is an eligible expense under the plan).

Advantages and Disadvantages of Flexible Benefit Plans

Flexible benefit plans offer employees and employers a number of advantages.

- Employees may receive more benefit value because they can tailor their benefits to their needs. Employees can change benefits as their lives change (e.g., when they marry or divorce, as their salaries increase, or as their children mature and leave home).

- Employees may become more appreciative of their benefits. This may improve employee morale and productivity.
- Employees may become more involved in controlling benefit costs. Moreover, when employees want a new benefit, they are asked to trade another benefit for it rather than to expect their employer to provide additional benefits.
- Flexible compensation plans can be used to convert workers' earnings into tax-free employee benefits, thereby producing a more valuable compensation dollar.

Flexible compensation plans also present potential disadvantages to employees and employers (although most of these can be minimized by careful planning).

- Some employees may not understand their choices well enough to choose the most needed benefits; thus families could suffer from losses in areas where they did not select adequate coverage. This problem can be addressed, in part, by a mandatory core program that assures basic protection and also by an effective communications program.
- Flexible plans may result in increased utilization and adverse selection, both of which may cause problems with group insurance underwriting requirements and result in higher benefit costs. Plan features can be added to minimize adverse selection (for example, limits can be placed on coverage levels and the frequency of election periods). The options can be priced to prevent the higher costs that can be caused by adverse selection.
- The requirement for health care spending accounts to provide uniform coverage throughout the plan year could expose an employer to additional liability if employees incur large claims early in the year and terminate employment before fully funding their accounts. This danger can be minimized by plan design features and by defining lower annual maximums or limiting midyear changes.
- Greater benefit flexibility is likely to result in greater administrative complexity and costs. To some extent, administrative costs can be controlled by restricting employee options and the frequency of benefit election periods. These restrictions limit the amount of flexibility under the plan, however. A number of available packaged computer

systems for handling enrollment, benefit payment, and recordkeeping can reduce the time and costs of implementing flexible benefit plans.

Deciding on a Flexible Plan

Before deciding to offer a flexible benefit plan, an employer should determine whether this type of plan is consistent with the organization's overall philosophy and is likely to advance its management goals and objectives. The design of a specific plan is often preceded by a survey to determine whether employees are receptive to the concept of flexible benefits and to identify the benefit choices employees most need and want. Once a decision is made to proceed, the employer must confront a number of basic issues. The most basic issue is probably, "How much do I want to spend and how can I maximize employee satisfaction or minimize employee dissatisfaction while limiting costs to that figure?" Some questions plan designers should decide are whether, and how, to include currently offered benefits in the plan; whether to provide a core of benefits; what benefits to make optional; what value to place on each option; how to distribute flexible credits; how to price options to prevent adverse selection; and under what circumstances to permit employees to change elections.

Bibliography

Brackey, Marianne, et al., eds. *Fundamentals of Flexible Compensation.* Second edition. New York, NY: John Wiley & Sons, 1992.

Employee Benefit Research Institute. *Databook on Employee Benefits.* Third edition. Washington, DC: Employee Benefit Research Institute, 1995.

Foley, Jill. "Flexible Benefits, Choice, and Work Force Diversity." *EBRI Issue Brief* no. 139 (Employee Benefit Research Institute, July 1993).

Harger, J. Lawrence. *Flex Plan Handbook.* Washington, DC: Thompson Publishing Group, 1992.

Hewitt Associates. *Survey on Flexible Compensation Programs and Practices.* Lincolnshire, IL: Hewitt Associates, 1993.

Manin, Mark, and Francesca Sciandra. *Flexible Benefits Answer Book.* New York, NY: Panel Publishers, 1994.

U.S. Department of Labor. Bureau of Labor Statistics. *Employee Benefits in Medium and Large Private Establishments, 1993.* Washington, DC: U.S. Government Printing Office, 1994.

_____. *Employee Benefits in Small Private Establishments, 1992.* Washington, DC: U.S. Government Printing Office, 1994.

Additional Information

Employers Council on Flexible Compensation
927 15th St., NW, Suite 1000
Washington, DC 20005

PART FIVE
PUBLIC SECTOR BENEFITS

38. The Public-Sector Environment

Introduction

More than 19 million individuals are employed by public jurisdictions in the United States. These public entities include the federal government; state, county, and municipal governments; school districts; and a host of other special-purpose districts and authorities. Approximately 15 percent of the employed labor force, or more than one in six working Americans, works for a public entity.[1]

Nearly all of these public employees are covered by employee benefit programs. While there is enormous diversity among the programs, taken together, they exhibit a certain family resemblance and differ in important respects from private-sector programs. This chapter highlights these differences and provides an overview of the current status of employee benefits in the public sector.

Many of the differences between public-sector and private-sector benefit plans stem from the different environments in which they operate. Indeed, the environmental differences are so important that some discussion of them is necessary to provide a context for the differences in individual benefits.

Centrality of Politics

The most significant difference between public- and private-sector benefit programs lies in their relationship to the legislative process. Private-sector plans are strongly affected by laws passed by national and state legislatures, but within these constraints private plan sponsors are relatively free to establish, maintain, and modify their plans. Public employee plans, on the other hand, are not so much affected by the legislative process as they are products of that process. These plans' basic features—eligibility, contributions, types of benefits, etc.—are often described in statutes or in local ordinances. (This is especially true in the pension area.) Moreover, even where collective bargaining over benefit issues is allowed, the legislatures generally retain some measure of control. Furthermore, public employee programs usually exist within a highly structured personnel system

---

[1] Employee Benefit Research Institute tabulations of the March 1995 Current Population Survey.

that is itself prescribed, often in great detail, in public law.

Because they are legislative products, public employee benefit plans necessarily reflect the interplay of political forces. Since large sums of public money are involved as well as the welfare of those who implement public policy, it is regarded as entirely appropriate that major benefit issues should be decided through the political process. This process is not the most efficient means of decision making, however, nor is it the best adapted to consideration of complex, technical issues. It inevitably involves the clash of multiple interest groups. Moreover, where public employee benefit plans are concerned, the "interested" groups usually extend far beyond the public administrators and employees (and their unions and associations) that are directly affected to include provider groups, insurers, the business and financial community, and taxpayer organizations.

The influence of organized labor on public employee benefits is particularly strong. Approximately 44.7 percent of public employees are represented by labor unions, compared with 12.0 percent of private employees (U.S. Department of Commerce, 1995). This influence is exercised directly where bargaining over benefit issues is allowed, but it is also exercised indirectly through the legislative process. In fact, where public employee benefits are concerned, labor-management negotiations and legislative politics are often inextricably intertwined.

Relationship to Federal Law

A second fundamental difference in the environment of public employee plans as opposed to those sponsored by private companies is the role played by federal tax and benefits law and regulation. The taxing power of the federal government has been used to encourage the provision of employee benefits by private business since 1916, when corporations were first allowed to deduct payments to retired employees, their families, and dependents as ordinary and necessary expenses (Graebner, 1980). The federal government's taxing power has also been used to compel certain behavior (e.g., participation in Social Security) by the levying of payroll taxes. Public jurisdictions are not taxpaying entities, however, and their behavior cannot be influenced by opportunities to reduce federal tax on their revenues.

State and local jurisdictions also coexist with the federal government in a system of federalism, and while the powers and prerogatives of the various levels of government have changed over time, the balance among them is always a politically delicate issue. Even when the federal government has formally asserted that its laws apply to benefit plans for state and local employees, it has for the most part shown little interest in enforcing them. (Attention to public plans has increased in the last several years, however; see chapter 40 on defined benefit plans in the public sector for more detail.) For reasons unrelated to federalism, the federal government has also chosen to exclude its own employees' benefit programs from major parts of the law applicable to private plans. The special status of governmental plans can be seen most readily in their relationship to two landmark pieces of federal legislation, the Social Security Act of 1935 and the Employee Retirement Income Security Act of 1974 (ERISA).

Benefit Systems

For many public employees, the immediate employing entity is not the sponsor or the administrator of the benefit plans under which they are covered. Particularly in the pension area, the public sector is characterized by a relatively small number of large systems and a large number of small systems. According to the Bureau of Census, there are 2,307 state and local retirement systems, with the 209 systems administered by the states accounting for 88 percent of the total covered population (U.S. Department of Commerce, 1995). At the federal level, most civilian employees are covered by the Civil Service Retirement System or the Federal Employees Retirement System. Certain relatively small groups—e.g., Foreign Service and military personnel—have their own, entirely separate arrangements.

Health and life insurance plans are more likely to be operated by each jurisdiction for its own employees and, unlike pension plans, they are often collectively bargained. However, New York and California operate statewide health benefit programs in which local government employees can elect to participate. Where they exist, state-run long-term disability and sickness and accident insurance plans may also be open to local government entities.

Occupational Divisions

Another salient feature of public employment for benefit purposes is that the work force is subdivided along certain occupational lines. In most jurisdictions law enforcement and firefighting employees have their own programs apart from those for other public employees. Alternatively, they may participate in a general system but in plans that take into account their unique career patterns. (These occupations are, of course, unique to the public sector.) Public school teachers also sometimes have separate plans or separate arrangements, whether they participate in a state-run or a local plan. The special status of these occupational groups is partly historical (they were among the first to obtain pension coverage), partly a consequence of the occupations' characteristics and requirements, and partly a reflection of their ability to protect their interests in the political arena.

One characteristic of private-sector plans that is extremely rare in the public sector is the provision of separate benefits for executives. In the public sector, benefit provisions tend to apply equally to all levels of the work force. Even where separate "executive services" have been recognized, separate benefit provisions are rare. This egalitarian tradition does not extend to members of the judiciary or the legislature, however. Judges almost always have their own separate pension plans, typically with higher benefit accrual rates, while legislators enjoy faster pension vesting, eligibility, and computation provisions. The judges' plans are justified on the grounds that the judiciary must be provided a sufficient measure of security to allow them to carry out their responsibilities in an impartial, disinterested way and also because they typically enter the system at a late age. The special provisions for legislators are justified by the uncertain nature of their tenure.[2]

Commonalities

Finally, in highlighting the differences between public- and private-sector employee benefit plans, the numerous commonalities should not be overlooked. In a competitive marketplace, all employers need to attract and retain workers and to maintain a healthy and vigorous work force. To the extent that benefit programs serve these needs, they are based on common motives and directed at common goals. Furthermore, while public pension systems developed early and more or less independently of private business practice, the later addition of health and welfare plans was often a response to the availability of such benefits in private employment. Indeed, in determining many aspects of compensation for public employees, legislators look first to the practices prevailing in the business community. Thus, many

---

[2] For a discussion of the legal forms and occupational divisions in public-sector pension plans, see McGill, 1992.

developments in private-sector employee benefit plans eventually surface in public employee programs, albeit in a form tailored to the public entity's traditions and circumstances.

Bibliography

Employee Benefit Research Institute. *Databook on Employee Benefits*. Third edition. Washington, DC: Employee Benefit Research Institute, 1995.

_____. *Fundamentals of Employee Benefit Programs for Education Employees*. Washington, DC: Employee Benefit Research Institute, 1993.

Graebner, William. *A History of Retirement*. New Haven, CT: Yale University Press, 1980.

McGill, Dan M. "Public Employee Pension Plans." In Jerry Rosenbloom, ed., *Handbook of Employee Benefits: Design, Funding, and Administration*. Homewood, IL: Business One Irwin, 1992.

National Education Association. *Status of the American Public School Teacher, 1990–1991*. Washington, DC: National Education Association, 1992.

Salisbury, Dallas L. "Pension Tax Expenditures: Are They Worth the Cost?" *EBRI Issue Brief* no. 134 (Employee Benefit Research Institute, February 1993).

U.S. Department of Commerce. Bureau of the Census. *Statistical Abstract of the United States, 1995*. Washington, DC: U.S. Government Printing Office, 1995.

U.S. Department of Labor. Bureau of Labor Statistics. *Employee Benefits in State and Local Governments, 1994*. Washington, DC: U.S. Government Printing Office, 1996.

_____. *1992 Census of Governments*. Washington, DC: U.S. Government Printing Office, 1995.

Additional Information

Public Employee Department
AFL-CIO
815 16th Street, NW
Washington, DC 20006
(202) 393-2820

U.S. Department of Commerce
Bureau of the Census
Washington, DC 20233
(301) 457-4100

39. Regulation of Public-Sector Pension Plans

Introduction

Like their private-sector counterparts, public-sector pension plans are extensively regulated by the federal Internal Revenue Code (IRC), the common source of rules governing the deferral of taxation for each type of pension plan. In fact, this regulation has been significantly expanded in recent years. In exchange for the deferral of taxation and for certain other favorable tax treatment, the IRC sets forth certain pension plan requirements some of which apply to both government and private-sector plans and others from which government plans are exempt.[1]

In addition to IRC regulations, public-sector plans are extensively regulated and governed by state constitutional, statutory, and decisional law. These plans are, in fact, highly regulated, and in the past three decades the states have voluntarily adopted regulations, procedures, and practices—legal, actuarial, accounting, administrative, and investment—that have led to strong, responsible, and effective public employee retirement systems (PERS) across the country. Because of their well-developed benefit programs, the significant size of their assets ($1.5 trillion), and their large numbers of active and retired members (15 or more million), they are naturally the subject of interest to all stakeholders involved in their operation, including public employers; employer associations; plan members and employee organizations; taxpayers; legislators on the state, local, and federal level; and, last but not least, the beneficiaries.

Federal Regulation

Due to the unique nature of public pension plans, they are regulated largely by state and local law, while federal regulation of these plans has been evolutionary. When the Employee Retirement Income Security Act of 1974 (ERISA) was enacted,[2] Congress intentionally excluded government

---

[1] Joseph G. Metz, *The Federal Taxation of Public Employee Retirement Systems: A Handbook for Public Officials* (Chicago, IL: Government Finance Officers Association, 1988).

[2] The Employee Retirement Income Security Act of 1974 established federal rules regarding private-sector pension plans, including funding; fiduciary standards; and reporting and disclosure of plan information.

pension plans from some sections of ERISA because "additional time was considered necessary to determine the need for federal regulation of these plans."[3] ERISA called for a congressional study of several aspects of goverment pension plans, including the adequacy of their financing arrangements and fiduciary standards. The study, *The Pension Task Force Report on Public Employee Retirement Systems*, which was completed four years later, reported some deficiencies in public plans—including plans covering federal employees—in the areas of funding, reporting and disclosure, and fiduciary practices. However, the report found public pension plan terminations and insolvencies to be rare. (Later the same year, the federal government imposed reporting and disclosure requirements on pension systems for its own employees.) Based on the study, proposals partly or wholly paralleling ERISA were advanced for federal regulation of other public plans.

Many sections of ERISA do apply to public-sector plans, including Title III and significant sections of Title II. Government plans are exempt from ERISA's reporting, disclosure, and funding requirements (Title I) and plan termination insurance (Title IV). Although ERISA excluded public plans from several sections, public plans were required to comply with pre-ERISA requirements of the IRC.[4] These pre-ERISA requirements form the bedrock of plan qualification rules on which both private- and public-sector plans have been shaped.

While some observers continue to believe that state and local plans would benefit from the federal imposition of ERISA-like standards, state and local plans are financially sound. Even though some underfunded plans can still be found (primarily at the local level), public pension systems are generally well financed. A 1993 study by the Public Pension Coordinating Council concluded that, "To meet their pension obligations, the respondent plans have accumulated substantial assets and generally demonstrate strong financial health" (Zorn, 1994). According to the study, 75 percent of

---

[3] U.S. Congress, House, Committee on Education and Labor, *Pension Task Force Report on Public Employee Retirement Systems*, Committee Print, 95th Congress, 2nd Session, March 15, 1978 (Washington, DC: U.S. Government Printing Office, 1978).

[4] The Internal Revenue Code (IRC) speaks in terms of *governmental plans* rather than public pensions. A governmental plan is any plan established and maintained by a federal, state, or local government or by an agency or instrumentality of that government. The term also includes plans sponsored by certain international organizations.

all systems conducted actuarial valuations on an annual basis, and 91 percent conducted them at least every two years (Zorn, 1994).

Tax Laws and Public-Sector Plans

The federal government continues to impose regulations on public pension plans. In recent years, especially since the Tax Reform Act of 1986 (TRA '86), public plans have increasingly shared more of the same IRC rules with private-sector plans, making the ERISA-nonERISA distinction largely irrelevant in the late 1980s.

Beginning in 1977, the Internal Revenue Service (IRS) observed a 12-year moratorium on disqualifying public retirement systems for violating applicable qualification rules.[5] In May 1989, the IRS lifted the moratorium on adverse qualification decisions based on discrimination requirements and determined that government and church plans must satisfy certain nondiscrimination requirements (Federal Register, 1989). Furthermore, in May 1990, rules issued by the IRS on coverage,[6] participation, and general nondiscrimination explicitly provided transition rules for government plans to give these units sufficient time to come into compliance (Federal Register, 1990). To date, these transition rules have not been issued by the IRS. This lack of guidance by the IRS has resulted in the agency extending the effective date to plan year 1999.

On the legislative level, a series of tax laws enacted in the mid and late 1980s modified the legal framework for benefit plans, and many of their provisions—unlike those of ERISA—were made applicable to government plans. Amendments made by TRA '86, in particular, added new requirements that apply to public plans as well as private-sector plans.

For example, the IRC sec. 401(a)(17) limit on compensation ($150,000 in

---

[5] The Internal Revenue Service (IRS) has had the issue of whether and how to regulate public pension plans under study for some time. In 1977, it announced that it was going to reconsider application of IRS' qualification requirements to public plans, and until the reconsideration process was completed, qualification issues would be resolved in favor of the taxpayer or the governmental employer by continuing to treat the plan as if it were qualified. As of the start of 1982, public plans have no longer been required to file the annual pension plan information form that had been used as the basis for review of governmental plans for compliance with the tax qualification rules.

[6] Coverage rules govern the age and service requirements employers may set for allowing employees to participate in pension plans.

1996, indexed) applies to governmental plans through a grandfather rule. The regulations governing the sec. 401(a)(17) annual compensation limit generally took effect on January 1, 1996. There have been efforts to exclude governmental plans (e.g., sec. 403(b) annuities) from the nondiscrimination requirements because the regulations written for the private sector are unworkable within the unique structure of public plans. The IRS has delayed the effective date of most of the pension nondiscrimination regulations under 401(a)(4) due to an inability to create workable regulations for IRC sec. 403(b) tax-sheltered annuity plans and for qualified retirement plans maintained by governmental employers.[7]

Most public employee retirement plans are contributory, and TRA '86 replaced a special "three year recovery" of contributions rule that had applied primarily to public employees. Where public employees had earlier been granted up to three years of tax-free benefit payments to recover their own post-tax investment in pension plans, TRA '86 stipulated that their benefits were to be treated as partly taxable and partly tax free, based on an "exclusion ratio." Furthermore, if those employees received a preretirement starting date distribution, even if the distribution equaled their accumulated contributions, it would be treated as partly a tax-free return of contributions and partly a taxable distribution. The ratio of the tax-free to the taxable part of the distribution would reflect the ratio of the total employee contributions to the total value of the plan's expected benefits.

TRA '86 recognized that public employee plans provide normal retirement benefits at an earlier age, on average, than most private-sector plans due to the inclusion of public safety employees. The IRC sec. 415(b) benefit limitations apply,[8] although sec. 415 (b)(2)(F) provides special protection for governmental employees by substituting age 62 for the Social Security normal retirement age. Specifically, governmental plans were allowed to remain under pre-TRA '86 sec. 415 limits regarding maximum benefits and actuarial reductions for retirement before a specified age. Because retirement at younger ages is common in the public sector, compliance with the new, more severe sec. 415 rules would have forced some public jurisdictions to reduce benefits to current employees below promised amounts, violating

---

[7] For sec. 403(b) plans, the effective date of the nondiscrimination regulations has been delayed until January 1, 1997. In the case of governmental plans, the effective date has been delayed until 1999 or later.

[8] The Small Business Job Protection Act of 1996 modified the 415 limits in a manner that the 100 percent of compensation limit will not apply to government plans.

pension plan law and in some cases constitutional law that prohibits cutbacks in public employees' benefits. Special sec. 415 rules were also enacted for police and firefighters, who typically retire at younger ages than other public workers. Because some state and local plans had promised benefits even beyond those allowed under pre-TRA '86 limits, an additional option was provided under the Technical and Miscellaneous Revenue Act of 1988. This law allowed jurisdictions to "grandfather" and excuse any sec. 415 violations resulting from benefit payments made to employees who became plan members before January 1, 1990, although the jurisdiction had to apply the new sec. 415 limits applicable to private plans to all future plan members.

State and Local Regulation

In addition to federal regulation, governmental plans are governed by state constitutional law and statutory law. Constitutional and contractual law guarantees, which may be expressed in state statutes and decisional law, afford members of public employee retirement plans many of the protections granted to members of ERISA-regulated plans by federal statutory law. In fact, it is safe to say that the public employees have stronger protection than private-sector employees today. A private-sector company can simply do away with its pension plan, subject to Pension Benefit Guaranty Corporation rules; merge; or terminate. This does not happen in the public sector because of the strong legal guarantees in place.

In those instances where ERISA rules are not applicable to public plans, such as reporting and disclosure, it is interesting that public plans are adopting the rules (through their state legislatures) on a voluntary basis. State statutes most often spell out benefit formulas, age and service require-ments, and vesting and contributions and typically include ancillary provi-sions such as disability and death benefits. These statutes constitute a "plan document" that contains the plan provisions of a private-sector plan.

Many states have also established pension commissions. In fact, New York had established a successful commission as early as 1971, and by the late 1980s, permanent pension commissions and legislative retirement committees had been formed in 21 states, temporary commissions had been formed in 3 states, and legislative committees with pension activities had been formed in 3 states. These commissions and committees were formed for the purpose of providing "guidance to public executives, administrators, and legislators in developing public retirement objectives and principles, identi-fying problems and areas of abuse, projecting costs of existing systems and modifications to those systems, and designing and implementing pension reform programs" (Foster Higgins, 1988). In some cases, the pension commissions also oversee nonpension benefit programs (e.g., studying the costs of providing postretirement medical coverage for public employees) and serve as a buffer between the legislature and special interest groups.

Investment Practices

The investment policy of most of the $1.5 trillion public employee retirement systems is governed by state or local statute. Most states incorporate "prudent person" rules, which require that investments be made with the care of a prudent individual, solely in the interest of plan participants, echoing ERISA's definition of the prudent person principle. Many states also have "legal lists" of permissible or prohibited investments, percentage limits on certain types of investments, or rules covering diversification of pension assets. For example, some states limit the percentage of assets that can be invested in equities (perhaps to 50 percent or less), while other states permit allocation of a percentage of assets to in-state investments (occasionally defined as a percentage in residential mortgages). Other common investment restrictions include limiting the maximum amount of assets that can be placed in one company, in foreign stocks or bonds, or in real estate.

Public pension plans are leaders in corporate governance, sound investment policies, asset allocation, and international investments, while at the same time they tend to be more risk averse, on average, than private plans. During the last decade, many jurisdictions have broadened permissible investment opportunities for their pension plans, allowing them to prudently pursue a higher return for participants. While public pension funds invested 95 percent of their assets in bonds in 1950, this share had declined to 45 percent by 1994. Meanwhile, the investment in equities increased from 1 percent in 1950 to 43 percent in 1994 (Employee Benefit Research Institute, 1995).

Public pension plans have been largely successful in increasing returns through these changes. With a notable pool of assets, public plans are facing issues such as the propriety of using public pension fund investments to further social goals (e.g., bringing pressure on the South African government to end apartheid or a prohibition against investing in Northern Ireland munitions manufacturers); to shore up the local, state, or regional economy (targeted investing); or to finance such controversial measures as hostile takeovers and leveraged buyouts. The Bankruptcy Reform Act of

1994 gave state and local government pension plans seats on creditors' committees in corporate bankruptcies.

Conclusion

Public pension plans have been substantially strengthened by federal, state, and local laws and regulations over the past three decades. In many instances, these new rules have narrowed the gap between public- and private-sector plans. Ironically, due to their strong constitutional and statutory guarantees on the state level, employees' rights and benefits may have even greater protection today in the public sector than they have in the private sector. The cadre of professional pension administrators, informed legislators, and state and local government administrators involved in the public pension policymaking process on a day-to-day basis has, in fact, ushered in a new era for PERS.

Bibliography

Advisory Commission on Intergovernmental Relations. *State and Local Pension Systems.* Washington, DC: Advisory Commission on Intergovernmental Relations, 1980.

Charles D. Spencer & Associates, Inc. "Public Employer Plans Are Exempt from Title I of ERISA But Are Snared Under the Tax Code." *Spencer's Research Reports on Employee Benefits* (July 7, 1995): 108.03–108.04.

_____. "Standards and Investment Policies of State Employee Retirement Systems." *Spencer's Research Reports on Employee Benefits* (July 1989): 108.02-1–108.02-9.

_____. "State Pension Commissions Assist Legislatures in Designing and Funding Public Employee Plans." *Spencer's Research Reports on Employee Benefits* (January 1989): 108.01-1–108.01.-4.

Congressional Research Service Research Team. *Public Pension Plans: The Issues Raised Over Control of Plan Assets.* Washington, DC: Congressional Research Service, 1990.

Employee Benefit Research Institute. *Quarterly Pension Investment Report, 2nd Quarter 1995.* Washington, DC: Employee Benefit Research Institute, 1995.

Hushbeck, Clare. *Public Employee Pension Funds: Retirement Security for Plan Participants or Cash Cow for State Governments?* Washington, DC: American Association of Retired Persons, 1993.

Federal Register (18 May 1989): 21437.

Federal Register (14 May 1990): 19897, 19935, and 19947.

Foster Higgins. *Foster Higgins Report on State Pension Systems*, 1994. Twelfth edition. New York, NY: A. Foster Higgins & Co., Inc., 1994.

_____. *Pension Commission Clearinghouse, Report on the State Pension Commissions*. New York, NY: A. Foster Higgins & Co., Inc., 1988.

Metz, Joseph G. *The Federal Taxation of Public Employee Retirement Systems: A Handbook for Public Officials*. Chicago, IL: Government Finance Officers Association, 1988.

National Council on Teacher Retirement. *Report of the National Council on Teacher Retirement on State Law Conformance with PEPPRA*. Austin, TX: National Council on Teacher Retirement, 1984.

Nesbitt, Stephen L., Jeanne M. Shearer, and Daniel Stern. *1994 Wilshire Report on State Retirement Systems: Funding Levels and Asset Allocation*. Santa Monica, CA: Wilshire Associates Inc., 1994.

Salisbury, Dallas L., and Nora Super Jones, eds. *Pension Funding & Taxation: Implications for Tomorrow*. Washington, DC: Employee Benefit Research Institute, 1994.

Schmitt, Ray, Carolyn L. Merck, and Jennifer A. Nesiner. *Public Pension Plans: A Status Report*. Washington, DC: Congressional Research Service, 1991.

U.S. Congress. House Committee on Education and Labor. *Pension Task Force Report on Public Employee Retirement Systems*. Appendix A. Washington, DC: U.S. Government Printing Office, 1978.

U.S. Congress. House Committee on Education and Labor. Subcommittee on Labor-Management Relations. *Hearings on the Public Employee Retirement Income Security Act of 1982*. Washington, DC: U.S. Government Printing Office, 1983.

Zorn, Paul. *Survey of State and Local Government Employee Retirement Systems*. Chicago, IL: Public Pension Coordinating Council, 1994.

Zorn, Paul, and Michael Hanus. *Public Pension Accounting and Reporting: A Survey of Current Practices*. Chicago, IL: Government Finance Officers Association, 1987.

Additional Information

American Academy of Actuaries
1729 Eye Street, NW, 7th Floor
Washington, DC 20006
(202) 223-8196

Government Finance Officers Association
180 North Michigan Avenue, Suite 800
Chicago, IL 60601
(312) 977-9700

40. Defined Benefit Pension Plans in the Public Sector

Introduction

There are many differences between public-sector defined benefit plans and private-sector defined benefit plans, including the requirement in many public plans that employees contribute toward the cost of the plan and the prevalence of cost-of-living adjustments (COLAs) in most public plans but few private plans. Also, public-sector employees are more likely to be covered by defined benefit pension plans than workers in private-sector establishments employing 100 or more workers (establishments similar in size to state and local governments). According to surveys by the U.S. Department of Labor, Bureau of Labor Statistics (BLS), among full-time workers in 1994, 91 percent of state and local government employees participated in a defined benefit pension plan, compared with 56 percent of private-sector employees in medium and large private establishments in 1993 (U.S. Department of Labor, 1994 and 1996). Approximately 90 percent of all federal employees are covered by defined benefit pension plans (U.S. Office of Personnel Management, 1995).

Federal Government Plans

The Federal Retirement Program includes two pension plans: the Civil Service Retirement System (CSRS) and the Federal Employees' Retirement System (FERS).

CSRS was enacted in May 1920 and has been amended by many subsequent acts of Congress. CSRS is a stand-alone retirement system intended to provide reasonable benefits for long-service federal employees and is administered by the U.S. Office of Personnel Management (OPM).

FERS was established in June 1986 and was created by Congress as a result of the expansion of Social Security to federal workers beginning in 1984,[1] although many other considerations went into the development of the new system. FERS is a three-part pension program that became effective on January 1, 1987. Using Social Security as a base, it provides an

---

[1] For further discussion of Social Security coverage of public employees, see chapter 2 on Social Security and Medicare.

additional defined benefit and a voluntary thrift savings plan. Only the defined benefit portion of FERS is administered by OPM. The Thrift Savings Plan is administered by a separate independent agency. (For further discussion of the Federal Thrift Savings Plan, see chapter 41 on supplemental savings plans in the public sector.) As of the beginning of fiscal year 1994, there were 2.8 million active participants and 2.3 million annuitants (retirees and survivors) in CSRS and FERS (U.S. Office of Personnel Management, 1995).

Financing—The Civil Service Retirement and Disability Fund (CSRDF) finances the operation of CSRS and FERS. By law, the entire fund is available for payment of either CSRS or FERS benefits.

Coverage—Both CSRS and FERS include as members appointed and elected officers and employees in or under the executive, judicial, and legislative branches of the U.S. government, except those excluded by law or regulation.

CSRS covers most federal employees hired before 1984 and is closed to new members. FERS generally covers those employees who first entered a covered position on or after January 1, 1984. Since the FERS program did not become effective until January 1, 1987, an interim plan (created under the Federal Employees' Retirement Contribution Temporary Adjustment Act) was in effect from January 1, 1984, through December 31, 1986. Any employee hired during that period received credit for all service toward FERS. Employees covered by CSRS had the opportunity to transfer to FERS from July 1, 1987, through December 31, 1987.[2] About 86,000 employees took advantage of this opportunity.

Eligibility for Retirement, Disability Retirement, and Death Benefits—

CSRS—CSRS provides a full range of pension benefits and wage insurance protections, including: annuities for employees who meet age and service criteria for voluntary retirement, annuities for employees whose jobs are terminated after they have reached certain specified levels of age and/or service, benefits to employees who become unable to perform in their positions because of a disabling condition, and benefits to deceased employees' and deceased retirees' survivors who meet certain conditions.

Employees covered by CSRS qualify for normal retirement or full annuity at age 55 with 30 years of service, age 60 with 20 years of service,

---

[2] For CSRS employees who met special criteria, there was an extended open season from January 1, 1988, through June 30, 1988.

or age 62 with 5 years of service. The average CSRS retirement age is about 61.5 (U.S. General Accounting Office, 1995). Deferred annuities are payable at age 62, provided the employee has completed at least five years of service before separation from service. Involuntary retirement is permitted at any age after 25 years of service or at age 50 with 20 years of service. Disability retirement is permitted at any age with five years of service.

An employee's widow or widower and children may qualify for a survivor annuity if the employee's death occurs while the employee is employed and a member of the retirement system and after the employee has completed at least 18 months of creditable civilian service.[3] A retiree's widow, widower, or former spouse will receive benefits in the event of the death of the retiree, provided the retiree elected a survivor annuity when he or she retired. Election of a survivor annuity at retirement will result in a reduction of the full retirement annuity in order to offset part of the cost of the additional protection afforded survivors.

FERS—Like CSRS, FERS provides benefits for normal retirement or early retirement due to involuntary separation, disability, and death. In addition, FERS provides reduced benefits for early retirement, an option that is not available under CSRS. Certain FERS retirees are also eligible for an annuity supplement.

FERS provides for full retirement benefits at the minimum retirement age (MRA) with 30 years of service, age 60 with 20 years of service, or age 62 with 5 years of service. The MRA is 55 for those born before 1948 and increases gradually to age 57 for those born in or after 1970.[4] Workers may retire at the MRA with only 10 years of service, but those who do so receive reduced benefits. Employees in FERS have retired, on average, at age 63.5 (U.S. General Accounting Office, 1995). Deferred retirement benefits are payable at age 62 with at least 5 years of service or at age 55 with at least 10 years of service. In cases of involuntary separation, full immediate benefits are payable at age 50 with 20 years of service or at any age with 25 years of service. Disability benefits are payable at any age with

---

[3] For more information on survivors' eligibility for benefits, see Mace and Yoder (1996).

[4] The minimum retirement age (MRA) is age 55 until 2002, when it begins to climb by two months per year in coordination with the gradual rise in the normal retirement age under Social Security. The MRA reaches age 56 in 2009, where it remains until the year 2020. The MRA begins rising again by two months per year in 2021 and reaches age 57 in the year 2026.

18 months of service.

In general, the same conditions required for survivors of CSRS participants to be eligible for benefits must be met in order for survivors of FERS participants to be eligible for benefits.

A special annuity supplement is payable until age 62 to certain eligible retirees. Those eligible include employees who retire at the MRA with 30 years of service or at age 60 with 20 years of service, or those on involuntary retirement. The supplement approximates the Social Security benefit earned while employed under FERS and is subject to reduction if earnings exceed a specified amount. The supplement was created in order to bring FERS benefits nearer to those of CSRS participants. (For more information on the special annuity supplement, see Mace and Yoder, 1996.)

Computation of Benefits

CSRS—The CSRS benefit formula uses an average salary that is based on the highest three years of salary (high-3 average salary). The general retirement annuity formula provides 1.5 percent of high-3 average salary for the first five years of service, 1.75 percent of high-3 average salary for the next five years, and 2 percent for any remaining years, up to a maximum of 80 percent of average salary. This annuity will be reduced if the retiree elected the survivor annuity.[5]

In the case of deferred retirement, the computation of benefits is performed as if the former employee is retiring from his or her former federal job at that point, using the highest three years of salary at the time of separation.

In the case of involuntary retirement, if the retiring employee is under age 55, the general retirement annuity rate is permanently reduced by one-sixth of 1 percent for each full month (2 percent a year) the retiree is under age 55.

For disability retirement, the annuity payable is the lesser of either 40 percent of high-3 average salary or the amount computed under the general formula using service projected to age 60. The general formula for annuity computation will be applied if a larger annuity would result.

The law also contains special eligibility and computation requirements for annuity and disability benefits of plan participants who fall into one of the following categories: certain law enforcement officers, firefighters, air

---

[5] For more information on the amount of the reduction, see Mace and Yoder (1996).

traffic controllers, bankruptcy judges, congressional employees, members of Congress, and certain other groups.

In the case of death, qualifying widows and widowers of deceased employees receive 55 percent of the disability formula as a benefit. This amount is generally equal to 22 percent of the deceased employee's high-3 average salary. Widows and widowers of deceased annuitants receive 55 percent of the annuity unless the employee annuitant waived provisions of a survivor benefit or elected to provide less than a full survivor benefit. Children of deceased annuitants and employees receive a flat monthly amount.

FERS—The average salary used in FERS benefit computations is also based on the highest three years of salary. The general annuity formula provides 1 percent of high-3 average salary times the years of creditable service. If retirement is at age 62 or later with at least 20 years of service, a factor of 1.1 percent is used rather than 1 percent. For workers who choose the reduced benefit option (i.e., workers who retire at the MRA with 10 years of service), the reduction is 5 percent for each year the employee is under age 62 at retirement.

In the case of deferred retirement, separated workers will have benefits computed as if they are retiring from their former federal jobs at that point. For separated workers who elect the deferred benefit at age 55 with at least 10 years of service, the benefit computation will include the applicable reductions of 5 percent for each year of age under age 62.

For FERS participants retiring under the involuntary separation rules, benefits are not reduced. However, the annuity supplement referred to earlier is not payable until the employee reaches the MRA (age 55–57).

In the case of disability, annuitants in the first year of retirement generally receive 60 percent of their high-3 average salary minus 100 percent of their Social Security disability benefits. In subsequent years, annuitants receive 40 percent of their high-3 average salary, minus 60 percent of their Social Security disability benefits. At age 62, FERS disability benefit is recomputed.

For annuity and disability benefits, the law also contains special eligibility and computation requirements for certain law enforcement officers, firefighters, air traffic controllers, congressional employees, members of Congress, and military reserve technicians.

In the case of death, qualifying widows and widowers of deceased employees receive a lump-sum payment of $15,000 (indexed to CSRS COLAs since 1987) plus either one-half of the annual rate of pay at death or one-half of the high-3 average pay as of the date of death, whichever is higher. If the employee had at least 10 years of service, the surviving spouse also receives an annuity equaling 50 percent of the accrued basic retirement benefit, unless the employee annuitant and spouse waived provision of a survivor benefit or elected a benefit of 25 percent. If the surviving spouse is under age 60, a FERS supplement is added to the FERS survivor benefit. Children of deceased annuitants and employees receive a flat monthly amount, minus the amount of Social Security benefits payable to them.

Employees who transferred from CSRS to FERS will have part of their annuities computed using CSRS general formula.[6]

Employee Contributions and Refunds of Contributions

CSRS and FERS both require contributions from employees. Except in certain special circumstances, amounts contributed have no bearing on amounts received. The contributions are deducted from an employee's pretax pay.

CSRS—Employees covered by CSRS must pay 7 percent of their basic pay in order to participate in the program. Basic pay includes salaries for regularly scheduled work.[7] These involuntary contributions are credited to the program under the employee's name. Employees who separate from government service or transfer to a position not covered by CSRS are eligible for a refund of their accumulated contributions. A separating employee who exercises the right to withdraw contributions waives the right to collect further benefits from CSRS, although participants can restore their lost rights under the program if they are reemployed by the federal government by repaying the withdrawn amounts, plus interest.

CSRS also allows for voluntary contributions by participants. Employees covered by CSRS who want to receive a larger annuity than would be payable based on salary and service may make voluntary contributions.[8]

---

[6] For more information on the benefits of employees who transferred from CSRS to FERS, see Mace and Yoder (1996).

[7] Exclusions include pay for special services such as night duty as well as for bonuses, allowances, overtime, and lump-sum payments for unused leave.

[8] Voluntary contributions cannot be deducted from an employee's salary. An employee may make voluntary contributions whenever he or she chooses, and contributions must be in multiples of $25.

Voluntary contribution annuities are not increased by COLAs. Total contributions may not at any time exceed 10 percent of the accumulated base pay the employee has received during federal service. Since 1985, voluntary contributions earn a variable interest rate,[9] based on the average yield of new investments purchased by CSRDF during the previous fiscal year, as determined by the U.S. Department of the Treasury.

FERS—Employees covered by FERS are also required to make contributions in order to participate in the program. FERS participants pay at a rate of total basic pay that, combined with the employee Old-Age, Survivors, and Disability Insurance (OASDI) portion of Social Security taxes, equals 7 percent. In 1996, the rate for FERS involuntary contributions was 0.8 percent of basic pay. (The 1996 OASDI employee tax rate was 6.2 percent.) Mandatory payments decline to 0.8 percent for wages above the Social Security wage base ($62,700 in 1996). Employees who separate from government service or transfer to a position not covered by FERS are eligible for a refund of their contributions. Participants who receive refunds of their contributions at separation are not able to recapture the lost service in the event that they return to federal employment.

There are no voluntary contributions for FERS participants, due to the existence of the Federal Thrift Savings Plan.

Cost-of-Living Adjustments—

CSRS—In accordance with the Omnibus Budget Reconciliation Act of 1983, civil service retirees and survivor annuitants receive annual COLAs. Initial COLAs for newly retired employees (or their survivors) are prorated, depending on the month in which the annuity begins. The COLA reflects the yearly change in the third calendar quarter average Consumer Price Index for Urban Wage Earners and Clerical Workers (CPI-W).

FERS—In general, retirees aged 62 and over receive COLAs. Survivors, disabled retirees, and certain other special groups receive COLAs regardless of age. Annuities are adjusted annually to reflect cost-of-living increases as measured by the yearly change in the third calendar quarter's average CPI-W.[10] Initial COLAs of retiring employees (or survivors of an employee)

---

[9] Prior to 1985, the interest rate was fixed at 3 percent.

[10] If the CPI-W increase is 3 percent or more, the cost-of-living adjustment (COLA) is one percentage point less than the CPI-W increase. If the CPI-W increase is greater than or equal to 2 percent but less than 3 percent, the COLA is 2 percent. If the CPI-W increase is less than 2 percent, the COLA is equal to it.

are prorated based on the number of months the employee is in receipt of an annuity prior to the effective date of the increase. The annuity supplement for retirees is not increased by COLAs, but the supplement for survivors is increased.

Coordination with Social Security—The FERS defined benefit plan is coordinated with Social Security, since (except for totally and permanently disabled workers) FERS benefits are added to Social Security benefits. When CSRS began in the early 1920s, Social Security had not yet been established. CSRS employees were excluded from Social Security when it became effective in 1937, and as Social Security expanded the type and generosity of benefits over the years, CSRS made appropriate changes so that coverage for federal workers and coverage for other workers remained roughly comparable. When Congress decided to expand Social Security coverage to federal employees in 1984, restructuring federal civilian retirement benefits became necessary. The product of this restructuring is FERS. Participants in FERS are also covered by Social Security, whereas most[11] participants in CSRS are not covered by Social Security. The benefit formulas under CSRS and FERS are different, due to coordination of FERS with Social Security. Like other individuals covered by Social Security, FERS participants have Social Security and Medicare (Federal Insurance Contributions Act (FICA)) taxes deducted from their pay.

State and Local Government Plans

Total membership in state and local government retirement systems was approximately 13.6 million in 1992. State systems had 11.9 million members and local systems had 1.7 million. There are 209 state-administered systems and 2,097 locally administered systems, for a total of 2,307 public employee retirement systems. Benefit payments totaling $44.2 billion were made to 4.7 million persons, for an average monthly payment of $768 per beneficiary (U.S. Department of Commerce, 1995).

The first group to be covered by a public employee retirement system (PERS) was the police force of New York City in 1857. By the early 1900s,

---

[11] Federal employees separated from service for at least one year are automatically covered by Social Security if they resume federal employment after 1983. Due to this separation in service, some employees are participants in both Social Security and CSRS. In these cases, CSRS benefits are reduced by the amount of Social Security benefits earned through federal employment. For more information, see Mace and Yoder (1996).

many other municipal employee retirement systems were in existence. In many of the early systems, coverage was confined to teachers or to firefighters and police officers. The first state employee retirement system was established by Massachusetts in 1911, covering the general service employees of the state. By 1930, 12 percent of the larger state-administered pension systems currently in existence had been established, and by 1947, every state provided retirement benefits. The percentage of full-time state and local government employees participating in a defined benefit pension plan has continued to grow; in 1994, approximately 9 of 10 such employees were defined benefit pension plan participants (U.S. Department of Labor, 1996). PERS plans range in size from those with more than 400,000 participants (e.g., the New York State Employees' Retirement System) to plans covering fewer than five employees (e.g., plans in townships or boroughs).[12]

Funding—A majority of state and local retirement systems are supported by both employer and employee contributions. Employee contributions provide a steady source of income to PERS plans. Contributions of the employing agencies are subject to the approval of the legislature (or other financing agency) and usually come out of general revenues. Employer contributions may also come from special taxes or levies.

Coverage—Plans may cover all types of employees, but benefit formulas and other plan provisions may be different for certain categories of employees (i.e., general employees, teachers, firefighters, police officers, judges, legislators, and elected officials). Such differences may result from historical distinctions or varying retirement policies. For example, public school teachers may have plans different from those for general employees, often because the system for teachers preceded that for general employees. Firefighters and police officers are often permitted to retire with full benefits at a younger age than most other employees, since such positions require young and vigorous employees. For judges, legislators, and elected officials, a career may encompass a much shorter period of time than for other categories of employees, so plan provisions may allow for accrual of benefits at a faster rate.

Eligibility for Retirement, Disability Retirement, and Death Benefits—According to a 1994 BLS survey of state and local government employees, 43 percent of all state and local employees could retire with normal, unreduced pensions, regardless of age, after satisfying a service

---

[12] See Rosenbloom (1992).

requirement (usually 30 years) (U.S. Department of Labor, 1996). Twenty-one percent could retire on attaining age 55, usually with a 30-year service requirement. Even earlier retirement eligibility (sometimes with no minimum age) is common for law enforcement and firefighting personnel at all levels of government, usually on completion of a service requirement of as little as 20 to 25 years (Rosenbloom, 1992). Not all public employees are eligible for retirement at younger ages, however. Thirteen percent of state and local employees were in plans with minimum age requirements of 60 to 65 in 1994 (U.S. Department of Labor, 1996).

In 1994, 91 percent of teachers and 85 percent of other government pension participants were in defined benefit plans that permitted them to retire early and receive an immediate but reduced pension. Almost all plans that permit early retirement make it the employee's option, but a few plans require employer approval. Early retirement is generally available only to participants with a certain number of years of service. Plans permitting early retirement at age 55 generally require at least 10 years of service; plans permitting early retirement prior to age 55 usually require 10–25 years of service.

Almost all state and local government employees are covered by disability retirement benefits. Participants must often meet a service requirement (e.g., 5 or 10 years) in order to be eligible for disability retirement benefits.

Preretirement survivor benefits (i.e., benefits for the survivors of a state or local government employee who dies before retirement) were provided to 87 percent of state and local government employees in 1994. Generally, participants must be vested before preretirement survivor benefits are available. Postretirement survivor benefits (i.e., benefits provided to the survivors of a state or local government employee who dies after retirement) were available to all state and local government pension plans participants in 1994.

Computation of Benefits—For normal retirement, the nearly universal defined benefit formula is the terminal earnings-based formula, which typically pays a flat percentage of earnings (an average of 1.9 percent in 1994) per year of service, based on earnings in the final years of employment (terminal earnings). For example, an employee who worked for 30 years and is covered by a plan that pays 1.5 percent per year of service would earn annual benefits equal to 45 percent of terminal earnings. For 61 percent of participants in 1994, terminal earnings were defined as a three-year average (often an employee's highest average earnings for three consecutive years). Some plans have alternative formulas that are used to provide a minimum level of benefits for individuals with short service or low earnings. The alternative formula may be a second terminal earnings formula or a formula that pays a flat dollar amount per year of service.

The amount of an early retirement pension is reduced because benefits begin at an earlier age and are paid over a longer period of time. The early retirement benefit is generally calculated by reducing the normal retirement benefit by a percentage for each year between the early and normal retirement ages. For example, if a plan's normal retirement age is 62 and the reduction factor is 5 percent, a person retiring at age 60 would receive 90 percent of the normal retirement benefit. The reduction factor may be uniform (e.g., 3 percent, 5 percent, or 6 percent for each year of early retirement) or may vary by age or service.

Disability retirement benefits often begin immediately, provided the employee's disability satisfies the pension plan's definition of total disability. In 1994, 42 percent of full-time state and local government employees were in plans with an "unreduced normal formula," in which case the disabled worker's pension is computed under the plan's normal benefit formula and is paid as if retirement had occurred on the plan's normal retirement date, either based on years of service actually completed or projected to a later date. Other methods of calculating disability benefits include: flat amount benefits, dollar amount formulas,[13] percentage of unreduced normal benefits less Social Security, and percentage of earnings formulas both with and without Social Security offsets. A few state and local government pension plans have deferred disability retirement benefits. The workers in these plans are often given long-term disability insurance benefits that typically provide 50 percent, 60 percent, or 67 percent of earnings at the time of disability. Once the long-term disability benefits cease, disability retirement benefits begin.

According to the BLS, of those full-time state and local government employees with a preretirement survivor annuity provided, nearly 81 percent had plans in which the surviving spouse would receive an annuity equivalent to the amount payable if the employee had retired (early retirement is usually assumed) on the day prior to death, with a joint-and-survivor form of payment in effect (U.S. Department of Labor, 1996). For those with preretirement survivor annuities based on early retirement, the most common annuities were 50 percent and 100 percent of the deceased

---

[13] Dollar amount formulas specify a flat dollar amount times years of service.

employee's pension. Most full-time state and local government employees with a postretirement survivor annuity have plans with an annuity that provides income during the lifetime of both the retiree and the surviving spouse. Many participants are in plans that give them a choice of two or more alternative percentages (usually 50 percent, 67 percent, or 100 percent), to be continued to the spouse. Depending on the alternative percentage chosen, reductions in the retiree's annuity are made accordingly. The few participants not in the plans noted above are in plans that provide the survivors with between 50 percent and 100 percent of the retiree's pension. For those participants in plans without the joint-and-survivor annuity, survivor benefits are typically a portion of the retiree's accrued benefit, in which case there is no reduction to the employee's pension to account for survivor benefits.

Employee Contributions and Refunds of Contributions—The majority of state and local government employees are required to contribute to their defined benefit plans; 72 percent of full-time state and local plan participants had to pay part of the cost of their plans in 1994 (U.S. Department of Labor, 1996).

Most public employees' mandatory contributions are made on an after-tax basis. However, in the 1994 BLS survey, 47 percent of contributory plan participants were allowed to have regular contributions deducted from their salaries on a pretax basis. One form of pretax contributions is the employer pickup. Employer pickups are permitted under sec. 414(h)(2) of the Internal Revenue Code (IRC). Although sec. 414(h) took effect in 1974, few systems adopted employer pickups until the 1983 amendments to the Social Security Act, which clarified that picked-up contributions are subject to the FICA tax.[14] Under the employer pickup provision, the employee's salary is reduced for tax purposes by the contributed amount. These contributions are then "picked up" and are treated as if they were made by the employer instead of the employee.

Public employees in a contributory system who terminate employment before becoming eligible for retirement benefits are generally entitled to a refund of their own contributions. Such refunds usually include credited interest that may be established by statute or may depend on the fund's earnings or on current economic conditions. Many systems allow employees

---

[14] It should be noted that the Deficit Reduction Act of 1984 specified that after 1983 only pickups made under "a salary reduction agreement" would be included in Federal Insurance Contributions Act wages.

to reinstate service credit that was forfeited after a break in service. Reinstatement may be allowed only after the employee has refunded the withdrawn contributions (and perhaps interest from the time of original payment), although some systems allow the employee to repay on an installment basis.

Employee contributions that were made on an after-tax basis are not subject to income tax or penalties when refunded, although the portion of the refund that has not yet been taxed (e.g., credited interest or picked-up contributions) is taxable and may also be subject to the 10 percent penalty under IRC sec. 72(t).[15]

The refund of contributions to employees who terminate employment with limited service is generally in the form of a lump sum. Employees of most systems also have the option of deferred vested benefits, provided they terminate employment after meeting certain service or age and service requirements. Service-related qualifications for vesting are typically five years.

Forms of Benefit Payments—Although defined benefit pension plans typically pay their benefits in the form of annuities covering the life of the retiree and spouse, some plans offer an option in the form of a lump-sum payment that provides the employee with the actuarial equivalent of the annuity. In 1994, lump-sum payments were available to 11 percent of full-time state and local employees. In most of these plans, a partial lump sum with annuity was available, in which case the participant generally receives a reduced annuity for the remainder of his or her life. The participant receives no further benefits from the pension plan if a full lump-sum distribution is taken.

In an effort to add benefit flexibility for plan participants without increasing costs, a growing number of public safety and other public-sector employers are considering delayed/deferred retirement option plans (DROPs). DROPs are optional payment forms under defined benefit plans similar to the traditional or partial lump-sum options that allow participants to elect to receive a lump sum in exchange for a reduced monthly benefit for life.

Cost-of-Living Increases—Public employee plans are widely known

---

[15] This tax is imposed unless the refund occurs following death, disability, attainment of age 59$\frac{1}{2}$, or separation from service after age 55. This tax burden may be overcome if the employee rolls over the contributions into an individual retirement account.

for their COLAs, a feature not often seen in the private sector. According to a 1994 BLS survey, among state and local jurisdictions, 45 percent of employees are in plans that have automatic adjustments, with a majority basing annual adjustments on increases in the BLS CPI. Such adjustments are usually made annually and are often subject to a maximum of 3 percent or less. (A few plans have lifetime ceilings on increases.) In those states that do not have automatic COLAs, the legislatures may grant ad hoc adjustments that are not directly linked to a cost-of-living index. In 1994, 13 percent of participants were in public plans that granted ad hoc increases. Under an ad hoc increase, retirees' current pensions are usually increased by a percentage of the present benefit (e.g., 8 percent). The public sector—which comprises more or less permanent entities that rely on the tax base rather than on operating results for their resources—has historically been more willing than the private sector to commit to postretirement benefit adjustments.

Integration with Social Security—Unlike employees in the private sector, those in state and local governments are not universally covered by Social Security.[16] The Social Security Act originally excluded all state and local government employees from coverage because of uncertainty concerning whether the federal government could legally tax state and local employers. In 1950, the Social Security Act was amended to allow state and local employees not already covered under a retirement system to acquire Social Security coverage in a manner consistent with their employers' sovereignty—through voluntary agreements between the state and federal governments. In keeping with the voluntary nature of the coverage agreements, public jurisdictions were allowed to opt out of Social Security after a five-year period of participation, if they gave two years' notice. In 1954, groups of employees who were already covered by retirement systems became eligible for Social Security, provided a majority of the members of the group voted for coverage in a referendum. (Police officers and firefighters, at the request of their representatives, were excluded.) Two years later, specified states and interstate authorities were allowed to cover parts of groups (including police officers and firefighters) on the condition that all newly hired members of the group in question would be covered. In 1967, the law was further amended to allow all states to provide Social

---

[16] For further discussion of the history of the relationship between Social Security and state and local governments, see chapter 2 on Social Security and Medicare.

Security coverage for firefighters (but not police officers) who were already covered under a state or local retirement system (U.S. Congress, 1982).

Since the withdrawal of state and local governments from the Social Security system resulted in a loss of much needed revenue and since employees of disaffiliated agencies continued to be entitled to some Social Security benefits, Congress revised the Social Security Act again in 1983. A provision in the Social Security Amendments Act of 1983 prevented state and local governments that had elected Social Security coverage from terminating the coverage. State and local governments that had already withdrawn were also permitted to reenter the system. The Omnibus Budget Reconciliation Act of 1986 contained further amendments to the Social Security Act. As a result of the 1986 amendments, all persons hired by state and local governments that do not participate in Social Security must be covered under the Hospital Insurance (Medicare) segment of the Social Security program. As a result of the Omnibus Reconciliation Act of 1990, Social Security coverage of PERS employees became mandatory on and after July 1, 1991, for any employee not covered by a retirement system providing benefits comparable with Social Security.

Although 76 percent of full-time state and local government employees were covered under Social Security in 1994, only 4 percent were in plans that were specifically integrated with Social Security. Reasons that few public plans are integrated with Social Security include the establishment of many public systems before Social Security benefits were available (modification of these programs may have required a reduction in benefits) and the complexity of designing benefits integrated with Social Security.

Employees who are not covered by Social Security have significantly different replacement rates under employment-based pension plans than those who are covered by Social Security. Generally, employees without Social Security receive consistently higher pension benefits. However, these higher pension benefits do not fully compensate for lack of Social Security coverage. When total income replacement from employer pensions plus Social Security is compared with the pension benefits provided by governments not participating in Social Security, replacement rates for participants with Social Security were significantly higher (chart 40.1). However, these replacement rates are achieved with substantial employee contributions.

Plans that do integrate with Social Security typically use either an offset approach or an excess formula. Under the offset approach, an employee's retirement benefits are reduced by part of his or her Social

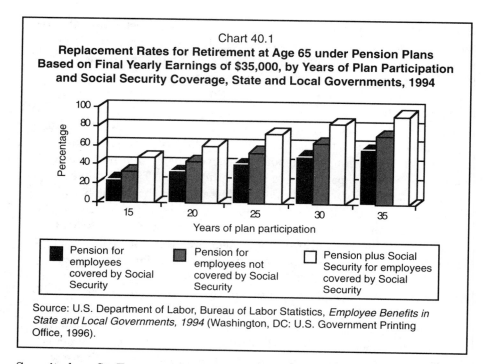

Chart 40.1

Replacement Rates for Retirement at Age 65 under Pension Plans Based on Final Yearly Earnings of $35,000, by Years of Plan Participation and Social Security Coverage, State and Local Governments, 1994

Years of plan participation

Legend:
- Pension for employees covered by Social Security
- Pension for employees not covered by Social Security
- Pension plus Social Security for employees covered by Social Security

Source: U.S. Department of Labor, Bureau of Labor Statistics, *Employee Benefits in State and Local Governments, 1994* (Washington, DC: U.S. Government Printing Office, 1996).

Security benefit. For example, the pension benefit of an employee who has worked for a state or local government for 30 years may be reduced by 30 percent of his or her Social Security benefit (1 percent times each year of service). The maximum offset is usually limited to 50 percent of the Social Security payment. Under an excess formula, a lower pension benefit rate is applied to earnings below the integration level, and a higher rate is applied to earnings above that level. The integration level is typically equal to the Social Security taxable wage base ($62,700 in 1996). Benefit accrual rates applied to earnings below the integration level may range from 0.75 percent to 2.0 percent; rates applied to earnings above the integration level may range from 1.5 percent to 2.5 percent.[17] A final approach, known as a pure excess formula, provides that earnings below the integration level are disregarded.

Social Security integration may also reduce disability benefits by the amount of benefits received from Social Security, workers' compensation, or both.

---

[17] See Zorn (1994).

Bibliography

Bleakney, Thomas P., and Jane D. Pacelli. *Benefit Design in Public Employee Retirement Systems*. Chicago, IL: Government Finance Officers Association, 1994.

Congressional Research Service. *Federal Civil Service Retirement: Comparing the Generosity of Federal and Private-Sector Retirement Systems*. Washington, DC: Congressional Research Service, 1995.

Congressional Research Service Research Team. *Public Pension Plans: The Issues Raised Over Control of Plan Assets*. Washington, DC: Congressional Research Service, 1990.

Foster, Ann. *Comparing Public and Private Pensions*. Paper presented at the 1995 Retirement and Benefits Forum in San Francisco, CA. Washington, DC: U.S. Department of Labor, 1995.

Foster Higgins. *Foster Higgins Report on State Pension Systems, 1994*. Twelfth edition. New York, NY: Foster Higgins, 1994.

Mace, Don, and Eric Yoder, eds. *Federal Employees Almanac 1996*. Forty-third edition. Reston, VA: Federal Employees New Digest, Inc., 1996.

Merck, Carolyn L. *Federal Retirement Systems: Background and Design Concepts*. Washington, DC: Congressional Research Service, 1994.

Rosenbloom, Jerry S., ed. *The Handbook of Employee Benefits: Design, Funding, and Administration*. Volume 2. Third edition. Homewood, IL: Business One Irwin, 1992.

Salisbury, Dallas L., and Nora Super Jones, eds. *Pension Funding & Taxation: Implications for Tomorrow*. Washington, DC: Employee Benefit Research Institute, 1994.

The Segal Company. *Government Employees Benefits Update*. New York, NY: The Segal Company, 1996.

U.S. Congress. House. Committee on Ways and Means. Subcommittee on Social Security. *Termination of Social Security Coverage for Employees of State and Local Governments and Nonprofit Groups*. Appendix A. Committee Print. Washington, DC: U.S. Government Printing Office, 1982.

U.S. Department of Commerce. Bureau of the Census. *1992 Census of Governments: Government Finances, Employee-Retirement Systems of State and Local Governments*. Washington, DC: U.S. Government Printing Office, 1995.

U.S. Department of Labor. Bureau of Labor Statistics. *Employee Benefits in Medium and Large Private Establishments, 1993*. Washington, DC: U.S.

Government Printing Office, 1994.

_____. *Employee Benefits in State and Local Governments, 1994.* Washington, DC: U.S. Government Printing Office, 1996.

U.S. General Accounting Office. Statement of Johnny C. Finch, Assistant Comptroller General, General Government Programs. *Overview of Federal Retirement Programs.* Testimony before the Subcommittee on Post Office and Civil Service Committee on Governmental Affairs, United States Senate. Washington, DC: U.S. General Accounting Office, May 22, 1995.

U.S. Office of Personnel Management. Retirement and Insurance Service. *Civil Service Retirement and Disability Fund Report for the Year Ended September 30, 1994.* Washington, DC: U.S. Office of Personnel Management, 1995.

_____. Budget and Program Information Division. *Statistical Abstracts: Federal Employee Benefit Programs, Fiscal Year 1993.* Washington, DC: U.S. Office of Personnel Management, 1994.

Wiatrowski, William J. "On the Disparity between Private and Public Pensions." *Monthly Labor Review* (April 1994): 3–9.

Workplace Economics, Inc. *1995 State Employee Benefits Survey.* Washington, DC: Workplace Economics, Inc., 1995.

Zorn, Paul. *Survey of State and Local Government Employee Retirement Systems.* Chicago, IL: Public Pension Coordinating Council, 1994.

Additional Information

American Federation of State, County, and Municipal Employees
1625 L Street, NW
Washington, DC 20036
(202) 429-1000

National Association of Government Deferred Compensation Administrators
167 W. Main Street, Suite 600
Lexington, KY 40507
(606) 231-1904

Public Pension Coordinating Council
c/o Government Finance Officers Association
1750 K Street, NW, Suite 650
Washington, DC 20006
(202) 429-2750

U.S. Department of Labor
Pension and Welfare Benefits Administration
200 Constitution Avenue, NW
Washington, DC 20210
(202) 219-8776

41. Supplemental Savings Plans in the Public Sector

Introduction

The availability and use of defined contribution pension plans in the public sector differs from their availability and use in the private sector. In contrast to the prevalence of sec. 401(k) plans in the private sector, the principal public-sector defined contribution pension plans are sec. 401(a) money purchase plans and, to a much lesser extent, target benefit and other "hybrid" plans. These plans are used as primary defined contribution pension plans. Federal tax law permits public-sector employers to adopt profit-sharing plans under sec. 401(a)(27). The sec. 401(k) feature, which was permitted in the public sector prior to 1986, is no longer available as a result of the Tax Reform Act of 1986 (TRA '86). However, a grandfather provision permits government employers that maintained a 401(k) plan prior to May 6, 1986, to continue to offer 401(k) plans to their current employees.

In addition to the availability of sec. 401(a) money purchase and profit-sharing plans, public-sector employees may also take advantage of sec. 457 deferred compensation plans, which are generally available on a voluntary basis as supplemental plans. Sec. 457 plans, which are nonqualified plans and are not considered pension plans, are available to most state and local government employees, allowing these employees to defer compensation to provide for supplemental retirement income.

Other organizations that are tax-exempt under Internal Revenue Code (IRC) sec. 501(c)(3) are eligible to set up a sec. 403(b) plan. These include nonprofit organizations whose purposes are religious, charitable, scientific, literary, educational, or safety testing, including certain state and local hospitals, and also public school systems, including publicly supported colleges and universities. One of the largest 403(b) plan sponsors is the Teachers Insurance Annuity Association-College Retirement Equities Fund (TIAA-CREF), which covers employees in 5,400 colleges, universities, independent schools, teaching hospitals, and nonprofit educational research and cultural organizations.

In 1986, the Federal Thrift Savings Plan (TSP) was authorized for federal employees. This plan functions in many respects like a 401(k) cash or deferred arrangement.

The Federal Thrift Savings Plan

The Federal TSP is a key component of the three-part Federal Employees' Retirement System (FERS) that became effective on January 1, 1987,[1] and covers those employees who first entered a covered position on or after January 1, 1984. The TSP is a tax-deferred defined contribution retirement savings and investment plan that contains features typically found in private-sector IRC sec. 401(k) plans. Even though the TSP was established by the FERS Act of 1986, employees in both the Civil Service Retirement System (CSRS) and the FERS may participate in the TSP, although the TSP is only a supplement to CSRS, and the contribution rules are different.

According to a Congressional Research Service (CRS) report, Congress included the TSP as a part of FERS for three reasons: (a) to increase retirement income replacement rates under FERS, especially for higher paid employees for whom Social Security replacement rates are low; (b) to provide a portable benefit and thereby reduce retirement income penalties associated with changing jobs, and (c) to replicate benefits available to private-sector workers (Merck, 1994). As of March 31, 1996, thrift savings fund accounts were maintained for more than 2.2 million participants. The participation rate among FERS employees has risen from 28.9 percent in 1987 to 78.4 percent in 1995 (Mace and Yoder, 1996).

Administration—The Federal Retirement Thrift Investment Board, an independent federal agency, manages the TSP. The board consists of five members who are nominated by the president and must be confirmed by the Senate. The board members serve part time and appoint a full-time executive director of the agency.

Open Seasons—Open seasons occur twice a year: May 15 to July 31 and November 15 to January 31. During open seasons, employees may begin or terminate contributions, alter contribution amounts, and change the way future contributions are invested. In late May and November, employees receive participant statements showing employee and employer

---

[1] The three-part Federal Employees Retirement System (FERS) program uses Social Security as a base and provides an additional defined benefit and the voluntary Thrift Savings Plan (TSP). Since the FERS program did not become effective until January 1, 1987, an interim plan was in effect from January 1, 1984, through December 31, 1986. Any employee hired during that period received credit for all service toward FERS. (For further discussion of the Social Security and defined benefit components of the FERS program, see chapter 40 on defined benefit pension plans in the public sector.)

contributions and gains or losses due to investment experience.

Employer and Employee Contributions—TSP participants may contribute either a percentage of basic pay each pay period or a fixed dollar amount. All contributions must be made through payroll deductions; lump-sum contributions are not permitted. Employee contributions to the TSP reduce the individual's taxable current income for federal (and usually state and local) income tax purposes. FERS employees may contribute up to 10 percent of basic pay on a pretax basis; CSRS employees may contribute up to 5 percent of basic pay on a pretax basis.[2] All participants are also subject to the annual deferral limit set by IRC sec. 402(g)—the same limit as for sec. 401(k) deferrals. The limit is subject to annual adjustment and was set at $9,500 in 1996. Employees may change their contribution rates only during the open seasons.

The government (acting in the role of employer) automatically contributes 1 percent of basic pay for all eligible FERS participants, regardless of whether the employees make personal contributions. For FERS participants who choose to make their own contributions, the government matches the first 3 percent of employee contributions at 100 percent and the next 2 percent of employee contributions at 50 percent. As noted, CSRS participants may make tax-deferred contributions to the plan, but there are no automatic or matching employer contributions for CSRS participants.

Eligibility to Make Personal Contributions and to Receive Employer Contributions—FERS participants newly hired in any month from January to June become eligible to participate in the TSP the first full pay period starting the next January. They begin to receive the automatic 1 percent employer contribution, and, if they elect to contribute, the employer matching contribution. FERS participants newly hired July through December become eligible to particpate the first full pay period starting the next July. They begin to receive the automatic 1 percent employer contribution and, if they elect to contribute, the employer matching contributions. CSRS participants can begin making contributions to the TSP during any open season.

An employee may stop contributing at any time. If a participant stops during an open season, he or she may resume making contributions the next open season. If a participant stops outside an open season, he or she must wait until the second open season to resume making contributions.

---

[2] Basic pay for TSP purposes is defined by law. The definition does not include things such as awards or many forms of premium pay.

Vesting—All TSP participants (both CSRS and FERS employees) are immediately vested in their own contributions and investment earnings on those contributions. FERS enrollees are also immediately vested in the government matching contributions, plus associated investment earnings. Most FERS participants vest in the automatic 1 percent employer contribution and its earnings after *three* years of federal civilian service. However, members of Congress, congressional staff, and certain political appointees to the Executive Branch vest in the automatic 1 percent employer contribution after two years of such service. If an employee leaves federal service before vesting, the automatic 1 percent employer contribution and its earnings are forfeited. In the case of death, vesting is immediate.

Investment Options—There are three TSP investment funds: the Government Securities Investment Fund (G Fund), the Common Stock Index Investment Fund (C Fund), and the Fixed Income Index Investment Fund (F Fund). Individuals who choose to invest in the C and/or F Funds are required to sign a statement saying that they understand and accept the risk of investing in these funds. If a FERS participant does not submit an investment election form, the automatic 1 percent employer contribution is invested in the G Fund. During open seasons, an employee may change his or her investment allocations for *new* contributions. For FERS employees, the investment allocations chosen apply to personal contributions and to agency automatic and matching contributions. Interfund transfers of *previously* contributed amounts are permitted in any month.

The G Fund consists of investments in short-term nonmarketable U.S. Treasury securities specially issued to the TSP. By law, all investments in the G Fund earn interest at a rate equal to the average of market rates of return on U.S. Treasury marketable securities that are outstanding with four or more years to maturity. The G Fund is managed by the Federal Retirement Thrift Investment Board.

The C Fund and the F Fund are managed by BZW Barclays Global Investors, N.A. (Barclays). The C Fund is invested primarily in the Barclays Equity Index Fund, a stock index fund that tracks the Standard & Poor's 500 (S&P 500) stock index.[3] The F Fund is a bond index fund invested primarily in the Barclays' U.S. Debt Index Fund, which tracks the Lehman

---

[3] The C fund also includes temporary investments in the G fund and certain other short-term securities pending purchase of stocks. These temporary investments also cover liquidity needs such as loans and withdrawals from the plan.

Brothers Aggregate (LBA) bond index.[4]

Plan Loans—Those eligible for the TSP Loan Program include current employees with a TSP account that has at least $1,000 in employee contributions and investment earnings. TSP loans are available for purchase of a primary residence, educational expenses, medical expenses, and financial hardship. The interest rate charged is the G Fund rate in effect at the time the loan application is received. Repayment is made through payroll deductions. To obtain a TSP loan, FERS employees must obtain spousal consent, and the spouses of CSRS employees must be notified of the loan application by the TSP.

Withdrawal of a TSP Account Balance—Employees who separate from federal service are eligible to withdraw their TSP accounts. An individual must be separated from federal service for 31 or more full calendar days before the TSP account can be paid out. Withdrawal options include a TSP life annuity, a single payment, or a series of monthly payments. A participant may choose to have the payment(s) begin immediately or at some future date.[5] A participant may also request that the TSP transfer all or a part of a single payment to an individual retirement account (IRA) or other eligible retirement plan. (In some cases, a series of monthly payments can be transferred.) Participants also have the option of leaving their accounts with the TSP on separation and making a withdrawal decision later. Amounts paid to participants from TSP accounts are considered taxable income for federal income tax purposes in the year in which payment is made. Payments not subject to these rules include TSP annuity purchases and direct transfers by the TSP to IRAs or other eligible retirement plans, since such payments are not made directly to the individual.

The withdrawal option known as the TSP annuity is a monthly benefit paid for life. A participant can request a single life annuity (with level or increasing payments), a joint life annuity with his or her spouse, or a joint life annuity with someone other than a spouse. As with the single life annuity, a participant with a joint life annuity can choose to have level or increasing payments. For participants with TSP account balances of at least $3,500, an annuity can be purchased from the TSP's annuity provider. If an

---

[4] The F fund may also have temporary investments in the G fund and in certain other short-term securities pending purchase of notes and bonds and for liquidity requirements.

[5] An individual cannot choose a future date that is later than April 1 of the year following the year in which he or she attains age 70 $1/2$.

account balance is less than $3,500, the participant can request an annuity with a specific future date. (The account must be at least $3,500 before the annuity can be purchased.) Annuity payments will be taxed as ordinary income in the years in which they are received.

Another withdrawal option is the single payment option, which is simply a withdrawal of the entire TSP account balance in a single payment. If the amount withdrawn in a single payment is paid directly to the participant (and is not transferred to an IRA or other eligible retirement plan), the payment is subject to mandatory 20 percent withholding. In addition to the ordinary income tax an individual must pay on money received directly from the TSP account, the IRS imposes a 10 percent penalty tax on amounts received from the TSP if the individual separates or retires before the year he or she reaches age 55 and receives the money before age $59^{1}/_{2}$.[6] In this case, the individual is subject to the penalty tax on all amounts received before age $59^{1}/_{2}$.

The third withdrawal option is a series of monthly payments. Participants may choose the *number* of monthly payments they want to receive. Another option available to participants is to choose a specific dollar amount for each monthly payment. A final alternative is for participants to have monthly payments computed by the TSP based on an Internal Revenue Service (IRS) life expectancy table. As with the single payment option, an individual who chooses the monthly payments option (unless the payments are based on life expectancy) is subject to a 10 percent penalty tax on all amounts received before age $59^{1}/_{2}$ if he or she separates or retires before the year he or she reaches age 55. Individuals who reach age $70^{1}/_{2}$ and are receiving a series of monthly payments from their TSP accounts are subject to IRS minimum distribution requirements.

Participants with vested account balances of $3,500 or less are subject to automatic cash-out procedures. Under the automatic cash-out procedure, the account balance is automatically paid directly to the participant unless the participant makes another withdrawal election or chooses to leave the money in the TSP. An automatic cash out is subject to the same taxes as other cash payments from the TSP.

Transferring TSP Accounts—On termination of federal employment, an individual may transfer all or a portion of a TSP account to an IRA or

---

[6] For individuals separating or retiring during or after the year in which they reach age 55, or for individuals who retire on disability, the withdrawal is not subject to the penalty tax.

other eligible retirement plan. If this option is chosen, the participant continues to defer taxes on the amounts transferred, and savings continue to accrue tax-deferred earnings until the money is withdrawn.

Leaving Money in a TSP Account—After a participant terminates employment with the federal government, he or she may leave the entire TSP account balance in the TSP (only until age 70$^{1}/_{2}$). Accounts continue to accrue investment earnings, and individuals can continue to change investment allocations among the three TSP funds by making interfund transfers.

Death Benefits—A participant may designate beneficiaries (including a surviving spouse, children, parents, or other named beneficiary) to receive the TSP account balance if the participant dies with a TSP account. Payments to spouses of deceased participants are subject to 20 percent mandatory federal income tax withholding. The withholding tax cannot be waived, although spouses of deceased participants can avoid the withholding by having the TSP transfer all or a portion of the payment to an IRA (but not to another eligible retirement plan). Payments to beneficiaries other than a spouse are subject to 10 percent withholding, which *may* be waived. Payments to nonspouse beneficiaries cannot be transferred to an IRA or other plan.

State and Local Government Plans

In contrast to the private sector, the overwhelming majority of state and local government employees continue to participate in defined benefit pension plans. According to a survey by the Bureau of Labor Statistics (BLS), 91 percent of full-time state and local government employees participated in defined benefit plans in 1994. Little has changed from 1987, when 93 percent participated in defined benefit plans.

While BLS data also show that the percentage of full-time state and local government employees in defined contribution plans has remained stable at 9 percent over the 1987–1994 time period, an increasing number of governmental employers have recently been giving consideration to defined contribution plans. Money purchase pension plans cover more state and local government employees than any other form of defined contribution plan (7 percent in 1994). Profit-sharing plans, providing discretionary employer contributions, are made available by some governments but to a much lesser extent.

Money Purchase Plans—

Contributions—Employers must annually make fixed, determinable contributions that are typically specified as a percentage of the worker's pay. Employees may be required to make contributions and may be allowed to make voluntary, after-tax contributions. The IRC allows annual maximum contributions of 25 percent of a participant's taxable earnings or $30,000 (indexed for inflation), whichever is less.

Taxation of Contributions—Employer contributions are not subject to Social Security (if applicable), federal, and most state taxes. Employee contributions may be made on an after-tax or pre-tax basis if "picked-up" by the employer. Pick-up contributions are mandatory employee contributions that are treated as though they were made by the employer for federal income tax purposes. An IRC provision specific to governmental plans allows the pick-up contributions to be pre tax. Pick-up contributions are subject to Social Security taxes, if applicable. State tax treatment of employee contributions varies by state, although most states follow the federal rules.

Distributions—Vested plan assets may be withdrawn at separation from service due to retirement, resignation/termination, death, or disability. In-service withdrawals of voluntary after-tax amounts may be permitted.

Distribution must begin by April 1 following the calendar year in which the participant attains $70^{1}/_{2}$ or retires, whichever is later.

Hardship withdrawals are not permitted from money purchase plans.

Taxation of Distributions—At the time of distribution, all amounts received from the money purchase plan not previously taxed are subject to federal and perhaps state taxes. This includes withdrawals of employer contributions, picked-up contributions, and associated earnings.

Money purchase plan assets eligible to be rolled over to another qualified plan or an IRA that are not directly rolled over are subject to 20 percent withholding. Distributions may be subject to early distribution, minimum distribution, and excess distribution penalty taxes.

Lump-sum distributions may be eligible for special tax treatment such as 5- or 10-year forward averaging. (See chapter 4 for more details on five-year averaging.)

Direct Rollovers—An employee separating from service may transfer his or her account to an IRA or another employer's qualified plan. As long as the transfer is made between plans and not through the employee there is no current taxable income to the employee. Amounts not directly rolled over are subject to a 20 percent withholding tax and may be subject to the early distribution tax.

Loans—If permitted by the employer's plan, active particpants may borrow assets from the vested portion of their accounts.

Administration and Regulation—As qualified plans, governmental money purchase plans must comply with numerous sections of the IRC.

Unlike private-sector plans, governmental plans are exempt from the Employee Retirement Income Security Act of 1974 (ERISA) and associated provisions of the IRC. While private-sector plans are required to follow strict guidelines when establishing, for example, vesting schedules, governmental employers have a great deal more flexibility. Despite this, many governments establish plans that conform to ERISA guidelines.

Private-sector employers must comply with nondiscrimination rules to maintain the qualified status of their plans. State and local government employers are currently in "deemed compliance" with these rules.

The application of several nondiscrimination provisions in the IRC to qualified plans maintained by state and local government employers has been delayed a number of times since 1977. In August of that year, the lRS released IRS News Release 1869, stating it would not enforce any nondiscrimination requirements against governmental plans. Since 1977, the application of the rules to these plans has been postponed several times.

In May 1995, the lRS issued announcement 95-48, which provided that a majority of the nondiscrimination regulations would begin to apply to governmental qualified plans beginning in 1999 and that two of the rules would apply beginning in 1997.

According to the announcement, the nondiscrimination rules associated wth voluntary employee pre-tax deferrals (in the small number of 401(k) plans) and employee after-tax and employer matching contributions will apply to governmental plans for plan years beginning on or after January 1, 1997. These regulations include a numerical test ensuring that the average contribution as a percentage of compensation for highly compensated employees (as defined by the IRC) is not excessively above that for nonhighly compensated employees.

The IRS has delayed the effective date for governmental plans until plan years beginning on or after January 1, 1999 for nondiscrimination regulations commonly referred to as "general nondiscrimination, minimum participation, minimum coverage, and definition of compensation."

The IRS will have to provide significant guidance before the current nondiscrimination rules for private-sector plans are applied to governmental plans. Guidance is necessary because the rules that currently exist were not designed to accommodate the special nature of governmental plans.

Profit-Sharing Plans—State and local governments that adopted profit-sharing plans with 401(k) features prior to May 6, 1986, are eligible to offer the 401(k) feature allowing participants to elect the amount of their voluntary pre-tax contributions on an individual basis. Even though the 401(k) feature can no longer be adopted by state and local governmental employers, IRC sec. 401(a)(27) specifically permits profit-sharing plans for employers who do not have profits and are tax exempt.

The profit-sharing and money purchase plans established by governments are similar in most respects. The principal difference is that in the money purchase plan employers must make fixed, determinable contributions, while in the profit-sharing plan employer contributions are discretionary and are not required to be made in the same amount or made every year. However, the IRC provides that contributions to a profit-sharing plan must be "substantial and recurring." Two other distinctive features are that profit-sharing plans may provide for withdrawal at 59$^1/_2$ and/or in cases of hardship.

Receiving Consideration of Defined Contribution Plans by State and Local Government—Increasingly, to continue providing quality retirement benefits at an affordable cost, state and local governments are considering defined contribution plans as an alternative to traditional defined benefit plans. In fact, a growing number of government employers have already established defined contribution retirement plans for their employees to complement or replace existing defined benefit pension plans.

There are a number of ways by which governments can "convert" from a defined benefit to a defined contribution plan. The three basic conversion trademarks are: 1) *complete* conversion; 2) *partial* conversion; or 3) *new employee-only*-conversion.

Under a *complete* conversion, the employer's defined benefit plan is terminated, and all current and future employees are enrolled in a defined contribution plan. Current employees are typically given credit for the greater of the present value of their accrued benefit in the defined benefit plan or their individual contributions.

In a typical *partial* conversion, all new employees are enrolled in the defined contribution plan, and current employees have the option of enrolling in the defined contribution plan. Current employees enrolling in the defined contribution plan are normally credited with the present value of their accrued benefit from the defined benefit plan. The defined benefit plan is retained for retirees and for current employees who elect not to participate in the defined contribution plan.

As its name implies, under a *new-employee-only* conversion, all new employees are enrolled in the defined contribution plan, while all existing employees remain in the defined benefit plan.

Sec. 457 Plans—Congress passed IRC sec. 457 as a part of the 1978 tax act, primarily in response to the IRS's effort to tax elective deferred compensation in the year in which it was *deferred* rather than in the year in which it was *received*. Sec. 457 allows state and local government entities to establish unfunded deferred compensation arrangements for their employees. Sec. 457 deferred compensation plans are not qualified plans but must meet a separate set of requirements under the IRC. These plans are similar to 401(k) plans for private-sector employees, although there are several important differences. According to a 1995 sec. 457 plans survey by the National Association of Government Deferred Compensation Administrators (NAGDCA), the three largest state plans (in terms of assets held) were California, New York, and Ohio; the two largest local plans were the City of New York and the County of Los Angeles. Total sec. 457 assets are estimated to be $28.5 billion.

As a result of the TRA '86, deferred compensation arrangements of other tax-exempt organizations are now subject to sec. 457. Examples of eligible tax-exempt organizations include civic organizations and local associations of employees; religious, charitable, scientific, literary, and educational organizations; business leagues; certain credit unions; nonprofit hospitals; trade associations; and mutual insurance funds. Eligible participants include employees of the governments or tax-exempt organizations previously noted as well as independent contractors of eligible employers. As a practical matter, only key management and highly compensated employees of nongovernmental tax-exempt employers may benefit from sec. 457 plans due to the applicability of ERISA to nongovernmental plans.

Contributions—Employees may defer up to one-third of includable compensation[7] (net of tax-deferred deductions) or $7,500[8] per year, whichever is less. The $7,500 limit is applied annually on a per-person basis. That

---

[7] Includable compensation is defined in the Internal Revenue Code as compensation for service performed for the employer that is currently includable in gross income (taxable in the current year). Since the definition of includable compensation does not include any amounts deferred, the one-third limitation is the mathematical equivalent of a 25 percent of total compensation (including deferrals) limitation.

[8] The $7,500 limit will be indexed for inflation and rounded to the next lowest multiple of $500.

is, an individual must aggregate all of his or her sec. 457 plans from all employers during a particular year to determine if the $7,500 threshold has been exceeded. The $7,500 limit applies not only to any elective deferrals but also to any nonelective deferrals the employer contributes to the plan. However, the one-third of includable compensation test only applies on a per-plan basis. Compensation may be deferred only if an agreement to defer has been made before the beginning of the month in which it is deferred, except for new employees who may participate in the month of hire. Some state and local plans have a minimum deferral requirement (e.g., $21.00–$24.00 per month). According to the 1995 NAGDCA survey of sec. 457 plans, the average annual participant deferral for 1995 ranged from $764 to $5,500, averaging $2,892 among the 84 plans that reported a figure. Most sec. 457 plans do not have matching employer contributions. Sec. 457 plans typically allow participant-directed investments. Loans to employees are not permitted, since assets are deemed to be owned by the employer.

Unlike 401(k) plans, 457 plans have a catch-up provision. The ceiling amount discussed previously may be increased, if the plan so provides, during one or more of the last three taxable years before normal retirement age. If the catch-up provision exists, participants may make contributions of the lesser of $15,000 or the sum of the ceiling that normally applies for a year (i.e., $7,500 or one-third of includable compensation) and the unused ceiling amounts from prior taxable years.

For 457 plan participants who also participate in a tax-deferred annuity under sec. 403(b), a salary reduction simplified employee pension (SARSEP), or a sec. 401(k) plan, the $7,500 (or $15,000, in the case of a catch-up provision) limit is reduced by the amount contributed to any of the other salary reduction plans. Participants who contribute to a 457 plan and to a 401(k) and/or 403(b) plan are subject to the lower 457 limit as opposed to the higher limits available under these plans.

The amount set aside in a 457 plan through payroll deduction and any increase from investment earnings is excluded from income subject to current federal income taxation until paid or otherwise made available to the participant.

Participation—According to the 1995 NAGDCA survey, over 4.2 million state and local government employees were eligible to participate in the 100 plans that provided an eligibility figure. Of those eligible to make deferrals, about 22 percent actually did so (another 6 percent maintained inactive accounts). Unless participation is limited to a specific defined group by an adopting resolution or personnel policy,[9] the plan is available to all employees.

Distributions—Deferred amounts and income may be made available on separation from service, retirement, death, attainment of age $70^1/_2$, or an unforeseeable emergency.[10]

An employee separating from service may transfer his or her account balance (tax free) to another 457 plan. As long as the transfer is made directly between the plans—and not to the employee—there is no current taxable income to the employee. (This is similar to the trustee-to-trustee transfer or direct rollover requirements for qualified plans.) Unlike 401(k) plans, amounts received from a 457 plan are not eligible to be rolled over into an IRA or into a qualified plan.

Another option for an employee separating from service is to receive a lump-sum distribution within 60 days of election, if the total amount payable is $3,500 or less. No additional amounts may be deferred under the plan.

Sec. 457 plans that provide hardship withdrawals must define "unforeseeable emergency" as severe financial hardship to a participant resulting from the sudden and unexpected illness or accident of the participant or his or her dependents, the loss of a participant's property due to casualty, or other similar extraordinary and unforeseeable circumstances that result from events beyond the control of the participant. If the hardship may be relieved through reimbursement, compensation, or insurance; liquidation of assets; or ceasing deferrals, then the 457 plan is prohibited from making a distribution. The emergency withdrawal is limited to what is reasonably required to satisfy the emergency need.

If distribution begins prior to a participant's death, the amount must be over the single life expectancy of the participant or joint life expectancy of the participant and a designated beneficiary, subject to certain restrictions. Distributions *must* begin no later than April 1 following the calendar year in which the employee either attains age $70^1/_2$ or retires, whichever is later. Any amount not distributed to the participant by the time of his or her

---

[9] Since sec. 457 plans are not subject to any nondiscrimination tests, employers may set eligibility criteria that might not be permitted in qualified plans.

[10] In-service distributions will be permitted from accounts of $3,500 or less if no contribution had been made in two years and no prior distributions had been made in-service.

death must be paid in a manner at least as rapidly as the method of distribution being used at the date of death. If distribution has not begun prior to a participant's death, the entire amount must be paid within 15 years. However, if the beneficiary is the spouse, then payments may be made over the spouse's life expectancy.

Taxation of Distributions—The only favorable tax treatment for 457 plan distributions is the plan-to-plan transfer option. A distribution from a 457 plan is taxed as ordinary income; there is no special tax treatment such as partial rollover or 10- or 5-year forward averaging. However, the following taxes are not applicable to distributions from 457 plans: early distribution penalty taxes, excess contribution taxes, excess distribution tax, or prohibited transaction excise tax. Amounts deferred under sec. 457 plans are subject to Social Security (FICA) taxes in the year the amounts are deferred.

Administration and Regulation—The amounts participants choose to defer are set aside by the employer and invested. Participants in state and local 457 plans are usually given a variety of investment options. The assets may be invested by insurance companies; banks and savings and loan institutions; mutual fund companies; or credit unions, brokerage firms, in-house managers, and other independent money managers. The Small Business Job Protection Act of 1996 requires that all amounts deferred under a sec. 457 deferred compensation plan of state and local governments be held in trust for the exclusive benefit of employees (effective on date of enactment, but allows for establishment of a trust by Jan. 1, 1999 for amounts deferred before the date of enactment).

Sec. 457 plans for *governmental* employers are not subject to the discrimination tests to which 401(k) plans must comply. Minimum vesting or participation standards and disclosure requirements are also not applicable to sec. 457 plans for *governmental* employers, since these plans are nonqualified plans exempt from Title I of ERISA.[11]

Sec. 403(b) Plans

Sec. 403(b) plans are deferred tax arrangements (similar to a 401(k) cash or deferred plan) available to employees of certain types of organizations. Participants can set aside a portion of their compensation for retire-

---

[11] Sec. 4(b) of the Employee Retirement Income Security Act of 1974 excludes governmental plans, church plans, and certain other types of plans from Title I.

ment purposes. The employer may also make contributions on behalf of the employee. Public school systems, colleges, universities, and certain state and local hospitals that are tax exempt under IRC sec. 501(c)(3) are eligible to set up 403(b) plans. (For further discussion of 403(b) plans, see chapter 15.)

TIAA-CREF Plans—Teachers Insurance and Annuity Association (TIAA) is a nonprofit, legal reserve life insurance and annuity company incorporated in the state of New York. Established in 1918 for the benefit of educational institutions and their faculty and staff, it was founded jointly by the Carnegie Foundation for the Advancement of Teaching and the Carnegie Corporation of New York.

The College Retirement Equities Fund (CREF), a separate, nonprofit companion corporation to TIAA, was established in 1952 by a special act of the New York state legislature to provide a variable annuity component for the TIAA-CREF retirement system. Originally a common stock-based fund, CREF currently offers seven separate variable annuity accounts (the Stock, Money Market, Bond Market, Social Choice, Growth, Equity Index, and Global Equities accounts).

Sec. 501(c)(3), the nonprofit provision of the IRC that gives tax exemption to colleges, private schools, and similar educational and scientific institutions, applies to TIAA and to CREF pension and annuity operations. The majority of TIAA-CREF retirement plans in educational institutions are operated under and subject to the provisions outlined in IRC sec. 403(b) However, many TIAA-CREF plans are qualified under sec. 401(a) or sec. 403(a), whose provisions are the same as or are similar to the provisions to which pension plans of business and industrial employers are subject. An educational employer may qualify its regular pension plan under sec. 401(a) or sec. 403(a) and at the same time provide employees with plans for supplementary, elective tax-deferred retirement annuity savings under sec. 403(b) under formal salary reduction agreements.

The fully funded, portable TIAA-CREF pension system is designed for staff members of private and public U.S. colleges, universities, independent schools, and related nonprofit research organizations and educational associations.[12] In 1996, some 5,800 institutions participated in the TIAA-

---

[12] The Teachers Insurance Annuity Association-College Retirement Equities Fund (TIAA-CREF) also provides eligible employees with tax-deferred annuity (supplemental retirement annuity) plans for additional (elective) retirement savings as well as individual and group life insurance, group long-term disability income plans, and long-term care insurance.

CREF system, which covered approximately 1.8 million participants.

TIAA-CREF Plans in Public Institutions—Although the majority of TIAA-CREF retirement plans are in privately supported colleges, universities, and other educational or research organizations, many plans are also provided by public colleges and universities, for their faculty and staff. TIAA-CREF plans in public institutions of higher education are generally designed to aid the institutions in attracting faculty and other professionals by reducing the barriers to geographic mobility represented by public plans that are limited by their state boundaries and have delayed vesting provisions.

In some cases, TIAA-CREF plans are offered as the only plan for faculty and other professional employees. In other cases, TIAA-CREF plans are offered as an alternative to the public employee or state teacher retirement system. In the latter situation, the plans operate concurrently, and information is usually provided to aid individuals in deciding which plan best suits their needs and career plans. In still other cases, a TIAA-CREF retirement plan supplements a public employee or state teacher retirement plan.

Contributions—Contribution rates are stated as a percentage of employee salary and are normally set at levels which will, at a given (normal) retirement age, produce a replacement ratio[13] of benefits to final salary that is expected to meet the institution's benefit objective for a career of service. Shorter periods of service at a given institution will produce commensurably lower benefits at retirement. Participants who work for successive employers having TIAA-CREF plans will receive benefits based on annuity accumulations derived from all such employers.

Under TIAA-CREF plans, contribution rates are generally set at a level percentage of an employee's salary, e.g., 10 percent or 15 percent. Contribution rates may also be set on a "step-rate" basis, with one stated percentage of salary up to a stipulated amount and a higher percentage of salary above that amount. For example, a contribution rate of at least 10 percent on the lower portion of salary and a contribution rate ranging from 11 percent to 15 percent on the higher portion of salary. Institutions with step-rate contribution levels need to assure that the contribution differential falls within limits permitted by nondiscrimination regulations under TRA '86. A plan may be either contributory, i.e., require contributions from both employer and employee, or it may be noncontributory, i.e., paid for exclu-

---

[13]Replacement ratio refers to retirement income relative to preretirement income.

sively by employer contributions. Approximately two-thirds of the plans are contributory.

Most institutions require new employees to complete one or two years of service (and perhaps attain a stipulated age) before participating in their TIAA-CREF retirement plans. However, in order to encourage mobility, many of these institutions include provisions permitting certain new employees to participate immediately. A typical provision, for example, credits "related" service performed with a previous educational employer toward meeting the one or two year service requirement.

TIAA-CREF Premium Allocations and Fund Investments— Participants in most TIAA-CREF retirement plans can allocate their annuity premiums (including the employer's contributions) to TIAA's traditional annuity and/or among the CREF variable annuity accounts. Allocations of future premiums may be changed at any time, subject to any restrictions imposed by the institution. Although most institutions permit their employees to allocate premiums in any proportion among TIAA and the various CREF accounts, some institutions limit the percentage allocations or restrict the availability of some of the CREF accounts under their retirement accounts.

The TIAA traditional retirement annuity guarantees principal (i.e., the amount of premiums paid) and a specified rate of interest, and provides the opportunity for additional growth through dividends. The seven CREF investment accounts offer participants the opportunity to diversify their retirement savings with a variable annuity, complementing the traditional TIAA annuity. Like all variable annuities, CREF does not guarantee principal or earnings.

Contributions to CREF purchase accumulation units in the CREF fund or funds to which an individual allocates premiums. The dollar value of the accumulation unit in each CREF account reflects changes in the market prices of the securities held by that account plus net dividends and other income received.

In the late 1980s, the TIAA-CREF system underwent changes related to the transfer of assets between the two funds. Until that time, assets placed in TIAA funds were not allowed to be transferred to CREF funds or any other funds. Participants were allowed to remove their money only at retirement or death and only in the form of annuities (no lump-sum distributions were allowed). Money placed in CREF funds has always been allowed to be transferred to TIAA.

The changes began when CREF decided it wanted to offer other investment options that brought the fund under Securities and Exchange Commission (SEC) rules. When CREF proposed these changes, the National Education Association and other related groups went to the SEC and requested that the entire TIAA-CREF system be opened up. The SEC consent agreement that TIAA-CREF now abides by says that money can be cashed out of TIAA funds over a 10-year period, that money in TIAA funds may be transferred to CREF funds, and that money in CREF funds may be transferred to funds held by other companies as specified by the plan participant's employer. In addition, the agreement says that TIAA-CREF would not prevent other pension companies from soliciting business on campuses where they currently have accounts. Also, under the terms of this agreement, states and private employers are able to negotiate separately with TIAA-CREF for other types of arrangements concerning the transfer of assets, investment options, and distributions.

There are two payment methods under which retirees may receive life annuity income from TIAA: the standard method and the graded benefit methods. All TIAA income may be received under either payment method or part may be received under each method.

Under the standard method, the full dividend interest rate is included in each annuity check from the start. Monthly payments under this method remain level from one year to the next as long as there is no change in TIAA's dividend scale for pay-out annuities.

Under the graded method, monthly payments of retirement income start out much lower than under the standard method because most of the dividend is added to the annuity reserve; rather than being paid out during each year, it is used to purchase an additional amount of lifetime annuity at the end of each year. Each year, the benefit increases by a percentage that is generally equal to the difference between the assumed investment return (AIR) of 4 percent and the current dividend rate.

TIAA-CREF Plans and Federal Pension and Tax Legislation— ERISA affects employee benefit plans of educational institutions, except for plans excluded because they are established or maintained "by the government . . . of any state or political subdivision thereof, or by any agency or instrumentality of the foregoing," or by a church. Thus, TIAA-CREF retirement plans established or maintained by a private, nonprofit organization are generally subject to the provisions of ERISA, but those operated by public educational institutions are not. However, the provisions of the IRC affect participants in all pension plans, public and private.

Since 1942, the IRC has provided tax deferral for contributions by nonprofit organizations to purchase annuities for their employees, and the current provisions are stated in sec. 403(b).

Originally, there was no limit on the amount of an educational employer's contributions that were excludable from an employee's gross income. The 1958 amendments to the IRC limited the exclusion to the employee's "exclusion allowance," and a 1961 amendment confirmed the applicability of the section to employees of public educational institutions. In 1974, ERISA added sec. 415 to the IRC, which imposed further limitations on benefits and contributions under qualified pension plans as well as sec. 403(b) plans.

Bibliography

Bleakney, Thomas P., and Jane D. Pacelli. *Benefit Design in Public Employee Retirement Systems.* Chicago, IL: Government Finance Officers Association, 1994.

Charles D. Spencer & Associates, Inc. "Employees of Public Schools, Tax-Exempt Entities May Participate in Sec. 403(b) Tax Deferred Annuities." *Spencer's Research Reports on Employee Benefits* (March 15, 1991): 207.04.-1–201.04.-4.

_____. "Majority of Government Employers Offer Sec. 457 Plans, Buck Survey Finds Only 16% of Eligibles Are Enrolled." *Spencer's Research Reports on Employee Benefits* (March 1988): 207.02.-1.

_____. "Sec. 457 Plans for State, Local Government, and Employees of Nonprofit Organizations." *Spencer's Research Reports on Employee Benefits* (November 26, 1993): 201.01.-2.

_____. "Thrift Savings Plan for Federal Employees Is Similar to Sec. 401(k) Plan; Investment Restrictions Lifted in 1991." *Spencer's Research Reports on Employee Benefits* (August 2, 1991): 108.04.-1–108.04.-2.

_____. "TIAA-CREF Assets Reach $127 Billion; 1993 Investment Experience Summarized." *Spencer's Research Reports on Employee Benefits* (February 11, 1991): 108.04.-3–108.04.-6.

Employee Benefit Research Institute. *EBRI Databook on Employee Benefits,* Third edition. Washington, DC: Employee Benefit Research Institute, 1995.

_____. *Fundamentals of Employee Benefit Programs for Education Employees.* Washington, DC: Employee Benefit Research Institute, 1993.

Federal Retirement Thrift Investment Board. *Summary of the Thrift*

Savings Plans for Federal Employees. Washington, DC: Federal Retirement Thrift Investment Board, 1995.

Franz, Steven J., et al. *401(k) Answer Book.* Second edition. New York, NY: Panel Publishers, 1995.

Harm, Kathleen Jenks. *State and Local Government Deferred Compensation Programs.* Chicago, IL: Government Finance Officers Association, 1993.

Mace, Don, and Eric Yoder, eds. *Federal Employees Almanac 1996.* Forty-third edition. Reston, VA: Federal Employees News Digest, Inc., 1996.

Merck, Carolyn L. *Federal Retirement Systems: Background and Design Concepts.* Washington, DC: Congressional Research Service, 1996.

National Association of Government Deferred Compensation Administrators. *1995 Survey of 457 Plans.* Lexington, KY: The National Association of Government Deferred Compensation Administrators, 1996.

TIAA-CREF. *Prospectus: College Retirement Equities Fund.* New York, NY: TIAA-CREF, 1995.

_____. *Retirement Annuities.* New York, NY: TIAA-CREF, 1994.

_____. *This is TIAA-CREF.* New York, NY: TIAA-CREF, 1995.

U.S. Department of Labor. Bureau of Labor Statistics. *Employee Benefits in State and Local Governments, 1994.* Washington, DC: U.S. Government Printing Office, 1996.

U.S. General Accounting Office. *Federal Pensions: Thrift Savings Plan Has Key Role in Retirement Benefits.* GAO/HEHS-96-1. Washington, DC: U.S. General Accounting Office, 1995.

Vonachen, James C. "Deferred Compensation Plans for Governmental and Tax-Exempt Employees." *Journal of Pension Benefits* (Spring 1995): 61–64.

Yakoboski, Paul, and Annmarie Reilly. "Salary Reduction Plans and Individual Saving for Retirement." *EBRI Issue Brief* no. 155 (Employee Benefit Research Institute, November 1994).

Additional Information

Government Finance Officers Association of the United States and Canada
180 N. Michigan Avenue, Suite 800
Chicago, IL 60601
(312) 977-9700

National Association of Deferred Compensation Administrators
167 W. Main Street, Suite 600
Lexington, KY 40507
(606) 231-1904

Thrift Savings Plan (TSP) Service Office
National Finance Center
P.O. Box 61500
New Orleans, LA 70161-1500
(504) 255-8777

TIAA-CREF
730 Third Avenue
New York, NY 10017-3206
1-800-842-2733

42. Health Insurance in the Public Sector

Introduction

Eighty-seven percent of public employees had employment-based health insurance in 1994 (Employee Benefit Research Institute, 1996). Moreover, coverage tends to be very broad, encompassing all of the traditional categories of medical expense, including hospital care, physicians' services, and diagnostic x-ray and laboratory services. Mental health care and coverage for treatment of alcoholism and drug abuse—although subject to limitations—are available to nearly all participants in state and local plans and to all federal employees. Coverage of dental care is also available to a majority of public employees.

One salient characteristic of public employee health plans is that employees usually become eligible to participate immediately on being hired. This is true at the local, state, and federal levels. In situations in which waiting periods apply, they tend to be three months or less (U.S. Department of Labor, 1996).

Postemployment Coverage

State and local employers are subject to the continuation of coverage provisions of the Consolidated Omnibus Budget Reconciliation Act of 1985 (COBRA), as amended. While the federal government, as employer, was not originally subject to the act, similar requirements were subsequently imposed on federal agencies by separate legislation. (See chapter 19 on health insurance in the private sector for more information on COBRA's requirements.)

Retiree Coverage

Seventy-five percent of full-time state and local employees participating in health plans received wholly or partially employer-paid health benefits during retirement in 1994 (U.S. Department of Labor, 1996). Federal workers enrolled in a plan under the Federal Employees Health Benefits Program for the five years immediately preceding retirement may continue coverage during retirement with the same level of employer-paid premiums as active workers. Where postretirement coverage exists in public plans, it almost always continues for the retiree's lifetime. (If a survivor annuity is payable, coverage may continue for the deceased worker's survivor.) In most cases, the level of coverage for retirees is the same as that for active workers, although employment-based benefits are usually coordinated with Medicare for retirees aged 65 and over.

Types of Plans

In the public sector, the law authorizing a health insurance program for employees sometimes sets forth the number and types of plans to be offered and the funding intermediaries that may be used. According to the Bureau of Labor Statistics (BLS), 38 percent of full-time state and local workers were in traditional fee-for-service plans in 1994. Among state and local workers participating in medical plans in 1994, 26 percent had policies underwritten by Blue Cross and Blue Shield, 15 percent were insured by commercial carriers, and 30 percent were in self-insured plans (U.S. Department of Labor, 1996). In 1992, approximately 40 percent of federal civilian employees participating in the Federal Employees' Health Benefits Program were enrolled with Blue Cross and Blue Shield, 32 percent were in employee organization plans (which are sponsored by employee organizations or unions and are only open to employees or annuitants who are members of the sponsoring union or organization), while 28 percent were enrolled in comprehensive medical plans (Employee Benefit Research Institute, 1995). (Technically, the federal government does not insure any plans for its employees, but several employee organizations that participate in the federal program self-insure their plans.)

A relatively high percentage of public employees are enrolled in health maintenance organizations (HMOs). BLS reported that 30 percent of state and local employees were enrolled in HMOs in 1994. A 1995 study of the 50 states found that 35 percent of the employees covered by state plans were enrolled in HMOs (The Segal Company, 1995). State and local governments were subject to mandate by HMOs under the original Health Maintenance Organization Act of 1973. In addition, some states legislated their own independent dual-choice laws. The federal government's program for civilian workers has included HMOs and has been continuously open for participation by new HMOs since its enactment in 1959. Approximately 29 percent of federal civilian employees, retirees, and their dependents were enrolled in HMOs in 1995 (National Academy on Aging, 1995).

The combination of public policy favorable to HMOs and the inherent political difficulty involved in limiting the number of HMOs that can participate in the public sector has led to a strong representation of these organizations in public-sector programs. However, the number of HMOs offered by public plan sponsors varies greatly. According to a 1995 survey, the number of HMOs offered among state governments ranges from none in 5 states to 10 or more in 14 states (The Segal Company, 1995). The federal government offers approximately 370 HMOs.

Over the past few years, there has been a dramatic increase in the number of full-time state and local employees covered under preferred provider organizations (PPOs). According to BLS, 30 percent of state and local employees were covered by PPOs in 1994, compared with 7 percent in 1987 (U.S. Department of Labor, 1988 and 1996). (For more information on PPOs, see chapter 24.)

Contributions

Among full-time state and local plans, it is common for the employer to pay the entire premium for the employees' coverage but to require a contribution from employees who elect coverage for their dependents. The 1994 BLS survey showed that 47 percent of participants contributed to their own coverage, whereas 71 percent made a contribution for dependents (U.S. Department of Labor, 1996). However, the incidence of noncontributory coverage for the worker may be declining as state and local jurisdictions, like all other employers, seek to manage their health care costs. At the federal level, substantial contributions (about 28 percent on average) are required of all participants regardless of the coverage selected.

Cost Management

During the past decade, many employers sponsoring employee health plans have struggled with the problem of how to manage what appear to be ever-escalating costs. In 1982, the massive federal employee program introduced mandatory coinsurance and deductibles in all health plan offerings in an effort to curb utilization and, consequently, costs. Public employers have tried many of the same strategies that private employers have used to eliminate unnecessary service and to control costs. These strategies include second surgical opinion, hospital precertification programs, concurrent review and discharge planning, incentives for outpatient surgery, audit of hospital and doctor bills, individual case management, home health care benefits, hospice benefits, wellness benefits, and mail order drug and preferred pharmacy programs.

Health care costs have continued to rise for both private and public employers despite their efforts to manage them. Recently, some employers in both sectors have attempted to curb utilization and price by using managed care arrangements. A few public jurisdictions have adopted point-of-service health plans under which the method of service delivery (fee for service, HMO, etc.) is selected at the time of treatment, with the expectation that patients will respond to financial incentives to use more cost-effective HMO or PPO arrangements. Other jurisdictions are encouraging employees to opt for HMOs by providing relatively greater financial support to those making this choice. Some smaller jurisdictions have tried negotiating favorable arrangements directly with providers. Finally, at least a few jurisdictions have ceased to offer traditional indemnity coverage altogether, relying instead exclusively on managed care arrangements.

Funding

In the public sector, as in the private sector, health care costs, including those for retirees, are treated as a current operating expense. Since public jurisdictions are not taxpaying entities, they could prefund benefits for retired workers without adverse tax consequences in much the same manner as pension benefits are prefunded. However, recognizing and prefunding a future liability increases current costs, and few jurisdictions are in a position to do so. The existence of a similar liability and a proposed requirement to disclose that liability on the financial statements of the sponsoring employer have recently caused concern in the private sector. While there appears to be less concern about calculating or disclosing the liability among public jurisdictions than in the private sector, postretirement health benefits constitute a potentially difficult political issue. Retiree groups are pressing for employer-supported benefits where they are not now available and for greater employer cost sharing where partial support is currently provided. This desire for greater support directly conflicts with many jurisdictions' fiscal problems.

Bibliography

Employee Benefit Research Institute. *EBRI Databook on Employee Benefits.* Third edition. Washington, DC: Employee Benefit Research Institute, 1995.

Fronstin, Paul, and Edina Rheem. "Sources of Health Insurance and Characteristics of the Uninsured: An Analysis of the March 1995 Current Population Survey." *EBRI Issue Brief* no. 170 (Employee Benefit Research Institute, February 1996).

National Academy on Aging. *The Federal Employee Health Benefits Program, Managed Competition, and Considerations for Medicare.* Washington, DC: National Academy on Aging, 1995.

The Segal Company. *Summary of Findings, The Segal Company's 1995 Survey of State Employee Health Benefit Plans.* New York, NY: The Segal Company, 1995.

U.S. Department of Labor. Bureau of Labor Statistics. *Employee Benefits in State and Local Governments, 1987.* Washington, DC: U.S. Government Printing Office, 1988.

_____. *Employee Benefits in State and Local Governments, 1992.* Washington, DC: U.S. Government Printing Office, 1994.

Workplace Economics, Inc. *1994 State Employee Benefits Survey.* Washington, DC: Workplace Economics, Inc., 1994.

Additional Information

Workplace Economics, Inc.
P.O. Box 33367
Washington, DC 20033
(202) 223-9191

The Segal Company
One Park Avenue
New York, NY 10016
(212) 251-5000

National Governors' Association
444 Capitol Street, NW
Washington, DC 20001
(202) 624-5300

43. Life Insurance and Related Protection in the Public Sector

Introduction

Most public jurisdictions make group life insurance coverage available to their employees, and many pay all or a portion of the cost. According to the Bureau of Labor Statistics, in 1994, 87 percent of full-time state and local government employees were covered by group life insurance funded wholly or partly by their employers (U.S. Department of Labor, 1996). A more recent survey covering only state employee benefits indicated that 41 states provide at least a basic life insurance benefit at no cost to the employee (Workplace Economics, Inc., 1995). Approximately 90 percent of active and retired federal employees participated in the basic federal group life insurance program in fiscal year 1993 (U.S. Office of Personnel Management, 1994).[1]

Federal Program

The Federal Employees' Group Life Insurance (FEGLI) Program was established by the Federal Employees' Group Life Insurance Act of 1954 and was significantly modified by the Federal Employees' Group Life Insurance Act of 1980. Modifications included an increased level of insurance under basic life insurance (discussed below), introduction of new optional forms of coverage, and a more competitive premium structure. Prior to the FEGLI Program, life insurance coverage was offered to groups of federal employees by beneficial associations. There were 27 such associations in 1954. Under the FEGLI Act of 1954, the Civil Service Commission was authorized to purchase a qualified life insurance policy to insure all or portions of the agreements assumed from the beneficial associations. Beneficial association insurance still has members, although it is closed to new enrollment.

As a result of improvements in the financial condition of the FEGLI Fund,[2] the U.S. Office of Personnel Management (OPM) effected premium

---

[1] Participation in the basic program by both active and retired federal employees has held consistently at 90 percent since the program was expanded and revitalized in 1981.

[2] The financial condition of the Federal Employees' Group Life Insurance fund improved as a result of lower mortality rates, expected gains from more favorable interest rate assumptions, and positive predictions concerning its reserve levels.

rate reductions and conducted an open enrollment period between March 29, 1993, and April 30, 1993—the first FEGLI open enrollment since 1985. During this period, eligible employees were given the opportunity to change their life insurance coverage.

Coverage—With few exceptions, all federal civilian employees are eligible to participate in the FEGLI Program. Those covered by the FEGLI Program include the president, members of Congress, federal government employees, Gallaudet University[3] faculty, and others not excluded by OPM statute or regulation.

Administration—The insurance program is administered by OPM, but each federal agency is responsible for daily program operations with respect to its own employees. Benefits are provided by the Metropolitan Life Insurance Company, under contract with OPM. More than 200 other companies participate as reinsurers.

Basic Life Insurance—During employment, the group policy provides both life insurance and accidental death and dismemberment (AD&D) insurance. The basic life insurance benefit equals the employee's annual pay rounded upward to the next thousand, plus $2,000. In 1996, the maximum amount of insurance coverage could not exceed $136,000. For employees earning $8,000 or less annually, the minimum amount of insurance coverage was $10,000 (Mace and Yoder, 1996). Additional benefits at no additional cost are provided for employees under age 45.[4] The AD&D benefit provided to employees is twice the basic life insurance benefit in the case of accidental death and one-half the basic life insurance benefit for the loss of one limb or sight of one eye. (The full amount is paid for two or more such losses.)

Basic insurance cost is shared by the employee and the government as the employer. The employer pays one-third of the cost (contributed from agency appropriations or other funds available to pay salaries), and the employee pays two-thirds (withheld from his or her salary).[5] Unless eligible

---

[3] Gallaudet University is a private four-year institution located in Washington, DC, with undergraduate programs open only to deaf individuals. The university was federally chartered in 1864 and continues to receive a portion of its funding from the federal government.

[4] Additional benefits range from 2 times the basic life insurance benefit for employees aged 35 or under to 1.1 times the basic life insurance benefit for employees at age 44.

[5] The employee paid $0.165 per $1,000 of basic coverage in 1996 (Mace and Yoder, 1996).

employees state in writing that they do not want basic insurance, they are automatically covered.

Basic life insurance enrollment is a prerequisite for enrollment in any of the following optional life insurance coverage.

Standard Optional Life Insurance—Federal employees under the basic life insurance program have the option of purchasing additional insurance known as standard optional life insurance. Standard life provides $10,000 of life insurance and an equal amount of AD&D coverage. The full cost of standard life is paid by the employee and is dependent on his or her age. The premium is withheld from the employee's salary. The monthly withholding ranges from $0.87 per $10,000 of coverage for employees under age 35 to $15.17 per $10,000 of coverage for employees aged 60 or over.

Additional Optional Insurance—Additional optional insurance is also available to employees covered by the basic life insurance program. Additional life is offered in amounts equal to one, two, three, four, or five times annual basic pay (after the pay has been rounded to the next higher $1,000).[6] The full cost of additional life is paid by the employee and is dependent on his or her age. The premium is withheld from the employee's salary. Unlike standard life, AD&D coverage is *not* included in additional life. The monthly withholdings for additional optional insurance range from $0.087 per $1,000 of coverage for employees under age 35 to $1.517 per $1,000 of coverage for employees aged 60 and over.

Family Optional Insurance—Federal employees covered by the basic life insurance program also have the option of purchasing insurance to cover eligible family members (spouse and unmarried dependent children). Family optional insurance is offered with $5,000 coverage for a spouse and $2,500 coverage for each child under age 22.[7] The full cost of family optional insurance is paid by the employee and is withheld from his or her salary. The premium depends on the employee's age. Monthly withholdings range from $0.65 for employees under age 35 to $5.63 for employees aged 60 and over. Family optional insurance does *not* include AD&D coverage.

Coverage after Retirement—Basic life insurance continues into retirement, with three elections offered. (The AD&D benefit provided to

---

[6] The maximum amount of basic pay used in this calculation was set at $133,600 in 1996 (Mace and Yoder, 1996).

[7] This coverage may include children aged 22 and over, provided the child is incapable of self-support due to a mental or physical disability that existed prior to age 22.

employees under basic life insurance does *not* continue into retirement.) The first option is a reduction in basic life insurance coverage of 2 percent a month after age 65 (maximum reduction of 75 percent of the basic policy value), with no additional cost to the retiree. The second option is a lesser reduction of 1 percent a month after age 65 (maximum reduction of 50 percent of the basic policy value). In 1996, the additional premium for this lesser reduction is $0.52 a month per $1,000 of basic insurance for those aged 65 and over and $0.8775 a month for those under age 65 (Mace and Yoder, 1996). The final option is no reduction in basic life insurance coverage after age 65. In 1996, the additional premium required for no reduction in the amount of basic insurance is $1.69 a month per $1,000 of basic insurance for those aged 65 and over and $2.0475 a month for those under age 65 (Mace and Yoder, 1996). If either of the last two elections is canceled, the amount of life insurance is computed as if the retiree had originally elected the 75 percent reduction.

The FEGLI Act of 1980 requires that employees who retire before reaching age 65 make a supplemental contribution in order to continue their basic life insurance coverage. This supplemental coverage applies regardless of which of the three postretirement options the retiree has elected. The supplemental contribution ceases when the retiree reaches age 65, at which point the elected option becomes effective. The optional insurance programs (standard, additional, and family) may also be continued into retirement (at the same cost to the retiree as when he or she was employed), although the cost and coverage change when the retiree reaches age 65.

Retirees aged 65 and over do *not* pay premiums for standard optional life insurance. However, the $10,000 standard optional insurance begins to decline at the rate of 2 percent per month until it reaches $2,500 (i.e., one-fourth of the face value). Similarly, premiums for additional optional insurance and family optional insurance are no longer required of retirees who have reached age 65. However, the amount of coverage will begin to decline at the rate of 2 percent per month for 50 months, at which point coverage ends.

State and Local Programs

In 1992, of those state and local government employees who were life insurance participants, approximately 58 percent were in plans sponsored by local governments. Another 42 percent were in plans sponsored by state governments, and a few were in plans in which the government contributed to union-sponsored trust funds that provided benefits.

Generally, the cost of basic life insurance in state and local government plans is paid entirely by the employer. In 1994, for example, 86 percent of life insurance plan participants were in plans that were *wholly* employer financed; the remainder were in plans that were *partly* employer financed. Workers in plans requiring employee contributions generally pay a dollar amount based on coverage—the employee typically pays no more than $0.20 per $1,000 of coverage. Some plans, however, require a set contribution that covers more than one benefit.

Coverage—Among all state and local government employees who were full-time life insurance participants in 1994, 26 percent were required to work a minimum period (commonly one or three months) to qualify for the plan; 36 percent were in plans with no service requirement, and 15 percent were in plans for which the service requirement was not determinable. Minimum age requirements were rare (U.S. Department of Labor, 1996).

Basic Life Insurance Benefit Formulas—For full-time employees of state and local governments, the most common method of determining basic life insurance is a flat dollar amount of coverage. Flat dollar coverage is especially prevalent among teachers. Teachers had the highest average flat dollar amount of life insurance in 1994 ($20,409); the average flat dollar amount for all participants in state and local government plans was $17,578. Flat dollar insurance ranging from $2,000–$25,000 accounted for 70 percent of life insurance participants in 1994 (U.S. Department of Labor, 1996).

The second most common method of determining the amount of basic life insurance is to base it on earnings. Earnings-based coverage provides a level of protection that automatically increases with pay. The most prevalent method of tying life insurance to pay is to multiply the employee's annual salary by one or two and then round the result to the next higher $1,000. For example, an employee whose annual pay is $43,600 would receive $88,000 of coverage under a plan providing two times pay.[8] Some plans place limits on the amount of life insurance available; such limits are typically in the range of $50,000–$250,000. According to a 1995 state employee benefits study, a majority of states base the amount of coverage on the employee's salary or on a combination of salary and age (Workplace

---

[8] The annual pay of $43,600 is multiplied by two, which yields $87,200. This amount is then rounded up to $88,000.

Economics, Inc., 1995).

Accidental Death and Dismemberment (AD&D) Coverage—
Accidental death and dismemberment (AD&D) insurance was available to
56 percent of state and local government life insurance plan participants in
1994. AD&D insurance provides additional benefits if a worker dies or loses
an eye or a limb in an accident. For most workers, the benefit is equal to the
basic life insurance benefit in the case of accidental death and a portion of
that benefit for dismemberment, although a few workers receive a flat
amount of AD&D coverage. Some states provide optional AD&D coverage at
the employee's expense.

Supplemental Benefits—The typical supplemental plan provides term
life insurance in multiples of one to three times annual pay, at the
employee's option. Supplemental benefits are more common among state
and local employees who have their basic life insurance determined by a flat
dollar amount than among employees with a multiple of earnings formula.
Among the 55 percent of state and local government employees with the
option of supplemental benefits in 1994, about 87 percent were required to
pay the full premium for such benefits.

Coverage for Dependents—Of the 46 percent of state and local
government employees with dependent life insurance coverage in 1994,
76 percent were required to pay the entire premium to obtain coverage; the
remainder had coverage paid either partly or entirely by the employer. The
most prevalent method used to provide dependent coverage is a flat dollar
amount, and the employee often has the option to select specific benefits.

Survivor Benefits—Life insurance plans providing a monthly benefit
to surviving members of a state or local government employee's family are
rare. When survivor income payments are available, they are generally
either a percentage of the employee's pay or a flat dollar amount. Survivor
benefits usually continue for 24 months, although some plans provide
benefits until the surviving spouse either remarries or attains age 65 or
until surviving children reach a specified age.

Coverage for Older Active Workers—In some life insurance plans,
coverage of older active workers is reduced to account for the increased cost
of insuring older workers. Coverage may be reduced once or in several
stages. Plans with reduced coverage typically make the first reduction at
age 65 or 70. If coverage is reduced only once, it is typically reduced to
50 percent of the original life insurance amount. For plans that reduce
coverage in several stages, a common provision is to reduce coverage to
65 percent at age 65 and then to 50 percent at age 70. In 1994, 31 percent of

participants were in plans in which older active workers faced reduced benefits.

Coverage for Retirees—Plans that extend basic life insurance coverage into retirement almost always continue coverage for the remainder of the retiree's life. However, the amount of the benefit is usually reduced at least once during retirement. Some plans require that continued coverage be paid fully by the retiree. In 1994, 46 percent of the full-time participants in state and local governments had basic life insurance that continued into retirement.

Bibliography

Mace, Don, and Eric Yoder, eds. *Federal Employees Almanac 1996.* Forty-third edition. Reston, VA: Federal Employees News Digest, Inc., 1996.

U.S. Department of Labor. Bureau of Labor Statistics. *Employee Benefits in State and Local Governments, 1994.* Washington, DC: U.S. Government Printing Office, 1996.

U.S. Office of Personnel Management. Budget and Program Information Division. *Statistical Abstracts: Federal Employee Benefit Programs, Fiscal Year 1993.* Washington, DC: U.S. Office of Personnel Management, 1994.

U.S. Office of Personnel Management. Retirement and Insurance Service. *Federal Employees' Group Life Insurance: Description and Certification of Enrollment in the FEGLI Program.* Washington, DC: U.S. Office of Personnel Management, 1995.

Workplace Economics, Inc. *1995 State Employee Benefits Survey.* Washington, DC: Workplace Economics, Inc., 1995.

Additional Information

U.S. Office of Personnel Management
1900 E Street, NW
Washington, DC 20415
(202) 606-1212

Workplace Economics, Inc.
P.O. Box 33367
Washington, DC 20033-0367
(202) 223-9191

44. Leave Programs in the Public Sector

Introduction

Leave, or paid time off from work, is a particularly significant benefit for public-sector workers. These workers are entitled to slightly more paid holidays on average than their private-sector counterparts, and annual and sick leave often play a somewhat different role in their total benefits package.

Sick Leave

Public employees rely on accumulations of paid sick leave to provide income during periods of illness and temporary disability. In 1994, state and local employees accrued an estimated 13 days of sick leave (U.S. Department of Labor, 1996). Federal employees also accrued just over 13 days of sick leave annually (U.S. Code, 1995). Persons employed in medium and large private establishments accrued an estimated 12 days of sick leave annually, in 1993 (U.S. Department of Labor, 1994a). Most public employees accrue sick leave on an annual basis (the rate of accrual may vary by service) and are entitled to carry forward unused sick leave balances indefinitely and without limitation. Thus, long-service employees who have enjoyed reasonably good health can have large sick leave accumulations during the later years of their careers.

In some jurisdictions, employees are compensated for their unused sick leave on termination of employment. However, a more common practice is to compensate them for this unused leave at the time of retirement. This compensation can take several forms. Some states and the federal Civil Service Retirement System credit unused sick leave for purposes of computing retirement benefits. (Under the federal system, this practice adds six months to the average employee's length of service.) Other states pay some percentage of unused sick leave or pay subject to certain dollar maximums. A few states credit the value of some amount of unused sick leave toward insurance premiums (Workplace Economics, 1995).

Annual Leave

Annual leave (vacation time) is generally accrued according to length of service, with average accruals for state and local employees of 12.3 days at one year of service, 18.3 days at 10 years of service, and 21.9 days at 20 years of service (U.S. Department of Labor, 1996). Federal employees accrue 13 days of annual leave during their first three years of employment, 20 days during years 3 through 14, and 26 days thereafter (U.S. Code, 1995). This compares with 9.4 days at one year of service, 16.6 days at 10 years of service, and 20.4 days at 20 years of service that persons in medium and large private establishments accrued in 1993 (U.S. Department of Labor, 1994a).

Unused annual leave can usually be carried forward to subsequent years, although the amount that can be carried forward is generally subject to a maximum. Most federal and state and local employees are able to carry over 30 days of annual leave. Three states (Indiana, Louisiana, and Mississippi) allow leave to be carried over without limit. Among states specifying a maximum, Hawaii allows the greatest accumulation, at 90 days. Accumulated leave is generally cashed out on termination or retirement, although the cashout may be subject to a limit that is different from that imposed on accumulation (Workplace Economics, 1995).

Leave Sharing/Leave Banks, and Compensatory Time

Since public employees often have accumulation in excess of their own needs, some jurisdictions have undertaken programs whereby employees can transfer leave to colleagues in need. Sixteen states are currently maintaining some form of "sick leave pool." In addition, nine other states allow employees to donate their annual leave to fellow employees in need of sick leave, under certain guidelines (Workplace Economics, 1995).

The federal government also has several leave-sharing programs. Under the Federal Employees Leave Sharing Amendments Act of 1993, all federal agencies are required to operate a leave-transfer program. The act also allows agencies to establish leave banks at any time.

Under the leave-transfer program, employees who have exhausted all of their leave and are in need of additional leave (due to medical or family emergencies) can accept annual leave donations from fellow employees.

Under the leave bank program, employees who are in need of additional leave and who have contributed a portion of their own annual leave to the agency's leave bank that year are eligible to apply for a withdrawal of annual leave from the bank, should a medical or family emergency arise.

Compensatory time ("comp-time") is another form of leave used in the public sector. It is a method employers in the public sector can use to compensate employees for overtime work. Under the Fair Labor Standards Act, public employers are able to provide compensatory time off instead of monetary overtime compensation, providing there is an agreement between the employer and the employee. Compensatory time off must be at least one and one-half hours for each hour of overtime worked.

Family and Medical Leave

Paid leave—apart from annual and sick leave accumulations—that may be used expressly to care for children is extremely rare in the public sector. However, under the federal Family and Medical Leave Act of 1993, employers are required to provide 12 weeks of unpaid, job-protected leave each year to eligible employees for the birth or adoption of a child or for the serious illness of the employee or the employee's child, parent, or spouse (see chapter 36 on dependent care). In addition to the federally mandated Family and Medical Leave Act, most states have their own family leave laws that apply to public-sector workers. For example, some states provide up to a year of unpaid parental leave, while other states provide employees with some paid parental leave.

Bibliography

Abrahams et al. *The Employer's Guide to the Fair Labor Standards Act (1995)*. Washington, DC: Thompson Publishing Group, 1995.

Mace, Don, and Eric Yoder. *Federal Employees Almanac 1995*. Reston, VA: Federal Employees News Digest, Inc., 1995.

U.S. Code. Chapter 63, Title 5. 1995.

U.S. Department of Labor. Bureau of Labor Statistics. *Employee Benefits in Medium and Large Private Establishments, 1993*. Washington, DC: U.S. Government Printing Office, 1994a.

_____. *Employee Benefits in State and Local Governments, 1994*. Washington, DC: U.S. Government Printing Office, 1996.

Workplace Economics, Inc. *1995 State Employee Benefits Survey*. Washington, DC: Workplace Economics, Inc., 1995.

Additional Information

Center for Personnel Research
1617 Duke Street
Alexandria, VA 22314
(703) 549-7100

Society for Human Resource Management
606 North Washington Street
Alexandria, VA 22314
(703) 548-3440

PART SIX
PUBLIC POLICY ISSUES

45. Pension Tax Expenditures

Introduction

The provision of tax incentives to encourage pension coverage reflects a longstanding policy of the U.S. government. Under the Internal Revenue Code, an employer's contribution to a qualified plan is deductible within specified limits. Taxes on employer contributions and investment income are deferred for pension plan participants until the pension benefit is received and declared as income. Any individual who participates in a pension plan, whether he or she works for the federal government, a state or local government, or a private nongovernment organization, receives a deferral on income tax as the benefit accrues.

Individuals tend to focus on the immediate reduction in taxes that comes with pension tax treatment rather than on a calculation of the ultimate net tax gain or loss that will occur many years in the future. Because tax rates may be higher in the future than they are today, individuals may ultimately pay more taxes when they receive their benefit. Some people, as a result, would be better off never putting in the money.[1] On the other hand, others may end up in a lower tax bracket in retirement than they were in when working, meaning they would have been better off in tax terms having received a pension rather than cash. In short, although it is generally assumed that everyone wins with lower tax payments when they invest in tax-deferred pensions, not everyone does.

Nevertheless, the federal government gives a value to this "gain from deferral," which is referred to as a "tax expenditure," i.e., a tax the government does not get paid today because the value of the pension benefit accrual is not taxed as income today. Each year a set of tax expenditure estimates is developed by the U.S. Department of the Treasury and published as part of the federal budget. The total reported pension tax expenditure (which includes civil service, state and local, and private pension plans) is $69.6 billion for fiscal year (FY) 1996.

At the same time, pension funds and their taxation have come to the forefront because of the tremendous accumulation of pension assets in the

---

[1] Although it is beyond the scope of this chapter, a detailed analysis of the relative advantage of contributing to a qualified retirement plan would also include the potential relative advantage produced by the tax-sheltered investment income.

economy. Private and public pension plans now hold more than $4 trillion in assets. Some policymakers have looked to this large pool of assets as a means to fund economic development projects such as infrastructure. Moreover, the ever-increasing federal budget deficit has caused policymakers to assess whether the "cost" of lost federal revenues, which is measured by tax expenditure estimates, is appropriate.

When we ask if pensions are worth the cost, we are focusing on the tax expenditures attributed to pensions. Are the tax incentives accorded to pensions meeting their public policy objectives? Do pensions provide enough benefit to individuals and the economy as a whole to justify the tax expenditure?

Several factors must be taken into account when evaluating the appropriateness of tax expenditures. First, analysts must determine what the numbers actually measure. It is especially important to distinguish between the types of plans represented by tax expenditure estimates. Often, pension tax expenditure estimates are referred to as if they only represent revenue associated with private pension plans. However, the number reflects all pension plans, including civil service; military; state and local governments; and private plans.

Second, to assess whether pensions are worth the cost, it is important to recognize the impact that the funding practices of different plan types have on the revenue numbers. Because the tax expenditure estimates for pensions are calculated by the government on a cash flow basis, no value is placed on the pension promise itself, only on the advance funding of that promise. With the exception of Social Security and federal employee defined benefit plans, most pension plans now seek to advance fund as a means of assuring that promises made will be kept. Federal law requires private pension plans to set aside funds for the purpose of paying benefits as they become due. However, public pension plans may operate on a pay-as-you-go basis, distributing benefits from current receipts. Defined contribution plans are always fully funded for accrued liabilities by definition because the participants' pension benefit consists of the contributions and investment returns on these contributions.

The Value of Tax Expenditures

Pension Costs—The concept of tax expenditures was developed in the 1970s. The Congressional Budget and Impoundment Act of 1974 (sec. 3(a)(3) defines tax expenditures as: "those revenue losses attributable to provisions of the Federal tax laws which allow a special exclusion, exemption, or deduction from gross income or which provide a special credit, a preferential rate of tax, or a deferral of tax liability" (Employee Benefit Research Institute, 1983).

Pension, Keogh (pensions for self-employed individuals) and individual retirement account (IRA) tax expenditures are different from most other tax expenditures because they represent tax-deferred expenditures rather than tax-exempt expenditures. For example, payments for health benefits are never taxed, while pensions are taxed when paid to the individual.[2]

The tax expenditure estimates for pensions are calculated by the government on a cash flow basis. This is significant because it has the effect of placing no value on the pension promise itself, only on the advance funding of that promise. First, the contributions made to plans and estimated investment earnings are treated as taxable wages. Second, benefits paid by the plans are treated as taxable income. Third, the tax to be paid on benefits is subtracted from the tax that would have been paid on contributions and earnings to get a net tax expenditure estimate. Thus, a "tax expenditure" is only considered to have occurred if advance contributions are made.

According to the Congressional Joint Committee on Taxation, the pension tax expenditure is $69.6 billion for FY 1996. The tax expenditure number reported by the government should represent all types of pension plans—civil service, military, state and local, and private—because pension participants gain economic value and tax deferral regardless of where they work. However, the number reportedly does not currently include military plans. The estimate does cover both defined benefit and defined contribution plans.

The total reported pension tax expenditure of $69.6 billion for FY 1996 has been broken down by the Congressional Joint Committee on Taxation. Based on present law and funded status of plans, the largest portion of the tax expenditure, $37.6 billion (or 54.0 percent), is attributable to public pension plans. Private-sector plans account for $32.0 billion (46.0 percent).

---

[2] For a full discussion of pension taxation, see Employee Benefit Research Institute, "Retirement Program Tax Expenditures," *EBRI Issue Brief* no. 17 (Employee Benefit Research Institute, April 1983); "Pension-Related Tax Benefits," *EBRI Issue Brief* no. 25 (Employee Benefit Research Institute, December 1983), and Dallas L. Salisbury, "Pension Tax Expenditures: Are They Worth the Cost?" *EBRI Issue Brief* no. 134 (Employee Benefit Research Institute, February 1993).

The Employee Benefit Research Institute (EBRI) estimates that private-sector defined benefit plans are about $8 billion (11.5 percent) and private-sector defined contribution plans are $24 billion (34.4 percent). This compares with the tax expenditure for IRAs of $8.8 billion, $3.5 billion for Keogh plans, and $23.1 billion for the exclusion from taxation of a portion of Social Security and railroad retirement benefits.

Generally, the pension tax expenditure number is discussed as if it only applies to private employer plans, and then sometimes only to private defined benefit plans. As the foregoing discussion makes clear, the number covers all plans, with a near equal split between the tax expenditure for private and public employees.

As a result, the tax expenditure attributed to private pensions has often been exaggerated. Public pension plans are seldom mentioned as part of the equation. More often than not during a call for private pension plan "reform" an advocate states that change must be made because of the "$69.6 billion tax expenditure." Would this be less compelling if the number was limited to the $8 billion for private defined benefit plans? Suddenly, the elements of the total pension tax expenditure would be significantly smaller relative to that for mortgages, medical premiums, capital gains at death, or accelerated depreciation. It would also show that the number attributable to private plans has grown little from the number published in the 1983 budget and earlier as the tax expenditure for pensions. Finally, it would show that the tax expenditure for private defined benefit plans had declined significantly as the system matured.

Private Expenditures for Retirement Income

Private employers contributed $24 billion to defined benefit and $13 billion to defined contribution plans in 1975, growing to $35 billion contributed to defined benefit plans and $94 billion to defined contribution plans in 1992. Defined contribution plans represented 35 percent of contributions in 1975 and 73 percent in 1992 (Employee Benefit Research Institute, 1995). Private retirement plans have about 82 million active, separated, and retired participants.

Private employer contributions to defined benefit plans grew to $48 billion in 1982 as plans responded to The Employee Retirement Income Security Act of 1974's (ERISA) funding requirements. Excellent investment returns during the 1980s, combined with federal legislation during the decade that placed limits on funding and benefits, have caused contributions to decline. More than 85 percent of private defined benefit plans reached full funding in the mid-1980s, compared with less than 25 percent when ERISA was enacted in 1974 and 42 percent in 1995. Contributions to defined contribution plans can generally be viewed as a percentage of income. As incomes have increased and as the number of workers given the opportunity to participate has grown, contributions have grown as well (Salisbury, 1989).

The Pension Benefit Guaranty Corporation (PBGC) was created under ERISA to strengthen retirement income security by guaranteeing some benefits for defined benefit plan participants. PBGC is funded by premiums paid by private defined benefit plans sponsors. PBGC reports that the single-employer private defined benefit system had $987 billion in assets to cover $853 billion in liabilities in 1995. Therefore, while there is underfunding within individual plans, there are also sufficient resources available within the defined benefit system itself—the payers of PBGC premiums—to cover this underfunding.

The ERISA requirements for pension plan funding have generally provided the benefit security sought by the law.

State and Local Expenditures for Retirement Income

State and local governments generally provide defined benefit pension plans to their work force. About 12 million active employees and another 5 million former employees, retirees, and survivors are covered. Employer contributions to these plans grew from $15 billion in 1975 to an estimated $47 billion in 1990. Most of these plans have been advance funded, resulting in significant investment earnings in addition to contributions. Total assets reached $1.176 billion in 1994 (Employee Benefit Research Institute, 1995).

Federal Direct Expenditures for Retirement Income

The most significant retirement income programs funded by the federal government are Social Security, the military retirement programs, and the civil service retirement programs. This discussion focuses on the latter two, the pension programs provided to federal workers. These federal employee programs include about 6.5 million active participants and 4 million participants who are retired or have left federal employment but will receive a benefit at a later date. These programs represent a sizable liability to the federal government and thus to the American taxpayers.

Budgeted outlays (inclusive of interest paid on bonds held as assets by the plans) for these employee pension programs grew from $21 billion in 1975 to $67 billion in 1995 and are projected to grow to $89 billion in 2002 (U.S. President, 1996).

The Civil Service Retirement and Disability Fund consists of two programs that are part of both the pension tax expenditure and the direct federal outlays. The Civil Service Retirement System (CSRS) covers those hired as federal civilian employees prior to 1984, and the Federal Employee Retirement System covers those hired after 1984. Data indicate that the programs represent a larger future obligation for taxpayers than cash outlays imply. The present unfunded liability for CSRS is equal to $69,000 per active CSRS participant.

For the federal civilian plans, the actual contributions being made as a percentage of pay are substantial at 56.4 percent, compared with a reported 3.9 percent for private employers. Funding for the value of one year's growth in promised benefits for present workers ("normal cost") requires a contribution equal to 7.3 percent of pay.

The Military Retirement System (MRS) presents a future financial challenge for taxpayers and policymakers as well. The MRS had an un-funded liability of $589.2 billion as of September 30, 1994, compared with $682.5 billion as of September 30, 1989. The actual contributions to the MRS were a substantial 132.7 percent of pay, compared to the MRS normal cost of 33.5 percent of pay.

Many analysts write as if every dollar of tax expenditure increases the federal deficit. When one looks at the tax expenditure represented by civil service and military plans, one sees that it is more complicated. When a pension promise is made to a civilian or military employee, a liability is created that effectively increases the federal deficit because it represents a promise taxpayers must eventually pay. However, it creates no tax expendi-ture and is not reported as part of the deficit because of cash accounting. Only if a contribution is made to secure the benefit will a tax expenditure arise or the reported deficit be affected. The future taxpayer's obligation has in theory been reduced because a contribution has been made and the plan now has lower liabilities and more assets. Yet, in the case of the CSRS and other federal plans, most of the assets are Treasury securities that repre-sent a liability of the federal taxpayer, which means the nation accounts for the liability explicitly.

Federal employees may have implicit benefit security because the promise is made by the federal government, which is expected to be here to pay its bills. However, the magnitude of the liabilities of the plans now in place, and the level of future payments required, justify concern.

What Would Taxpayers Save by Ending Federal Pensions?

Because federal pensions are not being funded at the rate ERISA requires for private plans, the tax expenditure that would otherwise be attributable to them is quite low. Ironically, a higher contribution would produce both a higher direct federal expenditure and a higher reported tax expenditure. If applied to the federal government, ERISA would have required a CSRS contribution in excess of $64 billion. This higher contribution would have increased the pension tax expenditure number in the budget by $8.5 billion, or more than 15 percent.

The size of the forgone revenues would indeed be large, but would the taxpayer be better off making no contributions to public pension plans? Lower contributions would lower the reported tax expenditure but would in no way reduce what must eventually be paid in taxes to provide the promised pension benefits. Taxpayers must eventually pay for public employee pension promises. Focusing on the tax expenditure for pensions makes much less sense than focusing on whether pension promises should be made, and if they are, how and when should they be paid for. For all pension participants, it is better to know that there is already "money in the bank" than to depend on future goodwill.

Who Benefits from the Tax Incentives?

The benefits of the pension system can be viewed in many ways, and the same numbers can be presented as positive or negative indicators. An analysis of who benefits most from the system based on the earnings distribution of participants finds most of the coverage going to those earning between $10,000 and $50,000 per year. An analysis of the system based on rates of participation reinforces this finding.

The Joint Committee on Taxation publishes statistics on taxpayers and tax expenditures, including the distribution of returns and taxes paid. Using the EBRI Tax Estimating and Analysis Model (TEAM), the pension tax expenditure was allocated across taxpayers in the same way. (The government last published its own income distribution of the pension tax expenditure in 1983.)

One percent of all tax returns report income above $200,0000; these taxpayers pay 26 percent of all individual income taxes (U.S. Congress, 1992a). EBRI TEAM data allocate the value of pension tax incentives by income class and show that high income taxpayers obtain 6.7 percent of the value of total pension tax expenditures. If this group of taxpayers were to lose pension tax incentives, they could experience a financial loss equal to a 3 percent tax increase.

Seven percent of the value of tax expenditures is received by taxpayers with income between $20,000 and $29,999, who pay 6 percent of all individual income taxes. This group could experience a financial loss equal to a tax increase of 14 percent if pension tax incentives were removed.

Middle income households gain the most from pension tax incentives. Taxable returns showing income between $30,000 and $50,000 (29 percent of taxable returns) paid 18 percent of taxes, received 28 percent of the pension tax incentive value, and could experience a financial loss equal to an 18 percent tax increase if the incentives were removed. Upper middle income households, at $50,000–$100,000 (24 percent of taxable returns), paid 33 percent of taxes, received 43 percent of the tax expenditure, and could experience a financial loss equal to a 15 percent tax increase with the end of pension incentives.

What If We Used Accruals for Tax Expenditures?

Using pension contributions, earnings, and benefits to calculate tax expenditures produces a low number if low contributions are made. Because federal plans make low contributions relative to the benefit being earned, they are not "charged" with as much tax expenditure as they would be if they contributed at a faster rate. Using the benefit being earned—the benefit accrual—as the basis of calculation would lead to a different distribution of value. Using accruals would have produced a tax expenditure of $67.2 billion rather than $56.5 billion.

This approach shows that the actual value of pensions is distributed more heavily at the middle and lower end of the income spectrum than the present method of calculating tax expenditures implies.

Pension plans are distributing more benefits to lower and middle income individuals than tax expenditure numbers imply. Those between $30,000 and $50,000 represent $15.9 billion of the cash flow tax expenditure, while earning $21 billion in accruals. Were all public and private pensions being fully advance funded, the numbers would be the same.

People Not Percentages

Most analysts focus on the proportion of those at given income levels who participate in pension plans and declare that this indicates that pensions favor high income persons. Among workers earning less than $10,000, 10.1 percent participated in pensions in 1991, or 3.6 million persons. This compares with a participation rate of 64.8 percent for those earning above $100,000, but this group includes only 71,728 people, according to EBRI tabulations. Eighty-nine percent of those covered by pensions and 86.7 percent of participants had earnings below $50,000 in 1991.

In addition, analysts have focused on retirees' share of income as represented by pension payments. The foregoing analysis points out that Census surveys treat only annuity payments from pensions as pension income. As a result, lump-sum distributions paid prior to retirement are not "credited" to the pension system. For 1989, this resulted in a major difference in the number reported by the Social Security Administration as retiree pension income and the number reported by the Commerce Department in the National Income and Product Accounts as pension benefit payments (Employee Benefit Research Institute, 1995).

As a result of current tax laws and methods of data collection, an assessment of the results of the pension system must focus primarily on the current work force, rather than the retiree population. This is, in fact, an unfortunate result and may argue for both policy change and for much improved data collection.

Pension Plans and Benefit Payments

Pension plans have had a history of significant increases in benefit payments. Pension plans paid more in benefits in 1994 ($313.4 billion) than Social Security retirement ($312.1 billion).

Employer pensions are an important source of retirement income and are growing. The data available understate pension plans' contribution to retirement income because they do not include lump-sum distributions made prior to and at retirement. In spite of this, the number of retirees with pension income continues to grow. Fifty-four percent of married couples and 42 percent of all "units" of individuals aged 65 and over reported pension income in 1994 (Grad, 1996). According to the 1991 Advisory Council on Social Security, the percentage of elderly families receiving income from employer-sponsored pensions is expected to increase from the current

44 percent to 76 percent by the year 2018 (Reno, 1992). Among married couples currently aged 45–59, nearly 70 percent are earning a pension right, and others who are not now participating in a pension plan report a pension right from a former employer (Goodfellow and Schieber, 1992).

In 1994, private pension benefits, estimated by the U.S. Department of Commerce at $179.4 billion, accounted for 29 percent of the $625.4 billion in total estimated retirement benefit payments.[3] By comparison, private pension benefits totaled $7.4 billion in 1970. Combined with benefits paid by the federal civilian and military retirement system and state and local government employee retirement systems, employer payments of $313.3 billion accounted for 51 percent of total benefits in 1994. Social Security benefits for retirees and their spouses and dependents totaled $312.1 billion and accounted for the other 49 percent of total benefits.

Pension payments to individuals have increased over the years as the pension system has matured. The maturity of the pension system is shown by tax return data that reveal 44 percent of retirees reported pension income in 1990, compared with 31 percent in 1976.

These numbers represent annuity payments only, so that the billions of dollars now paid each year in lump-sum distributions and taken into income would result in earnings reported as asset income. As the pension system continues to change, it will become increasingly important to find a way to identify this pension-created wealth. The growth in the previous numbers, it should be stressed, would be significantly greater if all income attributable to past pension distributions could be documented.

Pensions and Savings

Pension plans that are advance funded serve to expand total savings (VanDerhei, 1992). The magnitude has been debated, and studies show wide variation, from a low of $0.32 per $1.00 of pension savings to a high of $0.84. At either level, this translates into billions of dollars each year, with total pension assets exceeding $5 trillion in 1995. As previously noted, federal pension plans have combined unfunded liabilities of more than $1.6 trillion. If federal plan participants have saved less because of the pension income promise, then federal plans may have served to decrease personal savings, as private and state and local plans have served to increase personal savings with substantial advance funding.

---

[3] U.S. Department of Commerce estimates of private pension benefit payments lag actual data by three years.

The Need for More Complete Presentations

Some analysts and policymakers have suggested raising revenue by imposing taxes on pension funds. Often, however, they have not considered the potential effects that changing the tax treatment could have on the availability and extent of pension benefits, the financial markets, and the U.S. economy.

A 1992 Congressional Research Service (CRS) analysis includes the following paragraph:

"To tax defined benefit plans can be very difficult since it is not always easy to allocate pension accruals to specific employees. It might be particularly difficult to allocate accruals to individuals not vested. This complexity would not, however, preclude taxation of trust earnings at a specified rate." (U.S. Congress, 1992b)

Policymakers would also need to consider (1) the implications for the federal budget and state and local budgets (and benefit security) of requiring the payment of a portion of accumulated assets as an excise tax by public pension plans; (2) the implications for PBGC of decreasing the assets in private defined benefit plans by taxing them away; and (3) the implications for plan terminations and ultimate retirement income if defined benefit assets are taxed but the assets of defined contribution plans are not.

When making changes in the pension system, these interrelationships should be considered before policy actions are taken. And, the primary objective of pensions—economic security—should not be overlooked.

Bibliography

Employee Benefit Research Institute. *Databook on Employee Benefits. Third edition.* Washington, DC: Employee Benefit Research Institute, 1995.

_____. *Pensions in a Changing Economy.* Washington, DC: Employee Benefit Research Institute, 1993.

_____. *Pension Funding & Taxation: Implications for Tomorrow.* Washington, DC: Employee Benefit Research Institute, 1994.

_____. *When Workers Call the Shots: Can They Achieve Retirement Security?* Washington, DC: Employee Benefit Research Institute, 1995.

_____. "Pension-Related Tax Benefits." *EBRI Issue Brief* no. 25 (Employee Benefit Research Institute, 1983).

Goodfellow, Gordon P., and Sylvester J. Schieber. "Death and Taxes: Can We Fund for Retirement Between Them?" Paper. Washington, DC: The Wyatt Company, 1992.

Grad, Susan. *Income of the Population 55 or Older, 1994.* U.S. Social Security Administration. Washington, DC: U.S. Government Printing Office, 1996.

Metz, Joseph G. *The Federal Taxation of Public Officials.* Washington, DC: Government Finance Officers Association, 1988.

Munnell, Alicia H. "Are Pensions Worth the Cost?" *National Tax Journal* (September 1991): 393–403.

Reno, Virginia P. "The Role of Pensions in Retirement Income: Trends and Questions." Paper. Washington, DC: National Academy on Aging, 1992.

Salisbury, Dallas L. "Employee Benefits in a Flat Tax or Consumption Tax World." *EBRI Notes,* no. 9 (September 1995): 1–11.

_____. "Pension Tax Expenditures: Are They Worth the Cost?" *EBRI Issue Brief* no. 134 (Employee Benefit Research Institute, February 1993).

_____. "Individual Saving for Retirement—The 401(k) and IRA Experiences." *EBRI Issue Brief* no. 95 (Employee Benefit Research Institute, October 1989).

U.S. Congress. Joint Committee on Taxation. *Estimates of Federal Tax Expenditures for Fiscal Years 1993–1997.* Washington, DC: U.S. Government Printing Office, 1992a.

U.S. Congress. Senate. Committee on the Budget. *Tax Expenditures.* Prepared by Congressional Research Service. Washington, DC: U.S. Government Printing Office, 1992b.

U.S. President. Office of Management and Budget. *Budget of the United States: Fiscal Year 1997.* Washington, DC: U.S. Government Printing Office, 1996.

VanDerhei, Jack. "Pensions, Social Security, and Savings." *EBRI Issue Brief* no. 129 (Employee Benefit Research Institute, September 1992).

Additional Information

The Pension Research Council
The Wharton School
University of Pennsylvania
Philadelphia, PA
(215) 898-7620

International Foundation of Employee Benefit Plans
P.O. Box 69
18700 West Bluemound Road
Brookfield, WI 53008-0069
(414) 786-6700

National Academy on Aging
1275 K Street, NW
Washington, DC
(202) 408-3375

U.S. Department of the Treasury
Office of Tax Analysis
15th Street and Pennsylvania Avenue, NW
Washington, DC 20220
(202) 622-0269

46. Health Insurance Portability and COBRA Expansion

Introduction

The original purpose of the continuation of coverage provision of the Consolidated Omnibus Budget Reconciliation Act of 1985 (COBRA) was to assure individuals access to health insurance during periods of unemployment and job change. However, COBRA coverage premiums may be outside the range of one's budget constraint, making it ineffective for people trying to maintain health insurance coverage with limited resources. As a result, portability and affordability were the central issues surrounding the health insurance debate in 1996. The Health Insurance Portability and Accountability Act of 1996 attempts to address portability and affordability by including measures such as preexisting condition exclusions,[1] guaranteed access[2] to health insurance, guaranteed renewal[3] of health insurance, increases in the health insurance deduction for the self-employed, and medical savings accounts (MSAs). (For further discussion of MSAs, see chapter 47.) The main purpose of the bill is to increase individuals' opportunity to maintain health insurance as they change jobs. While the resulting legislation allows individuals to change insurers without being subjected to a new waiting period for preexisting conditions and reforms the market for individual and group health insurance, it does not radically change the 1985 COBRA law. Unemployed individuals still face the issue of affordability, and since the legislation does not include an employer mandate for health

---

[1] Preexisting condition exclusions are mechanisms that insurers use to restrict an enrollee's access to health care benefits relating to the individual's previous medical condition. These waiting periods are typically 6 months or 12 months; however, a group health plan has to take into account an individual's prior creditable coverage when applying any preexisting condition limit.

[2] Guaranteed access requires insurers that offer coverage to make coverage available to any individual or group that applies, regardless of the health conditions of the individual or the individuals in that group.

[3] Guaranteed renewal requires an insurer to renew coverage for an individual or group at the option of the covered individual or group. Typically, policies may be canceled or not renewed for nonpayment of premiums, fraud or misrepresentation, termination of the plan, or the failure of the plan sponsor to meet contribution or participation requirements.

insurance coverage, job lock may continue to be an issue for many individuals and employers. This chapter presents background information on issues surrounding portability, job lock, and COBRA.

Background Issues

Portability—Concern about the portability of health insurance primarily arises in situations where an individual is leaving, or would like to leave, a job. The circumstance can be one of completely withdrawing from the job market or wanting to move to a new employer. For example, portability could help alleviate the loss of insurance benefits when a worker is offered a new job that could alter his or her insurance status. If health insurance is not offered by a prospective employer, if the worker must satisfy a waiting period before becoming eligible for coverage, or if the benefits package offered through the prospective employer is less generous, the employee may opt to remain with his or her current employer. This may result in job lock, or in employees forgoing job opportunities that could potentially increase their productivity. In other words, workers may forgo job opportunities in which a better match between the worker and the employer would enable the worker to perform his or her job more effectively.

For employers that want employees to leave or retire and for employees who would prefer to change jobs, job lock can be undesirable. The original purpose of the coverage continuation provisions of COBRA was to assure workers an ability to maintain health insurance during a period of transition to other health insurance coverage. However, many individuals who qualify for COBRA forgo the continued coverage because of its high price relative to their income. Employees cannot be charged more than 102 percent of the employer's average health insurance premium, which may be less than the employer's actual cost but more than the employee was used to paying for health insurance. Because COBRA requires individuals to pay up to 102 percent of the average cost, persons leaving jobs may not always take advantage of the insurance.

Job Lock—Job lock may occur either because a worker cannot get health insurance coverage through a prospective employer or because, while the worker can obtain coverage, his or her share of the premium is higher at the prospective job than it is at the current job or the benefits package is less generous. Prior to the implementation of the Health Insurance Portability and Affordability Act of 1996, preexisting condition limits may also have contributed to job lock.

Limiting preexisting condition exclusions is one method that states have used to reduce job lock, yet there is no conclusive evidence assessing the impact of these laws on job mobility. However, in the presence of COBRA, among plans that cover a preexisting condition following a waiting period, preexisting conditions are not necessarily the primary motivating factor behind individuals' decision not to change jobs. This is because individuals can continue their current coverage for a maximum of 18–36 months even after moving into a new job, as long as they are willing to pay 102 percent of the premium for their old health insurance. Thus, individuals could carry two plans until the waiting period is satisfied. Regardless of the existence of COBRA, cost, comprehensiveness of the benefit package, and availability of coverage remain important.

COBRA Basics—COBRA, as amended in legislation subsequent to its passage in 1985, requires employers with health insurance plans to offer continued access to group health insurance to qualified beneficiaries if they lose coverage under the plan as a result of a qualifying event. COBRA requires continued access for 18 months (or 29 months if the qualified beneficiary is disabled) for covered employees, spouses, and dependent children who lose coverage when a covered employee terminates employment (for reasons other than gross misconduct) or there is a reduction in his or her hours of employment. COBRA requires continued access for 36 months for spouses and dependent children who lose coverage as a result of a covered employee's death, divorce, or legal separation. In addition, spouses and dependent children qualify for continued access for 36 months if a covered employee becomes entitled to Medicare benefits.

Prior to enactment of the Omnibus Budget Reconciliation Act of 1989 (OBRA '89), coverage could be terminated prior to the end of the maximum required period if the qualified beneficiary became covered under another group health plan. However, OBRA '89 provides that COBRA need not terminate before the maximum period if the qualified beneficiary becomes covered under another group health plan that excludes or limits a preexisting condition.

The Health Insurance Portability and Affordability Act of 1996 includes additional COBRA clarifications affecting individuals with disabilities, newborns, and adopted children, effective January 1, 1997. First, the act clarifies that any qualified beneficiary who becomes disabled within the first 60 days of his or her initial COBRA qualifying event is eligible for 29 months of coverage, along with his or her dependents. Second, newborns and adopted children will be allowed to enroll immediately under a qualified beneficiary's COBRA coverage, without being required to wait until the next open enrollment period. Third, COBRA coverage may be terminated as soon as any preexisting condition limitation in the new plan has been satisfied.

The coverage offered must be identical to that available prior to the change in the worker's employment status. The qualifying employee or dependent may be required to pay up to 102 percent of the premium (disabled qualified beneficiaries may be required to pay up to 150 percent of the premium for months 19 through 29). At the end of the coverage period, the employer must offer conversion to an individual policy if the group plan includes a conversion privilege (an option required in some states).

Group health plans for public and private employers with fewer than 20 employees are excluded from these provisions, as are plans offered by churches (as defined in sec. 414(e) of the Internal Revenue Code (IRC)); the District of Columbia; or any territory, possession, or agency of the United States.

COBRA Survey Results—The original purpose of COBRA's coverage continuation provisions was to assure workers an ability to maintain health insurance during a period of transition to other coverage. Several surveys have been conducted regarding issues surrounding the use of COBRA. Some key results of the Charles D. Spencer & Associates, Inc. survey, conducted in the spring of each year, include the following:

- Of the 14.5 percent of employees and dependents eligible for COBRA coverage, about one in five (18.2 percent) elected the coverage in 1994, down from 19.6 percent in 1993 and 19.3 percent in 1992, and a high of 28.5 percent in 1989.
- Among all spouses and dependents eligible for coverage, 26.0 percent elected coverage in 1994, compared with 9.6 in 1993, 37 percent in 1992, 23.4 percent in 1991, 25 percent in 1990, and 36.6 percent in 1989. Among employees eligible for coverage, 16.2 percent elected coverage in 1994.
- Among the entire surveyed population, 1.3 percent of the active employee work force elected COBRA coverage in 1994, down from 2.9 percent in 1993.
- Among all eligibles electing coverage, 21.9 percent were spouse/dependent elections in 1994 (4.4 percent selected coverage because of termination or reduction in hours, and 17.5 percent elected coverage because of death, divorce, or plan ineligibility). This is up from 15.9 percent in 1993.
- Average COBRA costs were $5,301, compared with $3,420 for active

employees in surveyed health plans in 1994. Thus, average continuation of coverage costs were 155 percent of the active employee claims costs. Large differences between active employee costs and COBRA costs have been typical since 1990, when average active employee costs were $2,769, compared with $4,208 for COBRA costs.

- Costs of COBRA coverage to companies with employees electing coverage varies greatly. Data indicate that within the 1994 plan year, COBRA costs bore little relationship to active employee costs. In 1993, the most common range (for 68 percent of responding companies) was between 102 percent and 200 percent of the average costs for an active employee. On the extreme end, 9 percent of responding employers had COBRA costs in excess of three times the cost of active employees. COBRA costs more closely resemble individual (as opposed to group) plan costs in that they are not consistent from year to year.

- For 18-month qualifying events, the average length of coverage was 10.3 months. For 36-month qualifying events, the average length of coverage was 25 months. Among individuals electing coverage, 1.6 percent converted to an individual policy.

- Difficulties surrounding COBRA coverage, according to surveyed employers, included adverse selection/claims costs (21 percent); difficulties in collecting premiums (30 percent); administrative difficulty such as paperwork and record keeping (28 percent); excessive time for beneficiary response and tracking eligibility (17 percent); notification from continuee of election or change in status (18 percent); and lack of final rules and complexity of law (14 percent) (Charles D. Spencer & Associates, Inc., 1994 and 1995).

COBRA coverage can be considered advantageous for some employees. Consider the following example of a firm with a traditional fee-for-service health plan offered by Blue Cross/Blue Shield plan in the Washington, DC region for plan years starting on March 1, 1995. Under the health plan, the annual premium for a family plan is $10,859. However, the actuarial cost of the plan varies greatly across workers. The actuarial cost for workers under age 30 would be $4,524, and the actuarial cost for workers aged 55 and over would be $12,759. If a worker chooses COBRA coverage, the premium would be $11,076, or 102 percent of the annual premium faced by the employer. Young individuals would have an incentive to forgo COBRA coverage, while older workers would have an incentive to accept COBRA coverage. As a result, the COBRA coverage pool of insured workers is adversely selected—meaning only relatively older, relatively unhealthy individuals will choose

COBRA coverage, and the cost of providing health insurance coverage will increase for all workers. If the firm is self-insured, it would receive $11,076 from each COBRA covered worker but would expect to pay $12,759 in claims for workers aged 55 and over and their families. If the firm's COBRA pool is adversely selected, it can expect to pay an even higher amount in health care claims, as evidenced by the Spencer survey. Even if a firm was able to require that COBRA beneficiaries pay 102 percent of their age-rated premium, the firm could pay an even greater amount in health care claims if the pool of COBRA beneficiaries was adversely selected. Older employees would prefer that employers use the average premium in determining COBRA costs, while employers and young employees would prefer to use age-adjusted premium levels.

Many employers consider COBRA to be a costly mandate. Assuming that individuals electing COBRA coverage are a relatively higher risk population than the general work force, any expansion in the current law that affects either the size of the firm covered under COBRA or the length of time that former employees could receive continuous coverage would almost certainly increase employer costs for health insurance. In addition, COBRA subsidies would increase the percentage of eligible workers electing COBRA coverage, driving up the costs to employers. On the other hand, if employers are able to offer plans that are substantially similar to the current plan, with the primary difference being the level of the deductible, employees electing this type of COBRA coverage may be less costly to insure.

Reform Issues

Job lock is a primary motivation behind proposals to increase portability of health insurance. Researchers, policymakers, and the general public give varying estimates of the extensiveness of job lock.

Public Opinion—The Employee Benefit Research Institute (EBRI), in conjunction with The Gallup Organization, Inc., conducted several public opinion surveys regarding Americans' perspective on job lock between 1991 and 1993 (Employee Benefit Research Institute/The Gallup Organization, Inc., 1991, 1992, and 1993). In 1993, 20 percent of surveyed Americans indicated they or a family member passed up a job opportunity based solely on health benefits, up from 11 percent in 1992 and 13 percent in 1991. Among age groups, 18–34 year olds were most likely to have passed up a job opportunity based solely on health benefits (28 percent). This compares with 21 percent among individuals aged 35–54 and 7 percent among individuals aged 55 and over. Individuals with an annual income of $20,000–$75,000 were most likely to have passed up a job opportunity based solely on health insurance (23 percent). When asked in further detail the reason for not changing jobs based on health benefits, the reason most often cited was that health benefits were not offered by the prospective employer (58 percent in 1991). The likelihood of this reason declined to 33 percent in 1993 yet remained the most commonly cited reason. (COBRA would allow these individuals to maintain coverage if they are willing to pay up to 102 percent of the premium.) Among other reasons cited, having a preexisting condition showed the largest increase, rising from 10 percent in 1991 to 20 percent in 1993.

In addition to public opinion surveys, several studies have been conducted regarding job mobility and health insurance. The findings are mixed and do not uniformly support or refute the existence of job lock. Studies that do support the theory of job lock show wide variation in the magnitude of its effects based on demographic and employment-based characteristics. Findings from these studies can be reviewed in Mitchel (1982 and 1983), Madrian (1993), Cooper and Monheit (1993), Gruber and Madrian (1994), Monheit and Cooper (1994), and Holtz-Eakin (1993).

Conclusion

Concern about the portability of health insurance primarily arises in situations where an individual is leaving, or would like to leave, a job. If health insurance is not offered by a prospective employer, if the worker must satisfy a waiting period before becoming eligible for coverage, or if the benefits package offered through the prospective employer is less generous, the employee may opt to remain with his or her current employer—a situation known as job lock. Expansions in COBRA may not have any effect on portability. Employers can charge up to 102 percent of the premium for COBRA coverage, making COBRA coverage unaffordable for many workers. Because cost is a major factor, if there is no reduction in cost (or health care cost inflation), there could be little or no increase in coverage.

Bibliography

Charles D. Spencer & Associates, Inc. "1995 COBRA Survey: Almost One in Five Elect Coverage, Cost Is 155% of Actives' Cost." *Spencer's Research Reports* (August 25, 1995): 329.04-5–329.04-7.

_____. "1994 COBRA Survey: One in Five Eligible Employees Takes COBRA; Employees Pay One-Third." *Spencer's Research Reports* (August 19, 1994): 329.04.-1–329.04.-6.

Cooper, Philip F., and Alan C. Monheit. "Does Employment-Related Health Insurance Inhibit Job Mobility?" *Inquiry* (Winter 1993): 400–416.

Employee Benefit Research Institute/The Gallup Organization, Inc. "Public Attitudes on Benefit Trade Offs, 1991." *EBRI/Gallup Survey* G-28 (Washington, DC: Employee Benefit Research Institute, December 1991).

_____. "Public Attitudes on Health Benefits, 1993." *EBRI/Gallup Survey* G-50 (Washington, DC: Employee Benefit Research Institute, November 1993).

_____. "Public Attitudes on Health Benefits, Part 1." *EBRI/Gallup Survey* G-30 (Washington, DC: Employee Benefit Research Institute, February 1992).

Fronstin, Paul. "Medical Savings Accounts: Issues to Consider." *EBRI Notes* (July 1995): 1–7.

_____. "Portability of Health Insurance: COBRA Expansions and Small Group Market Reform." *EBRI Issue Brief* no. 166 (Employee Benefit Research Institute, October 1995).

Gruber, Jonathan, and Brigitte C. Madrian. "Health Insurance and Job Mobility: The Effects of Public Policy on Job-Lock." *Industrial and Labor Relations Review* (October 1994): 86–102.

Madrian, Brigitte, C. "Employment-Based Health Insurance and Job Mobility: Is There Evidence of Job-Lock?" *Working Paper Series*, no. 4476. Cambridge, MA: National Bureau of Economic Research, 1993.

Manning, Willard G., et al. "Health Insurance and the Demand for Medical Care." *American Economic Review* (June 1987): 251–276.

Mitchell, Olivia S. "Fringe Benefits and Labor Mobility." *The Journal of Human Resources* (Spring 1982): 286–298.

_____. "Fringe Benefits and the Cost of Changing Jobs." *Industrial and Labor Relations Review* (October 1983): 70–78.

Monheit, Alan C., and Philip F. Cooper. "Health Insurance and Job Mobility: Theory and Evidence." *Industrial and Labor Relations Review* (October 1994): 68–85.

Morrisey, Michael A., Gail A. Jensen, and Robert J. Morlock. "Small Employers and the Health Insurance Market." *Health Affairs* (Winter 1994): 149–161.

U.S. General Accounting Office. "Health Insurance Regulation: Variation in Recent State Small Employer Health Insurance Reforms." GAO/HEHS-95-161FS. Washington, DC: U.S. General Accounting Office, 1995.

Additional Information

American Federation of Labor and Congress of Industrial Organizations
815 16th Street, NW
Washington, DC 20006
(202) 637-5000

Health Insurance Association of America
Public Affairs
1025 Connecticut Avenue, NW, 12th Floor
Washington, DC 20036
(202) 223-7783

National Federation of Independent Business
600 Maryland Avenue, SW, Suite 700
Washington, DC 20024
(202) 554-9000

The Urban Institute
Health Policy Center
2100 M Street, NW
Washington, DC 20037
(202) 833-7200

47. Medical Savings Accounts: Issues to Consider

Introduction

Given concerns regarding rising health care costs and utilization, policymakers, employers, analysts, and the media are directing their attention to proposals that put more control in the hands of the consumer, in the hope that less money will be spent on health care.

Medical savings accounts (MSAs) represent one such approach. MSAs can be viewed as savings accounts for uninsured medical expenses. They resemble flexible spending accounts (FSAs).[1] In an MSA, employers and individuals are allowed to contribute to a savings account on a pretax basis and roll over the unused funds at the end of the year. A primary difference between an FSA and the proposed MSA is the absence of the FSA "use-it-or-lose-it" provision. At year end, any FSA contributions that have not been spent are forfeited by the individual. MSAs would allow unused balances and earnings to accumulate on a pretax basis or be paid to the account balance holder in taxable cash. However, unlike FSAs, MSAs incorporate a move to high deductible, or catastrophic, health insurance and, if broadly used, they would fundamentally change the way in which health care is financed.

Nineteen states had enacted MSA legislation as of July 1996. In general, the provisions of the MSA that employers can offer vary considerably among the states until tax years beginning after December 31, 1996. Individuals in these states are still subject to federal tax laws that do not currently allow pretax contributions to MSAs or accumulation of tax-deferred earnings. Beginning with tax years after December 31, 1996, certain eligible individuals will be allowed to make tax-deductible contributions to an MSA, or to exclude MSA contributions made by the individual's employer from income and FICA wages. Eligible individuals must be covered under a high deductible health plan established by an employer with 50 or fewer employees. Self-employed individuals and their spouses with high deductible health plans are also eligible for tax-deductible MSAs.

---

[1] See Jill Foley, "Flexible Benefits, Choice, and Work Force Diversity," *EBRI Issue Brief* no. 139 (Employee Benefit Research Institute, July 1993).

The number of individuals eligible for tax-favored MSAs is limited to 750,000, with the total determined over a four-year period beginning in 1997 and ending in 2000. After December 31, 2000, no new MSA contributions may be made except for those with previously established MSAs, unless Congress votes to extend or expand the MSA provision.

The effect of MSAs on cost management, health care utilization, and risk selection depends heavily on plan design and just as heavily on consumer behavior and whether workers view their MSA as personal savings or as an extension of their health insurance.

The Theory Behind MSAs

The theory behind MSAs is that they should reduce health care costs and utilization by allowing the employer to replace low deductible health plans with high deductible (or catastrophic care) health plans. The high deductible, when combined with the individual's ability to keep MSA money not spent, is intended to provide a double incentive for less consumption of discretionary health care, thus lowering current health spending. It is argued that current health insurance markets lead to health care cost inflation because many events covered under most health insurance plans represent discretionary health consumption and are not truly "insurable." An insurable event is one whose occurrence is outside the control of the insured individual, such as a car accident caused by the other driver (auto insurance) or an unexpected injury or illness (health insurance). Health insurance with low deductibles is generally viewed as providing coverage for conditions for which insured individuals might otherwise choose to forgo treatment. For example, individuals may choose to see a physician for a bad cold if part or all of that visit is paid for by an insurance plan, while they might not visit the physician for the cold if they were paying the bill with their own money. Comprehensive coverage for health care services, through third party payers, is widely viewed as having the effect of increasing the demand for health care services. This is known as moral hazard. MSA proponents believe moral hazard would be mitigated with MSAs.

MSAs are premised on the argument that individuals should play a greater role in purchasing health care services. In an MSA setting, individuals would spend their own money—money that would be set aside for them by their employer due to savings from lower premiums, combined with their own contributions—for routine care and treatment of minor ailments, until the high deductible coverage takes effect. If the MSA works as planned, insurance would be less expensive, both because coverage would be less extensive and because the problem of moral hazard (unnecessary consumption) would be mitigated. MSAs would bear the burden of some of the out-of-pocket expenses that normally are covered under comprehensive coverage, and individuals desiring or needing care would have an incentive to search out the most cost-effective health care provider because they would be spending their own money. The health care system would have to find ways to provide cost-effective treatments to meet the demands of patients if all individuals with traditional fee-for-service health insurance enroll in high deductible health plans with MSAs and behave as proponents believe they will.

MSA Design Issues

A number of employers have begun offering MSAs to their employees. Employers can vary the design of the MSA in numerous ways. The Golden Rule Insurance Company, for example, has claimed great success with its MSA plan.[2] Beginning in May 1993, Golden Rule began offering its employees a high deductible health plan, coupled with an after-tax MSA, in addition to offering a traditional indemnity plan. Under the indemnity plan, single coverage plans include a $500 deductible and 20 percent coinsurance thereafter, up to a $5,000 out-of-pocket maximum. Under the high deductible health plan with the MSA option, single coverage plans have a $2,000 deductible, and Golden Rule places $1,000 into the worker's MSA. Workers are allowed to withdraw funds from the MSA under these circumstances: medical expenses, end of year, and termination. At the end of the year, workers are given the choice to withdraw the remaining funds or roll the funds over into an annuity with 7 percent interest. Since the implementation of the MSA option in 1993, neither the traditional fee-for-service health plan nor the high deductible health plan with the MSA has experienced increases in premiums.

The high deductible health plan with the MSA option at Golden Rule Insurance Company is just one example of how an MSA can be designed. Other plan design options that could be implemented include the following:
- MSA could earn interest on the account, either pre tax or post tax;
- unused balances could be rolled over each year and could eventually be

---

[2] Golden Rule Insurance Company, headquartered in Indianapolis, IN, is an industry leader in marketing medical savings accounts.

used to finance long-term care;

- if MSAs were allowed to move with the individual from job to job, they could be used to pay for insurance premiums and health care expenses during periods of unemployment.

Issues to Consider

Many issues related to the effects of MSAs have not yet been fully researched due to the newness of the concept. Among the most significant issues that merit analysis are the following:

- MSAs may discourage the use of necessary care. Individuals may not seek preventive care or interventive services because they might not think they need the care. Instead, they might choose either to save the MSA money for future use or spend it for other purposes. Individuals who forego preventive care and interventive services run the risk of necessitating more costly services in the future. This may increase total health care expenditures and utilization because individuals may be in poorer health once they seek treatment for a health problem.
- MSAs may introduce adverse selection into the system. Adverse selection occurs when healthy individuals choose high deductible, relatively low premium health plans, leaving relatively unhealthy individuals in low deductible, relatively high premium health plans. As a result, premiums for the low deductible, high premium health plan will increase, and premiums for the high deductible, low premium health plan will decrease. In addition, if adverse selection occurs, preexisting conditions may be excluded from coverage and waiting periods may be implemented in the low deductible, high premium health plan.
- Employers and insurers have typically been able to negotiate discounts with health care providers in exchange for guarantees of high volume. If individuals become the primary agent for health care decision making through the use of MSAs, they may not be able to negotiate discounts on low dollar value claims.
- Health care costs may not decrease under an MSA setting. The effectiveness of an MSA depends on how the individual views the account. If the account is viewed as personal savings, the individual may weigh the benefits and the costs of utilizing health care services. However, if the account is viewed as an extension of the insurance plan, health care costs and utilization may not be affected. In this

case, individuals would not view the account as personal savings and may consume health care services at the same level as they would under the low deductible, high premium health plan. Higher utilization may occur if the definition of reimbursable health care expenses is different from the specification in the health plan. Inclusion of items not covered under a health plan, such as eyeglasses and cosmetic surgery, could increase utilization of health care services. Using the Internal Revenue Code definition of reimbursable health care items for FSAs may remedy this; however, individuals must know whether or not each MSA reimbursable expense counts toward a health plan's deductible in order to budget effectively.

- Individuals may incur out-of-pocket expenses beyond those that are funded through the MSA. An individual may use his or her MSA to cover health expenses that do not count toward the plan's deductible. If MSA funds have been spent on qualified expenses that are not covered plan expenses, the individual would have to pay for additional services with after-tax, out-of-pocket dollars until the deductible is met and the plan would start covering services. In addition, after the MSA funds have been depleted and the deductible has been met, individuals may still be required to pay coinsurance for additional health expenses with after-tax dollars.
- The availability of MSAs may reduce participation in cost-effective managed care arrangements. Integration of MSAs with managed care arrangements is very difficult. Federally qualified health maintenance organizations (HMOs) are restricted from using deductibles for primary care. Both federal and state HMO laws would have to be modified to allow for the integration of MSAs with high deductible managed care arrangements. Managed care organizations would have to reorganize the provision of services in an attempt to integrate MSAs with their benefit package. In addition, under a closed panel HMO coupled with an MSA, individuals would not have the freedom to choose from an array of providers in order to find the most cost-effective treatment. MSAs may achieve savings when integrated with a fee-for-service health plan, but the likelihood of realizing any reduction in health care utilization will be more difficult if they are coupled with a managed care arrangement because utilization and premiums are already lower in managed care arrangements.
- Low income individuals might have difficulty saving sufficient amounts to fund necessary health care. These individuals may also

choose to forgo preventive care. The RAND Health Insurance experiment found that low income individuals with lower coinsurance rates experienced specific health improvements for three prevalent chronic problems—high blood pressure, myopia, and dental care—relative to individuals enrolled in high cost-sharing health plans. All three conditions are relatively inexpensive to diagnose and treat. Conversely, a high deductible might discourage low income individuals from seeking treatment for such maladies, increasing the cost of treatment at a later stage of the ailment.

- Do individuals have the ability to evaluate the quality of care they receive? The present market does not provide individuals with adequate information or training for assessing the quality or effectiveness of medical care. In the absence of such information, individuals may use other criteria in choosing among competing providers or treatments. Proponents of MSAs argue that once individuals have the need for such information, a market for these services will be created. However, given that such information would likely benefit not only those paying for it but also all users, it can be argued that the health care market would produce less than the desired amount of information. With adequate information accompanying education and analytic capability, individuals may be able to evaluate the quality and effectiveness of medical care. To the extent that the current market does not provide adequate information and individuals do not possess the other noted characteristics, MSAs might exacerbate current inefficiencies in the health care market.

- Another issue to consider is whether individuals are better off financially under the MSA option. Consider the following illustrative example for a worker with single coverage.[3] Under the current system, the worker participates in a health plan with a $2,699 premium. This plan imposes a $200 deductible and 20 percent coinsurance thereafter. Maximum out-of-pocket payments are $1,000 per year. Assume that the individual placed $500 in an FSA. This $500 is used to pay for qualified medical expenses during the year. Any amount that is not used is returned to the employer. The individual's exposure is $500, which is the maximum amount the individual would have to pay out of

---

[3] The plan designs under the low deductible plans are based on table II-4A and table II-5 in American Academy of Actuaries, 1995.

pocket. Under the MSA option with a high deductible, the premium is $1,921 with a $1,800 deductible and 20 percent coinsurance thereafter. Maximum out-of-pocket payments are limited to $2,800. Under this scenario, the individual places $1,278 into the MSA. The $1,278 is composed of the original $500 from the FSA account and $778 from the employer contributions. The employer contribution comes from savings from the lower premium. The employee's exposure under this option is $1,522. Some individuals may be worse off under the MSA option because of the higher exposure. However, individuals may be better off for the following reasons. First, individuals will not be subject to a "use it or lose it" provision. Second, if individuals roll over the unused portion of the savings account, funds can roll over so that the future exposure level is reduced. It can be expected that 24 percent of individuals will incur expenses greater than the $1,500 exposure limit.[4] If individuals choose to roll over account balances at the end of each year, the percentage of individuals at risk of exposure will be lower. Individuals with little or no health care expenditures will benefit financially under the high deductible health plan. This is just one example of how an MSA might work. Whether or not the exposure level of individuals changes depends heavily on how the high deductible health plan is designed.

MSAs versus FSAs

MSAs build on the plan design of FSAs that employers are currently permitted to offer. Flexible spending arrangements may exist as stand-alone plans or within a cafeteria plan. Employees choose how much money they want to contribute to the FSA at the beginning of the plan year. Any funds remaining in the FSA at the end of the plan year are forfeited to the employer, so the employee has an incentive to spend as much of the FSA as possible. This use-it-or-lose-it provision might have the effect of increasing use of health care services because individuals would rather seek health care services than lose the funds. In addition to the absence of a rollover provision in FSA accounts, FSAs do not generate earnings for the individual. FSAs can easily be coupled with both fee-for-service health plans and managed care arrangements. Money placed into FSAs can be used to

---

[4] Employee Benefit Research Institute estimates based on the 1987 National Medical Expenditure Survey.

finance such health care expenses as prescription drug purchases, eye-glasses, or other uncovered medical expenses. The funds may also be used to pay for medical expenses incurred as part of health plan deductibles or copayments.

Current federal laws that allow employers to offer MSAs do not change employers' ability to offer FSAs. Employers are allowed to offer both MSAs and FSAs. If individuals with FSAs simply moved their funds into MSAs, they would not have the incentive to spend the funds each year because of the rollover/withdrawal provisions. Individuals may not be conservative about the amount they put into the fund, consequently putting more money into an MSA than into an FSA. However, because the MSA can earn interest and unused balances can be rolled over each year, individuals may put less money into an MSA than they put into an FSA. In addition, individuals not previously participating in an FSA may choose to participate in the MSA because of rollover/withdrawal provisions.

The effects on tax revenue depend largely on how the MSA is designed, whether FSAs are allowed to coexist with MSAs, and how individuals and employers respond to the availability of MSAs. According to evidence on FSA eligibility and participation, growth in eligibility has been slow and steady, but participation rates have been generally low. In 1993, 52 percent of full-time employees in medium and large private establishments were eligible to participate in an FSA, up from 13 percent in 1988, 24 percent in 1989, and 37 percent in 1991.[5] In addition, 14 percent of full-time employees were eligible in small private establishments in 1992, and 50 percent of state and local government workers were eligible in 1992.

Studies have shown that only a small percentage of employees actually take advantage of the potential savings available to them. In 1992, 21 percent of eligible employees contributed to a health care FSA. If the use-it-or-lose-it provision in FSAs were removed, and individuals were allowed to roll over unused balances and earn interest on the account, participation in FSAs may rise. However, because MSAs are allowed only when coupled with high deductible health plans, patterns of eligibility and participation in FSAs may not be indicative of what might occur with MSAs.

---

[5] U.S. Department of Labor, Bureau of Labor Statistics, *Employee Benefits in Medium and Large Firms,* 1988 and 1989 (Washington, DC: U.S. Government Printing Office, 1989 and 1990); and *Employee Benefits in Medium and Large Private Establishments,* 1991 and 1993 (Washington, DC: U.S. Department of Labor, 1992 and 1994).

Conclusion

It is difficult to predict whether we will see a strong movement toward MSA use. Given that the main advantage to workers for choosing an MSA over an FSA is the absence of the use-it-or-lose-it provision in the MSA, MSAs may become a competing alternative to FSAs. However, workers must understand that the use of MSAs represents a move toward responsibility and accountability for purchasing health care services and procedures. Workers would need time to understand the function of MSAs and their role in a world of catastrophic health insurance coverage before they can decide whether to participate. Time is also needed to determine what the market effects of MSA availability mean for health care cost containment.

Bibliography

American Academy of Actuaries. *Medical Savings Accounts: Cost Implications and Design Issues.* Public Policy Monograph no 1. Washington, DC: American Academy of Actuaries, 1995.

Fronstin, Paul. "Medical Savings Accounts: Issues to Consider." *EBRI Notes,* no. 7 (Employee Benefit Research Institute, July 1995): 1–7.

Geisel, Jerry. "Costs Savings by All Accounts." *Business Insurance* (April 3, 1995): 32–33.

Manning, Willard G., et al. "Health Insurance and the Demand for Medical Care." *American Economic Review* (June 1987): 251–276.

Mechanic, Robert E. "How Would MSAs Work in the Real World?" *Business & Health* (November 1995): 29–30, 34, 37.

Additional Information

American Medical Association
Center for Health Policy Research
515 North State Street
Chicago, IL 60610
(312) 464-5022

Health Insurance Association of America
1025 Connecticut Avenue, NW, 12th Floor
Washington, DC 20036
(202) 223-7783

International Foundation of Employee Benefit Plans
Box 69
18700 West Bluemound Road
Brookfield, WI 53008-0069
(414) 786-6700

RAND
1700 Main Street
P.O. Box 2138
Santa Monica, CA 90406-2138
(310) 393-0411

Washington Business Group on Health
777 North Capitol Street, NE,
Suite 800
Washington, DC 20002
(202) 408-9320

48. Tax Reform and Employee Benefits

Introduction

Employee benefits and economic security programs are rapidly being transformed. Some in Congress are now considering tax reforms that would create a new tidal wave of change. Therefore, it is important to assess proposals for comprehensive tax reform and what these proposals would mean for human resources and employee benefits. Major tax reform would come on top of the dramatic change in the employer-employee relationships already being experienced, and tax change that removes relative tax advantages for employment-based programs could serve to accelerate existing trends away from traditional paternalism and toward individual responsibility. Taken together, they have significant potential implications for future economic security.

Characteristics of Proposed Reforms

Tax reform proposals are being categorized as flat taxes, progressive "flat" taxes, value-added taxes (VAT) or national sales taxes, consumption taxes, or "fundamental" reform of the present system through base broadening (elimination of deductions and exclusions). Characteristics of these proposals include:

- All of the proposals are intended to largely eliminate taxation as a factor in individual and corporate decision making by eliminating most existing deductions and exclusions from taxation.
- Most of the proposals seek to encourage employer asset accumulation in retirement plans by allowing deferral of tax on contributions to, and investment earnings within, the traditional "pension" plans—defined benefit and money purchase pension plans. The exception is the progressive "flat" tax proposal that taxes all income as it flows into retirement plans.
- Most of the proposals would not tax interest, dividends, or investment income as it is earned. Some would tax investment income only when it is spent. The progressive "flat" tax proposal is an exception in that it taxes *all* investment earnings as they accumulate.
- The proposals differ in how they treat health and other welfare benefits and participant contributions to defined contribution programs. For example, Rep. Richard Gephardt's (D-MO) proposal would

allow no tax-free contributions to any plan—employees would be taxed. The proposal advanced by House Majority Leader Richard Armey (R-TX) and Sen. Richard Shelby (R-GA) allows only after-tax contributions to plans that involve employee contributions such as 401(k), 403(b), and 457 plans, according to language in one section of the bill (the "back-ended individual retirement account (IRA)" approach but with earnings not subject to tax). However, under other sections it would allow pretax contributions to such plans.

Compared with the current tax system, which provides differential tax treatment for employee benefit programs and differential investment sheltering for tax-exempt bonds, life insurance, and annuities, the proposals—except the progressive "flat" tax—would establish a level playing field with all savings eligible for either tax deferral of investment earnings or no taxation of investment earnings.

How the Proposals Will Be Evaluated

How an individual reacts to employment and economic changes now occurring and would react to tax reform depends on the point of reference. Do I analyze as an employer, an employee, or as an individual taxpayer? How old am I? How big a firm do I work for? How "responsible" am I, or, will I take full responsibility for my actions (e.g., poverty in old age if I have never saved)?

For employers, the issues are work force age, the organization's size and profitability, the relative ease or difficulty of attracting and keeping the right people, whether it is difficult to move older workers into retirement, and the extent to which employees might be expected to "demand" benefits that have a tax advantage to them even if not to the employer and/or demand benefits that have no relative tax advantage.

The fundamentals of the tax system in terms of employer and employee decisions have changed little since the 1920s, even as tax rates and rules have changed a great deal. Major tax reform proposals would fundamentally change the system, relationships, and decision making.

The Kemp Commission as a Touchstone

The National Commission on Economic Growth and Tax Reform (the Kemp Commission, appointed in 1995 by former Senate Majority Leader Bob Dole (R-KS) and House Speaker Newt Gingrich (R-GA) and chaired by former congressman Jack Kemp, was charged with setting forth a tax reform proposal that could be embraced by the Republican Party for the 1996 election campaign. The commission's members included advocates of a number of different tax reform approaches.

In January 1996, the commission released a report recommending general principles that it thought any tax reform plan must meet in order to replace the current tax code with a more fair and simple system. The report recommends a single, low tax rate with a generous personal exemption. The chairman noted that the single tax rate should be no more than 20 percent. The report recommended abolishing taxation of capital gains and allowing full deductibility of the payroll tax for workers. The report noted that consideration must be given to deductions such as that for home mortgage interest and charitable giving. It also noted the need for strengthening private retirement saving and stated that any tax system "should encourage people to save for their own retirement." While this is not outright support for maintaining tax-favored treatment of retirement savings, the inclusion of such language is important.

The Armey-Shelby Flat Tax Proposal

The flat tax proposal, as introduced by Rep. Armey and Sen. Shelby (H.R. 2060 and S. 1050) in July 1995 would lower all tax rates (to 20 percent immediately and to 17 percent after 12/31/97) and allow employers to deduct the cost of business inputs, cash wages,[1] and retirement contributions to defined benefit and money purchase plans. All employers (including tax-exempt employers in the public and private sectors) would have to pay taxes on the value of noncash compensation other than retirement contributions. For example, an employer providing health insurance would pay tax (income and FICA) on the value of this insurance. Many provisions of the Internal Revenue Code (IRC) that apply to retirement plans, such as limits on allowable compensation (401(a)(17) and limitations on benefits, distributions, and contributions (415 and 4980A), would be repealed. As currently drafted, the bill could *end* pretax contributions (and tax-deductible contributions for employers) to stock bonus, profit-sharing, and other defined contribution plans except for money purchase plans, but would allow tax-exempt and government organizations to establish such plans. The bill

---

[1] All expenditures for employee life, health, disability, and similar benefits woud become nondeductible, and the employer would pay tax on the value of such expenditures.

contains conflicting language, with one section suggesting unlimited pretax contributions (and tax-deductible contributions for employers) to salary reduction plans, and another repealing the deductibility of contributions to such plans by employers.

Employer reversions of pension assets would once again be allowed—however, only in excess of 125 percent of current liability—once each year (with vesting of participants), and employers would be required to pay regular income tax but not excise taxes. At one and the same time this could serve to encourage employers to maintain defined benefit plans and discourage them from maintaining sufficient fund balances to take care of "rainy day" periods of down investment markets. The proposal would also define self-employed individuals as having an employer, so that they could also have defined benefit and money purchase plans.

The proposal would not tax interest, dividend, or capital gains generated by savings on which taxes have been paid. "Sheltering" and "deferral," as differential tax treatment in terms of qualified plans and life insurance products, would no longer be meaningful or relevant concepts.

The proposal includes other provisions that could have an indirect effect, including a super-majority requirement in order for Congress to pass future tax increases; repeal of estate and gift taxes; zero-based budgeting and decennial sunsetting;[2] spending caps on the growth of entitlements, excluding Social Security, for fiscal years through 2002; maximum spending limits; and a provision for automatic sequestration if revenue falls short of the spending caps.

The Archer View

House Ways and Means Committee Chairman William Archer (R-TX) set forth five "guiding lights" for reform. First, to achieve simplicity and freedom from the Internal Revenue Service as it exists today, all loopholes and exceptions in the Internal Revenue Code would be eliminated. Second, the new system would be made savings friendly by ending the taxation of interest earned and investments. Third, the "underground economy" would

---

[2] The bill would serve to sunset programs and require full reenactment, as compared with the present law, where the vote would be to repeal the present law. Currently, the "burden" is on having as much as a two-thirds majority in favor of elimination of an existing program. Under this provision, the burden would shift to a positive vote to maintain the program.

be curtailed by taxing the purchase of goods and services. Fourth, international competitiveness would be improved by removing the tax from U.S. goods sold overseas and adding it to imported foreign goods. Fifth, to assure fairness, those able to spend more would pay more in taxes; the system would recognize and account for the needs of low income Americans; and, since homes are not consumed items, their purchase would not be taxed.

Archer's principles would allow individuals to set aside an unlimited amount of money in savings and not pay tax on interest and earnings. Taxes would only be paid when funds are spent on consumption. Interest, dividends, or capital gains would be taxed only if used for consumption. For employers, neither cash nor noncash compensation would be given a deduction for tax purposes, allowing the employer to decide on the provision of cash compensation and employee benefits purely against human resources objectives.

The Unlimited Savings Allowance Tax Plan

The proposal of Sens. Pete Domenici (R-NM) and Sam Nunn (D-GA) would combine an 11 percent VAT on business, with graduated consumption tax rates, up to 34 percent, on individuals on the annual aggregate value of consumption expenditures. (Ultimate tax rates would be 9 percent, 19 percent, and 40 percent in 1999). The proposal can be thought of as creating one big savings account for individuals since no income, interest, dividends, or capital gains would be taxed until spent for consumption.

This proposal would allow limited individual deductions for charity, mortgage interest, and education. It would allow unlimited savings without immediate taxation or immediate taxation of earnings on assets, with taxation occurring only when savings and earnings are spent. The savings portion of the proposal has been described as "quite complicated" as it would require careful tracking of dollars by the individual and an annual detailed tax return. Employment-based plans and IRAs would be allowed, but they would have no relative tax advantage over any other savings since no income or earnings on assets would be taxed until spent. As currently proposed, the Nunn-Domenici plan does not change qualified plan rules per se, but contributions to plans would not be deductible from the 11 percent VAT. As savings, they would not be taxed to the individual until taken as distributions and then only when spent. In the current tax system context, this would appear to be a form of double taxation of employer contributions to plans.

The Nunn-Domenici proposal would also change the tax treatment of all other employee benefit expenditures that provide in-kind benefits by making them subject to the 11 percent VAT and treating them as taxable income to the individual.

The Nunn-Domenici proposal would also change the tax treatment of FICA taxes by providing a tax credit against income taxes and then making an explicit allocation to the programs in order to pay benefits. This would appear to eliminate some of the insulation from the annual budget process that the programs now experience, as benefits are now paid from the trust funds and are off budget. Under this proposal, Social Security benefit and spending levels would experience added pressure each year as budget appropriations are decided.

While the Nunn-Domenici proposal does not provide simplicity, it is savings friendly; it would attack the "underground economy"; and it would attempt to deal with international competitiveness.

The Gephardt Progressive "Flat" Tax

Rep. Gephardt's proposal contrasts with others by providing an income tax with full taxation of interest, dividends, and capital gains; with progressive rates; and with the elimination of virtually all deductions except the mortgage interest and standard deductions.[3] His proposal as currently stated would eliminate the favorable tax treatment of all employee benefit programs by providing for immediate taxation of either the employer or the individual. The progressive "flat" tax Gephardt proposal differs from the other proposals by not favoring savings over consumption as much as the present system, whereas the other proposals favor savings more than the present system.

Gephardt's proposal would encourage employers to pay employees cash only, leaving all retirement saving, health, life, disability, and other economic security decisions to the individual. The employer would have an incentive to provide benefits through a flexible choice program, if at all, to avoid tax complications, similar to the incentives provided by the Nunn-Domenici proposal.

---

[3] Seventy-five percent of taxpayers would pay a 10 percent rate, with rates of 20 percent, 26 percent, 32 percent, and 43 percent above that. The standard deduction would be $5,000 for a single taxpayer, $7,350 for head of household, and $8,350 for married couples. The personal exemption would be $2,750.

Gephardt's proposal contains significant simplification provisions. Thus, he sets the stage for debate with a message that all tax reform proponents favor simplification but highlights the different positions concerning who pays the taxes, at what rates, and when.

Issues for Consideration

This mix of proposals offers significant contrasts in the tax treatment of qualified retirement plans and other employee benefits. Most of these tax reform proposals essentially take most or all of the retirement savings tax incentives away from the employer and give them directly to the individual. These proposals focus on individual opportunity and responsibility, consistent with the growth of defined contribution programs over the past 15 years. Policymakers face a number of design questions.

- Should all qualified plans be treated the same, as under current law, or should defined benefit and money purchase plans be given unique treatment as "retirement" plans versus "savings" plans, as provided for in the Armey-Shelby proposal? How would this affect behavior?
- Employers might choose to maintain funded defined benefit plans on a strategic basis for work force management, or consider the adoption of money purchase defined contribution plans for that purpose. Employers would be likely to continue to focus on the value of prefunded programs, competitive advantage, and disciplined saving through these plans. Where employers have already moved away from defined benefit plans and toward individual responsibility, we would likely see acceleration of this movement. Where contributions are from after-tax dollars, a new form of savings plans that would not have to be qualified, using payroll deduction, might be offered in partnership with financial institutions. Prior to 1978 and the advent of 401(k) plans, it was common for employers to maintain savings plans, but they then had the advantage of more favorable treatment of investment earnings than was accorded regular savings. This difference would not exist under most tax reform proposals.
- Employees might ask employers the simple question, "Will I receive in added wages the money that would have been contributed to a pension plan if there is no plan to which you contribute? If yes, give me the money, a means of payroll deduction, and a route to unlimited investment choice."
- Employers would be likely to find it more expensive to pay employees

than to contribute to retirement savings plans, particularly considering the difficulty involved in attributing exact dollar amounts to each employee in traditional defined benefit plans. This attribution would be even more difficult for those plans with deferred vesting and integration with Social Security.

- Are employer contributions treated as taxable income to me so that I must pay tax? If yes, will I have the cash to pay the taxes on the money contributed to the plan? If not, I might again prefer the income to the plan contribution. This choice would be most pronounced under the Gephardt proposal.

- Should all plans and savings be treated as nondeductible for the employer but sheltered for the individual as provided for in the Nunn-Domenici proposal? Should savings be the goal, versus retirement savings? How would this affect behavior?

For the individual, the ability to save after-tax dollars eliminates the emotional driver of immediate tax savings. Given the option, would employees prefer the immediate tax savings and the deferral of tax on investments as provided for in Armey-Shelby as an option, thus causing them to urge employers to maintain defined benefit and money purchase plans?

IRAs provide a basis for assessment of how individuals would react. Nondeductible IRAs are being used by fewer than 5 percent of the eligible taxpayers. Fully deductible IRAs were used by 16 percent in the last year of full deductibility, while among employees with incomes above $50,000 per year nearly 60 percent contributed. Given the presence of employment-based plans, one might not expect better. The question: without employment-based plans available, how much would people save? And, how much less might be saved for retirement or might still be available at retirement due to the shift of focus to general savings?

How Might the System React?

- Employees would likely find defined benefit and money purchase plans attractive if they *did not* feel employers would give them *the full value of contributions as added cash* if the plans were not offered. Full cash payment would be unlikely. With other defined contribution plans, where employer deductions would be lost under several proposals, employers would likely choose to pay some added cash, simply eliminate the plans, or offer the plan with payroll deduction only in order to provide the employee a group administrative cost advantage. They might also offer expanded financial planning opportunities.

- Should health and welfare benefits contributions be nondeductible/ taxed for the employer and nontaxable for the employee as proposed by Armey-Shelby, or nondeductible for the employer and taxable for the employee as proposed by Gephardt and Nunn-Domenici? Since there is a tax, would there be no difference? Or, would taxes affect behavior in different ways? Taxes paid by the employer would be on aggregate health expenditures and would not affect the individual; thus employee behavior would be unlikely to change in terms of health care consumption. However, were employees to be taxed, they might seek or demand less health insurance in order to reduce their taxes.
- Either approach would likely lead to the expansion of health care choice and flexibility for individuals, a trend that began in 1978 but is not yet the general rule. The argument made by former Rep. Jim Cooper (D-TN) in his 1993 comprehensive health reform proposal in favor of the equivalent of the Armey-Shelby employer tax treatment would apply: taxation of health costs would make employers more careful purchasers. Facing taxes on contributions, they would find it more advantageous to funnel deductible cash compensation into a flexible benefits plan that offers health insurance options and in which many employees would choose lower cost health insurance than they now have.

The behavioral questions are beginning to be discussed by analysts, employers, and employees. However, the assessments are filled with contradictions. Some argue that, in the absence of relative tax advantages, employers and individuals would not want employment-based plans. Others believe that many employers would still want to maintain some plans for competitive advantage and to assure a savings pool to facilitate work force exit, and that employees will want the ease and discipline of payroll deduction savings.

Consequences for the Nation

Demographics are quickly bringing us an older work force and a growing retiree population. Many employers, reporters, and policymakers are beginning to focus more on questions of retirement savings adequacy and people's ability to retire in the decades ahead. Many employers are just beginning to win the savings education battle with employees. Public- and private-sector organizations are just starting to engage in a national savings education effort. How would these savings concerns interact with changes in the tax law? Would change disrupt the system so dramatically that savings would drop during the adjustment period? Retirement savings programs such as defined benefit plans, money purchase plans, or matched 401(k)s would become much more clearly "coercive" as a forced allocation of compensation in the absence of today's relative tax advantage. Having just begun to explain the virtues of tax deferral to employees, would we slide backward? How much would a required change in message serve to confuse individuals?

Some proposals allow employer deductibility for some plan types and not for others, further complicating decision making. What would this mean for employee relations? Would employers be sufficiently motivated by the need to manage exit from the work force to maintain plans when contributions are not deductible and when there is no special treatment for investment earnings in plans relative to other savings?

What would be the consequences for the nation if individuals cannot afford to retire? We know from the Social Security trustees' report of April 1995, that future retirees will get less from Social Security and Medicare, and at later ages. This reduction will serve to increase the resources they need from personal savings to retire before they begin drawing Social Security, and after, to maintain a desired lifestyle. What if employer plans disappear just as the public programs decline? Will individuals at all income levels save the same amount as would have been provided through employment plans, and more?

We know that individuals have not universally taken advantage of employment-based defined contribution plans even when generous matching contributions were offered. Would these nonparticipating workers be more likely to save with a consumption tax? Available research on qualified plans and IRAs suggests that the answer is no, leading to the prospect of lower rather than higher savings. On the other hand, research by economists such as Nobel prize winner Franco Modligliani suggests that access to funds without access restrictions based on age or the imposition of special taxes would probably encourage many individuals to save more. Would the end result be more or less total savings? What would be the effect on retirement income? What would be the implications for the ability to get individuals to retire? What would be the employment and political fallout if even fewer individuals reached the "golden" years with savings than is the case today? What if there were more savings in the aggregate after tax reform, but they were concentrated among fewer people? Would that produce a groundswell for a new round of reforms?

Finally, what would be the ultimate impact of these proposals on public demand for expansion of Social Security and Medicare? Some suggest that these programs will essentially be privatized in the years ahead, making these concerns moot. Would they remain moot if elderly poverty rates began to grow over time as a result of lower retirement savings due to fewer employment-based retirement plans?

The Future of Employee Benefits in a Tax Reformed World

Each of the tax reform proposals, if enacted, would raise fundamental questions about the future of employment-based plans and other employee benefits that partially rely on tax advantages to draw participation. Given no relative tax advantage for contributions to a defined contribution plan, or for investment earnings within the plan, fewer individuals would be likely to contribute to an employment-based plan. Fewer individuals would purchase group universal life rather than multiyear fixed-rate term insurance. Employers see it as advantageous to provide a match in a plan when the match is tax deductible but may not see an advantage if that match is not deductible. If given the choice between a qualified plan and cash in a flexible benefits plan, with the accompanying ability to make their own decisions, many workers would prefer the latter.

Health and welfare benefits have been moving toward a system of options and flexibility. This movement could be expected to become nearly universal, and many employers could choose simply to pay cash, open the door to health firms to market to employees, and provide payroll deduction premium payment.

Some major employers are contemplating such changes without tax reform, and tax reform would certainly increase their numbers. Outsourcing has been a movement of the early 1990s as employers seek to focus on the real "businesses" they are in for a profit, letting specialists profit from work that supports the firm. In addition, the use of part-time and contract workers has expanded as employers seek to operate with lean work forces that can expand or contract with customer or production demands. Both trends could be expected to accelerate, with implications for employee benefits, in a post-tax reform work place as individuals see even less reason to remain with one firm for long periods.

The ability of employers (including the self-employed) to maintain defined benefit and money purchase plans with the unrestricted design and contribution flexibility allowed by the Armey-Shelby proposal would allow an end of any unfunded nonqualified deferred compensation. Individuals might well prefer payment in current cash instead of deferred compensation under a new tax system, while employers might seek to maintain plans to provide an incentive for employees to remain and to retain some ability to manage work force exit.

Small employers, having always been motivated largely by the tax advantages, would be less likely than ever to maintain defined benefit or money purchase plans, even with the elimination of much regulation. However, the end of heavy regulatory requirements, including recordkeeping and testing, might lead more small employers to allow financial institutions to offer payroll deduction defined contribution programs to their employees.

Conclusion

Many organizations are thinking about the macroeconomic implications of tax reform. Many individuals are thinking about the impact on their own tax bill. Fewer are thinking about the business, profitability, human resources, employee benefit, and retirement income security implications, but that analysis is beginning. These implications will be far-reaching. The combination of unintended consequences and intended consequences that do not materialize could leave us short of meeting the proposals' objectives. Or, we could exceed them.

Bibliography

American Institute of Certified Public Accountants. *Flat Taxes and Consumption Taxes: A Guide to the Debate.* Washington, DC: American Institute of Certified Public Accountants, 1995.

Conte, Chris. "Comprehensive Tax Reform: Implications for Economic Security and Employee Benefits." *EBRI Notes,* no. 6 (Employee Benefit Research Institute, June 1996) 1–5.

Employee Benefit Research Institute. Comprehensive Tax Reform: Implications for Economic Security and Employee Benefits. EBRI-ERF Policy Forum held April 30, 1996, Washington, DC. Tapes available. Washington, DC: Employee Benefit Research Institute, 1996.

_____. *Comprehensive Tax Reform: Implications for Economic Security and Employee Benefits.* Washington, DC: Employee Benefit Research

Institute, forthcoming.

_____. *Pension Funding & Taxation: Implications for Tomorrow.* Washington, DC: Employee Benefit Research Institute, 1994.

Hall, Robert E., and Alvin Rabushka. *The Flat Tax.* Second edtion. Stanford, CA: Hoover Institution Press, 1995.

Heitzman, Robert E. *Pensions in a Flat World.* Washington, DC: American Academy of Actuaries, October 1995.

McTeer, Bob. "Tax Reform: An Opportunity To Increase Our Saving." *Economic Insights.* Vol. 1, no. 2. Dallas TX: Federal Reserve Bank of Dallas, n.d.

Pechman, Joseph A. *Federal Policy.* Fifth Edition. Washington, DC: The Brookings Institution, 1987.

Salisbury, Dallas L. "Employee Benefits in a Flat Tax or Consumption Tax World." *EBRI Notes,* no. 9 (Employee Benefit Research Institute, September 1995): 1–11.

U.S. Congress. Joint Committee on Taxation. *Selected Materials Relating to Federal Tax System under Present Law and Various Alternative Tax Systems, Prepared in Connection with House Ways and Means Committee Retreat Held March 1–3, 1996, Issued March 14, 1996.* Washington, DC: Bureau of National Affairs, Inc., 1996.

Tax Analysts. *Tax Notes.* Special Reports and Policy sections (January 22, 1996).

Woodbury, Stephen A., and Wei-Jang Huang. *The Tax Treatment of Fringe Benefits.* Kalamazoo, MI: W.E. Upjohn Institute for Employment Research, 1991.

Additional Information

American Enterprise Institute for Public Policy Research
Economic Studies Program
1150 17th Street, NW
Washington, DC 20036
(202) 862-5800

Cato Institute
1000 Massachusetts Avenue, NW
Washington, DC 20001
(202) 842-0200

The Brookings Institution
Economic Studies Program
1775 Massachusetts Avenue, NW
Washington, DC 20036
(202) 797-6121

Heritage Foundation
Domestic Policy Department
214 Massachusetts Avenue, NE
Washington, DC 20002
(202) 546-4400

U.S. Department of the Treasury
Office of Tax Analysis
15th Street and Pennsylvania Avenue, NW
Washington, DC 20220
(202) 622-0269

Appendix A: SIMPLE Plans

The Small Business Job Protection Act of 1996 creates a simplified retirement plan for small business called the savings incentive match plan for employees (SIMPLE) retirement plan. SIMPLE plans can be adopted by employers who employ 100 or fewer employees on any day during the year and who do not maintain another employment-based retirement plan.

A SIMPLE plan can be either an individual retirement account (IRA) for each employee or part of a 401(k) plan. If established in IRA form, a SIMPLE plan is not subject to the nondiscrimination rules generally applicable to qualified plans (including the top-heavy rules) and simplified reporting requirements apply. Within limits, contributions to a SIMPLE plan are not taxable until withdrawn.

A SIMPLE plan can also be adopted as part of a 401(k) plan. In that case, the plan does not have to satisfy the special nondiscrimination tests applicable to 401(k) plans and is not subject to the top-heavy rules. The other qualified plan rules continue to apply.

SIMPLE Retirement Plans in IRA Form

A SIMPLE retirement plan allows employees to make elective contributions to an IRA. Employee contributions have to be expressed as a percentage of the employee's compensation and cannot exceed $6,000 per year. The $6,000 dollar limit is indexed for inflation in $500 increments.

The employer is required to satisfy one of two contribution formulas. Under the matching contribution formula, the employer generally is required to match employee elective contributions on a dollar-for-dollar basis up to 3 percent of the employee's compensation. Under a special rule, the employer can elect a lower percentage matching contribution for all employees (but not less than 1 percent of each employee's compensation). A lower percentage cannot be elected for more than two out of any five years.

Alternatively, for any year, in lieu of making matching contributions, an employer may elect to make a 2 percent of compensation nonelective contribution on behalf of each eligible employee with at least $5,000 in compensation for such year. No contributions other than employee elective contributions and required employer matching contributions (or, alternatively, required employer nonelective contributions) can be made to a SIMPLE account.

Each employee of the employer who received at least $5,000 in compensation from the employer during any two prior years and who is reasonably expected to receive at least $5,000 in compensation during the year generally must be eligible to participate in the SIMPLE plan. Self-employed individuals can participate in a SIMPLE plan.

All contributions to an employee's SIMPLE account have to be fully vested.

Contributions to a SIMPLE account generally are deductible by the employer. In the case of matching contributions, the employer is allowed a deduction for a year only if the contributions are made by the due date (including extensions) for the employer's tax return. Contributions to a SIMPLE account are excludable from the employee's income. SIMPLE accounts, like IRAs, are not subject to tax.

Distributions from a SIMPLE retirement account generally are taxed under the rules applicable to IRAs. Thus, they are includable in income when withdrawn. Tax-free rollovers can be made from one SIMPLE account to another. A SIMPLE account can be rolled over to an IRA on a tax-free basis after a two-year period has expired since the individual first participated in the SIMPLE plan. To the extent an employee is no longer participating in a SIMPLE plan (e.g., the employee has terminated employment) and two years have expired since the employee first participated in the SIMPLE plan, the employee's SIMPLE account is treated as an IRA.

Early withdrawals from a SIMPLE account generally are subject to the 10 percent early withdrawal tax applicable to IRAs. However, withdrawals of contributions during the two-year period beginning on the date the employee first participated in the SIMPLE plan are subject to a 25 percent early withdrawal tax (rather than 10 percent).

Employer matching or nonelective contributions to a SIMPLE account are not treated as wages for employment tax purposes.

Each eligible employee can elect, with the 30-day period before the beginning of any year (or the 30-day period before first becoming eligible to participate), to participate in the SIMPLE plan (i.e., to make elective deferrals), and to modify any previous elections regarding the amount of contributions. An employer is required to contribute employees' elective deferrals to the employee's SIMPLE account within 30 days after the end of the month to which the contributions relate. Employees must be allowed to terminate participation in the SIMPLE plan at any time during the year (i.e., to stop making contributions). The plan can provide that an employee who terminates participation cannot resume participation until the following year. A plan can permit (but is not required to permit) an individual to make other changes to his or her salary reduction contribution election during the year (e.g., reduce contributions). It is intended that an employer is permitted to designate a SIMPLE account trustee to which contributions on behalf of eligible employees are made.

For purposes of the rules relating to SIMPLE plans, compensation means compensation required to be reported by the employer on Form W-2, plus any elective deferrals of the employee. In the case of a self-employed individual, compensation means net earnings from self-employment. The term employer includes the employer and related employers. Related employers include trades or businesses under common control (whether incorporated or not), controlled groups of corporations, and affiliated service groups. In addition, the leased employee rules apply.

SIMPLE 401(k) Plans

In general, a cash or deferred arrangement (i.e., 401(k) plan), is deemed to satisfy the special nondiscrimination tests applicable to employee elective deferrals and employer matching contributions if the plan satisfies the contribution requirements applicable to SIMPLE plans. In addition, the plan is not subject to the top-heavy rules for any year for which this safe harbor is satisfied.

The safe harbor is satisfied if, for the year, the employer does not maintain another qualified plan and (1) employees' elective deferrals are limited to no more than $6,000, (2) the employer matches employees' elective deferrals up to 3 percent of compensation (or, alternatively, makes a 2 percent of compensation nonelective contribution on behalf of all eligible employees with at least $5,000 in compensation), and (3) no other contributions are made to the arrangement. Contributions under the safe harbor have to be 100 percent vested. The employer cannot reduce the matching percentage below 3 percent of compensation.

Appendix B: Safe Harbor Tests for 401(k) Plans

Safe Harbor for Cash or Deferred Arrangements

The Small Business Job Protection Act of 1996 provides that a cash or deferred arrangement satisfies the special nondiscrimination tests if the plan satisfies one of two contribution requirements and satisfies a notice requirement.

A plan satisfies the contribution requirements under the safe harbor rule for qualified cash or deferred arrangements if the plan either first, satisfies a matching contribution requirement or second, the employer makes a nonelective contribution to a defined contribution plan of at least 3 percent of an employee's compensation on behalf of each nonhighly compensated employee who is eligible to participate in the arrangement without regard to whether the employee makes elective contributions under the arrangement.

A plan satisfies the matching contribution requirement if, under the arrangement: first, the employer makes a matching contribution on behalf of each nonhighly compensated employee that is equal to (a) 100 percent of the employee's elective contributions up to 3 percent of compensation and (b) 50 percent of the employee's elective contributions from 3 percent to 5 percent of compensation; and second, the rate of match with respect to any elective contribution for highly compensated employees is not greater than the rate of match for nonhighly compensated employees.

Alternatively, if the rate of matching contribution with respect to any rate of elective contribution requirement is not equal to the percentages described in the preceding paragraph, the matching contribution requirement will be deemed to be satisfied if first, the rate of an employer's matching contribution does not increase as an employer's rate of elective contribution increases and second, the aggregate amount of matching contributions at such rate of elective contribution at least equals the aggregate amount of matching contributions that would be made if matching contributions satisfied the above percentage requirements.

Employer matching and nonelective contributions used to satisfy the contribution requirements of the safe harbor rules are required to be nonforfeitable and are subject to the restrictions on withdrawals that apply to an employee's elective deferrals under a qualified cash or deferred arrangement.

The notice requirement is satisfied if each employee eligible to participate in the arrangement is given written notice, within a reasonable period before any year, of the employee's rights and obligations under the arrangement.

Alternative Method of Satisfying Special Nondiscrimination Test for Matching Contributions

The Small Business Job Protection Act of 1996 provides a safe harbor method of satisfying the special nondiscrimination test applicable to employer matching contributions (the ACP test). Under this safe harbor, a plan is treated as meeting the special nondiscrimination test if first, the plan meets the contribution and notice requirements applicable under the safe harbor method of satisfying the special nondiscrimination requirement for qualified cash or deferred arrangements, and second, the plan satisfies a special limitation on matching contributions.

The limitation on matching contributions is satisfied if: first, the employer matching contributions on behalf of any employee may not be made with respect to employee contributions or elective deferrals in excess of 6 percent of compensation; second, the rate of an employer's matching contribution does not increase as the rate of an employee's contributions or elective deferrals increases; and third, the matching contribution with respect to any highly compensated employee at any rate of employee contribution or elective deferral is not greater than that with respect to an employee who is not highly compensated.

Any after-tax employee contributions made under the qualified cash or deferred arrangement will continue to be tested under the ACP test. Employer matching and nonelective contributions used to satisfy the safe harbor rules for qualified cash or deferred arrangements cannot be considered in calculating such test. However, employer matching and nonelective contributions in excess of the amount required to satisfy the safe harbor rules for qualified cash or deferred arrangements can be taken into account in calculating such test.

Index

Page references in *italic* type refer to charts or tables

A

Accidental death and dismemberment insurance, 315-316, *424, 425, 428*

Activities of daily living, 301, 306

Actual deferral percentages
ADP tests, 96-97
maximum ADPs for top paid employees, *98*

AD&D insurance. *See* Accidental death and dismemberment insurance

ADLs. *See* Activities of daily living

Adoption benefits, 349, 453-454

ADPs. *See* Actual deferral percentages

Adult day care centers, 301, 306

Advisory Council on Social Security
percentage of elderly families receiving pension income, 445-446
reform recommendations, 28

Age Discrimination in Employment Act, 194
group life insurance and, 316

Age Discrimination in Employment Act Amendments of 1986, mandatory retirement and, 296

Age factors, demographic changes in the work force, 7-10, 343, 353, 479

Age-weighted profit-sharing plans, 111, 119

AIDS, long-term care and, 302

Alcohol abuse. *See* Employee assistance programs; Mental health and substance abuse benefits

Allocation groups, new comparability profit-sharing plans and, 119-120

Alzheimer's disease, 305-306

American Bar Association, public's uncertainty about obtaining legal advice, 337

American Council of Life Insurance, number of life insurance policies, 313

American Express Company, private employer pension plan, 3

American Managed Care and Review Association, PPO participation, 243

Annual leave, public sector programs, 431-432

Annuities. *See also* Joint and survivor annuities; Tax-deferred annuities; Teachers Insurance and Annuity Association-College Retirement Equities Fund; *specific plans by name*
cash balance pension plans and, 116
as plan distributions, 60-61
retirement planning and,

compressed work week and, 347
demographic changes in the
labor force and, 343
direct financial assistance with
child care expenses, 345
elder care, 345-346
flexible spending accounts, 345
flexible work options, 346-347
flextime, 346-347
job sharing and, 347
number of two-earner couples
and, 343
parental leave, 349
part-time work and, 347
resource and referral services,
344-345
tax issues, 347-348
types of child care, 344-345
Dependent care assistance
programs, 347-348
Dependent life insurance, 315
Disability benefits. *See also specific
plans by name*
pension plan distributions, 63
profit-sharing plan distributions,
84
thrift plan distributions, 89-90
for veterans, 185
Disability income plans. *See also*
Old-Age, Survivors, and
Disability Insurance; Social
Security
disability-related costs, 289
employment-based private
programs, 294-297
financial impact of disability, 297
history of, 289
informal programs, 289
long-term disability plans,

296-297
nonoccupational temporary
disability insurance plans,
293-294
number of workers covered,
289-290
public programs, 290-294
retirement income, 3, 7
short-term disability plans,
295-296
workers' compensation, 292-293
Distributions. *See* Lump-sum
distributions; Premature
distributions; *specific plans by
name*
District of Columbia, continuation
of health insurance coverage
and, 218
Divorced persons, IRAs and, 166
DoL. *See* U.S. Department of Labor
Dole, Sen. Bob, tax reform proposal,
472-473
Domenici, Sen. Pete, tax reform
proposal, 475-476, 478, 479
DROPs. *See* Delayed/deferred
retirement option plans

E

EAPs. *See* Employee assistance
programs
Early distributions. *See* Premature
distributions
Early retirement. *See also specific
plans by name*
adjustments for integration, 146,
146
OASDI and, 19
pension plan distributions, 63

raising the age for, 28
state and local government
defined benefit pension plans
and, 386, 387
EBRI Tax Estimating and Analysis
Model, 443-444
Economic Recovery Tax Act of 1981
adoption of "special needs" child
or children belonging to a
sibling set, 349
ESOPs and, 105-106
IRAs and, 163
Keogh plans and, 174
SEPs and, 126
tax incentives for employer-
sponsored child and
dependent care benefits, 347
Educational assistance benefits
federal assistance programs,
333-335
growth of participation in higher
education, 331
program design and types of
assistance, 331-332
State Student Incentive Grant
Program, 335
tax issues, 331-332
veterans' programs, 335
work place availability, 333
Elder care, 345-346
retirement planning and, 191
Employee assistance programs
alcohol and substance abuse and,
285, 287
confidentiality of records, 286
employer cost of, 287
health promotion and, 277, 285
mental health care, 266
mental illness and, 285

participation estimate, 285
range of services, 286
referral to, 286-287
structure of program, 286
types, 285-286
uses for, 285
Employee Benefit Research
Institute. *See also* EBRI Tax
Estimating and Analysis
Model
job lock perspective survey,
456-457
pension tax expenditures
estimates, 439-440
Employee benefits. *See also specific
benefits by name*
brief history of, 3
demographic changes in the
work force and, 7-10
federal budget and, 10-11
flexible benefit plans, 10
intention of, 3
mandatory programs, 3, 4, *6*
as partnership among
businesses, individuals, and
the government, 3
role of, 4-5
selected benefits chart, *6-7*
specialized benefit programs, 5
tax treatment of, 5, 7
voluntary programs, 3, *6-7*
Employee Retirement Income
Security Act of 1974 (ERISA)
assignment of benefits, 42
benefit accrual, 45
benefit payment form, 44-45
cash balance pension plans and,
113
contribution and benefits, 47-48

description, 256-257, 353
flexible spending accounts, 256,
257-258, 354
funding, 355
impact on cost, 356
IRS requirements, 356-357
number of employers offering,
353
premium conversion plans, 354
tax advantages, 256, 258
tax issues, 353-354
Flexible spending accounts, 256,
257-258, 345, 354
compared with medical savings
accounts, 461, 465, 466,
467-469
use-it-or-lose-it provision, 468
Flextime, 346-347
Floor-offset pension plans, 111,
118-119
Forfeitures, defined contribution
plans, 70, 120*n*
Form SSA-7004-SM (Request for
Earnings and Benefit
Estimate Statement), 27
Formulas for determining benefits.
See specific plans by name
401(k) cash or deferred
arrangements. *See* Sec. 401(k)
cash or deferred
arrangements
FSAs. *See* Flexible spending
accounts
Funding of retirement plans. *See
specific plans by name*

G

G Fund. *See* Government Securities

Investment Fund
Gallatin Glassworks, profit-sharing
plan, 3
Gallaudet University, FEGLI
coverage, 424
The Gallup Organization, Inc., job
lock perspective survey,
456-457
GAO. *See* U.S. General Accounting
Office
Gephardt, Rep. Richard,
progressive "flat" tax proposal,
471, 476-477, 478, 479
Gingrich, Rep. Newt, tax reform
proposal, 472-473
Golden Rule Insurance Company,
medical savings account
example, 463-464
Government Securities Investment
Fund, 398
Grandfather provisions, cash
balance pension plans,
112-113
Group health plans. *See also* Health
insurance; *specific plans by
name*
retirement planning and, 190
Group life insurance plans. *See also*
Life insurance in the public
sector
accidental death and
dismemberment insurance,
315-316
amounts of insurance, 315
beneficiary provisions, 316
benefits for retired persons and
older active workers, 316
conversion options, 316-317
dependent life insurance, 315

development of, 313-314
disability benefits, 317
eligibility, 314-315
employee cost, 315
group term life insurance
definition, 314
group universal life programs,
318-319
insurance contract, 314
living benefits, 319
number of employer-sponsored
plans, 319
optional forms of payment, 317
percent of employees covered by,
313-314
plan provisions, 314-317
standard rates table for
premiums, 314
tax issues, 317-318
waiver-of-premium disability
benefit, 317
Group model HMOs, 236-237
Group universal life programs,
318-319
GULPS. *See* Group universal life
programs

H

Hawaii
annual leave carryover policy,
432
Prepaid Health Plan, 37
HCPPs. *See* Health care
prepayment plans
Health care
increase in health care costs, 9,
251, 259-260
national health expenditures as

percentage of Gross Domestic
Product, 9
Health care coalitions and
cooperatives, 259
Health care cost management
cost-sharing strategies, 214-216
delivery system spectrum chart,
256
employer health care coalitions
and cooperatives, 259
flexible benefit plans, 256-258
health care costs as percent of
Gross Domestic Product, 251
inappropriate use of benefits
and, 254-255
incentives to use health care
economically, 252-254
increase in health care costs, 9,
251, 259-260
plan design changes and,
251-252
raising deductible or copayment
provisions, 253
range of services changes,
253-254
service delivery restructure,
255-256
Health care costs after retirement
HMOs and, 190-191
long-term care and, 191
Medicaid and, 191
Medicare and, 189-190
preventive care considerations,
189
Health Care Financing
Administration, risk HMO
payments by, 271
Health care prepayment plans, 272
Health club discount programs, 278

I

rollovers from qualified pension plans, 65, 66
SEP-IRAs, 125-128, 167
SIMPLE plans, 485-487
tax expenditures and, 439, 440
tax reform and, 478
tax treatment, 169-170
Instrumental activities of daily living, 301
Integration of pension plans
average annual compensation, 144-145
cash balance pension plans, 112
covered compensation, 145
defined benefit plans
adjustments, 146
average annual compensation, 144-145
career caps, 146
excess approach, 142, 145
integration levels, 145
offset approach, 141, 145-146
defined contribution plans, 141, 143-144
integration levels, 142, 143, 144, 145, 146
maximum offset or spread, 143
nondiscrimination rules and, 135, 142, 143
overview, 67
permitted disparity, 143
profit-sharing plans, 82
retirement age determination for, *145*, 145
SEPs, 127-128
TRA '96 and, 141-142
two-for-one rule, 143
value of retirement package, 141-142

Internal Revenue Code. *See* Internal Revenue Service; *specific section numbers*
Internal Revenue Service. *See also* Tax issues; Tax reform; *specific tax legislation*
benefit liabilities definition, 49
flexible benefits plans, 353-354, 356-357
life expectancy table, 400
pension plan death benefits and, 326-327
public-sector pension plans and, 371-373
Tax Benefits for Older Americans, 192
waivers of minimum funding contribution for pension plans, 46
Interpersonal relationships after retirement, 193
InterStudy, HMO participation projection, 235
Investments of pension plans. *See specific plans by name*
IPAs. *See* Independent practice associations
IRAs. *See* Individual retirement accounts

J

Job lock, 452-453
Job-search seminars, 188
Job sharing, 347
Joint and survivor annuities, 44. *See also* Survivor benefits; Survivor income benefit plans; *specific plans by name*

cash balance pension plan
distributions, 114
IRA distributions, 167
Keogh plan distributions, 176
pension plan distributions, 64
retirement planning and, 182
Joint individual retirement
accounts, 166
Judges, pension plans for, 366

K

Katz, Sidney, index of independence
in activities of daily living,
301n
Kelso, Louis O., 103
Kemp, Jack, tax reform proposal,
472-473
Kemp Commission. *See* National
Commission on Economic
Growth and Tax Reform
Kennedy, President John F., ERISA
and, 35
Keogh, Eugene J., 173
Keogh plans
contributions and benefits, 175
development of, 173
distributions, 176
earned income computations,
175n
eligibility, 174-175
growth of, 177
legislative history, 179-180
loans, 177
nondiscrimination rules, 177
retirement income from, 185-186
rollovers, 165, 176
tax expenditures and, 439, 440
tax treatment, 176

Key employees, 58-59, 174
Kingsport, TN, health care
coalitions, 259

L

Labor-Management Relations Act of
1947, 149, 152
Labor unions, public-sector benefit
plans and, 363-364
Late retirement benefits. *See also*
specific plans by name
pension plan distributions, 63-64
Law enforcement employees. *See*
Public-sector environment
Leave bank programs, 432
Leave programs in the public sector
annual leave, 431-432
compensatory time, 432-433
description, 431
family and medical leave, 433
leave bank programs, 432
leave-transfer programs, 432
sick leave, 431
Leave-transfer programs, 432
Legal issues. *See also specific laws*
by title
PPOs, 246-247
Legal services plans
access plans, 338
closed panel plans, 339
comprehensive plans, 338
consultation services, 339
delivery of benefits, 338-339
description, 337
domestic relations services, 340
enrollment, 338
exclusions and limitations, 340
general nonadversarial services,

M

maintenance prescription drugs
and, 270
Medicare HMOs, 271-272
Medigap and, 271
noncovered benefits, 270-271
option to divert contributions to
IRAs, 28
outlook, 27-30
prospective payment system for
inpatient hospital care, 9
recovering value of, 24-26
resource based relative value
system for outpatient
physician services, 9
retirement planning and,
189-190
trust funds, 29, 30, 31, 271, 272
Medicare Select, retirement
planning and, 190
Medigap policies, 271
retirement planning and, 190
Memphis, TN, health care coalition,
259
Mental health and substance abuse
benefits
appropriateness of treatment,
265
carve-outs of benefits, 266
cost variation factors, 264-265
employee assistance programs,
266, 286
employer plan design, 265-266
federal legislation requirements,
265-266
intensity of treatment, 264-265
limits on benefits relative to
other health benefits, 265
mental illness treatment costs,
263-264, 266

public-sector coverage, 417
social stigma and, 266
subjectivity of treatment, 264,
266-267
Metropolitan Life Insurance
Company, 424
Military pensions, 185
Military plans, 184
Military Retirement System, 442.
See also Military pensions;
Military plans
Minimum coverage requirements.
See also Nondiscrimination
rules; Tax Reform Act of 1986;
specific plans by name
aggregation of plans, 139
average benefit test, 136
compliance, 140
excludable employees, 138
facts and circumstances test, 138
former employees, 139-140
general rule, 136
mandatory disaggregation of
plans, 138-139
collectively bargained units, 139
ESOPs, 139
Sec. 401(k) and 401(m)
arrangements, 139
multiemployer/multiple
employer plans, 139
nondiscriminatory classification
test, 136-137
plans deemed to pass, 138
ratio percentage test, 136
safe harbor/unsafe harbor tests,
137, 137-138
Minimum participation
requirements, 136. *See also*
Nondiscrimination rules; Tax

Reform Act of 1986; *specific
plans by name*
Minneapolis, MN, health care
coalition, 259
Mississippi, annual leave carryover
policy, 432
Mixed model of HMOs, 237
Modligliani, Franco, 480
Money purchase plans, 395,
401-402, 480. *See also specific
plans by name*
cash balance pension plans
compared with, 115
description of, 57, 71, 120n
Montgomery G-1 Bill, 331, 335
Montgomery G-1 Selected Reserve
Program, 335
Montgomery Ward, group health,
life, and accident insurance
program, 3
MPPAA. *See* Multiemployer
Pension Plan Amendments
Act
MRS. *See* Military Retirement
System
Multiemployer Pension Plan
Amendments Act of 1980
(MPPAA)
automatic benefit guarantee,
49-50
full and partial withdrawal, 51
guaranteed benefits level, 50
premium rates, 49
Multiemployer plans
advantages, 154
benefit formulas and payments,
153-154
characteristics, 150-151
contributions and benefits,

152-153
coverage, 149
description of, 149
development of, 149-150
establishing, 151-152
growth of, 154
minimum coverage
requirements, 139
qualified plan rules, 151
reciprocity, 153
types of, 149
Multiple employer plans, 139, 150.
See also Multiemployer plans

N

NAGDCA. *See* National Association
of Government Deferred
Compensation Administrators
National Association of Government
Deferred Compensation
Administrators, survey on
Section 457 plans, 405, 406
National Association of Insurance
Commissioners, long-term
care insurance and, 309
National Center for Employee
Ownership, on ESOP growth,
105
National Commission on Economic
Growth and Tax Reform,
472-473
National Income and Product
Accounts, 445
National Institute of Mental
Health, mental illness
estimate, 263
National Resource Center for
Consumers of Legal Services,

on, 9-10
long-term care and, 306
Medicare and Medicaid coverage, 303
Nutrition programs, 278

O

OASDI. *See* Old-Age, Survivors, and Disability Insurance
OBRA. *See* Omnibus Budget Reconciliation Acts
Office of Personnel Management, 184
Ohio, Sec. 457 plans, 405
Old-Age, Survivors, and Disability Insurance (OASDI). *See also* Social Security
  alternative monthly test, 20
  amount paid out during 1994, 22
  benefits overview, 17-22
  benefits table, *19*
  cost-of-living adjustments, 20, 291
  divorced spouses, 19, 322, 323-324
  early retirement and, 19
  earnings limitations, 20
  effects of aging population on, 8-9
  eligibility, 16-17
  fully insured person definition, 18
  funding, 16, 23
  maximum taxable earnings base, 24
  primary insurance amount, 18
  ratio of workers to beneficiaries, 8

spouse benefits, 18-19
tax increases and, 8-9
trust funds, 28, 30
work year credits, 18, 290*n*, 322
Omnibus Budget Reconciliation Act of 1983 (OBRA '83)
  COLAs for civil service retirees, 383
  federal pensions and, 184
Omnibus Budget Reconciliation Act of 1986 (OBRA '86), Social Security Act amendments, 391
Omnibus Budget Reconciliation Act of 1987 (OBRA '87)
  accelerated contributions to pension plans, 46
  single-employer pension plan premium, 48
Omnibus Budget Reconciliation Act of 1989 (OBRA '89)
  COBRA coverage, 453
  COBRA termination and, 218
  ESOPs and, 103, 108
  single-employer pension plan premium, 48
Omnibus Budget Reconciliation Act of 1990 (OBRA '90), Social Security Act amendments, 391
Omnibus Budget Reconciliation Act of 1993 (OBRA '93)
  educational benefits and, 332
  maximum taxable earnings base for HI, 24
  SEPs and, 126
  Social Security benefits taxation, 21
Ophthalmologists, 231
OPM. *See* U.S. Office of Personnel Management

participation and cost, 269
Retirement, apprehension about,
   179-180, 194
Retirement age
   determination of for integration
      purposes, 145, *145*
   federal pensions and, 184
   raising, 9, 27-28
   retirement planning and, 179,
      181-182, 196
Retirement benefits. *See specific*
   plans by name
Retirement bonus plans, 111,
   117-118
Retirement Confidence Survey, 180
Retirement Equity Act of 1984
   break in service and, 44
   pension plan death benefits and,
      327
   qualified joint and survivor
      annuity, 327-328
Retirement income. *See also*
   Retirement planning
   from continued employment, 188
   from homeownership, 187-188
   from investment instruments,
      188
   from Keogh plans and IRAs,
      185-186
   from life insurance, 188
   from military plans, 184
   from personal savings, 186-188
   from private pension programs,
      182-184
   from public welfare programs,
      189
   from Social Security, 181-182
   from state and local government
      pensions, 185

from veterans' pensions, 185
   workers' confidence in prospects
      for, 180
Retirement planning
   employee considerations,
      180-194
   employer considerations, 194-196
   estate planning, 193-194
   financial planning
      considerations, 180-186
   health care cost considerations,
      189-191
   importance of, 179-180, 196
   independent living
      considerations, 191-193
   interpersonal relationship
      considerations, 193
   key areas to focus on, 180
   leisure time use, 193
   personal savings and, 186-188
   public welfare programs and, 189
   retirement planning programs,
      194-196
   savings tables, *207*
   savings worksheet, 201-206
Retirement planning programs
   content of, 195
   design of, 195
   group size, 195
   interest in, 194
   participants' ages, 196
   timing and length of counseling
      sessions, 195
   who should attend, 195
Retirement Protection Act of 1994
   accelerated contributions to
      pension plans, 46
   excise tax waiver, 47
   single-employer pension plan

premium cap, 48
value of vested benefits and, 48-49
Revenue Act of 1978. *See also* Internal Revenue Service
educational assistance benefits, 331-332
flexible benefit plans and, 256
SEPs and, 126
SEPs established by, 125
Revenue Ruling 71–446, pension plan integration and, 141
Reverse mortgages, 187
Rhode Island
nonoccupational temporary disability insurance, 293
utilization review success, 255
Risk HMOs, 271-272
Rollovers. *See specific plans by name*
Roosevelt, President Franklin D., 15

S

Safe harbors, 132-133, 134-135, *137*, 137-138, 487, 489-490. *See also* Minimum coverage requirements; *specific plans by name*
Sale leaseback plans, 187
Savings. *See also* Supplemental savings plans in the public sector; Thrift plans
annual payment factor, *207*
annuity factor, *207*
personal, 186-188
retirement income and, 180
retirement planning worksheet, 201-206
savings growth factor, *207*
Savings incentive match plans for employees. *See* SIMPLE plans
Savings plans. *See* Supplemental savings plans in the public sector; Thrift plans
Scholarships. *See* Educational assistance benefits
SECA. *See* Self-Employed Contributions Act
Sec. 213, 65
Sec. 401(a)(4). *See* Nondiscrimination rules
Sec. 401(a)(26), 59. *See also* Nondiscrimination rules
Sec. 401(a) plans, public-sector employees and, 395
Sec. 401(h) plans, as funding vehicle for postretirement medical benefits, 273
Sec. 401(k) cash or deferred arrangements
administration, 100-101
advantages and disadvantages, 101
contributions and benefits, 58, 60, 95-96, 100
coverage, 93
description of, 57, 71, 93
determining financial need from reasonably available resources, 99
development of, 93
distributions, 97-99, 100
elective contributions, 95
eligibility, 94
financial hardship defined, 98, 161

plan distributions for, 61
SEPs and, 125
Social Security coverage, 17
Self-funding health plans, ERISA
    and, 37-39
Self-insured health plans, 212-213
SEOGs. *See* Supplemental
    educational opportunity
    grants
Shelby, Sen. Richard, flat tax
    proposal, 472, 473-474, 477,
    478, 479
Short-term disability plans. *See
    also* Long-term disability
    plans
    compared with long-term
        disability plans, 297
    definition of short-term
        disability, 295
    duration of, 295
    paid sick leave, 295
    Taft-Hartley trust funds and, 296
    waiting period, 295
Sick leave
    public-sector programs, 431
    as short-term disability plan, 295
SIMPLE plans
    contribution formulas, 485
    distributions, 486
    early withdrawals, 486
    eligibility, 486
    401(k) form, 487
    IRA form, 485-487
    nondiscrimination rules and, 96
    $6,000 limit, 485
    vesting, 486
Simplified employee pensions
    advantages and disadvantages,
        128

contributions, 126-127
description of, 125
distributions, 127
eligibility, 125-126
employee contributions, 126-127
employer contributions, 126
integration with Social Security,
    127-128
salary reduction and, 95, 159
tax treatment, 127
Skilled nursing facilities, Medicare
    certification, 303
Small Business Job Protection Act
    of 1996
    ADP test alternatives to be
        provided by, 96
    defined benefit/defined
        contribution plans and, 77,
        136
    educational benefits and, 332
    ESOPs and, 108
    integration and, 145n
    IRAs and, 163n, 166
    nondiscrimination tests, 489, 490
    SEPs and, 127
    SIMPLE retirement plans, 485
Small businesses. *See also* Keogh
    plans
    SEPs and, 125, 128
SMI. *See* Supplementary Medical
    Insurance
Smoking cessation programs, 278,
    279
SNFs. *See* Skilled nursing facilities
Social Security. *See also* Medicare;
    Old-Age, Survivors, and
    Disability Insurance
    benefit estimates, 26-27
    coordination with CSRS and

T

Insurance and Annuity
Association-College
Retirement Equities Fund
Top-heavy plans, 58-59, 174
TRA '86. *See* Tax Reform Act of
1986
TRASOPs. *See* Tax Reduction Act
stock ownership plans
Travelers Insurance Inc. v. Pataki,
213*n*
Treasury. *See* U.S. Department of
the Treasury
TSP. *See* Federal Thrift Savings
Plan

U

UCR charges. *See* Usual,
customary, and reasonable
charges
Unemployment Compensation
Amendments Act of 1992, 183
pension plan distributions under,
65
Uniformed Services Employment
and Reemployment Rights Act
of 1993, 185
UR. *See* Utilization review
U.S. Bureau of Labor Statistics
defined benefit plan
participation, 401
disability insurance coverage
estimate, 289-290
group life insurance coverage,
423
HMO participation, 235
life insurance coverage
determination, 315
long-term care insurance

eligibility, 304
long-term disability plan
participation estimate, 297
PPO participation, 243
public-sector health insurance
coverage, 418, 419
self-funded health plan
participation, 38-39
short-term disability plan
participation estimate, 296
state and local government
defined benefit pension plan
survey, 385-386, 387, 388, 390
U.S. Bureau of the Census
child care settings, 344-345
disabled worker estimate, 289
number of state and local
retirement systems, 365
pension income surveys, 445
U.S. Chamber of Commerce, survey
on employment-based
educational assistance, 333
U.S. Congress. *See also specific
legislation by title*
Medicare reform efforts, 272
Social Security legislation, 3
U.S. Department of Commerce
private pension benefits
estimate, 446
retiree pension income reports,
445
U.S. Department of Education,
student financial aid
programs, 333-335
U.S. Department of Health and
Human Services, Health
Maintenance Organization Act
of 1973 administration, 237

coverage, 232
deductibles, 233
schedule of benefits, 233
selection of, 234
services, 232
usual, customary, and reasonable cost criteria, 232
vision care providers, 231
Voluntary employees' beneficiary associations, as funding vehicle for postretirement medical benefits, 273
Voting rights for ESOP participants, 106-107

W

Weight loss programs, 278
Welfare benefit plans, 149. *See also* Multiemployer plans

Wellness programs. *See* Health promotion programs
William M. Mercer survey on EAP counseling services, 286
Wills, 193-194
Women
increase in number in the work force, 10, 343, 353
"sandwich generation," 346
workers with disabilities, 289
working mothers increase, 343
Workers' compensation
compared with disability income plans, 292
description, 292
eligibility, 292
lump-sum settlements, 293
state variability, 292-293
waiting period, 293
Worksheets, retirement savings, 201-206

EBRI Fact Sheet

THE MISSION

- EBRI's mission is to advance the public's, the media's, and policymakers' knowledge and understanding of employee benefits and their importance to our nation's economy and to contribute to, encourage, and enhance the development of sound employee benefit programs and sound public policy through objective research and education.

WHAT IS EBRI?

- EBRI provides credible, reliable, and objective research, data, and analysis. The belief: neither public nor private policy or initiatives, whether institutional or individual, can be successful unless they are founded on sound, objective, relevant information.

- EBRI is funded by membership dues, grants, and contributions. EBRI's financial base includes a cross section of pension funds; businesses; associations; labor unions; health care providers; insurers; banks; mutual funds; government organizations; and service firms, including actuarial firms, employee benefit consulting firms, law firms, accounting firms, and investment management firms.

- EBRI does not take advocacy positions on policy proposals, lobby for or against proposals, or recommend specific approaches/prescriptions. EBRI does provide objective data on and analysis of the range of identified options in order to provide others the opportunity to make more informed decisions than might otherwise be possible.

- EBRI is a nonprofit, nonpartisan organization established in 1978. EBRI's Education and Research Fund (ERF), which performs the charitable, educational, and scientific functions of the Institute, is a tax-exempt 501(c)(3) organization supported by contributions and grants (it is not a foundation).

THE CHALLENGE

- As employee benefit costs—already in the hundreds of billions of dollars—continue to escalate, as public policy continues to evolve, as the design of employee benefit plans becomes more complex, and as employers change their view of benefits, the need for data and analysis is greater than ever.

EBRI PROGRAMS TO MEET THE CHALLENGE

- EBRI's comprehensive program of research and dissemination covers health, retirement, and related economic security topics. This program includes policy forums, round tables, briefings, testimony, interviews, and speeches. Major studies in process include Social Security reform, individual investment education and results, health insurance coverage, health policy reform, and pension design and investment trends.

- The *EBRI Databook on Employee Benefits* and *Fundamentals of Employee Benefit Programs* are regularly updated as resources. They are augmented by monthly *EBRI Issue Brief* studies and monthly *EBRI Notes* (which summarize major data releases, public policy activity, and new studies). Special initiatives for public education include the American Savings Education Council (ASEC) and EBRI's World Wide Web site, <http://www.ebri.org>.

- EBRI's Fellows program allows individuals from the private sector, government, foundations, academia, and the media to undertake studies of economic security issues and work with EBRI teams on major projects.

EBRI
EMPLOYEE
BENEFIT
RESEARCH
INSTITUTE

You Don't Have to Sort Through Stacks of Data to Find the Information You Need . . .

Get All Your Benefits Data from One Source . . .

EBRI Issue Briefs and EBRI Notes annual subscription for only $224.

EBRI Issue Briefs—Published monthly, this periodical provides expert evaluations of employee benefit issues and trends, as well as critical analyses of employee benefit policies and proposals.

Each issue, ranging in length from 16–28 pages, thoroughly explores one topic. Recent topics include: Lump-Sum Distributions, Health Promotion and Disease Prevention, An Analysis of Large 401(k) Plan Data, Retiree Health Benefits, Health Insurance Portability, The Changing World of Work and Employee Benefits, Hybrid Retirement Plans: The Retirement Income System Continues to Evolve, Sources of Health Insurance and Characteristics of the Uninsured, and more.

EBRI Notes—Published monthly, this periodical provides up-to-date information on a variety of employee benefit topics. Each issue includes a feature article on an important benefit topic; a statistical article highlighting new benefits data; highlights of legislative, regulatory, and judicial activities; research and activities taking place at EBRI; and a list of new benefit-related publications and web sites.

A combined annual subscription to *EBRI Issue Briefs* and *Notes* is only $224. To subscribe or to receive more information, call EBRI at (202) 659-0670. Discount rates are available for nonprofit and educational organizations.

EBRI Issue Briefs and *EBRI Notes*—Two monthly information sources that go beyond the headlines to examine, analyze, and interpret the vital issues in employee benefits and tell you how they will affect your taxes, your employees, your benefit plans, your organization.

EBRI PUBLICATION SUBSCRIBERS RECEIVE THE FOLLOWING

EBRI Issue Briefs A monthly periodical providing expert evaluations of employee benefit issues and trends, as well as critical analyses of employee benefit policies and proposals. Each issue, ranging in length from 16–28 pages, thoroughly explores one topic.

EBRI Notes A monthly periodical providing up-to-date information on a variety of employee benefit topics. Each issue includes a feature article; a statistical piece; highlights of legislative, regulatory, and judicial activities; activities and research areas at EBRI; and a list of selected new publications related to employee benefits.

EBRI's Quarterly Pension Investment Report The *Quarterly Pension Investment Report (QPIR)* contains data on qualified private trusteed, qualified private life insurance, and state and local government pension funds. It provides historical data on net contributions to pension plans and investment allocation by plan type, total plan assets and their investment mix by plan type, and short- and long-term earnings.

Fundamentals of Employee Benefit Programs This book offers a straightforward, basic explanation of employee benefit programs in the private and public sectors. It is useful to employers, employees, human resource managers, and consumers. Each chapter focuses on a particular benefit plan or issue, offers an historical perspective on plan development, describes plan characteristics, and explains the tax implications of the benefits.

EBRI Databook on Employee Benefits This book compiles data from multiple authoritative sources in table and chart form, supplemented with brief explanations of the information. It is organized into four sections—overview, retirement programs, health programs, and other employee benefits, with an extensive appendix offering general economic and demographic statistics, a glossary, a selected legislative history, and a source list.

Other EBRI Publications All EBRI books and studies published during the subscription year and a 55 percent discount on additional copies of all EBRI publications.

For information on becoming an EBRI publication subscriber at $1,500/year, call EBRI at (202) 659-0670.